# The
# Liberal Conspiracy

# THE
# LIBERAL
# CONSPIRACY

*The Congress for*
*Cultural Freedom and the*
*Struggle for the*
*Mind of Postwar Europe*

## Peter Coleman

THE FREE PRESS
*A Division of Macmillan, Inc.*
NEW YORK

Collier Macmillan Publishers
LONDON

The Free Press
A Division of Macmillan, Inc.
866 Third Avenue, New York, N.Y. 10022

Collier Macmillan Canada, Inc.

Printed in the United States of America

printing number

1 2 3 4 5 6 7 8 9 10

**Library of Congress Cataloging-in-Publication Data**

Coleman, Peter
    The liberal conspiracy: the Congress for Cultural Freedom and the
struggle for the mind of postwar Europe / Peter Coleman.
        p.    cm.
    Bibliography: p.
    Includes index.
    ISBN 0-02-906481-3
    1. Congress for Cultural Freedom.    2. Anti-communist movements.
3. Europe—Politics and government—1945-        4. World politics—1945-
I. Title.
D839.C84283C65    1989
324'.1—dc19
                                                                    89–728
                                                                    CIP

*For*
*Roma Krygier*
*and in memory of the late*
*Richard Krygier*

I want to write on this theme when I get out [of prison]—on the need [for] and urgency of a continuing "liberal conspiracy."

RAJAT NEOGY
Editor of *Transition*
Kampala, Uganda, 1968

# Contents

*Contents*

APPENDIX C: Some of the Institutions That
   Co-sponsored Congress Seminars                    259
APPENDIX D: Books Published by the Congress for
   Cultural Freedom or Its Affiliated Groups         261
APPENDIX E: Congress for Cultural Freedom,
   Summary of 1966 Expenditures                      275

Notes                                                277
Bibliography                                         301
Acknowledgments                                      313
Index                                                315

# *Preface*

In June 1950, as the Cold War grew more intense in Europe and North Korea invaded South Korea in Asia, more than a hundred European and American writers and intellectuals met in Berlin and established the Congress for Cultural Freedom to resist the Kremlin's sustained assault on liberal democratic values. In the 1950s the Congress spread throughout the world, successfully creating magazines, publishing books, conducting conferences and festivals, organizing protests, establishing a network of affiliated national committees, and fostering personal contacts. The Congress continued into the 1960s, broadening its focus to lay the basis of an international community of liberal and democratic intellectuals. It was America's principal attempt to win over the world's intellectuals to the liberal democratic cause.

Then, in an era of the Vietnam War, a New Left, a new Conservatism and an emerging *détente,* the Congress began to falter in its purpose. It was finally dissolved in 1967 amid disclosures of its funding by the CIA. Its successor organization, the International Association for Cultural Freedom, never recaptured the *élan* or equaled the achievements of the earlier Congress.

My own interest in this story began in 1967 at the time of worldwide publicity about the disclosures. I was a member of the Australian outpost of the Congress for Cultural Freedom—the Australian Association for Cultural Freedom—and had just been appointed editor of the Australian magazine associated with the Congress, *Quadrant.* The Congress, now under attack, had for some

xi

years commanded my loyalty and through its magazines had helped form my view of the world. When interviewed by reporters about the disclosures, I said firmly and frankly (as did most, but not all, people in a position similar to mine around the world) that none of our editorial decisions had ever been influenced by outside pressures, least of all by any American agency such as the CIA. I added—with what I would now, in the light of a greater awareness of the issues, regard as unfeeling sanctimony—that any-one involved in or knowing of CIA funding should resign from the Congress or be dismissed.

But a doubt lingered. Did, for example, the idea for the Con-gress's massive cultural festival in Paris in 1952 emerge from de-liberations among Congress intellectuals or rather from the concern of the U.S. administration at the time that America was losing the "Battle of the Festivals"? Were all of the Congress's var-ied initiatives in Latin America and Africa in the 1960s sponta-neous Congress ideas, or were some of them produced by the activist mentality of the Kennedy administration? Were the Con-gress's forlorn attempts to reach Soviet writers entirely an expres-sion of solidarity or did the CIA also have an interest?

I decided to inquire into the details of the programs of the Con-gress for Cultural Freedom—its magazines and national commit-tees, its conferences and festivals, its protests and campaigns—to see if I could settle the doubts one way or another.

I wish, after ten years of research, that I had the final and com-plete story on the CIA's role. Some of its former officers—William Colby, Lyman B. Kirkpatrick, Jr., Thomas Wardell Brady—have written briefly about the CIA's funding of the Congress. Others, such as Cord Meyer, Jr., have written in some detail of the CIA's arrangements with the (U.S.) National Students' Association. But when I applied to the CIA under the Freedom of Information Act for records covering the years 1950 to 1967, all I received was a clipping from the *New York Times* published after the dissolution of the Congress and the statement: "No other records responsive to your request were located."

Given this absence of cooperation, I have no significant news from official sources about the extent of the CIA's involvement. But I do claim that I have found out more than anyone I have interviewed about the Congress's various activities around the world, about the plans and intentions of the people associated with it, and about their knowledge of any secret funding. I have also, in the course of seeking answers to my questions, come to the conviction that the cloak-and-dagger questions of who paid whom, how, and for what are in fact far less important than the astonishing story into which I was more fully drawn than I had originally been, of the idealistic, courageous, and far-sighted men and women of the Congress for Cultural Freedom who fought in this war of ideas—with its attendant suffering and atrocities— against Stalinism and its successors. It was, we now know, a necessary war, fought when much of the world was quite unaware of the fact that it was taking place.

The account herein summarizes my inquiry, discusses the Congress's successes and failures, and, perhaps, offers some useful suggestions for viewing our recent history.

# The
# Liberal Conspiracy

# 1

# *Out of No Man's Land*

The tight-rope had snapped, but there was a safety net under it. When I landed there [in 1938], I found myself in a mixed company—veteran acrobats who had lost their dialectical balance, Trotskyites, critical sympathizers, independent "cryptos," new statesmen, new republicans, totalitarian liberals and so on—who were sprawling in the net in various contorted positions. We were all hellishly uncomfortable, suspended in no man's land.

ARTHUR KOESTLER, *The God That Failed,* 1949

It was an exhilarating moment for Arthur Koestler, on the afternoon of Thursday, June 28, 1950, as he called to a crowd of 15,000 in a public park in the British sector of Berlin: "Friends, freedom has seized the Offensive!" (*Freunde, die Freiheit hat die Offensive ergriffen!*)[1] This was the final day of the international conference called the "Congress for Cultural Freedom," a name resonant of many Leftist rallies. Koestler, the forty-five-year-old author of *Darkness at Noon,* was exhausted after weeks of planning, days of arguing, and hours of drafting and redrafting a liberal, anti-Communist, anti-neutralist "Freedom Manifesto," which he now proclaimed.

But he was also triumphant: His point about *seizing the offensive* was that for at least fifteen years, and especially since the end of World War II, liberal opinion had excused the continuing expansion of Soviet totalitarianism and justified its relentless suppression of democratic possibilities in Central and Eastern Europe as

1

either necessary for Soviet security against Western imperialism or in any case a progressive alternative to the restoration of reactionary powers. According to George Orwell in 1946, "the poisonous effect of the Russian *mythos* on English intellectual life" had led to such suppression or distortion of facts that it was "doubtful whether a true history of our times can ever be written." In the same year *Partisan Review* published an editorial by William Barrett that condemned the " 'Liberal' Fifth Column" in America and its campaign of "concealment, misrepresentation and deception" in the interests of the Soviet Union.[2] But now at long last, in the ruins of post-Hitler Berlin, a coalition of liberals, social democrats, and anti-Communist Leftists was finally getting organized. On the other side of the world, in Korea, U.S. forces were preparing to repel the North Korean army, which had invaded South Korea and had just captured the capital city, Seoul. Perhaps, Koestler and his audience felt, this was a fateful moment in history.

Even when the Soviet *mythos* was strongest, there had always been dissenters on the intellectual Left—social democrats, liberals, libertarians, and Marxists. In the United States they included Trotskyists (Max Eastman, Max Schachtman, James Burnham), revisionist Marxist philosophers (Sidney Hook), refugee Mensheviks (Boris Nicolaevsky, Sol Levitas), and liberal pragmatists (John Dewey). In Britain there were Bertrand Russell, Malcolm Muggeridge, George Orwell, T. R. Fyvel, and the publisher Fredric Warburg. In France there were Boris Souvarine, Anton Ciliga, and André Gide (after his visit to Russia). In Germany Franz Borkenau and Richard Löwenthal (Paul Sering) could not accept the Stalinist identification of Social Democrats as "social-fascists," and in Austria Manès Sperber had broken with the Communist Party after the murder of his friends and comrades in the Moscow purges. In Mussolini's Italy, Ignazio Silone, fleeing the Fascists, and Altiero Spinelli, in Fascist detention, had also broken with the Communists over the Moscow purges. In Belgium there was Charles Plisnier, author of the influential anti-Stalin novel *Faux Passeports (False Passports),* and in Spain Andreas Nin and Julian Gorkin. In Australia the philosopher John Anderson had ceased to be "theoretical adviser" of the Communist Party and had become its principal critic on the Left. In Indian prisons, the revolutionary M. N. Roy, the Liberal Minoo Masani, and the Gandhian Jayaprakash Narayan each developed his own critique of Stalinism.

So it was around the world, but these and other anti-Stalinist writers and intellectuals of the Left remained a very small minority and had no significant organization, national or international, remotely capable of overcoming the Stalinist and fellow-traveling hegemony. They lived in an intellectual no man's land. Many of them were tentative, even deeply uneasy, in their anti-Stalinism. In 1934 Max Eastman, for example, explained how he had hesitated to publish his *Artists in Uniform,* a detailed account of Stalin's persecution of writers and artists, in case it would damage "the soviets";[3] in 1936 André Gide confessed to a similar anxiety before publishing his *Retour de l'URSS*; and in 1938 Arthur Koestler ended his letter of resignation from the German Communist Party with the words "Long Live the Soviet Union!" (*Es lebe die Sowjetunion!*).[4] In a world still recovering from the catastrophes of World War I and enduring the Great Depression and the spread of fascism, the Soviet Union seemed to many a last hope for humanity, and to cease to give it the benefit of doubt was a sort of treachery. But the number of defections increased with each new shock of Stalinist reality: collectivization, the Ukrainian famine, the Moscow Trials, the betrayal of the Social Democrats in Germany and of the Popular Front in Spain, the Hitler–Stalin pact, the assassination of Trotsky, the attack on Finland, the increasing reports of the gulag. Nevertheless, Stalin always kept the loyalty of millions, including a large part of the intellectual elites.

This was most dramatically illustrated in a series of international conferences of writers, artists, and scientists. In June 1935, for example, the First International Congress of Writers for the Defense of Culture in Paris brought together a wide cross-section of famous writers, including André Gide, Julien Benda, André Malraux, E. M. Forster, Aldous Huxley, Heinrich Mann, Bertolt Brecht, Waldo Frank, Theodore Dreiser, Boris Pasternak, Isaak Babel, and Ilya Ehrenburg. Yet it was, in the words of the historian Roger Shattuck, "one of the most thoroughly rigged and steam-rollered assemblages ever perpetrated on the face of Western literature in the name of culture and freedom." When the prominent Italian antifascist historian Gaetano Salvemini referred to the suppression of freedom in the Soviet Union, he was hissed down. Paul Eluard, then in an anti-Soviet phase, was given the platform only after midnight, when most *congressistes* had gone home.[5] Julien Benda was permitted to criticize Communism, but only, according to Forster, because his criticism was "academic."[6] The Stalinist organizer of the Congress, Johannes R. Becher, censured Gustav Reg-

ler because, while chairman, he had let Communist control become too obvious by allowing the assembly to burst into singing
*The Internationale.*[7]

This pattern of ideological control and manipulation was resumed after World War II. In October 1947 a German Writers'
Congress was held in East Berlin at the height of the Zdhanovist
purges of Soviet writers, philosophers, and musicians. It was also
the month after the creation in Poland of the Cominform (the
Communist Information Bureau), foreshadowing a new worldwide Communist offensive. The Soviets sent three well-known
writers and editors to Berlin, but no one was invited to represent
the liberal West or its tradition of dissent—and the Germans
would be discreet, if not silent, not yet having recovered their
voices after the Nazi era (and in any case they were subject to censure and possibly arrest if they criticized any representatives of
the four occupying powers). To frustrate the planned Communist
triumph, a twenty-seven-year-old American journalist, Melvin J.
Lasky, gave a sensational thirty-five-minute speech in which he
paid homage to the persecuted writers and artists of the Soviet
Union and pointedly named Anna Akhmatova, Mikhail Zosh-
chenko, and Sergei Eisenstein as victims of Stalinism. ("We feel
spiritual solidarity with the writers and artists in Soviet Russia. . . .
We know how soul-crushing it is to work and write when a political
censor stands behind us and behind him stand the police.") A Soviet apparatchik immediately denounced Lasky as "a repulsive,
war-mongering fascist" and a "cheap Hollywood imitation of Trotsky." But he received a standing ovation from the German writers.
In a city where anti-Soviet activists were not safe, his speech constituted a courageous act.[8] But that was only an isolated and personal
gesture. The U.S. authorities, eager to maintain postwar "Allied
harmony," considered expelling Lasky from Berlin.

In the following year, in September 1948, the larger Wroclaw
(formerly Breslau) Cultural Conference for Peace witnessed more
Western protest. The Soviet line was hammered hard against both
the Western democracies and Tito's Yugoslavia (which the Soviets
had recently expelled from the Cominform). The Kremlin spokes-
man, Aleksandr Fadeyev, Secretary General of the Soviet Writers'
Union, delivered the keynote address. "If hyenas could type and
jackals use a pen," he said, they would write like T. S. Eliot, Eugene
O'Neill, Jean-Paul Sartre, and André Malraux. Ilya Ehrenburg declared there was no such thing as "Western culture," and Georges

Lukacs explained that Soviet culture was beyond the understanding of the Western bourgeois intelligence.

Among the milder, personal "deviationists" at this conference were Julien Benda, philosopher, novelist, and author of *La Trahison des clercs*, who objected to being called upon to applaud at each detonation of Stalin's name, and Elio Vittorini, then editor of the modernist, pro-Communist *Il Politecnico*, who said that Soviet artists were "the Negroes of the Soviet Union." But the principal protesters were two historians, A. J. P. Taylor from Oxford and Bryn J. Hovde from New York. Taylor's speech lacked the detail of Lasky's in Berlin, and it was more neutralist in content, condemning equally "Wall Street" and "the Kremlin." But, like Lasky's, it was a courageous act in a forum behind the Iron Curtain and rallied enough delegates to prevent the conference's anti-American resolution from being adopted unanimously. But those "hiccups" of the conference were not at all due to solid oppositional planning. As Kingsley Martin, editor of the *New Statesman and Nation*, complained, the protestors lacked any "agreement, cohesion, or organization."[9]

Such was not the case at the next two Communist international Peace conferences of March and April 1949. The first, in New York, was sponsored by, among others, Albert Einstein, Charlie Chaplin, Paul Robeson, and Leonard Bernstein. Participants included Dmitri Shostakovich and Aleksandr Fadeyev from the Soviet Union, Paul Eluard (now toeing the Soviet line again) from France, Olaf Stapledon from Britain, and Howard Fast, F. O. Matthieson, Clifford Odets, Aaron Copland, and Lillian Hellman from America. The scene was set at the Waldorf-Astoria Hotel for a glittering disavowal of "U.S. war-mongering." But this time the anti-Communists had formed a counter-organization, the "Americans for Intellectual Freedom," whose numbers included Sidney Hook, Dwight Macdonald, Mary McCarthy, Nicolas Nabokov, and Arnold Beichman.[10] At each meeting one of them questioned the Conference speaker about the fate of Soviet artists. Dwight Macdonald asked Fadeyev why he had submitted to the Politburo's direction to rewrite his novel *Young Guard*. "The Politburo's criticism helped my work greatly," he replied.[11] Did Shostakovich agree, Nicolas Nabokov asked, with *Pravda* that such "lackeys of imperialism" as Hindemith, Schoenberg, and Stravinsky should be banned in the Soviet Union? Yes, said Shostakovich, trembling. (He wrote later that he thought: "When I get back, it's over for me.")[12] The "Americans for Intellectual Freedom" also organized a rally at Freedom House, with an overflow crowd of some thousands in Bryant Park, to hear Sidney Hook, Max Eastman, and Nicolas Nabokov speak of the harassment, persecution, and execution of Soviet intellectuals.

The official Stalinoid Conference's final resolution was weaker and less anti-American than the one proposed at Wroclaw. It simply called for the strengthening of the United Nations. The fellow-travelers had to wait for the final mass rally of 18,000 in Madison Square Garden for the full-throated denunciation of America.

The "Americans for Intellectual Freedom" had been far more effective than the isolated protesters at the earlier conferences. "We had frustrated one of the most ambitious undertakings of the Kremlin," Sidney Hook wrote later.[13] Dwight Macdonald was excited: "The anti-communist left has taken the offensive," he wrote at the time—words which Koestler echoed in Berlin in 1950.[14]

But William Barrett was not so sure; all that had happened, he said, was that a few embarrassing questions had been asked and an anti-Stalinist rally, far smaller than the official pro-Soviet rally, had been staged. He had "the melancholy impression that there is no American organization adequate in resources, energy, or direction to fighting Stalinist propaganda on a satisfactory intellectual level."[15] At least one other who attended, Michael Josselson, found the opposition a bit more inspiring. "We should have something like this in Berlin," Josselson said to his friend, the composer Nicolas Nabokov.[16] Josselson was at that time a U.S. State Department cultural officer in Berlin. He would later, as we shall see, play the central role in the management of the Congress for Cultural Freedom for the CIA.

The "Americans for Intellectual Freedom" had also encouraged the French socialist David Rousset in his plan to form a similar organization to combat the World Peace Congress to be held in Paris in April 1949, a month after the New York conference.[17] For the Peace Congress, the familiar faces were assembled again: Ilya Ehrenburg and Aleksandr Fadeyev from Russia, Paul Robeson and Howard Fast from America, Hewlett Johnson and Konni Zilliacus from Britain, Frédéric Joliot-Curie from France, and Pietro Nenni from Italy. There were also large delegations from the European colonies. Charlie Chaplin sent a message; Picasso released his Peace Dove; a Soviet priest blessed the conference; and Paul Robeson sang *Ole Man River*. When Nanking fell to the Chinese Communists, the "peace" delegates cheered wildly. The Paris organizers avoided the "errors" of Wroclaw and New York, and no dissenter was even given a hearing. Up to 30,000 people, thousands of whom arrived in trains and "peace caravans," rallied at the Buffalo Stadium for anti-American speeches, although a final resolution was couched in the same vague, anti-Western generalities that characterized the New York resolution.

David Rousset's counter-conference, the "International Day of Resistance to Dictatorship and War," was meant to frustrate the Kremlin in Paris in the way the "Americans for Intellectual Freedom" had tried to do in New York. But, despite careful planning, it was a failure. Eleanor Roosevelt, Upton Sinclair, John Dos Passos, Julian Huxley, and R. H. S. Crossman sent messages of support. Delegates included Ignazio Silone, Carlo Levi, Sidney Hook, James T. Farrell, Franz Borkenau, and Fenner Brockway. Raymond Aron, Arthur Koestler, and James Burnham were not invited because they were "too anti-Communist," and Jean-Paul Sartre, Maurice Merleau-Ponty, and Richard Wright boycotted the conference (although they sent a message condemning "the terrorism" of the Soviet Union and of the Atlantic Pact "equally and for the same reason"). At its main meeting at the Sorbonne most of the speeches were so "neutralistic" that Sidney Hook wrote later: "Not since I was a boy thirty years ago listening to the soap-boxers in Madison Square have I heard such banalities and empty rhetoric."[18] At the evening rally a group of anarchists seized the microphone and denounced the meeting. It was clear to anyone not yet aware of it that whatever plans were to be made for an international, liberal, and social democratic anti-Communist organization, "progressive," Sartrean Paris would always be a special and difficult case: This was the world capital of the fellow-travelers from which, Arthur Koestler dourly said, the Communist Party could take over France with one telephone call.

None of these dissenters, with the partial exception of the "Americans for Intellectual Freedom," had been able to play more than a spoiler's role against the Communists and their fellow-travelers, who remained in control. Throughout this period, with the exception of the twenty-two months of the Hitler–Stalin Pact, the dissenters remained a defensive, beleaguered minority. There was only one established magazine, *Partisan Review* in New York, that reflected their experience. Some of the writers among them found it hard to be published at all. When they managed to be published, contemptuous reviews of their books often minimized their sales. This was the period when Max Eastman's *Artists in Uniform* sold a total of five hundred copies;[19] when George Orwell's publisher, Victor Gollancz, refused to look at the anti-Communist *Homage to Catalonia* (and when Fredric Warburg published it, it sold a mere seven hundred copies); when Orwell's *Animal Farm* was turned down by several London publishers;[20] when Malcolm Muggeridge, quarantined for writing *Winter in Moscow,* could barely earn a living in England and had to find work in India;[21] when Boris Souvarine had difficulty finding a publisher for his now classic biography *Stalin,*[22] when the French translator of Koestler's *Darkness at Noon* found it prudent to withdraw first his name and then his pseudonym from the translation;[23] and when Hannah Arendt could not find a French publisher for her *Origins of Totalitarianism.*[24] "An anti-Communist is a rat," said Jean-Paul Sartre, reflecting a general view.[25] Anti-Communism, said Thomas Mann, is "the basic stupidity" (*die Grundthorheit*) of the twentieth century.[26]

But in the late 1940s opinion on the Left gradually began to change, spurred on by the Sovietization and the purges of social democrats in Eastern and Central Europe, the Berlin Blockade, and the campaign against Tito. The year 1949 brought the publication of three books that indicated the new mood on the Left: *The God That Failed* (edited by R. H. S. Crossman), George Orwell's *1984,* and Arthur M. Schlesinger, Jr.'s *The Vital Center.* Schlesinger's book, a manifesto of the American "Non-Communist Left," also showed how quickly this movement had spread from the intellectual ghetto to high government office under the influence of such figures as George Kennan, Charles E. Bohlen, and Isaiah Berlin. "Under Byrnes and Marshall," Schlesinger said, recounting a "quiet revolution,"

> ... the State Department moved in the direction of a philosophy of the non-Communist left. The very phrase, indeed, was reduced in the Washington manner to its initials; and the cryptic designation "NCL" was constantly used in inner State Department circles.

It was the widespread adoption in the more intellectual U.S. government circles of the belief that the non-Communist Left could be the most effective response to the totalitarian Left that created a receptive atmosphere for the formation and support of what would become the Congress for Cultural Freedom. It was to this non-Communist Left that Koestler was appealing when he uttered his *cri de triomphe* in the Berlin Sommergarten in June 1950.

There had never before been a conference quite like the 1950 Congress for Cultural Freedom, as anti-Soviet intellectuals gathered from all over the world, adopted an anti-Soviet, antineutralist manifesto, and agreed to establish a permanent organization of the democratic anti-Communist Left. It lasted for seventeen years and at its height had offices or representatives in thirty-five countries, employing a total of 280 staff members. Its history falls into three periods. In the first period, from 1950 to about 1958, it often thought of itself as "a movement" leading a liberal offensive against the Communists and their fellow-travelers. It was a period of creativity and expansion. It sponsored a network of magazines including *Encounter, Survey, Preuves, Tempo Presente,* and *Cuadernos* and helped others ranging from *Quest* in Bombay to *Quadrant* in Sydney. It conducted large and small international seminars, which J. K. Galbraith (for one) said were "by a wide margin, the most interesting, lively and informative I had ever attended."[27] It orchestrated international protests against oppression of intellectuals, most frequently in the Soviet bloc but also in Spain, Argentina, and Indonesia. It organized festivals and helped refugee writers. "I can think of no group of people," George F. Kennan wrote to Nicolas Nabokov, the Congress's General Secretary, "who have done more to hold our world together in these last years than you and your colleagues. In this country [the United States] in particular, few will ever understand the dimensions and the significance of your accomplishments."[28] Above all, the Congress in this period helped to shatter the illusions of the Stalinist fellow-travelers. It did not have the impact of Nikita S. Khrushchev's "secret speech" and the Soviet suppression of Hungary in 1956 (or of Aleksandr Solzhenitsyn later), but it prepared the ground. The Congress was a success; in Raymond Aron's blunt summary, it carried out its task.

In the second period—1958 to 1963–64—the record is mixed. If in the first, the Congress built an Atlanticist intellectual community, it set out in the second period to lay the basis for a world community, including, as far as possible, intellectuals in the Soviet bloc. In a time of "peaceful coexistence," Italian polycentrism, Polish revisionism, a continuing Soviet "thaw," and a Sino-Soviet split, the Congress somewhat moderated its public anti-Communism, cultivated "cultural contacts," and tried to encourage "liberalization" behind the Iron Curtain. It had its greatest success in Poland and Hungary. In the Third World, its program of seminars, magazines, and books helped keep liberalism alive in Sukarno's Indonesia and enjoyed a modest, brief success in Africa, as well as a limited success in Latin America. In this second period, the Congress also maintained the magazines already launched and sponsored new ones: *China Quarterly, Minerva,* and *Censorship* in England and *Transition* in Uganda.

In its third period—from 1963 to 1967, the Congress (or its Secretariat) was operating under the shadow of the now inevitable exposure of its funding by the CIA in a new age when the CIA and all of its works (especially in Vietnam) were being presented as expressions of evil. It was a period of retreat—the closing down or selling of magazines and the reduction of programs—and of the urgent arrangement of new sources of funds (from the Ford Foundation). The dominant hope was, as far as possible, to protect the Congress and its achievements from defamatory publicity. It was largely a vain hope in the late 1960s when, as the worldwide and sometimes hysterical campaigns against the Vietnam War developed, almost anything associated with the U.S. Government, and certainly anything associated with the CIA, was doomed to such publicity. Some of the magazines created by the Congress have actually survived to this day with their policies basically unchanged: for example, *Encounter, Survey, Minerva* in England, *New Quest* and *China Report* in India, and *Quadrant* in Australia. (*Survey* indeed went on to enjoy its period of greatest acclaim.) But what began with such high hopes in 1950 ended in "scandal," and the Congress was dissolved. Its successor organization, the International Association for Cultural Freedom, lasted ten years and continued some of the Congress's programs but lost a clear sense of its mission.

What, then, was the mission of the Congress for Cultural Freedom? It was obviously anti-Fascist as well as anti-Communist. Many of its supporters had been refugees from Hitler's Germany (Franz Borkenau, Golo Mann, Richard Löwenthal), from Mussolini's Italy (Ignazio Silone, Nicola Chiaromonte), or from Franco's Spain (Julian Gorkin, Salvador de Madariaga). The Congress throughout its life fought against the right-wing dictators General Francisco

Franco and Antonio Salazar (as well as against other dictators such as Juan Peron and Achmad Sukarno) (see chapters 8 and 12). It was also opposed to "McCarthyism" (although some of its American associates were so-called anti-anti-McCarthyites). James Rorty and Moshe Decter published, for the American Committee for Cultural Freedom in 1954, *McCarthy and the Communists,* which documented the damage the Senator had done and supported Sidney Hook's call, in the name of the American Committee for Cultural Freedom, for McCarthy's retirement from public life.

The Congress also kept its distance from political conservatism. Such conservatives as Michael Oakeshott and Eric Voegelin played a small, marginal role in the Congress, but magazines like the American *National Review* were considered outside the pale. Lionel Trilling's question to Jeffrey Hart—"You wouldn't ever write for *National Review,* would you?"[29]—was a characteristic attitude, and Michael Josselson, the Congress's chief administrator, rebuked Friedrich Torberg for reprinting in the Congress's Austrian magazine, *Forum,* a *National Review* exchange in 1957 by James Burnham and William Schlamm: " . . . it is beneath the dignity of a Congress journal to reprint something from the completely discredited *National Review* which devotes most of its columns to mudslinging and name-calling of the worst kind."[30] (At the same time *National Review,* deeply skeptical of the non-Communist Left, was a frequent critic of the Congress and the American Committee for Cultural Freedom.)

The Congress also had little in common with other centers of anti-Communism—churches and private business. Its coalition included some religious believers, such as Denis de Rougemont or Pierre Emmanuel, but most of its active members were secularist freethinkers in the style of Bertrand Russell, Benedetto Croce, or Sidney Hook. The theologians who supported the Congress were liberals like Reinhold Niebuhr and Jacques Maritain. With regard to business, the Congress's economist was J. M. Keynes, not F. A. Hayek. It appealed to intellectuals, a class of people for whom, Raymond Aron observed, "anticapitalism is an article of faith." For them even to agree to debate the possible merits of a free enterprise system, Aron said, would be an emotional and philosophical surrender.[31] Malcolm Muggeridge had illustrated this "article of faith" in 1945 when the editor of the conservative London *Daily Telegraph,* offering him a job, asked him if he believed in "private enterprise." Muggeridge was "unable to say whether he believed in it or not."[32] It is a far cry from the neoconservatism that succeeded the dissolution of Congress liberalism.

The basic hallmark, in short, of the Congress's anti-Communism was that it felt itself to be of the Left and on the Left. Arthur Koestler, in his New York address in 1948 on "The Radicals' Dilemma," had exposed "the deadly fallacies of the Babbits of the Left" because he himself was (as he said) a man of the Left: "To the Babbit of the Right I have nothing to say; we have no language in common."[33] Dwight Macdonald caught something of that spirit the following year in his account of a Stalinoid reception that he, Mary McCarthy, and other members of the "Americans for Intellectual Freedom" attended following the Waldorf Peace Conference, at the invitation of the Communist writer Howard Fast. He found communication easier than he had expected:

> We had a common culture ... we read the same books, went to the same art shows and foreign films, shared the same convictions in favour of the (American) underdog—the Negroes, the Jews, the economically underprivileged—and against such institutions as the Catholic hierarchy and the U.S. State Department.

Macdonald even preferred the Stalinoids to people who marched under what he referred to as the "repulsive" banners of religion and of patriotism.[34]

Many of the Congress's leading figures were active in social democratic political parties: Carlo Schmid, Ernst Reuter, and Willy Brandt in Germany; Ignazio Silone in Italy; David Rousset, André Philip, and Georges Altman in France; Hans Oprecht in Switzerland. The Americans were either socialists like Sidney Hook and Daniel Bell or progressive liberals like J. K. Galbraith or Arthur M. Schlesinger, Jr. Raymond Aron, Edward Shils, Michael Polanyi, and George Kennan were among the many who eluded such categories. But the sympathies of Congress supporters were usually with the Democratic Party in the United States, the Socialists in France, and the Labour Party in the United Kingdom. In the 1960s *Encounter* was for a period the main forum for the discussion of Gaitskellite ideas. It was in the same spirit that the Congress supported the decolonization of the Western empires (although it was slow to move in the case of French Algeria; when it did, its Paris office was bombed).

Along with all that strength of commitment, what else was nota-
ble, especially in the early years, was the zest with which the Congress went about its work. It enjoyed a sense of embodying an idea
whose moment had come. With the gradual disintegration of the
Soviet *mythos,* it felt itself in the *avant-garde,* at the very center of a
redefinition of civilization. Norman Podhoretz caught the mood
of the Congress when he described the intellectual atmosphere in
New York in 1953: The main element

> ... was an exhilaration at the sudden and overwhelming
> appearance of new possibilities, in life as in consciousness.
> There was a world out there which no-one, it seemed, had
> bothered to look at before, and everyone, happily shedding
> his Marxist blinkers, went rushing off to look.[35]

By the time the Congress dissolved in 1967, both the New Left
and the New Right would agree in scorning the achievement of
the non-Communist Left. But that was a long way from the day in
Berlin in the late 1940s when Michael Josselson and Melvin Lasky
watched trainloads of Soviet prisoners being carried from the
West to death in the gulags, and when, as Edward Shils put it,
"these two Russian Jews decided to save Western civilisation."[36]

# 2
# *The 1950 Offensive*

G ive me a hundred million dollars and a thousand dedicated people, and I will guarantee to generate such a wave of democratic unrest among the masses— yes, even among the soldiers—of Stalin's own empire, that all his problems for a long time to come will be internal. I can find the people.

SIDNEY HOOK, 1949[1]

Truth also needs propaganda.

KARL JASPERS, 1950[2]

In the late 1940s there were many calls, similar to Sidney Hook's quoted above, for an organization to combat the sustained cultural blitz of the U.S.S.R. and to counter the public appeal of the glittering international congresses of Communist fellow-travelers. George Orwell, Bertrand Russell, Arthur Koestler, André Malraux, Albert Camus, and many others all agreed on the urgent need for some sort of action to save the free world,[3] especially among writers, artists, scientists, and intellectuals. But little came of all these discussions (apart from Camus's short-lived *Groupes de liaison internationale*), until August 1949, when Ruth Fischer, Franz Borkenau, and Melvin J. Lasky met in a Frankfurt hotel to develop a plan for an international conference of anti-Communist Leftists to be held in 1950 in Berlin—"that traumatic synecdoche of the Cold War," as James Burnham called it. The idea was to invite leading European and American writers and intellectuals (Bertrand

15

Russell, George Orwell, Albert Camus, Ignazio Silone, and Sidney Hook were mentioned) and debate the Cold War for several days. The conference would culminate in a mass meeting and the formation of a permanent "International Committee for Cultural Freedom," committed to the "cultural reconstruction" of a still weak and devastated Europe, to a sort of cultural counterpart to the Marshall Plan. The conference would be sponsored by the magazine *Der Monat* (which the U.S. Military Government published in Berlin and which Lasky edited), and Lasky would be its organizing Secretary-General. The costs would be met by the newly formed and generally unknown CIA, whose staff in Berlin already included Michael Josselson.

Melvin Jonah Lasky was born in 1920 and had grown up in the Bronx, in the "looming presence"[4] of his bearded and learned grandfather, who spoke nothing but Yiddish (and to whose memory in 1976 he dedicated his major book, *Utopia and Revolution*). He was, in Daniel Bell's words (chosen before the term was debased by its application to the high-tech strategists of the Vietnam war) one of the "best and brightest"[5] graduates of that ideological hothouse, the City College of New York, which in the 1930s was the arena of a constant, tense confrontation between the Stalinists (and their fellow-travelers) and the anti-Stalinist Left, including Trotsky-ites (Cannonites and Schachtmanites), Lovestoneites, Norman Thomas socialists, and social democrats. In the end, most City College graduates were permanently inoculated against Stalinism and its fronts, although they still writhed in ideological quandaries. When Sidney Hook formed the Committee for Cultural Freedom in 1939 to combat fascist and Communist totalitarianism, Lasky joined a rival group, formed by Dwight Macdonald, called the League for Cultural Freedom *and Socialism*, and signed its manifesto, which declared that "the liberation of culture is inescapable from the liberation of the working class and all humanity."[6] (Other signatories included James Burnham, James T. Farrell, and the editors of *Partisan Review*, Philip Rahv and William Phillips.)

Educated as a historian, Lasky joined the civil service and worked as a historical aide and travel guide at the Statue of Liberty until he resigned to join the staff of the anti-Stalinist, anti–Popular Front fortnightly *The New Leader*, published by Samuel (Sol) Levitas, a Menshevik who had been imprisoned several times by the Bolsheviks. Drafted into the Army, Lieutenant Lasky became a combat historian with the U.S. Seventh Army in France and Germany and was demobilized in Berlin.

Lasky found Berlin (not yet a divided city and still under the government of the Allied Four-Power Kommandatura) a fascinating enclave; in turn he soon fascinated the Berliners. He cut a flamboyant figure, with his short, stocky figure, his oriental eyes, his Lenin-like black spade beard, his cosmopolitan culture, his easy-going New York manner, and his histrionic delivery, alternately whispering and thundering. He soon involved himself in two new German "resistance" movements, one political, based on Berlin's Social Democrats and in conflict not only with the Communists but also frequently with the Allied Occupation authorities, and the other cultural, reasserting Western liberal values in the post-Hitler turmoil.

Politically Berlin, where almost every family had a relative who had disappeared behind the Iron Curtain, and which was surrounded by Soviet Germany, was inevitably an anti-Stalinist city. Already in March 1946, in one of the first acts of the postwar conflict with the Soviet Union, Dr. Kurt Schumacher, the crippled survivor of ten years in Nazi concentration camps, had led his Social Democrats in a vote against a merger with the Communists, and in October of the same year the Social Democrats and Christian Democrats overwhelmingly defeated the Communists in the Berlin city assembly elections. When in June 1947 the city assembly elected Ernst Reuter mayor, the Soviets vetoed the election of such a well-known ex- and anti-Communist. In 1948 and 1949 the Berliners had held out against the Soviets' Blockade of Berlin and were saved by the Allied airlift.

This political struggle was further embittered by what George F. Kennan described as the "quite extensive" Communist penetration of the U.S. government services by the end of the war, "particularly in the hastily recruited wartime bureaucracies," such as the occupational establishment in Germany.[7] In the view of German Social Democrats and American anti-Stalinists, the American Military Government was heavily "penetrated," especially the Information Control Division, which licensed the staffs of German newspapers, radio stations, and theaters, and the Political Affairs Division, which was responsible for reestablishing German political life on a democratic basis. Peter Blake (a former political intelligence officer with the U.S. Army in Germany) spoke for these anti-Stalinist dissenters, who included Lasky of *Der Monat,* Boris

Shub of RIAS (Radio in American Sector), and Josselson of the State Department when he wrote in Dwight Macdonald's magazine *Politics*:

> The strange collection of American "liberals," Stalinoids, Russia-firsters etc. etc. that assembled to lend the U.S. Army a hand in accomplishing that mission [of reeducation] has, instead, spent the better part of the past three years in making our Zone of Germany ripe for Stalinism.[8]

The highest American officials, he wrote, were so naïve in their dealings with the Soviets that Communists controlled many important newspapers, radio stations, and trade unions, and it had been left to Schumacher's and Reuter's impoverished Social Democrats to lead the fight for democracy against Stalinism in Berlin. (George Orwell complained to Arthur Koestler in 1947 that the U.S. authorities in Munich had seized and handed over to Soviet authorities 1,500 copies of a Ukrainian translation of *Animal Farm.*)[9]

The second "resistance movement" Lasky joined was within Berlin's cultural life. In a sense Berlin had quickly become a city of dazzling culture. Winthrop Sargeant reported in 1946 that Berlin was already "the theatrical and musical capital of Europe. . . . You can see a wider variety of good theatre of all kinds in two months in Berlin than in two years on Broadway."[10] Judith Anderson acted and Yehudi Menuhin played there. Wilhelm Furtwängler conducted the Berlin Philharmonic and Jürgen Fehling directed Jean-Paul Sartre's *The Flies.* Plays by Shakespeare, Schiller, Shaw, and O'Neill were produced. But in another sense it remained an "authorized," "licensed," "permitted," and sponsored culture: Nowhere, Lasky complained in *Partisan Review,* were the principles of cultural freedom recognized or even paid lip service. The German intellectuals had been isolated since 1933 and knew little of such writers as James Joyce, T. S. Eliot, André Gide, Franz Kafka, or Ignazio Silone. "Never in modern history, I think, has a nation and a people revealed itself to be so exhausted, so bereft of inspiration or even talent," Lasky wrote.[11] Despite its glitter, it remained a wasteland where a shoddy Spenglerism prevailed. There was certainly little in the Western sectors to rival the galaxy of literary talent assembling in East Berlin and East Germany—Bertolt Brecht, Anna Seghers, Theodor Plievier, Arnold Zweig, Ernst Bloch, Hans Mayer.

Lasky was shortly in a position to do something. After his much publicized speech in East Berlin at the 1947 German Writers' Congress, in which he had paid tribute to persecuted Russian writers, the U.S. Commander, General Lucius D. Clay, in response to Soviet protests, had considered expelling him from Berlin. But now, as U.S. policy began to move away from appeasement of the Soviet side, the U.S. authorities sought Lasky's advice in the field of "cultural politics." Lasky recommended sponsoring and editing a cultural magazine that would bring to German intellectuals the best that was being written and thought in the free world. The result was *Der Monat.*

The first issue in October 1948 published Bertrand Russell, Arthur Koestler, Arnold J. Toynbee, and Jean-Paul Sartre. Later issues presented George Orwell, Thomas Mann, James T. Farrell, Benedetto Croce, Ernest Hemingway, and Aldous Huxley, among others. The magazine was an immediate success, and its liberating influence was felt not only in West Germany and West Berlin but also in the East, where its articles on Nazi–Soviet cooperation or on Lenin's testament (warning against Stalin's brutality) aroused intense interest and where reading it became a punishable offense. Sidney Hook wrote to Lasky, "you are getting out the best cultural magazine in the entire world."[12] *Der Monat* was the natural sponsor of the Congress for Cultural Freedom that assembled in a tense Berlin in June 1950 as the Korean War broke out.

The hundred invited writers, artists, and scientists were mainly of that generation born early in the century who had never experienced "the long Edwardian summer" of peace, and for whom the formative events—"our generation's Stations of the Cross," as Malcolm Muggeridge put it—were World War I, the Russian Revolution, Italian fascism, the world Depression, German Nazism, the Spanish Civil War, the Moscow purges, Munich, the Hitler–Stalin pact, World War II, and the Holocaust. Former political prisoners, refugees, and Resistance activists set the tone.

Former prisoners of the Nazis included Eugen Kogon (author *Der SS-Staat*), David Rousset (*L'Univers concentrationnaire*), Rudolf Pechel (*Deutsche Widerstand*), Luise Rinser (*Gefängnistagebuch*), Fritz Molden, Per Monsen, and Rémy Roure. Rudolph Brunngraber had been under civil arrest outside Berlin (until he escaped and went into hiding). Altiero Spinelli had been in a prison or under detention for seventeen years in Mussolini's Italy. Former gulag inmates included Josef Czapski (who had written *The Inhuman Land*); Elinor Lipper (*Eleven Years in Soviet Prison Camps*); Margaret Buber-Neumann, who had been in both Soviet and Nazi prisons (*Under Two Dictators*); and Boris Nicolaevsky, who had been exiled in Siberia under the Tsar and imprisoned, then deported, by the Bolsheviks (*Forced Labour in the Soviet Union*, with D. J. Dallin). Arthur Koestler had been a political prisoner in Spain (*Spanish Testament*) and an internee in France (*The Scum of the Earth*) and, briefly, in England. Panayotis Kanellopoulous had been interned by the Metaxas dictatorship in Greece; François Bondy and Walter Mehring had been political internees in France; and Ignazio Silone a political prisoner in Spain. (During World War I Bonaventura Tecchi had been a political prisoner in Italy and Hans Kohn had been a prisoner of war for four years in Russia.)

The refugees from Hitler included Franz Borkenau, Fritz Eberhard, Hermann Kesten, Richard Löwenthal, Golo Mann, Walter Mehring, Theodor Plievier, and Eugen Rosenstock-Huessy. Silone and G. A. Borgese had been refugees from Mussolini. There were ten refugees from the U.S.S.R., including Sol Levitas, Nicolas Nabokov, Boris Nicolaevsky, Sergei Utechin, Salomon Schwartz, and Anna Siemsen. There were two refugees from Poland, Josef Czapski and Jerzy Giedroyc; two from Czechoslovakia, Frantisek Kovarna and Karel Kupka; and one from Latvia, Mintauts Cakste. Sheba Strunsky of the International Rescue Committee, who had helped some of them escape, was also there.

Many of the others had been active in the Resistance. André Philip had been a Resistance leader in France. Henri Frenay had been a Minister in General de Gaulle's Free French government. Claude Mauriac had been de Gaulle's private secretary, and Raymond Aron (who could not attend the Congress but sent a paper attacking neutralism) had edited the Gaullist *la France libre* in London during the war. Jules Romains had worked for the Free French cause in the United States and in Mexico. Haakon Lie and Per Monsen ahd been Resistance leaders in Norway. Fröde Jakobsen had been commanding general of the Danish Home Army during the Nazi occupation. Panayotis Kanellopoulos had formed a Greek resistance movement and had been a minister in the Greek government-in-exile. Others had been well-known opponents of Hitlerism: the economist Wilhelm Röpke and the physicist Hans Thirring had both been removed from their university chairs because of their liberal views, and Franz Josef Schoeningh had had his Catholic literary review, *Hochland,* closed down becuase of its anti-Nazi articles.

Almost all the participants were liberals or social democrats, critical of capitalism and opposed to colonialism, imperialism, nationalism, racism, and dictatorship. They supported freedom of thought and the extension of the welfare state. Many had been active in the movement for a European Union (Julian Amery, Hendryk Brugmans, François Bondy, Henri Frenay, Eugen Kogan, Charles Plisnier, Denis de Rougemont, and Altiero Spinelli). A few were former Communists: Arthur Koestler, Spinelli, Ignazio Silone, Franz Borkenau, Richard Löwenthal, Ernst Reuter and Theodor Plievier. (The authorities had assigned bodyguards to Koestler and to Plievier, the author of *Stalingrad* and veteran of the 1918 mutiny of the German fleet at Kiel.) Others were former Marxists, including the Americans Sidney Hook, James Burnham, and James T. Farrell; the Belgian novelist Charles Plisnier; and the Swedish poet Ture Nerman.

The participants' occupations spanned the intellectual professions. There were philosophers (A. J. Ayer and Hook), historians (Hugh Trevor-Roper and Franz Borkenau), scientists (Hans Thirring and H. J. Muller), artists and novelists (Nicolas Nabokov and Jules Romains), editors (Sol Levitas, Jerzy Giedroyc), politicians (Carlo Schmid and Christopher Hollis), and labor leaders (Haakon Lie and Irving Brown). There were one actor (Robert Montgomery) and two men of the cloth (Pastor Adolf Grimme and Father Alberto de Onaindia). They came from almost all parts of Europe and from the United States. Two Americans were blacks, George Schuyler, author of *Slave Today* and *Black No More,* and Max Yergan, the first teacher of black studies on an American campus (at the City College of New York). Only one came from Latin America (German Arciniegas of Colombia) and only one from Asia (Keshev Malik of India). There was no one from Africa.

The Congress also had five Honorary Presidents—all philosophers—who did not attend but whose names exemplified the spirit of the occasion. Benedetto Croce was the most renowned of the Italian liberals who opposed Mussolini. A lifelong freethinker, all his works appeared on the Vatican Index of Prohibited Books. (When he died in 1952, he refused the last rites of the Church.) John Dewey, the American pragmatist and liberal educationist, had headed the famous commission of inquiry that exposed the Moscow trials of Leon Trotsky and other Russian revolutionaries.

Karl Jaspers, one of the founders of "existentialism," had been an unrelenting critic of the Third Reich. (The Nazis had removed him from his academic chair and banned many of his books.) Jacques Maritain was a liberal Catholic humanist of whom Pope Paul VI said (twelve years later, after the Ecumenical Council, Vatican II), "I am a disciple of Maritain." He had been awarded the Medal of French Resistance. Bertrand Russell, the author of *Principia Mathematica,* among other major works of philosophy, was awarded the Nobel Prize for Literature in 1950. Ten years earlier a New York State Supreme Court judge had declared him unfit to teach at the City College of New York because of his libertarian moral views.

Before the Congress started, about forty messages of support were received from kindred spirits around the world—usually of an older generation. They included Eleanor Roosevelt, André Gide, John Dos Passos, Hermann Broch, Upton Sinclair, Walter Reuther, Ralph Bunche, R. H. S. Crossman, Julian Huxley, Louis de Broglie, David Low, and George Grosz.

The two key, and polarizing, figures at the Congress were Arthur Koestler, then a pugnacious and energetic "cold warrior," and Ignazio Silone, a gentle socialist moralist. Koestler was born in Budapest in 1905 in "a typical Continental middle-middle-class family."[13] But "our idyll" collapsed in 1914 when he was nine, and his father was ruined in the postwar Austrian inflation (which Koestler came to see as evidence of the terminal crisis of capitalism). Educated in Vienna, he abandoned his studies to emigrate to Palestine, where he worked for a time as a secretary to Vladimir Jabotinsky. He then became a Berlin-based science journalist with the liberal Ullstein chain (and covered the Graf Zeppelin North Pole expedition in 1931).

His joining the Communist Party at this time was a true conversion. Every page of Marx, he wrote later, "and even more of Engels," had "the intoxicating effect of a sudden liberation." This was at the beginning of that abortive renaissance, the Pink Decade:

> The stars of that treacherous dawn were Barbusse, Romain Rolland, Gide and Malraux in France; Piscator, Becher, Renn, Brecht, Säghers in Germany; Auden, Isherwood, Spender in England; Dos Passos, Upton Sinclair, Steinbeck in the United States.... The cultural atmosphere was saturated with

Progressive Writers' congresses, experimental theatres, committees for peace—against Fascism, societies for cultural relations with the USSR, Russian films and avant-garde magazines.[14]

Koestler's Party cell in Berlin included the psychoanalyst Wilhelm Reich, author of *The Function of the Orgasm* and founder in 1930 of the "German Association for Proletarian Sexual Politics." In 1932 Koestler went to the U.S.S.R. and wrote a Soviet propaganda book, *Of White Nights and Red Days.*

After Hitler's triumph in Germany, Koestler joined the German exiles in Paris and for five years worked with Willi Muenzenberg, the propaganda genius who perfected the organization of Communist fronts. In 1936 Koestler went to Spain, nominally as a correspondent for the London *News Chronicle.* Captured by Franco's troops, he spend four months in prison, expected to be executed. The British Government secured his release, and his 1937 book, *Spanish Testament,* established him, in the words of George Orwell, as one of "a new breed of political writers" who combine propaganda, truth, and integrity.[15]

But the months in prison, during which he underwent mystical experiences, had changed his life, and in 1938, about seven years after joining the Communist Party—seven years of dialectically justifying each Party lie, slander, purge, or murder—he finally wrote a letter of resignation, ending it, as noted earlier, with the words: *Es lebe die Sowjetunion!* (Long live the Soviet Union!) He still believed, like Trotsky, in the Bolshevik Revolution. It was not until the swastika was hoisted on Moscow Airport in honor of Ribbentrop's arrival to sign the Hitler–Stalin Pact and the Red Army band broke into the *Horst Wessel Lied,* that he gave up this last illusion.

Arrested again, this time by the French when World War II began, he was interned in a prison camp where he wrote his novel about the Moscow Trials, *Darkness at Noon,* one of the most influential books of the century. On his release he joined the French Foreign Legion and finally escaped to England, where he was once more interned, but only for six weeks. He then enlisted in the Pioneer Corps and later joined the Ministry of Information as an anti-Nazi propagandist, although he felt compromised by the alliance with the Soviet Union: For him, it was a war of "a partial truth against a total lie."

After the war, he resumed his often desperate anti-Communist polemics. His tensions in this period led frequently to the bitter Left Bank quarrels chronicled in Simone de Beauvoir's *The Mandarins* (1954) and in Iain Hamilton's biography *Koestler* (1982). His despair culminated in the novel *The Age of Longing*, which is about the fall of France to the Soviet army and the ignoble conduct of the French intellectuals. The character Jules Commanche (based on Koestler's friend Pierre Bertraux) says:

> [E]ach time a god dies there is trouble in History. . . . The last time a god died was on July 14, 1789, the day when the Bastille was stormed. On that day the Holy Trinity was replaced by the three-word slogan which you find written over our town halls and post offices. Europe has not yet recovered from that operation, and all our troubles today are secondary complications, a kind of septic wound-fever.

It is Koestler's farewell not only to Revolution but, as it would turn out, to progressive politics. It was in this dark mood that he arrived, with his bodyguard, in Berlin.

At one stage when Ignazio Silone was addressing the Berlin Congress, Koestler scribbled a note to a colleague: "I always wondered whether basically Silone is honest or not. Now I know he is not."[16] This was not his real view, but Koestler and Silone were of opposite temperaments. When the Berlin Congress was over, Koestler told Silone how much he admired him, despite the fact that Silone had made things difficult for him during the week: Silone had acted, Koestler told him, as if he were some kind of broad-bottomed Abruzzi peasant and Koestler some kind of cosmopolitan gigolo.[17] In any case, Silone was an inevitable rallying point for many at the Congress who temperamentally resisted Koestler's militancy.

Silone, whose real name was Secondo Tranquilli, was born on May Day, 1900. His father had been a small Abruzzi landholder, and his mother a weaver. (He lost them both in an earthquake when he was fifteen.) He was educated to be a priest, but at seventeen, after being charged with inciting an antiwar riot, he became a socialist journalist. In 1921, when four factions split from the Italian Socialist Party to form a Communist Party, Silone joined it (with Antonio Gramsci), taking most of the Youth Federation with him.

This step, like Koestler's ten years later, was a true conversion and meant breaking with his family. "The Party," he wrote later, "became family, school, church, barracks." He edited Communist newspapers and went to Spain to organize Communist youth groups. (It was in a Spanish prison that he adopted the name Ignazio Silone: It meant nothing, and he wanted an unattractive name to show his disgust with the literary world of the time.) He became a member of the Central Committee of the Italian Communist Party and of the Executive of the Communist International. (No one else in this story held as high a position in the Communist movement as Silone.)

His visits to Moscow were progressively disillusioning. Discussion with Lenin or Trotsky was impossible. To disagree with them was to be an "opportunist," a "hireling," or a "traitor." Two incidents at meetings of the Executive of the Communist International became symbolic for him. At one an English Communist interrupted a discussion to complain that certain proposed tactics would involve lying.

> Loud laughter greeted this ingenuous objection, frank, cordial, interminable laughter, the like of which the gloomy offices of the Communist International had perhaps never heard before. The joke quickly spread all over Moscow, for the Englishman's entertaining and incredible reply was telephoned at once to Stalin and to the most important offices of State, provoking new waves of mirth everywhere. The general hilarity gave the English Communist's timid, ingenuous objection its true meaning.

The second incident was more decisive. Silone had refused at a 1927 meeting to vote for a resolution condemning Trotsky's assessment of the Chinese situation without having been able to read it. Stalin calmly said: "The proposed resolution is withdrawn." But after Silone had gone, the Executive announced that it had adopted the resolution.[18]

Cheated and disillusioned, he quietly dropped out of Party activity, retaining always "the ashen taste of a wasted youth." But the final break did not come until 1931, when the Communist Party asked him to make a public statement condemning Trotsky. He could have done so, but, seeing this as an unexpected "emergency exit," he refused, and the Party expelled him as a "clinical case"

("clinical" because, in one of his discussions with Communist officials, he had said that, in the Party sense of the word, he did not
regard himself as "normal").

But Silone did not feel liberated. He had jumped the wall, but
where was he to go? "It is not easy to free oneself from so intense
an experience as Communism. Something of it always remains to
mark one's character for the rest of one's life." Ex-Communists, he
said, remain a category apart, like former regular officers or ex-
priests.

> I continue to ponder it even today [he wrote in 1949], in an
> attempt to understand it better. If I have written books . . . it
> was to try and understand and to make others understand. I
> am not at all sure that I have come to the end of my
> reflections.[19]

The books were written at first in Switzerland, where Silone fled
after the Italian Fascists issued a warrant for his arrest. (His
younger brother was arrested and beaten to death in prison.) In a
series of novels and essays, beginning with *Fontamara* (1933), he
analyzed the totalitarian mind and the social democratic and
Christian alternatives to it. His emphasis was less intellectual and
more moralistic than Koestler's, and he did not share Koestler's
Rubashovite illusions about the noble character of the early Bolsheviks. Underground work (and almost all of Silone's work for
the Communist Party had been underground) places such a strain
on the nerves, he wrote, that you survive only by being narcotized,
by destroying your conscience. It attracts men of weak character
and makes them weaker still.[20]

He did not abandon his socialist millenarianism, but he now
gave it a Christian, if anticlerical, direction. December 25 in the
Year Zero was the most important date in history, and he saw the
unshakable Christian certainties as so built into human reality that
a man disintegrates when he denies them. His Christianity stressed
suffering (he was one of those, he said, whom God pursues, tears
to pieces, chews, and swallows) and heroism: The church won the
hearts of the masses when it offered them the boldest and most
difficult aims, and socialism too will progress only by scorning the
ideal of comfortable mediocrity.

When he returned to Italy in 1944 he was, for two uncomfortable years, a socialist deputy in the new Constituent Assembly. Few
men were as unsuited as he to Parliamentary life, and his natural

role (as he had acknowledged in 1942) was that of an isolated partisan behind the enemy lines. In 1948 he joined Giuseppe Saragat's anti-Communist Social Democratic faction in its struggle with Pietro Nenni's pro-Communist Socialists, and in 1949 he helped form a third socialist group. He also devoted himself to encouraging defections from the Communist Party.

Apparently he did not want to go to the Berlin Congress in 1950, suspecting (as his widow recalls)[21] that it was "a U.S. State Department operation." What he had written in 1942 remained his creed: "The most important of our moral tasks today consists in liberating our spirits from the racket of gunfire, the trajectory of propaganda warfare and journalistic nonsense in general" and in finding "the seeds beneath the snow." But he was persuaded to go, and this gentle, pensive, melancholy moralist became one of the Congress's leading figures—the alternative to the pugnacious Arthur Koestler.

The initiative, however, from the opening ceremony to the adoption of the "Freedom Manifesto" on the last day, remained with Koestler and his supporters, Sidney Hook, James Burnham, Irving Brown, and Melvin Lasky, who caucused each night to plan the next day's tactics.

Each day, and each of the four sessions after the opening ceremony, had its moments of high drama—defections from the East, political conversions, intellectual confrontations. But nothing was as dramatic as the international events: News of the Korean War was both the background and the foreground of the debates and was of life-or-death significance for the West Berliners, since the U.S. reaction would indicate their own fate, and the Berliners were an essential part of the conference audience.[22]

At the opening public ceremony at 3 P.M. on Monday, June 25, in the Titania Palace, the Berlin Philharmonic Orchestra played the darkly heroic *Egmont* overture (Koestler had wanted Benjamin Britten and Louis MacNeice to compose a "Free Europe Anthem," but nothing came of it) and Mayor Ernst Reuter called on the audience of four thousand to stand in silence for those who had died in the struggle for freedom or were still in concentration camps.

In their opening speeches Silone and Koestler soon stated the competing themes of the conference. This Congress, Silone said, answered a compelling, unfeigned need of writers and artists both to talk to each other across national boundaries and, while valuing their differences, to revive the comradely spirit of the Resistance. Koestler was more challenging: The Congress could or should be the historic turning point when intellectuals finally abandoned their "contemplative detachment" and acknowledged the international emergency created by aggressive totalitarianism. Addressing his "friends, fellow-sufferers, fellow-fighters," he spoke of this emergency as one in which, in Beethoven's words, "fate knocks at the gate of existence" and it is necessary to act with "the unhesitating assurance of an organic reflex." He scorned the "clever imbeciles" who preach neutrality toward the bubonic plague.

Tensions sharpened quickly the next morning at the session on "Science and Totalitarianism." The first paper, by A. J. Ayer, strayed far from the fears and hopes of Koestler, Hook, and Burnham. (He wrote later, no doubt whimsically, that he had only gone to Berlin for the free trip.) His "contemplative"—or, as he put it, "namby-pamby"—paper on J. S. Mill's conception of liberty aroused little interest in this assembly; the session chairman, the Greek politician Panayotis Kanellopoulous, was unsympathetic; and Ayer heard someone say: *In unserer Zeit hilft nicht John Stuart Mill* (in our time John Stuart Mill is no help). Ayer and his Oxford colleague, Hugh Trevor-Roper, were already in the anti-Koestler camp.

There was more interest in later developments in the session. Professor H. J. Muller, the American biologist (who had emigrated to the U.S.S.R. in 1933 and became head of the Institute of Genetics in Moscow before returning to the West in 1937) spoke of the damage done to Soviet biology by Lysenkoism, which the Central Committee of the Communist Party of the Soviet Union had officially adopted in 1948. The Austrian nuclear scientist Hans Thirring announced (to applause) that he had withdrawn his paper because the Korean War had shown that he had been wrong about the peaceful intentions of the U.S.S.R. Hans Nachtsheim of the Free University of Berlin illustrated the servility of science in the Eastern bloc by quoting a telegram the head of the Prussian Academy of Science in East Berlin had sent to Stalin congratulating him on his "scientific achievements." At this point (to further applause) Alfred Weber announced his immediate resignation from the Academy.

In this charged atmosphere, Hugh Trevor-Roper decided not to deliver his paper on "Truth, Liberalism, and Authority" (in which he described "totalitarian" trends in the Christian churches). Instead he took up Ayer's ideal of tolerance and his critique of Koestler's "dogmatism." Koestler replied that he was not asking the Congress to say *yes* to any program, but only for an alliance with ordinary people, millions of whom have fled to the West and have said *no* to totalitarianism: "If intellectuals cannot say *no* to concentration camps and totalitarianism, then I no longer understand the language."

The same uneasy mixture of academic discussion and drama, of reflection and calls to action, characterized most of the debates. At the hot afternoon session, on "Freedom and the Artist," chaired by Silone, it was the famous German novelist and refugee from the U.S.S.R., Theodor Plievier, who, by arriving with his bodyguard, stole the show—he and the American screen actor Robert Montgomery, who said: "There is no neutral corner in Freedom's room." There was little response to Herbert Read's gloomy paper on the death of Western capitalist culture ("We are staggering," he said "into a new stage of darkness, utility and ugliness"). An excited Nicolas Nabokov was the next to be applauded when he shouted:

> Out of this Congress we must build an organization for war. We must have a standing committee. We must see to it that it calls on all figures, all fighting organizations and all methods of fighting, with a view to action. If we do not, we will sooner or later all be hanged. The hour has long struck 12.

The session ended with Lasky reading a draft message to intellectuals behind the Iron Curtain, pledging "our moral and material support to all those who assert their right to freedom against oppression."

On the following day, Wednesday, at the session on "The Citizen in a Free Society," Franz Borkenau raised a major theme of this Congress and of the later years of the Congress for Cultural Freedom: the restoration and restatement of the idea of liberty. But in the discussion following Henri Frenay asked: "What is to be the result of the work of the Congress? I admire Berlin and I admire the speeches, but I did not come merely as a tourist or to listen to talk." (This was an unfair criticism, if only because in the same session Josef Czapski, the Polish artist, had outlined his plan for a university for exiled or refugee students—a plan close to the heart of James Burnham, who saw it as a potential weapon for the liberation of Central Europe.)

The fourth session, on Wednesday afternoon, on "Defense of Peace and Freedom," involved the angriest debates. As the participants assembled, the dominant news was that the United States and the United Nations had committed troops to the defense of South Korea—had decided, that is, to fight Communism on the battlefield. Fate, in Beethoven's words quoted by Koestler, had knocked on the gate of existence and had been answered. Koestler and his allies—and the West Berliners—were relieved and pleased.

The two most provocative papers were delivered by Koestler and James Burnham. Koestler's theme was the false dilemma of "Left" and "Right," of "Socialism" and "Capitalism." Anticipating later debates on "the end of ideology," he argued that the old debates between Left and Right, Socialism and Capitalism, were out of date, if not meaningless, semantic curiosities. The Left had been traditionally against injustice; today it had failed to lead the fight against the Soviet Union, the worst regime of terror and despotism in human history. (As if to enrage American progressives, he declared: "McCarthyism represents the wages of the American liberals' sins ... they were found wanting on the most crucial issue of our time.") The Left had also been traditionally internationalist, but today the "progressive" Labour Government of Britain was obstructing efforts toward European unity, while the nonsocialist governments of Germany, Italy, and France, along with British Conservatives like Winston Churchill, were more internationally minded. In response Haakon Lie claimed that it was British socialism that had destroyed British Communism, and Altiero Spinelli declared that ex-Communists of the Koestler variety had retained a "Communist intolerance" that would "reduce us all to rubble." This in turn provoked another ex-Communist, Franz Borkenau, in an overwrought speech, to call out that he was proud to be a convert from Communism. Then he asked: Is not everyone thrilled that President Truman has ordered arms for South Korea? When the Berliners loudly applauded him, David Rousset complained that "this is no way to debate a question," and Trevor-Roper, in a subsequent damaging report on the Congress declared that "this fanatical speech [Borkenau's] was less frightening than the hysterical German applause which greeted it."[23] (To which Lasky, thinking of Berlin's anti-Nazi, anti-Stalinist social democrats, replied that at least one reader of Trevor-Roper's *The Last Days of Hitler* has been forced to doubt whether Trevor-Roper really knew what the last days of Hitler were like, "or the first days, or any day.")[24]

James Burnham's paper, "The Rhetoric of Peace," delivered with "the dry and deliberately unemphatic smoothness of a YMCA teacher,"[25] ridiculed the sacred cows of the neutralist Left. On *anti-Americanism*: "I will grant all the horror of American comics and radio programs, but I will still choose them as against the MVD." On *the atomic bomb*: "I am not, under any and all circumstances, against atomic bombs. I am ... for those bombs made in Los Alamos, Hanford, and Oak Ridge, and guarded I know not where in the Rockies or American deserts. For five years, those bombs have defended—have been the sole defense of—the liberties of Western Europe." On *peace*:

> So long as the Communist power threatens the world, genuine peace, or even the prospect of peace, will prove impossible. Through a moral, psychological, and political counteroffensive, through a worldwide anti-Communist Resistance, we can disintegrate the Communist power without the last desperate resort—which otherwise will surely come— to atomic bombs. Such a counteroffensive, driven forward by the resolute will of free men, is today the only road to peace.

In the debate André Philip pointed out atomic bombs do not distinguish friend from foe, and, supported by Eugen Kogon, claimed that social reforms and European unification would be better, if not the best, defenses against Communism. Lasky and Reuter argued that welfare and defense policies should supplement each other, not conflict. To end the session Norbert Muhlen introduced a refugee student from the Soviet sector, who spoke of political and intellectual coercion in his former university, and Mayor Reuter announced that, although the Communist regime in East Germany would shortly cut off West Berlin's electricity, the city now had its own independent sources and would survive.

The final debate of the Congress was over the wording of the Freedom Manifesto, drafted by Koestler with Manès Sperber's help. The Manifesto was fourteen numbered paragraphs rejecting neutralism, calling for peace through the establishing of democratic institutions, and expressing solidarity with the victims of totalitarian states. Trevor-Roper and Ayer raised what Ayer himself later called "mischievous objections" in an attempt at "undermining" the Congress. In particular Trevor-Roper objected to one draft paragraph declaring that totalitarians "who deny spiritual freedom to others do not enjoy the right to citizenship in the free republic of the spirit." It was a clumsily expressed renunciation of neutralism, but Trevor-Roper claimed that it amounted to calling for a ban on the Communist Party. When Silone, Lie, and Fröde Jacobson, as well as Ayer, supported Trevor-Roper, Koestler with-drew the paragraph to preserve unanimity.

Koestler read the Manifesto to the fifteen thousand people who attended the closing ceremony on Thursday afternoon and shouted the echoing words: "Friends, Freedom has seized the of-fensive!" The Berlin Congress had been a triumph for Koestler—but at a price.

# 3
# *Good-bye to Berlin*

🖎

I have an elaborate plan for a music and arts festival
[which] will have much more *retentissement* than a
hundred speeches by Arthur Koestler, Sidney Hook, and
James Burnham, about the neuroses of our century.

NICOLAS NABOKOV, 1951[1]

I have ... a sense of real tragedy in relation to this
present crisis of the Congress.

JAMES BURNHAM, 1951[2]

## THE ARTHUR KOESTLER EPISODE

If Berlin was a triumph for Arthur Koestler, it was also the climax
of his swan song. He had been brilliant in Berlin, but for the next
few months the Congress for Cultural Freedom remained a faltering and uncertain organization, its future in doubt. When the
stumbling ended, about November and December 1950, and funds
had been secured, staff appointed, and goals clarified, Koestler
and his closest associates were no longer the dominant influences.
*"Ne koestlerisons pas,"* the French Leftist Catholic *Esprit* had warned,
and the Congress took careful note. To "Koestlerize" meant to attack contemptuously the fellow-travelers, whom Koestler indeed
regarded as—literally—neurotics or, as he described them twice in
one speech at Berlin, "imbeciles." His style, as even his admirer

33

Sidney Hook conceded, was such that he could not recite the multiplication tables without infuriating somebody. The alternative strategy adopted by the Congress for Cultural Freedom was to build a kind of "united front" with the democratic elements of the European Left and gradually win it over to the Atlanticist cause.

It is impossible to separate this *coup*—at once ideological and pragmatic—from the decision of the U.S. Central Intelligence Agency to assume responsibility for the continuing funding of the Congress. But before coming to that, and its consequences, it is necessary to examine what happened within the Congress in the second half of 1950.

In his final report on the Berlin Congress, Lasky outlined what he saw as the next steps. The Executive Committee (Irving Brown, Koestler, David Rousset, Carlo Schmid, and Ignazio Silone) would have to meet very soon, he wrote. It would have to draw up Articles of Association, appoint a secretariat, rent an office, prepare pamphlets, public meetings, broadcasts, protests, and newsletters. National Committees around the world should be formed, in accordance with a resolution adopted at Berlin. A publishing house, filmmaking, lecture tours, and encouraging defections from the Soviet bloc had all been suggested. Josef Czapski's plan for a university for refugee students and academics was still on the agenda. Lasky wrote:

> The Congress task is one of information, education, orientation, agitation. None of the existing organizations— surely not the UNESCO, nor the French-Anglo-American official services in Central Europe, nor the Marshall Plan publicists in the West—can properly meet this problem. The Congress for Cultural Freedom, on the platform of the broad democratic front created in Berlin, must take advantage of a unique historic opportunity.[3]

An informal steering committee—Koestler, Brown, and Lasky, joined later by Silone and François Bondy—met at Koestler's home at Fontaine-le-Port outside Paris in July and August 1950. Brown brought the resources of the American Federation of Labor to the work of the committee and raised the funds to keep the interim organization going. Born in New York in 1911, he was the bustling, European Representative of the AFL in its contest with the Communist front, the World Federation of Trade Unions—a contest that involved Brown in several public confrontations with the U.S. Military Government in Germany. Working under the general direction of Jay Lovestone (a former Comintern delegate and now a leading anti-Communist), Brown helped form independent anti-Communist unions in France and Italy and built up "the Mediterranean Committee" of vigilantes to stand guard while French dockworkers unloaded U.S. arms for NATO in the face of Communist threats to life. He also helped organize the International Confederation of Free Trade Unions and a Syndicate of Free Trade Unions in Exile, which kept in touch with anti-Communist unionists in the Soviet satellites. A *Reader's Digest* article at the time described him as a "one-man OSS" and "a character out of an E. Phillips Oppenheim novel."[4] François Bondy described Brown as "more helpful than all the Koestlers and Silones put together."[5]

The interim steering committee made some important decisions. It opened a temporary Paris office in the Hôtel Baltimore. It planned a French national committee, *Les Amis de la Liberté,* to hold meetings in Paris and the provinces. It had Articles of Association drafted and the "Berlin Manifesto" translated into French. It agreed that a special committee to deal with Soviet affairs would have to be formed and a French magazine launched when an editor could be found. Koestler began writing a pamphlet.

There was still disagreement and uncertainty about the precise role of the Congress they were forming. Koestler now believed that, in the light of the Korean War, it should be less a cultural organization and more a political movement, a "Deminform" to counter the Cominform. He wanted to set up a labor *Front de la Liberté* among the trade unions—a proposal with which Silone agreed—to supplement *Les Amis de la Liberté.* Koestler also proposed "mass rallies" on the crises in Korea, Persia, and Yugoslavia. Above all, he wanted militancy, and he opposed the acceptance of Nicola Chiaromonte (who had fought in Malraux's squadron in the Spanish Civil War) as Silone's alternate for the executive meetings: How, he asked, can you expect a man who remained a conscientious objector throughout World War II to be an aggressive, ideological fighter in the new struggles?[6] But Koestler was overruled, and the quiet, thoughtful Chiaromonte joined the melancholy Silone in the inner circle of the Congress.

Meanwhile the Leftist and neutralist press of France, Italy, and Britain continued to attack the Berlin Congress. The most damaging attack was H. R. Trevor-Roper's in the *Manchester Guardian*: "The Congress was in no sense an intellectual Congress. . . . It was simply Wroclaw in reverse," organized by American ex-Communists, "rootless" Europeans and "hysterical" German nationalists or even Nazis. G. A. Borgese made a similar attack on the "Manichean" conference in *Corriere della Sera.*[7] Koestler answered his critics in a series of interviews, and Lasky wrote a series of letters to British publications presenting the Congress as a liberal and social democratic initiative against totalitarianism. Nevertheless, the damage was done. Bertrand Russell, for example, resigned as an Honorary Chairman: "From the accounts which reached me through the Press and otherwise," he wrote to Lasky, "I feel I could not be in entire agreement with the majority as expressed in the Congress." He added: "I should like, nevertheless, to assure you that I am in general sympathy with your work and that my disagreements, such as they are, concern only fine shades."[8] Hook, Schlesinger, and Koestler were able on this occasion to persuade him to withdraw his resignation.

But at this stage the strains on Koestler (which included threats to his life and Communist surveillance of his home) led to what he called "a kind of nervous crack-up,"[9] and he decided to resign from the Executive Committee. He flew to the United States in September and watched with resentment as the Congress moved away from his ideas. His last gift to the Congress was its first pamphlet, *Que veulent Les Amis de la Liberté?* Koestler remained pleased with it and republished it in both *The Trail of the Dinosaur* (1955) and *Bricks to Babel* (1981). It developed the ideas of the Berlin Manifesto, settled a score with Trevor-Roper and Ayer, and defined the mission of the Congress:

> The task which the Congress for Cultural Freedom and the Friends of Liberty have set for themselves is to change the present confused and poisoned intellectual climate. If we fail, we shall become guilty of a new *trahison des clercs,* and the responsibility before history will be ours.

But the moment of Koestler's domination had now passed, although his influence as a "founding father" would remain.

## THE EXECUTIVE COMMITTEE

With Koestler in the United States and Lasky back in Berlin editing *Der Monat,* the steering committee gave way toward the end of 1950 to the formal Executive Committee elected in Berlin, with some variations. Nominally there were seven members and seven alternates. Brown (alternate: Haakon Lie), Koestler (Raymond Aron), Eugen Kogon (Carlo Schmid), Denis de Rougemont (no alternate), Rousset (Georges Altman), Silone (Chiaromonte) and Stephen Spender (T. R. Fyvel). Others joined them from time to time without standing on formalities—André Philip, Malcolm Muggeridge, Melvin Lasky, Sidney Hook, and Manès Sperber.

They were all prominent figures in public life, journalism, and letters. Lie was a leader of the Norwegian Labor Party. Kogon was a director of the *Frankfurter Hefte.* Schmid was a member of the German Federal Parliament and of the central committee of the German Social Democratic Party (and a translator of Baudelaire). Rousset was the author of *l'Univers concentrationnaire* and founder of the International Commission against Concentration Camps. (He was at this time fighting a libel action in Paris against a French Communist writer and newspaper, which alleged that he had falsified documents in order to attack the Soviet Union. He called several witnesses who had survived Soviet camps, and won his case.) Altman was editor of the daily *Franc-Tireur.* Spender, the poet, was a former editor of *Horizon.* Fyvel was a member of the English socialist group associated with *Tribune,* where he had succeeded Orwell as literary editor. Chiaromonte was an Italian essayist and theater critic.

Those and other figures will reappear in later pages. One whose continuing role in the Congress should be stressed now is Manès Sperber (1905–84). A "Galizianer," born in Zablotov, the son of a rabbi, he was an Adlerian psychologist and a novelist. His experiences as a Comintern agent from 1927 until the Great Purges (in which friends were murdered) form the basis of his trilogy, "the saga of the Comintern," *Like a Tear in the Ocean.* After a brief period under Nazi arrest in Berlin in 1933, he fled, via Yugoslavia, to France, where he remained for the rest of his life. During the war he served in the French Army and survived in hiding during the German occupation of France. After the war he became an anti-Communist (he described searching in vain through the European press in 1944 for any reports on the Katyn massacre or the Warsaw uprising) and André Malraux's adviser on the organization of press, radio, and publishing in the French zones of Germany and Austria. He helped Arthur Koestler draft the Freedom Manifesto of 1950 and remained actively involved in the Congress—its committees, publications, seminars, and protests—until the end.

His autobiography, *Ces Temps-là,* was published in three volumes in 1976, 1977, and 1979. He received the Peace prize at the Frankfurt Book Fair in 1983.

The President of this Executive Committee was Denis de Rougemont. Born in 1906 to an ancient Swiss family, he had achieved fame before the war with his book *L'Amour et l'Occident* (translated as *Passion and Society* and, in America, as *Love in the Western World*), in which he traced the cult of romantic love to the gnostic heresies of the Middle Ages. He had also been one of the founders in Paris of Emmanuel Mounier's monthly *Esprit,* a journal of the non-Marxist Left and had committed himself to the "personalist movement," to which he contributed the concept of "engagement" (meaning, in part, a refusal to submit to any party). In his own magazine, the personalist *Hic et Nunc,* he introduced the work of Karl Barth, Martin Heidegger, and Søren Kierkegaard to the French public. When Paris fell to the Nazis in 1940, he published in the *Gazette de Lausanne,* in neutral Switzerland, an anti-Nazi appeal for which he was sentenced to fifteen days' detention, but which also led the U.S. Office of War Information to seek his services as a broadcaster for the Voice of America's French-language program. After the war he worked with the European Union of Federalists, which had been formed by former inmates of concentration camps or prisons (Bondy, Henri Frenay) and members of the Resistance (Camus). In 1950 he became director of the "European Center for Culture" (with Salvador de Madariaga as President), which he hoped would develop into a European UNESCO. His prolific appeals for the creation of other Europeanist institutions led St. John Perse to call him the most representative of *l'homo europeanus.* A man of striking appearance with arresting eyes, a jutting jaw, and a sad smile, he looked, one friend said, like a "tough guy" from an American movie.[10] Eugène Ionesco called him the "incomparable de Rougemont."[11]

But the most influential of all the Executive Committee was Aron, who was to become a towering figure in twentieth-century intellectual life. Born in 1905 to a Jewish family of Lorraine (always preserving, he said, "a strain of Lorraine patriotism," which made him skeptical of some theories of a "united Europe"), he was a student with Sartre and Simone de Beauvoir at the *Ecole Normale Supérieure,* where he briefly joined the Socialist Party, then resigned, characteristically, because of his distaste for its romantic revolutionism. Compelled to make a living, since his family was financially ruined in 1929, he chose teaching. He taught for more than three years in Weimar Germany, where he studied the German sociologists, in particular Max Weber, with whose position as "the committed observer" he felt kinship. He also witnessed the rise of totalitarianism in Germany. Aron listened to Josef Goebbels at the notorious Nazi burning of books in May 1933 in Berlin (and tried to console the heartbroken Golo Mann). In 1933 he returned to France, of which he would later say: "Basically France didn't exist any longer. It existed only in the hatred of the French for each other. . . . I lived through it intensely, with profound sadness and a single obsession: to avoid civil war."[12] He published two books, *La Sociologie allemande contemporaine* (1935), which introduced Max Weber to France, and *Introduction à la Philosophie de l'Histoire* (1938). During World War II he joined General de Gaulle's Free French forces in England and managed the monthly review *la France libre,* contributing to almost all of its fifty-nine issues.

Returning once more to Paris in 1945, Aron found a city that was "mortally sad" (the victory had been that of the Allies "more than that of France"), but also found that his generation had a "truly profound determination for national renewal."[13] Although addicted to "metaphysical speculation," Aron decided to defer a return to academic life in order to throw himself into politics and journalism. He helped Sartre found *les Temps modernes* and joined Albert Camus's group around *Combat.* But faced with the spread of Eastern Communism and Western neutralism, Aron distanced himself from the Left (his break with Sartre being the most bitter) and became a columnist for the liberal-conservative *le Figaro.* He also served briefly in André Malraux's Ministry of Information (with his friend Manès Sperber) and in 1947 joined General de Gaulle's *Rassemblement du Peuple Français,* sharing both its anti-Communism and its critique of the French constitution. In 1950 he sent a paper to the Berlin Congress for Cultural Freedom, "Impostures de la Neutralité," in which he argued that the years of appeasement of the Soviets between 1944 and 1946 had increased the chances of war and that only the U.S. atomic weapons had saved the West; the choice now was between capitulation and active political resistance. He developed his liberal, Atlanticist position in the Cold War in three major polemics: *Le Grand Schisme* (1948), in which the first chapter was entitled: "Peace Impossible. War Improbable"; *Les Guerres en chaîne* (1951), translated as *The Cen-*

*tury of Total War*; and *L'Opium des Intellectuels* (1955), in which he scathingly exposed the illusions of the French fellow-travelers and neutralists. Those were the years in which Aron was ostracized and defamed by French intellectuals (rumors circulated that he was "a paid American agent"); and *Preuves* and the Congress, as well as *le Figaro,* became important sustaining milieus for him.

In 1955 he returned to academic life at the Sorbonne. His stature grew with a series of books on sociology, philosophy, and international affairs. But he maintained both his involvement with the Congress and his journalism. His biographer Robert Colquhoun estimated his output at forty books, six hundred essays, and four thousand articles.[14]

A man of absolutely independent judgment, Aron combined— and the adjective Aronian came to mean this—calm, even-tempered skeptical analysis with a deep adherence to liberal values. Always scornful of messianic prophesying, he remained a disciple of Kant, an adherent of the idea of reason and the ideal of a humane society. By the time of his death in 1983 he was honored throughout France and the world. Colquhoun tells an anecdote of a writer who sought Aron's pardon for having referred to his "paranoia." Aron, laughing, accepted the apology but later over lunch exclaimed: "I was wrong to forgive you. Paranoia! Paranoia! Is it my fault that I'm always right?"[15] The joke had some truth in it. Henry Kissinger called him "my teacher."[16]

## THE SECRETARIAT

At the same time as the Executive Committee was etablished in November 1950, the Secretariat was appointed in Paris. The key man, the enlivening spirit, first as Administrative Secretary, then as Secretary of the Executive Committee, and finally as Executive Director, was Michael Josselson, who for the next seventeen years made the Congress his life.

Born in Tartu, Estonia, on March 2, 1908, the son of a Jewish timber merchant, Josselson was educated in Russian and German, and at the time of the Bolshevik Revolution he was taken to Berlin as part of the Baltic diaspora. He completed his schooling and attended university in Berlin. He then earned his living in Paris as representative of the American chain stores of Gimbels–Saks and soon became the European managing director. As Nazi power grew in Europe (many members of his Estonian family were to be murdered), he undertook another emigration, this time to the United States in October 1936.

Josselson became an American citizen in June 1942 and was inducted into the U.S. Army in 1943. He served in an interrogation team of the Psychological Warfare Division in Germany. Discharged in 1946, he stayed on in Berlin with the American Military Government as a Cultural Affairs Officer and with the State Department and the U.S High Commission as a Public Affairs Officer. His work was de-Nazification and cultural politics. He befriended and helped rehabilitate such figures as the conductor Wilhelm Furtwängler and the theater director Jürgen Fehling. It was during this period that he met Melvin Lasky and Boris Shub and joined the dissenters from the then dominant pro-Soviet policy of the U.S. Occupation authorities.

He was in New York at the time of the Peace Conference in the Waldorf-Astoria in March 1949 and attended the counter-rally organized by Sidney Hook's "Americans for Intellectuals Freedom" in Bryant Square. Back in Berlin he became one of the founders of the Congress for Cultural Freedom. By then he was undoubtedly a CIA officer.

Daniel Bell has described Josselson as "a Prussian by day and a Russian by night." What has survived in his correspondence in the Congress archives is the Prussian—a controlled and orderly man attempting to organize a worldwide community of unruly and temperamental intellectuals, coordinate a dozen cultural-political magazines in as many languages, and sponsor a series of multilingual international and national seminars and conferences. (He himself had an accent-free fluency in English, Russian, German, and French.) The correspondence is often that of an irritable, impatient, and ailing man. What does not emerge in it is an underlying melancholy (seen in photographs, in the dark concentration of his eyes), the eruptions from time to time of tempestuous anger or enthusiasm, or the extraordinarily warm and generous personality described by so many friends, of whom the editor, novelist, and critic Robie Macauley will serve as an illustration. In 1960 Macauley wrote to Josselson, who was then recovering from one of his major heart attacks:

> I want to tell you, chiefly, what an extraordinary privilege and satisfaction it has been to have your friendship over the past

few years. In the course of a lifetime one is lucky enough, perhaps once or twice, to come across an intellect that is so dazzling and so beautifully concentrated that only the word "genius" will do for it. As I sat in your room Monday and listened to you talk, it struck me again, as it very often has, what a superb intelligence I was encountering—a combination of clarity, verve and imagination that is, God knows, the rarest thing in the human race. Your ability to produce an idea or to transform one swiftly into some kind of action is beautiful to watch. I've often heard people discussing the question of who could replace you in the Congress. Of course nobody ever can or will. There may be a substitute, but there never will be a replacement.[17]

This same sort of admiration for Josselson and his extraordinary achievements was also evidenced at his death in January 1978 in the hundreds of messages of condolence to his widow, Diana Josselson. They came from Madariaga, Schmid, Sperber, Boris Souvarine, Koestler, Kennan, Kristol, Aron, Bell, Patricia Blake, K. A. Jelenski, Pierre Emmanuel, Theodore Draper, Richard Pipes, George Urban, Jeanne Hersch, Jean Starobinski, and Josef Czapski. Typical of the messages were these:

LOUIS J. HALLE: "Mike lived a uniquely useful life, like that of no one else I have ever known."

SIDNEY HOOK: "He was wiser about human beings, more intelligent about things of the mind than most of those he worked with. His deep modesty probably prevented him from realizing it."

IGNAZIO AND DARINA SILONE: "perte inoubliable ami noble heroique extraordinaire."

WILLY BRANDT: "die Nachricht hat mich tief betroffen."[18]

Yet, despite these deeply felt tributes, the world remained generally unaware of his achievement, and his death went largely unnoticed. The lively and influential organization he had built no longer existed. For many it was still discredited. Some years later Raymond Aron wrote in his *Mémoires* (1983) one of the first sympathetic comments on Josselson to appear in print:

Je garde pour lui consideration, estime. . . . Il etait plus et autre chose qu'un agent de services secrets. Intellectuel doué du sens de l'action, il porte la double responsibilité de la réussite du Congrès et du mensonge originel. [I retain respect, esteem for him. . . . He was something else and more than an agent of the secret services. An intellectual endowed with the sense of action, he carries the double responsibility for the success of the Congress and for the original lie.]

That double responsibility was a huge and embittering burden. When a CIA officer at his funeral asked his widow what she wanted done with the medal and citation Allen Dulles of the CIA had conferred on him some years before (and then, as usual, taken back for safe-keeping), she waved it aside.

But in 1950–51 all this was barely imaginable, and Josselson was about to begin what has been called "one of the greatest epics of our era"[19] while carrying what Aron called "the burden of the lie."

The position of Secretary-General, which entailed full-time public representation of the Congress to the world at large, was filled by Nicolas Nabokov. Born in 1903, an effusive Russian from an old White Russian family (the novelist Vladimir Nabokov was his cousin) he had as a boy fled with his parents from the Bolsheviks, who had killed his eighty-seven-year-old grandmother. He grew up in the Russian diaspora, mainly in Berlin, where the bulk of the Russian intelligentsia had found refuge and had turned the city, he said, into a Russian camp. He studied music, became a composer, and achieved fame in Paris in 1928 when Sergei Diaghilev produced his ballet *Ode*. He continued his musical career in the United States, where the Ballet Russe de Monte Carlo presented his ballet *Union Pacific,* its first ballet with an American theme. Although sometimes drawn to the idea of returning to Russia (like his friend Sergei Prokofiev), he did not, and he became an American citizen in 1939. During the war he worked as a translator for the government in Washington, where he met Charles "Chip" Bohlen, a meeting which was a turning point in his life. Bohlen was to remain "always my model, my source of advice and often my comforter." It was under his influence that Nabokov turned to politics, or cultural politics—with the U.S. Military Government in Berlin, with the Voice of America, and finally with the Congress for Cultural Freedom. (The Voice of America involved him in an experience common to many Congress intellectuals, a humiliating brush with the U.S. authorities, in his case the FBI, as its agents grilled him over his bohemian private life before clearing him.)

A man of striking appearance with a great mane of silver hair, piercing eyes, aquiline nose, and high complexion, Nabokov brought a Slavic enthusiasm and a gift for bear-hugging friendship to his Congress work, especially to its festivals. If, for his critics, he was something of "a comedian from the *Balalaika*," for his friends he brought a lively liberalism and a sense of cultural excitement (along with the skills of a famous raconteur) that made the enterprise worthwhile. James Burnham was delighted with his appointment, and when he heard a report that Nabokov might not stay long with the Congress, he wrote: "With you arriving as a catalyst as well as a quantitative addition, the Congress staff is blossoming as an effective *équipe*, and it would be a shame to throw things back to the pre-Nabokov period."[20] Nabokov did stay, but Burnham had misjudged him. He was, it is true, an anti-Bolshevik, but more an impresario than an intellectual, and certainly neither a Burnhamite nor a Koestlerizer.

A further key appointment to the Secretariat was François Bondy, who became Director of Congress publications and soon editor of its French magazine *Preuves*. Born in 1915 in Berlin—his parents were citizens of the Habsburg Dual Monarchy—he grew up in Switzerland. As a young man he had been in the Communist Party until the Hitler–Stalin Pact (and also briefly, until his Swiss passport rescued him, a prisoner in a French internment camp). Bondy brought to his editorial work a great breadth of mind and information, an endless curiosity, and an irony far removed from the passions of, for example, Koestler. One friend, Peter Coulmas, saw the cosmopolitan Bondy as the product of more than a thousand years of European culture and "almost anachronistic." For another, Melvin Lasky, he was "the editorial adviser of our time *par excellence*."[21] (Another Swiss, René d'Epinay, became the Congress Treasurer.)

It was clear that these appointments would change the direction of the Congress, which the old guard—Koestler, Burnham, and Hook—had set. When the Secretariat met on December 30, 1950, and prepared a list of persons to be invited to a Congress in Paris in 1952, it included the names Sartre, Beauvoir, and Thomas Mann! That was too much for Koestler. He found it preposterous that, within six months of the adoption in Berlin of an antineutralist manifesto, such people could be invited to a meeting of the Congress for Cultural Freedom. He wrote to the new President of the Executive Committee, Rougemont: "If you insist on taking this course will you please accept my resignation?"[22] On the same day he wrote to Jay Lovestone of the AFL:

> Perhaps you could ask Irving Brown to warn the imbeciles to whom our hopeful movement has been handed over that on this issue I refuse to compromise. If these people intend to use our money and efforts to provide Messieurs Sartre and Mann with a platform for denouncing "Western Imperialism" I shall certainly not be an accomplice in this only too well-known kind of thing.
>
> Furthermore, I regard the attempt in itself to paralyze and castrate our movement by going back to the old muddle and confusion as sufficient reason for asking immediately on my return to Europe for the resignation of the whole present Secretariat.
>
> I hate quarrels among intellectuals. I hate even more connivance in intellectual suicide.[23]

To James Burnham he wrote: "I believe that you are an important political thinker in our time but a rotten judge of people." Bondy and Rougemont "were, so to speak, your inventions" and they "have now apparently succeeded in undoing all we have tried to do. Unless they immediately retrace their steps I am out of this."[24] In fact he went further, and in 1955 renounced political activity entirely. "Cassandra," he wrote, "has gone hoarse"—but he remained Cassandra.

As for Burnham, he came to see the Congress as becoming a province of "the Lovestone empire," that is, the AFL. "I would personally have below zero interest in a mushy leftist Lovestonite Congress." To Bondy he wrote complaining of the Congress's move to the Left. "I have . . . a sense of real tragedy in relation to this present crisis of the Congress. To destroy the Congress now would be to blast and betray hopes which, after a long darkness, have begun to stir again."[25]

But the die was cast: The Secretariat would not be sacked, and the Congress would no longer "Koestlerize." There would be no mass rally in Paris in the summer on the model of Berlin. "I have an elaborate plan," the new Secretary-General Nabokov wrote, with characteristic effusive optimism and questionable judgment,

to his friend Arthur M. Schlesinger, Jr., "for a music and arts festival" which "will have much more *retentissement* than a hundred
speeches by Arthur Koestler, Sidney Hook, and James Burnham
about the neurosis of our century."[26]

## FUNDING

Despite ambitious plans, nothing substantial could be done until
adequate and regular funding was secured. The CIA had secretly
funded the Congress in Berlin, and there was a general assumption that the U.S. Government would somehow continue to meet
the costs, perhaps by using Marshall Plan funds. Koestler, who had
always envisioned a "small, shoestring operation like Willi Muenzenberg's," wrote to Bertrand Russell in September 1950 that "we
have little money, only scant personnel and no Cominform behind
us. But if we can produce results in the next six months, support
will grow rapidly."[27] Meanwhile, Irving Brown of the American
Federation of Labor arranged funding for six months,[28] and others
tried to secure funds from various private American foundations.
Sidney Hook, for example, acting on behalf of the Executive Committee, asked the Fund for the Republic for $1 million, but on
June 27, 1951, he was curtly refused.[29] In the same month Nabokov
urged the American Committee to try to raise funds for the European program and wrote of a fundraising drive in Europe.[30]

In the end the recurrent costs of the Congress were met by the
Central Intelligence Agency. At this apocalyptic stage of the Cold
War, there was a further deepening of what Schlesinger called the
"quiet revolution" in the State Department of the late 1940s,
when, under the influence of such figures as Kennan, Bohlen, and
the British philosopher Isaiah Berlin, it came to understand and
support the ideas of the formerly isolated non-Communist Left
(the "NCL"). Now, at a unique historic moment, there developed
a convergence, almost to the point of identity, between the assess-
ments and agenda of the "NCL" intellectuals and that combination of Ivy League, anglophile, liberal, can-do gentlemen, academics, and idealists who constituted the new CIA. It is one of the
ironies of the story that the CIA gave its support secretly, conspira-
torially, and believed that it could not—as to this day it does not—
claim credit for one of its more imaginative and successful decisions.

The regular funding of the Congress was arranged by the CIA's "International Organizations Division," a division created on the suggestion of Thomas W. Braden. Braden, an Iowan, had served as an infantryman with the British Army in North Africa at the beginning of World War II and later as a parachutist in the U.S. Office of Strategic Services. The OSS, the forerunner of the CIA, was an intelligence and espionage "Office" of academics and adventurers that General William "Wild Bill" Donovan had organized during World War II at the request of President Roosevelt and over the opposition of the established military intelligence services and of the FBI. In their youthful book *Sub Rosa* (1946), Braden and Stewart Alsop wrote that the OSS "provided its men with opportunities for the most amazing adventures recorded in any war since that of King Arthur"! Braden himself was parachuted several times into occupied France to work with the *Maquis*. After the war he taught English at his old college, Dartmouth, and was executive secretary of the Museum of Modern Art in New York before joining the CIA to work with Frank Wisner, Director of Policy Coordination. A tall, craggy liberal Democrat (he later campaigned in California for the Democratic nomination for Lieutenant Governor and served on that state's Board of Education during the administration of Governor Edmund G. Brown), his concept of the International Organizations Division was that it would avoid the limitations of the CIA's geographic divisions (Far Eastern, West European, and so on) and would more effectively combat the international front organizations on which the Soviet Union was then spending (according to the CIA) some $250 million a year—such as the World Peace Council, the World Federation of Trade Unions, and the International Union of Students.[31] The basic idea was to create "counter-organizations" or, where they already existed, to help finance them. An assembly like the Congress for Cultural Freedom, already operating independently, if penuriously, easily fitted into the second category. Braden wrote later that: "in much of Europe in the 1950s, socialist people who called themselves 'left' ... were the only people who gave a damn about fighting Communism."[32]

Braden's assistant in administering the International Organizations Division was Cord Meyer, Jr. (who became head of the division when Braden resigned in 1954 to become the publisher-editor of a newspaper in Oceanside, California). Meyer was educated at St. Paul's boarding school and at Yale. During the war, as a Marine lieutenant, he was wounded (losing the sight of his left eye) during the invasion of Guam. After the war he joined the American Veterans' Committee, a liberal alternative to the conservative American Legion, and was deeply involved in the struggle to frustrate a takeover of the AVC by the Communist Party. He also spent two years as an organizer and lecturer for the liberal United World Federalists and wrote *Peace or Anarchy* (1947). The book was endorsed by Albert Einstein, and Moscow radio denounced Meyer as "the figleaf of American imperialism." In 1951 Allen Dulles urged him to join the CIA and, after consulting Walter Lippmann, he did. Within two years the CIA suspended him without pay while it investigated an FBI report that he might be a security risk because of his past association with pro-Communist individuals and organizations. He was cleared after several weeks, but the ordeal strengthened his hostility toward the "McCarthyist" type of anti-Communism, which Sidney Hook called "vigilantism." But Meyer still maintained that

> ... the real competition with the Communists for votes and influence was focused on the left side of the political spectrum, where the struggle for the allegiance of the European working class and the liberal intelligentsia would be decided.[33]

The CIA's method of providing funds was indirect, through actual foundations or ones created for the purpose. For the Congress, one of the principal conduits was the Farfield Foundation, which was incorporated on January 30, 1952, as a nonprofit organization in the State of New York. Its brochure stated:

> It was formed by a group of private American individuals who are interested in preserving the cultural heritage of the free world and encouraging the constant expansion and interchange of knowledge in the fields of the arts, letters, and sciences. To this end, the Foundation extends financial aid to groups and organizations engaged in the interpreting and publicizing of recent cultural advances and to groups whose enterprises in literary, artistic, or scientific fields may serve as worthy contributions to the progress of culture. The Foundation offers assistance to organizations whose programs tend to strengthen the cultural ties which bind the nations of

the world and to reveal to all peoples who share the traditions of a free culture the inherent dangers which totalitarianism poses to intellectual and cultural development. The Foundation dedicates its efforts to the hope that under modern conditions which are bringing about closer and closer relations among nations there may be a new growth of free and creative activity in every artistic and scientific field.[34]

The Foundation's President was Julius Fleischmann, a director of the Metropolitan Opera in New York, a fellow of the Royal Society of the Arts in London, a member of the advisory committee of the Yale Drama School, and a former director of Ballet Russe de Monte Carlo and of the Ballet Foundation of New York. He had been a financial backer of many Broadway productions. His personal wealth and his varied artistic patronage made the Farfield Foundation's patronage of the Congress plausible. The directors of the Foundation met every other month at a lunch meeting, where there would usually be a guest from the Congress—Nicolas Nabokov, Michael Josselson, or Malcolm Muggeridge. They approved the payments, asking no questions, acting out "the comedy" (in Muggeridge's words) as a patriotic duty.

In fact the attempt at cover was hardly successful. Sidney Hook has written that he, "like almost everyone else" had heard that "the CIA was making some contribution to the financing of the Congress but I was never privy to the amount or to the mechanism of its operation."[35] Nabokov wrote to Burnham in June 1951 about the importance of convincing anti-American French intellectuals that the Congress is "not an American secret service agency." Many of the English intellectuals, he also wrote, "think of our Congress as some kind of semiclandestine American organization controlled by you [Burnham], Koestler, and . . . Borkenau."[36]

The later consequences of the link between the CIA and the Congress will be discussed further in the chapter dealing with the controversies that followed the public exposure in 1967 of the scale of the CIA's funding of international organizations. But whatever the rumors or allegations, they were in the early 1950s of secondary importance to the Congress intellectuals, who had been desperately calling for a greater American commitment if European freedom were to survive. Raymond Aron spoke for them all when he said bluntly: "I am entirely convinced that for an anti-Stalinist there is no escape from the acceptance of American leadership."[37] In the same spirit Malcolm Muggeridge wrote in *Time* magazine:

> If I accept, as millions of other Western Europeans do, that America is destined to be the mainstay of freedom in this mid-20th century world, it does not follow that American institutions are perfect, that Americans are invariably well behaved, or that the American way of life is flawless. It only means that in one of the most terrible conflicts in human history, I have chosen my side, as all will have to choose sooner or later, and propose to stick by the side I have chosen through thick and thin, hoping to have sufficient courage not to lose heart, sufficient sense not to allow myself to be confused or deflected from this purpose, and sufficient faith in the civilization to which I belong, and in the religion on which that civilization is based, to follow Bunyan's advice and endure the hazards and humiliations of the way because of the worth of the destination.[38]

Some of the Congress intellectuals would later change their position, but in the late 1940s and early 1950s they all actively welcomed America's tardy assumption of leadership.

## "THE END OF IDEOLOGY"

Although the Congress now had a structure and secure funding, it still lacked a clear program or sense of direction. When the International Committee met in the AFL offices in Brussels in November 1950 to adopt formally its articles of association, Irving Brown referred to "the haphazard and provisional manner [in which] we have been operating since Berlin"[39] and to the need to settle objectives and priorities. But in the general discussion at Brussels there was still little agreement. The Norwegian Labor Party leader, Haakon Lie, and the Belgian novelist Charles Plisnier wanted the Congress to become a mass movement. Guido Calagero, director of the Italian Institute in London, gave the highest priority to the translation of the major classics of tolerance into all the major languages, European, Chinese, and Arabic. James Burnham, however, called for the exchange of students and teachers between the Soviet and non-Soviet worlds, and Ernst Tillich of the Kampfgruppe gegen Unmenschlichkeit (Battle Group against Inhumanity) wanted help with his clandestine work behind the Iron Curtain. German Arciniégas of Colombia wanted more attention paid to the threat of neofascism in Latin America, and the black American writer Max Yergan stressed the importance of Africa. There was even talk of changing the name from "Congress for Cultural Freedom" to "International Movement for Cultural Freedom." Silone spoke eloquently of the 15 million slave laborers in Soviet camps ("Here is the Paschal Lamb on the butcher's block since the beginning of time whose groans nobody hears") and of the Moscow Show Trials in which the accused lied against themselves. ("The liberal movement . . . began with the rehabilitation of *habeas corpus* . . . at the moment the watchword of the new resistance to totalitarianism should be *habeas animam:* the right of each creature to his soul."[40] But this was not a program. The meeting finally adopted four resolutions calling for the establishment of a university for refugees, a series of public debates with the "Partisans for Peace," an annual prize for literary or artistic achievement, and a mass meeting in Paris in 1951. When the conference was ending, Rougemont told the participants that they would surely leave Brussels with the impression of *"une organisation qui n'était pas parfaite. C'est exact."* But, he went on, *"le stage de la gestation est depassé. L'enfant est né."*

But since Nabokov returned to the United States and could not take up his position as Secretary-General in Paris until April 1951, and Michael Josselson as Administrative Secretary was still groping for viable directions, the Congress continued for several more months in a halting, uncertain way. When the Executive Committee met in Versailles in February 1951 and discussed the proposal (adopted in Brussels) to hold a Congress in Paris on the model of the one in Berlin, Raymond Aron strongly opposed it. The purpose in Berlin, he said, had been to create an international organization and then to make it work. To have another polemical Congress now, in imitation of Berlin, would only draw attention to the fact that very little had been done in the eight months since the excitement of Berlin.

The point was well taken. There had been a great deal of discussion but few practical actions since the publication of Koestler's brochure, *Que veulent les Amis de la Liberté?* The Partisans for Peace ignored the Congress's challenge in Brussels to a debate. There was a proposal for a traveling exhibition of photographs depicting oppression in Sovietized Central and Eastern Europe, but the idea reminded Aron of Hitler's anti-Bolshevik exhibitions, and it was dropped. Instead the Executive Committee set up a subcommittee to investigate the possibility of sponsoring some propaganda films. Rougemont agreed that his European Center for Culture in Geneva would administer a Feature Agency to distribute magazine articles. Most agreed on the need for a magazine in Paris, although no editor had been found, and Silone doubted that it would succeed, since it would have to rely on a core of writers in general agreement with each other, whereas the intellectuals of the Congress were often in serious disagreement, as was seen in Berlin and Brussels. At least Bondy was able to announce that the Secretariat would shortly publish a small bimonthly bulletin documenting developments behind the Iron Curtain.

"We need more drive, imagination, urgency," Melvin Lasky complained to Sidney Hook after the Versailles meeting of February 1951. None of the national committees affiliated with the Congress—in England, the United States, Japan, and India—was receiving clear leadership from Paris. Individuals associated with the Congress were already beginning to take their own individual steps to advance the cause. Arthur Koestler advocated a European "Legion of Liberty" as a first step toward an integrated European Army, and he had formed a "Fund for Intellectual Freedom" (and donated a percentage of his own royalties to it) to help exiled writers and subsidize emigré magazines. James Burnham was promoting the "Free University for Exiles," which the Congress supported in principle but for which it was unable to do anything beyond paying Josef Czapski's fare to the United States to raise funds. The newly formed American Committee for Cultural Freedom was in fact more active in international issues than the Paris Congress: It had, for example, in January 1951, released a statement condemning the election to the Presidium of the German PEN Club of Johannes R. Becher, the East German cultural commissar. Sidney Hook, in the name of the American Committee, had also sent a cable to Otto Grotewohl of the East German Republic protesting the threatened execution of an eighteen-year-old boy.

Here, then, was an international association of intellectuals who shared many common attitudes, particularly their opposition to totalitarianism, and who could argue with each other in trust and good faith, but who had no agreed position beyond the "Berlin

Manifesto"—about which, in any case, many had serious reservations. They did not have an agreed program. Besides, Raymond
Aron reminded them, if Stalin invaded Yugoslavia in the spring
and the third world war broke out, they would not then be worry-
ing about the future of their Congress. So are we, David Rousset
asked, after the great promise of Berlin, to become another PEN
Club "avec ses petites activités?"

It was in fact the launching in March 1951 of Bondy's bulletin,
*Preuves,* which first made it possible for the Congress intellectuals
to sort out where, and where not, they agreed and could act together. It was named *Preuves* because its emphasis was to be on
proof, evidence, documentation of the facts behind the ideology
in Communist countries and because it would at the same time
avoid ideological bombast. But from the beginning it was a more
general magazine for Congress writers and easily grew into the
independent *grande revue* that the Executive Committee and Secretariat had discussed for months. It also served as a bulletin of Congress news. More literary than Claude Mauriac's Gaullist *Liberté de
l'esprit* (which supported the Congress and published the Berlin
papers of Aron, Burnham, Czapski, and Alfred Weber) and more
political than Jacques Carat's *Paru* (from which it drew such writers
as Aimée Patri and Michel Collinet), it was a new voice in the heavily neutralist atmosphere of Paris at that time, and even today the
short, polemical articles of its early issues convey a tense vibrancy
and courage. *Preuves* demonstrated for the first time since Berlin
that despite a slow start the Congress was a movement with a future. The circles of Sartre's *les Temps modernes,* Hubert Beuve-Méry's
*le Monde,* and Claude Bourdet's *l'Observateur* quickly denounced and
boycotted it as a "right-wing . . . American . . . police" journal.

A *Preuves* consensus soon established itself. It was Atlanticist,
pro-NATO and pro-American. But it also gave, as it were, equal
space to criticizing many developments in American life. In its
pages George Kennan condemned "anti-Communist hysteria" in
the United States; Raymond Aron attacked the McCarran visa policy (which Bondy said would prevent most of the *Preuves* writers
from visiting the United States); and Mary McCarthy described a
new *trahison des clercs* among some American anti-Communists.
(She meant the "anti-anti-McCarthyites" like Burnham.)

*Preuves* was, of course, anti-Soviet, publishing evidence of Soviet
persecution of intellectuals. It discussed the slave camps and Han-

nah Arendt's theory of totalitarianism. (Her book *The Origins of Totalitarianism* still could not find a publisher in France.) It published Boris Souvarine on the Kremlin's contempt for Picasso; it defended André Gide against Moscow's attacks; it supported Czeslaw Milosz after his defection. It published Lasky on cultural subjugation in East Germany and Max Eastman on the persecution of Russian artists. Vladimir Weidlé celebrated the pre-Soviet Russian culture. (*Preuves* was anti-Soviet, not anti-Russian.)

*Preuves* was antineutralist and Europeanist. It published Rougemont's paper to the Bombay congress of the Indian Committee for Cultural Freedom in which he distinguished political neutrality, which can be justified ("I am Swiss"), from neutralism, which is neutral between free thought and servitude: Neutralism is a "lie against which we have to struggle." Rougemont also published many appeals for "the coming unity of Europe," East and West, and *Preuves* attacked, as betrayals of the European spirit, the dictatorships of Francisco Franco in Spain and Juan Domingo Peron in Argentina, as well as the new racist *apartheid* regime in South Africa.

Behind those polemics and positions, a new theme began to emerge with which the Congress was to become identified and which formed the real basis of its consensus. In an editoral in the second issue of *Preuves*, Rougemont wrote of the central importance of the critical, freethinking spirit. Bondy later wrote of the irrepressible pleasures of universal curiosity. An editorial of September 1951 contrasted dogmatic ideology with living ideas. With the decline of fascism and the growing disenchantment not only with Stalinism but also with Gaullism and neutralism, the Western world was entering a new age of reform without dogmas or totalist world views. By 1955, after the title of an article by Edward Shils in *Encounter*[41] and of a chapter by Raymond Aron in his *L'Opium des Intellectuels*,[42] this new age was to be characterized as "the end of ideology." (Both Shils and Aron punctuated the phrase with a question mark; in its best-known formulation—as the title of a book by Daniel Bell—the query was dropped.)

The Congress did not invent the idea of the evil of dogmatism, the wrongness of dividing the world into the powers of light and the powers of darkness and the unquestioning conviction that those with whom one disagrees will inevitably be defeated through the inexorable operation of the laws of history. It was developed between the seventeenth and nineteenth centuries in the liberal idea of toleration. By 1950 it was in the air again after decades of propaganda, dogma, and war. George Kennan's doctrine of containment assumed it. The writers of *The God That Failed* announced it. Karl Popper's critique of historicism and Michael Oakeshott's analysis of rationalism developed it. Rejecting the dogmas of both Communism and anti-Communism and relying on the critical resources of free traditions was the theme that Congress intellectuals needed and were seeking. No other organization devoted so much thought and time to exploring it.

What Shils and Aron called "the end of ideology" was in a sense the basis of almost all the Congress's activity. It encouraged the factual and calm examination of totalitarian regimes; the celebration of the free world in festivals without artistic dogmas; and the building of an international community of intellectuals based on civility. It meant conferences on economic growth and development unrestrained by theories of imperialism, or seminars on worker participation in industry unrestrained by doctrines of class war. If it sometimes confused the desirable with the actual (ignoring the question mark that Shils and Aron had added to the phrase), its mood was decidedly optimistic, emphasizing less "the God that failed" than the liberation from dogma.

With the launching of *Preuves* and the early exploration of "the end of ideology," the Congress was at last finding its form. There would be no more challenges to the Partisans for Peace for public debates and no more talk of forming a mass political party. There would be conferences and seminars, magazines and festivals, and a program of public education aimed at changing, in Koestler's words, "the present confused and poisoned intellectual climate."[43]

## "THE BATTLE OF THE FESTIVALS"

But if *Preuves* gave the Congress a voice, it was Nicolas Nabokov's massive Festival of Paris in May 1952 that put the Congress "on the map," especially in France. It was designed as a counterattack in "the battle of the Festivals," which the Soviet side appeared to be winning without a serious struggle. (In December 1951, for example, the *New York Times* had criticized "America's foolish disregard of the importance of the 'cultural offensive'"[44] and reported that the Soviet Union spent more on cultural propaganda in France alone than the United States did in the entire world.)

But in May 1952, in the course of thirty days, Nabokov presented Paris with one hundred symphonies, concertos, operas, and ballets by about seventy twentieth-century composers. Paris had its first productions of Alban Berg's *Wozzeck* (by the Vienna Opera), of Benjamin Britten's *Billy Budd* (by Covent Garden), of Gertrude Stein's and Vergil Thomson's *Four Saints in Three Acts* (by Harlem and ANTA, with Alice B. Toklas attending), and of Arnold Schoenberg's *Die Erwartung*. Igor Stravinsky conducted *Oedipus Rex*, for which Jean Cocteau designed the set and directed the choreography. There were performances by the Boston Symphony Orchestra and the New York City Ballet. William Faulkner, Katherine Anne Porter, and Allen Tate came from the United States for literary debates. There was an exhibition of 150 modern paintings and sculptures. As well as celebrating the cultural freedom of the West, the Festival also made its anti-Soviet point indirectly by performing works by Sergei Prokofiev and Dmitri Shostakovich that were banned in the Soviet Union, and directly by arranging church services for the victims of totalitarian oppression.

The festival was, as Janet Flanner of the *New Yorker* put it, "an extremely popular fiasco."[45] It attracted full houses but a bad press. The Parisian *beau monde* sneered at those great "Americans," Igor Stravinsky, George Balanchine, and Arnold Schoenberg. The tickets were expensive, the literary debates dull, and the art exhibition limited. Flanner also theorized that the performances of works by Pierre Monteux, Stravinsky, and Charles Münch, which Parisians had earlier scorned, now aroused guilt over past misjudgment. It was in any case still the high tide of French anti-Americanism. A "gypsy curse" hung over the festival.

Nabokov wrote defensively to Hook:

> Yes, I think, despite what it may have looked like to people reading the French press, the festival was a psychological success in the complex and depressingly morbid intellectual climate of France. Of course, in any other country we would have had both more sympathy and more support. We would also have had a finer press reaction, but then again the action we had undertaken was aimed at this area, and I still believe that it was the only kind of action we could have undertaken here in Paris which would have established the Congress in the minds of the European intellectuals as a positive, and not only a political, organization. I sincerely believe that now the

Congress is not only well-known, but is respected by many intellectuals who don't agree with us. And it is a fact that many other intellectuals who were afraid of us before have come to us now as friends and colleagues.[46]

For Arthur Koestler, the festival was "an effete gathering."[47] For Stephen Spender, it was a welcome "Goodbye to Berlin." But in either case the Congress for Cultural Freedom was now well and truly launched, and festivals were established as at least one of the Congress's forms of appeal. Nabokov held others in Rome in 1954, in Tokyo and New Delhi in 1961, and in Rio de Janeiro in 1962.

But if the festivals helped give the Congress "a presence," they played a minor role in the Congress's total commitment and could not be remotely compared with its programs for conferences and magazines. To these it now turned.

# 4

# Encounter:
## *"Our Greatest Asset"*

🖋

It takes a screwball like [Cyril] Connolly to put out a
lively British magazine.

IRVING KRISTOL, 1953[1]

*Encounter* . . . remains . . . the first, the best monthly
review in English.

RAYMOND ARON, 1983[2]

Of course we have always considered *Encounter* to be our
greatest asset.

MICHAEL JOSSELSON, 1964[3]

Speaking some thirty years after the event, Irving Kristol, the
founding coeditor of *Encounter,* remarked that it had been easy for
a young American to launch a new monthly magazine in England
in 1953 because—as he explained with characteristic *bravura* and
some exaggeration—there had been nothing to read in England
at that time.[4] It was indeed a bad time for English magazines. Both
Cyril Connolly's *Horizon* and John Lehmann's *Penguin New Writing*
had ceased publication in 1950, and both Michael Oakeshott's
*Cambridge Journal* and F. R. Leavis's *Scrutiny* ceased in 1953. Certainly there was no magazine expressing the Congress position in
the Cold War, while the Leftist, neutralist *New Statesman and Nation,*
with sales of 85,000 a week, was at the height of its influence.

59

The English magazine most sympathetic to the aims of the Congress was the bluffly named *The Nineteenth Century and After,* a famous monthly launched by James Knowles in 1877, which in its time had published such writers as W. E. Gladstone, A. V. Dicey, Prince Peter Kropotkin, and Oscar Wilde. When the Congress agreed to subsidize this magazine as a British beachhead of the liberal, Atlanticist, anti-Communist "movement," it changed its name to *The Twentieth Century* (in January 1951) and began introducing to English readers a range of writers associated with the Congress—Franz Borkenau, Mark Alexander (i.e., Walter Z. Laqueur), Ruth Fischer, Gertrude Himmelfarb, Hook, Kristol, Lasky, Herbert Lüthy, Czeslaw Milosz, Vladimir Weidlé, Alexander Weissberg, and Bertram D. Wolfe.

But *The Twentieth Century* did not develop into the sort of magazine the Congress was, however uncertainly, looking for. The Congress wanted a magazine that was as much literary as political, and *The Twentieth Century* almost ignored poetry, literature, and the arts. In December 1951, after a meeting of the Executive Committee in Paris, Stephen Spender warned the editors: "There are almost no good magazines in England today and there is a tremendous opportunity, either in *The Twentieth Century* or in *some new magazine. . . .*"[5] George Lichtheim replied on behalf of *The Twentieth Century*: "This kind of thing," he wrote to Bondy, "only confirmed people in their ingrained conviction that all Continentals were mad." The magazine is not being produced "for a set of cosmopolitan intellectuals in Paris," he said, and he was not going to turn *The Twentieth Century* into an "ivory-towerish" *Der Monat* or "a sort of pink *Horizon*" just to please the Congress. Poets carry very little weight in England, he went on, and there are "a hundred people who are interested in theology, philosophy, and psychology for everyone who is interested in poetry or the drama." The "whole *Horizon* period is now very much a thing of the past."

It was clear that the Congress would have to start its own magazine in London, but it was also clear that it had not sorted out its ideas or policy for the magazine, beyond wanting one that would combat neutralism. For example, when Nicolas Nabokov wrote to Irving Kristol in New York to ask him to coedit the proposed magazine, he explained that the Congress wanted an English-language publication "aimed primarily at the Far East" and other parts of the world, such as Scandinavia, where English was the second language and "where neutralism is the strongest force." The maga-

zine, he said, would be edited in Europe, "preferably in Paris."
About the same time Michael Josselson wrote to Stephen Spender,
the proposed English coeditor: "The Congress is not primarily interested in reaching readers in England and the U.S. because a
communist or neutralist problem does not exist in those two countries." Above all, he added obscurely, the magazine would have to
avoid "Anglo-American provincialism."

Kristol and Spender were willing to edit a magazine for the Congress, but not one of this kind. They had the support of the English
associates of the Congress, Malcolm Muggeridge, Fredric Warburg,
and T. R. Fyvel, who went to Paris to reason with Josselson, Nabokov, and Bondy—"the comedians," as Muggeridge called them.[6]
The Englishmen insisted that the magazine be edited in London,
be editorially independent, be both literary and political, and,
while internationalist, draw heavily on a hinterland of British
writers.

The disagreements were amicably settled in London's favor. For
Josselson the important thing was to have editors in whom he had
confidence; problems could then be sorted out as they arose. The
editors, it was agreed, would be independent of both the Paris
Secretariat and the British Society for Cultural Freedom (including Warburg, a tall, commanding veteran of Passchendaele, whose
wish "to keep in touch with affairs" alarmed both Kristol and Josselson). The magazine would be "published by Secker and Warburg"(not by the British Society for Cultural Freedom) and would
be "sponsored" by the Congress for Cultural Freedom (but not as
its organ). It would have its own office (not in the Secker & Warburg building), and there would be no editorial advisory board.
There were the usual discussions about the name of the new magazine. Suggestions included *Oasis* (Warburg's), *Outlook* (Josselson's),
and *The Contemporary* (Kristol's). Spender and Kristol also considered *Present, Turning Point, Moment,* and *Attack.* They settled on
Kristol's suggestion, *Encounter.* Kristol arrived in London in May
1953 (joined later by his wife, the historian Gertrude Himmelfarb,
and their new baby) and the editors began to produce volume 1,
number 1.

The coeditors were an odd couple, a partnership of City College
and Bloomsbury, of *Partisanski Review* and MacSpaunday. Kristol,
born in Brooklyn, New York, in 1920, the son of a garment worker,
had been a student at the City College of New York, where he was

one of the anti-Stalinist Left which met and argued in Alcove No. 1 off the college's "slummy and smelly" lunchroom. He later wrote of the CCNY debates at the time of the Trotskyist split over the Hitler–Stalin pact in 1939 and of the Soviet invasion of Finland in 1940 (the Cannonites like Trotsky supporting, the Schachtmanites opposing, the Soviets): "I have never seen or heard their equal as a learning experience. (When James Burnham's presentation lasted only two hours, many questioned his 'seriousness.')"[7] On graduation in 1940, he worked as a freight handler in Chicago and helped edit an ex-Trotskyist magazine, *Enquiry,* until he was called up. He said later in an interview: "I learned a lot in the Army. When I went in, I was still enough of a socialist to turn down officer training. I wanted to be an enlisted man, working among the common people. By the time I got out, I was convinced that the Army knew a lot more about people—real people—than I did."[8] After the war he spent two years in England, and in 1947 he became an assistant editor of *Commentary* (then edited by Elliot Cohen) in New York.

In 1952 *Commentary* published Kristol's extraordinarily controversial statement on McCarthyism: "'Civil Liberties', 1952—A Study in Confusion."[9] It developed the theme Arthur Koestler had stated in Berlin in June 1950, not long after Senator McCarthy had first become prominent: that the reason why a "vulgar demagogue" like McCarthy had won his following was that American liberal fellow-travelers, in their apologetics, had given "aid and comfort to Stalinist tyranny" abroad and to the Communist Party at home.

> Did not the major segment of American liberalism, as a result of joining hands with the Communists in a popular front, go on record as denying the existence of Soviet concentration camps? Did it not give its blessing to the "liquidation" of the kulaks? Did it not apologize for the mass purges of 1936–38, and did it not solemnly approve the grotesque trials of the old Bolsheviks? Did it not applaud the massacre of the non-Communist left, by the GPU during the Spanish Civil War?

As for the Communist Party, the heart of the matter (Kristol went on) is that fellow-travelers accept the myth that Communism is just another form of dissent. It is in fact, he said, a totalitarian conspiracy and is as counterrevolutionary as Louis XVI (and more dangerous than Nazism because of its ideological appeal). "If one wishes to defend the civil liberties of Communists ... one must do so on the same grounds that one defends the civil liberties of Nazis and fascists—no more, no less." The essay also included these sentences, which Kristol's critics quoted against him for years afterward:

> For there is one thing that the American people know about Senator McCarthy: he, like them, is unequivocally anti-Communist. About the spokesmen for American liberalism, they feel they know no such thing. And with some justification.

Later Kristol said he would accept the substitution of "believe" for "know" in the first sentence but saw nothing else to modify. The subsequent years only deepened his kind of populism, already apparent in this passage.*

But Kristol was no McCarthyite. It was he who drafted the first resolution of the American Committee for Cultural Freedom condemning McCarthyism. While he was executive secretary of the American Committee in 1952–53, it issued more statements criticizing Senator McCarthy than criticizing Stalinism. Before leaving for London he helped Sidney Hook draft his letter to the *New York Times* calling for a national movement to retire Senator McCarthy from public life.

Kristol came to London with a reputation as an anti-Communist polemicist, something of a "Koestlerizer." In fact he was already losing interest in anti-Communism, which was for him a stage in his passage from liberalism toward conservatism. Robert Nisbet was later to say that Kristol had really never been a liberal but was, even in this transitional phase, a conservative without knowing it. His early essays on religious themes ("Is Jewish Humor Dead?" and "God and the Psychoanalysts" )[12] gave hints of his later conservative development, which the English years would encourage, but which would also lead to difficulties with the Congress and, in the end, to his resignation from *Encounter.*

---

*Norman Thomas and Jay Lovestone enthusiastically endorsed Kristol's article[10] but Arthur Schlesinger, Jr., criticized it for confusing New Deal liberals (who were pragmatic, anti-Communist reformers) with "New York intellectuals" (who supported the Popular Front and knew "nothing about the New Deal except how to live off writers' and artists' projects of the WPA"—the Works Progress Administration).[11]

Stephen Spender was born in 1909 to a famous Liberal family, from whom he inherited an idea of great causes and an ease in political circles. At Oxford in the 1920s he came under the lifelong influence of W. H. Auden (who said "You will be a poet because you will always be humiliated").[13] Spender's first book, *Poems,* published when he was twenty-three, made him famous on both sides of the Atlantic. Its modernist, Left-wing, and homosexual romanticism appealed immediately to the political and erotic mood of the times. He was now to be classified forever with Auden, C. Day Lewis, and Louis MacNeice as the Poets of the Thirties—*"MacSpaunday,"* as Roy Campbell dubbed them. With his tall good looks, he was also called the "Rupert Brooke of the Depression." *Poems* was followed the next year by *Vienna* (about the Austrian Socialists' insurrection in 1934), and Spender continued to publish a book of verse, fiction, or criticism almost annually.

Politically he moved into the orbit of the Communist Party. *The Destructive Element* (1935) drew a Communist moral from studies of Henry James, T. S. Eliot, and W. B. Yeats (although he declared that "the Communist explanation of our society is not adequate to produce considerable art"). He joined the Communist Party— for a few weeks—in the winter of 1936–37, and in 1937 he published *Forward from Liberalism,* in which he declared: "I am a communist because I am a liberal." Drawing on the Webbs, he doubted (weakly) that there had been a Ukrainian famine, and defended (weakly) the Red Terror as a stabilizing force. He regretted Soviet mistakes but saw them as resulting from "unavoidable necessity." He recommended a democratic constitution for Russia. F. A. Voigt called the book "a characteristic product of English parlour Bolshevism";[14] this catches the note of naïveté but underestimates the element of calculation: It has always been impossible to pin Spender down.

He took various positions on the Cold War. In a *New York Times* article in 1948, "We Can Win the Battle for the Mind of Europe,"[15] he saw the decisive issue as the defense, with American support, of "cultural freedom" in the West. But a few weeks later he sent a message to the Communist-controlled Cultural Congress for Peace in Wroclaw, Poland, calling on writers to "take the lead in opposing power politics" and avoiding alignment with any bloc.[16] In 1949 he contributed a chapter to *The God That Failed* and declared: "No criticism of the Communists removes the arguments against capitalism." In 1951, in his autobiography *World Within World,* he wrote: "I do not *choose* America or Russia: I *judge* between them."

For Spender, a prolific autobiographical writer, his various changes of belief and commitment have been a matter of "my utter vulnerability and openness."[17] Where his friends saw "a Dostoevskyian Holy Fool" (Auden),[18] or "a parody Parsifal," an "essentially comic character" who reveals truth through farce (Christopher Isherwood),[19] his critics found a "wincing bewilderment" (Ian Hamilton),[20] or a "loose-jointed mind, misty, clouded, suffusive" in which "nothing has outline" (Virginia Woolf).[21] But it was from this mistiness that his poetry came, and he would not sacrifice it to any cause or "outline," be it the Communist Party in the 1930s or the Cold War in the 1950s. "Those who try to exploit people like Spender," Isherwood wrote, "always live to regret it."[22]

The first issue of *Encounter* appeared in October 1953. Ten thousand copies were printed, a press run chosen because *Horizon*'s sales once reached that figure. (It sold out in a week.) Kristol's editorial, "After the Apocalypse," foreshadowed the "end of ideology." It welcomed the passing of "messianic arrogance" and discerned "a breath of fresh air drifting through the fog." Stalin, Hitler, and Mussolini were now dead,

> . . . and with them, the mythologies of an epoch. The last surviving fable was exposed only yesterday in Eastern Germany and Czechoslovakia, where real factory workers were unambiguously dissociating themselves from a hypothetical Proletariat, achieving by that simple action what a thousand subtle arguments could not do: the destruction of the Marxist-Leninist creed. Now, perhaps, words will once again mean what they say, and we shall be spared the tedious sophistry by which despotism could pose as a higher form of freedom, murder as a supreme humanism.

*Encounter,* the editorial concluded, would have no "line" but would represent the diversity of opinion, the love of liberty, and the respect for culture of those associated with the Congress. It would be an international magazine and would aim at the uninhibited exploration of differences of opinion.

Volume 1, number 1, contained some unpublished diaries of Virginia Woolf, poems by Edith Sitwell and C. Day Lewis, memoirs by Albert Camus and Christopher Isherwood, and articles by Spender on American diction and poetry, Kristol on the Congress's Hamburg Conference on Science and Freedom, Denis de Rougemont on India, Nicolas Nabokov on music in the U.S.S.R., Mark Alexander (Walter Z. Laqueur) on the "almost incredible naïveté" of Isaac Deutscher's *Russia after Stalin,* and Leslie Fiedler on the Rosenberg case. The second issue had a similar balance of British, American, and European writers. Nicola Chiaromonte wrote a guest editorial, also foreshadowing the theme of "the end of ideology" and deploring the replacement, during the ideological age 1914–53, of the will to question by the nihilistic will to power: "The duty that no intellectual can shirk without degrading himself is the duty to expose fictions and to refuse to call 'useful lies' truths." There were poems by Auden and Frances Cornford, some of W. B. Yeats's letters, articles by Melvin Lasky on Japan and Norbert Muhlen on East Germany, and book reviews by Bertrand Russell, Arthur Schlesinger, Jr., and Golo Mann.

Kristol (if not his coeditor Spender) was excited with the new magazine. "I really think," he wrote to Josselson,

> that . . . in *Encounter,* the Congress has hold of something far more important than even you realize. . . . Potentially, we have it in us to become, in a few months, *the* English-language cultural periodical, and not only in England but for Asia too. . . . I mean this seriously; and if I'm wrong then you ought to get yourself another editor. But you've got to give us time, and editorial freedom, to achieve this. . . . I honestly think we have the opportunity to become, on a world-wide scale, what the NRF [*Nouvelle Revue Française*] was for France in the 20's.[23]

Philip Toynbee in *The Observer* also welcomed *Encounter* as "brilliant and encouraging,"[24] and at a meeting of the Executive Committee of the Congress in Rome in November 1953 Michael Polanyi said *Encounter* had released a "great movement" of ideas in England.[25]

But while *Encounter* was an exciting new voice, there were many critics. Some said there was too much politics. (Hook said there was not enough, but he was in a minority.) Graham Hough complained that it had "no sense of direction at all. . . . No drive, no community of feeling, none of that sense of personality in diversity that makes a periodical live."[26] Anthony Hartley complained of the "portentous platitudes" on the editorial page.[27] Writing in the Australian Leftist journal, *Meanjin,* someone named Patrick Carpenter called *Encounter* an antihumanist publication edited by "turncoats."[28] A. J. P. Taylor said it was too "high-minded" and did nothing to combat that enemy of cultural freedom, good taste:

> There is no article in the present number which will provoke any reader to burn it or even to throw it indignantly into the waste-paper basket. None of the articles is politically subversive; none will be condemned by a magistrate, even in Douglas, Isle of Man. All are safe reading for children. Most of them are written by the elderly and the established.[29]

T. S. Eliot considered it so obviously published under American auspices that he did not want to contribute to it[30]—which Spender took to mean that *Encounter* would have to overcome a reputation of disguising American propaganda under a veneer of British culture.

Some of the critics found an obsession with Communism. *The Times Literary Supplement,* for example, called *Encounter* a journal of "negative liberalism" whose main feature is "hatred and fear of Communism."[31] (Who in the 1930s, Kristol asked in his rejoinder, was ever called a "negative" because of his hatred or fear of fascism?)[32] The article that most concerned these critics was Leslie Fiedler's "A Postcript to the Rosenberg Case." In Melvin Lasky's view, *Encounter* would not have had to struggle so bitterly for two years to establish itself on the British literary scene if Fiedler's article had not appeared in the very first issue.

The Americans Julius and Ethel Rosenberg had been found guilty of spying for the U.S.S.R., of handing over to the Soviets sketches of the detonating device of an atomic bomb. Few doubted their guilt then or now,[33] but many, including almost everyone associated with the Congress (and Leslie Fiedler), attacked the death penalty imposed on them. An international Communist campaign of extraordinary scope and intensity took up their cause in an anti-American crusade, in which the Rosenbergs played their part, pretending with well-trained will and imagination (even in their letters to each other) to be innocent, patriotic, baseball-loving Americans martyred by fascists. Fiedler's article, with New York deftness, analyzed this myth, the self-conversion of human beings into Party symbols and their total subordination to the Soviet Union. "The final pity was that they could not say even so much aloud—except in certain symbolic outcries of frame-up and persecution, and only through the most palpable lies. It is for this reason that they failed in the end to become martyrs or heroes, or even men. What was there left to die?" Their own ideology, Fiedler implied, had already dehumanized them through and through.

Kristol wrote enthusiastically to Josselson about the Fiedler manuscript at the end of July 1953, when the first (October) issue was still being planned. He listed the reasons why *Encounter* must publish it: It was a fine article, it was provocative and would be talked about, it struck the right note politically, both profoundly anti-Communist and compassionate, and its publication would demonstrate *Encounter*'s boldness, its willingness to face up to problems and therefore its *bona fides* ("Make no mistake about it" he wrote, "such *bona fides* must be presented . . . if we are to gain the credence of our readers. It will be no secret—nor should it be one—that most of our funds will come from American sources, and this will inevitably cause people to examine our pages with a special skepticism and suspicion").[34]

Some readers welcomed the article.* A. J. P. Taylor called it "brilliant"[36] and Philip Toynbee "a carefully imaginative article."[37] But most condemned it. Graham Hough did not like to contemplate the concept of cultural freedom involved in the writing or publication of such a piece.[38] E. M. Forster resented its tone and especially its so-called compassionate ending. How would Fiedler act if he were ever condemned to death? Czeslaw Milosz disagreed with Fiedler and found nothing to scorn in the Rosenbergs' willingness to die as propaganda symbols. It was terrifying, but he compared them with the Catholic bishops depersonalized in the People's Democracies' prisons.[39]

Fiedler's essay has, in fact, stood the test of time as a contribution to the discussion of the Rosenberg case. In his 1986 *Journals* Spender still called it "the liveliest" article of the first issue of *Encounter,* and it was reprinted in 1986 in *The Penguin Book of Contem-*

---

*Hook, sensing that an article criticizing the role of a couple recently executed (June 1953) needed some explanatory introduction, suggested a note along these lines: "These remarks should not be construed as an attack against human beings who are dead—for we must respect the dead as human beings—but the point is that in their political life the Rosenbergs abandoned their role as human beings and put themselves forward as political symbols. We are therefore making an analysis not of human personalities but of a political myth."[35] Hook's suggestion was not adopted.

*porary American Essays.* Kristol's judgment in publishing it has been vindicated, but the anger it provoked in 1953 reminded him—and the Paris Secretariat—of the cultural distance between Manhattan and London.

When the magazine was first being planned, the editors of *Encounter* had had to assert their independence of the British Society for Cultural Freedom and of their publisher, Fredric Warburg. Later they had to assert their editorial independence of the Congress, especially of the Secretariat and the Administrative Secretary, Michael Josselson. The Executive Committee only occasionally debated over *Encounter* and in general supported it enthusiastically. At the Rome meeting of November 1953, for example, Malcolm Muggeridge said that since the editors had done a "magnificent job,"[40] they should be left in freedom to find their feet.* The others agreed. The principal Executive Committee debate was in Paris in January 1955, when Kristol and Spender submitted a statement of their policies. Called "Reflections on *Encounter*," it was clearly designed to meet their critics head on. They wrote that, at the time of the first few issues, *Encounter* was accused of "being a magazine of political propaganda with a cultural décor . . . we were accused of bad faith." Now, the editors reported, that criticism was no longer made; writers who once remained aloof were now happy to collaborate, and sales were already larger than *Horizon*'s ever were. However, they continued, there were still problems of policy to be settled. *Encounter* was an *international* review, but it also had to be firmly rooted in a national center, that is, Britain:

> The question arises: how "British" ought we to be? This is not
> an easy question to answer, partly because the facts of the
> case do some of the answering for themselves. In India, for
> instance, we are a British magazine *tout court*, by virtue of
> being published in London and being co-edited by Stephen
> Spender. The same is largely true in England itself. To the
> extent that we are accepted as British, we gain a considerable
> amount of good will throughout all the countries of the

*The January 17, 1954, entry in Muggeridge's diaries, *Like It Was* (1981), describes the early issues as "dead fruit." This must refer not to its political role, which he supported, but to its silence on spiritual or religious questions. He would in time withdraw from the Congress, regarding it as another expression of "the liberal death-wish."

Commonwealth that would otherwise be wanting. This goodwill is something that *Encounter* obviously does not want to squander.

However, being British to this extent has its responsibilities, too, as well as its advantages. For one thing, it means paying special attention to British writers, painters, musicians, etc.— even if our American and French friends don't think they are worth it. For another, being British imposes a certain tone on the magazine—one rather more muted than, say, that of most American political periodicals. Once these two things are done, we can—as we have done—practically fill up occasional issues with non-British writers, without anyone's minding, or even noticing it.

But "being British" also makes some other, more severe, demands upon us. It means, for instance, that we have to try extra hard to get British political writers as well as British short-story writers. It would be intolerable—and would not be tolerated by our readers—were the political features in *Encounter* written by Americans or Germans, while the British contributed the poetry. This means we must publish British political writers, with all their particular accents and emphases and prejudices. Some of these accents and emphases, even among writers friendly to the Congress, are not to everyone's taste. But they must, in the nature of things, be to *Encounter*'s taste.[41]

Muggeridge, unable to attend the Paris meeting, had written to Josselson that he was "in complete agreement" with the editors' "Reflections." "I can quite see that the Congress might wish it to be more specifically and voluminously ideological, but I am equally certain that, given the circumstances prevailing in this country and in Asia, this would be a mistake and would undermine the magazine's very real utility." At the Executive Committee meeting, Lasky also endorsed the editors' "Reflections" and warned against a "Johnny-One-Note ineffectiveness." To dramatize his attitude, Lasky said that if he were asked what would be in the next issue of *Der Monat* and he had to reply that Herbert Passin would be exposing the Japanese Communist Party again, that Nicolas Nabokov would be exposing Soviet music again, that Sidney Hook would be exposing the Leninist roots of Stalinism again, and that

we all had to continue in this way because the same grave problems persisted in the world, then the magazine would have "no
audience in no time."

Nabokov seemed to agree. He was bored stiff, he said, with exposing Soviet music; the problem was that the Soviet cultural offensive was becoming more intense and sophisticated. Moscow
was even organizing a Picasso exhibition, which would have been
unthinkable a few years earlier, and Soviet delegates were attending conferences all over the world. The Congress would have to
develop answers to this new challenge. Irving Brown disagreed.
He was "astonished" by Lasky's approach, he said. Everything the
Congress did should have a bearing on the Cold War, which the
free world was losing. The debate petered out in a general agreement that *Encounter* should sharpen its political edge.

But the criticism continued and bedeviled Kristol's brilliant editorship. The American Committee for Cultural Freedom remained scornful of *Encounter* and "its apparent unwillingness to
offend what it presumes are English sensibilities with explicit anti-
Communism."* *Encounter,* a memorandum of the American Committee said,

> . . . might have made a significant contribution to the health
> of the Western community of nations by being a
> counterweight to the *New Statesman & Nation,* both as regards
> forthright opposition to Communist totalitarianism and
> support of America's role in the free world. That it has not
> done so, that it has instead published primarily literary
> material, often of questionable merit, that it feels unwilling to
> accept the responsibility which Congress sponsorship should
> have entailed, is a further example to us of how far the
> Congress has moved from pursuit of its real objectives and
> how far it seems to be willing to compromise with an
> atmosphere far too tolerant of totalitarianism and hostile to
> America's role in the preservation of a free world.

*In a skit Daniel Bell wrote for the Paris office party to celebrate Michael
Josselson's fiftieth birthday in 1958, Kristol is presented with affectionate
malice as more English than the English: "He is faultlessly attired in a
black suit, black bowler hat, striped tie (Winchester), black tightly furled
umbrella. A thin blond moustache, slightly curled, adorns his lower lip."[42]

Josselson did not take seriously the American Committee's criticisms of *Encounter*'s "softness on Communism," but he was concerned about another persistent criticism, that *Encounter* failed to combat frivolous British anti-Americanism. In 1955 he asked Norman Jacobs, the chief political commentator of the Voice of America, to prepare a report on that question. Jacobs's report described *Encounter* as "the best magazine of its kind" in the English language but he agreed that it had failed "to offset the cliché that Americans are barbarians." He gave four examples: Leslie Fiedler's "The Middle Against Both Ends" (August 1955), on American conformity; Bertrand Russell's "Virtue and the Censor" (July 1954), which said that in America "anybody who knows much about Communism is suspect"; Aldous Huxley's "Faith and History" (February 1954), which has "a withering account of the vulgarity of the Mormons"; and Albert Dasnoy's "What Is Vulgarity?" (February 1955), which implied that vulgarity had reached its peak in the United States. (Nabokov wrote marginal notes defending as "true" the criticisms attributed to Fiedler, Russell, and Dasnoy.)

Further (Jacobs went on), *Encounter* did not provide its readers "with a sympathetic understanding of the role America must play as leader of the free world coalition." (Nabokov's note: "Let's not talk about leadership with Mr. F. Dulles [John Foster Dulles] in the saddle.") Nor did it report the vast economic and sociological changes that had taken place in America since the end of the World War II, such as the U.S. Supreme Court decision banning segregation in public schools. (Nabokov commented that if it dealt with desegregation it "would have to go into Lucie's [sic] case* which would be most embarrassing.") Finally, it did not review many important American books (to which Nabokov commented, "This is quite correct").

Josselson would defend *Encounter* against the American Committee, but he—himself an editor *manqué*—never seemed satisfied with Kristol's editorship. He wanted more emphasis on the Cold War (in a British rather than a New York way), more attention to Central Europe, more articles on the Third World, and more reports on the United States. In Kristol's view, Josselson did not un-

---

*The reference is to the international controversy concerning the exclusion of a black student, Autherine Lucy, from the University of Alabama in 1956.

derstand *Encounter*'s market. An exchange of letters between Josselson and Kristol in early 1955 illustrates the tensions. Kristol wrote
to Josselson:

> Your remarks about the Labour party, and about whether
> *Encounter* is doing enough to counteract its views on China,
> was an echo of the kind of thing I heard in New York.* I will
> repeat to you what I told them: This Labour Party fixation
> (sometimes even a *New Statesman and Nation* fixation) is quite
> absurd. The situation in England is not like that in France. . . .
> The editorials on China, as well as the special articles on the
> present crisis, which have been appearing . . . have been
> excellent on the whole. We could duplicate them—I honestly
> don't think we could do better. Perhaps we ought to duplicate
> them, and if you insist I'll see that we will. But have no
> illusions on one score: it would not do the magazine any
> good. . . .
>   There are certain things a magazine like *Encounter* can do.
> There are certain things we can't do—at least not well. We are
> *not* a substitute for a sensible Social-Democratic weekly, and
> can't try to act as one. We cannot save the Labour Party from
> itself—that is beyond our powers. What we *can* do is to create
> a certain kind of intellectual-cultural milieu, which would in
> turn have far-reaching, but indirect, effects.†
>   On China: yes, we can get an article, which will say exactly
> what is being said in the non-Labour press, in almost
> precisely the same way—and probably even written by the
> very same person (how many Far Eastern experts, anyway are
> there?) . . . You might say that it's better for The Cause to have
> a fair and familiar article, rather than none at all. I would say
> that it's worse—for the magazine, and therefore eventually,
> for The Cause. However, if you want to try the experiment,
> I'll agree.

*The context was China's anti-American cultural diplomacy and the Brit-
ish Labour Party Mission to China, led by Lord Attlee, in 1954.

†In fact Kristol published many Labour Party writers, including Hugh
Gaitskell, Roy Jenkins, C. A. R. Crosland, Richard Crossman, Patrick
Gordon-Walker, John Strachey, Rita Hinden, Denis Healey, and Roderick
Macfarquhar.

Josselson replied on February 13, 1955:

> I find it most depressing to receive the kind of letter you have just written me, after two years of talks, conferences, and discussions.
>
> Since you're talking about fixations, let me say frankly that I think you're the one who has a fixation. In fact a double one. First, that *Encounter* is published only for an English audience. And second, that the Congress is in the publishing business just to give readers what they want to read. . . . Your theory is absurd, because what it comes to is that any subject which is topical and therefore being discussed in English dailies and weeklies must not be discussed in *Encounter.* . . .
>
> You will remember that at our Executive Committee meeting [in January 1955 in Paris] everyone was in agreement that the period spent so far by *Encounter* in overcoming covert and overt resistance [in the English literary world] was time well spent, but that now it was time to go one step further.

(If it hadn't been for the American Committee's "extreme criticism," Josselson said, some would have been more outspoken.)

> As far as Congress publications go, *Encounter* is the weakest link in the chain—and this is the most important language. A good editor can't have a supercilious attitude and judge all contributions in terms of his own omniscience.

Kristol replied on February 16, 1955:

> Just got your letter. Look, let's call a moratorium on this sort of thing for a while. I believe I know the kind of magazine that you and the Congress want, and I shall do my best to deliver. Let's wait and see. The more we argue, the more entangled we become in vicious circles. Your suggestions are always welcome—but, basically, I have to do things my way, because I don't know how to do it any other. If my way turns out to be inadequate, there's always a "final solution."

In the same month—February, 1955, that is, less than eighteen months after the first issue—Nabokov explored that "solution." He wrote to ask Arthur Schlesinger if he could "very, very tactfully" sound out Dwight Macdonald about becoming a possible replacement for Kristol. Schlesinger did, and Macdonald was definitely interested. Schlesinger wrote to Nabokov: "I could not think of a better American prospect for the job." Spender was delighted at the prospect: "The chance of having D.M.," he wrote to Josselson, "is the most amazing piece of good luck and should be seized." Muggeridge was also enthusiastic: "This country," he wrote to Josselson, "has at the moment an anti-American obsession and an eccentric individualist as he is, would be a tremendous help in overcoming this. . . . The non-standard American is, as far as England is concerned, the best of all counter-irritants to anti-Americanism." Josselson agreed to discuss the possibilities with Macdonald in New York.

Dwight Macdonald (1906–82), tall, bearded, looking (Muggeridge said) like a mad professor with a butterfly net, as portrayed in old comic books, was from Yale, very far from City College. In his youth, when he and his friends wore monocles and carried canes, his heroes had been Oscar Wilde and H. L. Mencken. He had not read Marx until the age of thirty, when, as Mary McCarthy put it (in a novel where a character is modeled on him), he "made the leap into faith" and abandoned a well-paid career with Henry Luce's *Fortune* to espouse the life of a Left-wing intellectual dissenter. After a period as "a mild fellow-traveler" he joined the Committee for the Defense of Leon Trotsky headed by John Dewey and in 1937 joined Philip Rahv and William Phillips in reorganizing *Partisan Review.* "The speed with which I evolved from a liberal into a radical and from a tepid Communist sympathizer into an ardent anti-Stalinist still amazes me," he wrote some twenty years later.[43] In 1939 he was Secretary of the "League for Cultural Freedom and Socialism" (as distinct from Hook's "Committee for Cultural Freedom"), which, associating itself with André Breton and Diego Rivera, attacked Stalinism, Hitlerism, and Catholicism, and declared that "the liberation of culture is inseparable from the liberation of the working class." In the same year he joined the Trotskyist Socialist Workers' Party (taking as his Party name "James Joyce"). When it supported the Soviet invasion of Finland, he joined, with Max Schachtman and James Burnham, the breakaway Workers' Party, which condemned the Soviet invasion as "imperialist." He also opposed American involvement in World War II and maintained that position throughout the entire war. In 1941, with Clement Greenberg, he published "10 Propositions on the War" against "the Roosevelt–Churchill war régimes" and called for revolutionary mass action against both them *and* Hitler.

When the majority of the *Partisan Review* editors decided to support the American involvement in the war against Hitler, Macdonald resigned to launch the new magazine *Politics,* which would be, he said, less academic, "more informal, disrespectable and chance-taking" than *Partisan Review.* The magazine lasted five years. Its circulation was small (rising from two thousand at the beginning to five thousand) its standard high, and its influence considerable. It published a number of European writers—Andrea Caffi, Nicola Chiaromonte, Victor Serge, George Woodcock, Orwell, Camus, and Simone Weil—and such young Americans as C. Wright Mills and Melvin J. Lasky. It was relentlessly anti-Stalinist at the height of American official enthusiasm for "Uncle Joe" Stalin, and it organized the sending of books, paper, and typewriters to European intellectuals after the war. Culturally, it stood for "high culture" against the American "mass culture." Politically, under the influence of Nicola Chiaromonte, it came to espouse a sort of anarcho-pacifism. In *Politics,* Macdonald wrote, "my thinking took its natural bent towards individualism, empiricism, moralism, aestheticism. . . . It was also partly a reaction to Hiroshima and Nagasaki."[44]

In 1949 he joined Hook's "Americans for Intellectual Freedom" and published in *Politics* his detailed, contemptuous report of the Stalinoid (he coined the term) Waldorf Peace Conference.[45] In 1951 he joined the staff of *The New Yorker,* and in 1952 he delivered the address "I Choose the West" ("I support it critically").[46]

But when Michael Josselson finally met Dwight Macdonald in New York in June 1955, he quickly decided against appointing him as coeditor. He cabled Spender and Muggeridge that Macdonald was too provincial ("lacks knowledge and feeling for anything outside American scene") and too "lone wolf" for *Encounter.*[47] Most of the members of the American Committee for Cultural Freedom also strongly opposed Macdonald's candidacy. Borrowing Trotsky's *mot,* they said that "every man has a natural right to be stupid, but Dwight Macdonald abuses the privilege."[48] Hook threatened to resign from the Executive Committee of the Congress and "blow the Congress out of the water"[49] if Macdonald were appointed. Josselson was usually scornful of the American Committee, but he had to take some notice of its views. He wrote to Nabokov: "While I wholeheartedly agree that we have to replace Kristol,

I remain unconvinced as far as Dwight is concerned.... I absolutely refuse to hire Dwight at this point."[50]

On hearing of the New York arguments, Kristol had forthwith resigned, although he was later persuaded to stay on. A compromise was reached during the Congress's international conference on "The Future of Freedom" in Milan in September 1955. Macdonald joined the staff of *Encounter* as an associate editor but not as a coeditor, and Kristol (Josselson wrote to Muggeridge) was given "such a heavy dose of frank treatment bordering on brutality that a salutary change in his attitude can be expected."

The nagging complaints from New York and Paris about *Encounter*'s alleged "hesitancy on the great issues" continued, although in subsequent issues Kristol did give more attention to the Third World and to Central Europe, especially after the Polish October and the Hungarian Revolution. (In fact, Leopold Labedz's regular column, first carried in July 1957, on developments in Central Europe and the Soviet Union, "From the Other Shore," was so well received that it was separately distributed around the world.) Kristol also reached an agreement in 1957 to exchange articles with the editor of a proposed cultural magazine in Warsaw, although the agreement fell through when the Polish magazine was banned.

But, despite the critics, *Encounter* continued to enjoy a *succès d'estime* (and *de scandale*) with such famous articles as Nancy Mitford's "The English Aristocracy" (whose "U" and "non-U" became international catchwords) and Hugh Trevor-Roper's polemic against Arnold Toynbee. The original formula of mixing leading English writers with leading Americans (Lionel Trilling, Edmund Wilson, George Kennan, Edward Shils) and Europeans (Czeslaw Milosz, Bertrand de Jouvenel, Herbert Lüthy, Manès Sperber) continued to succeed. The editors reported to Paris in 1957 that the sneering remarks that greeted early issues were no longer heard and that "the most eloquent of our original critics, like A. J. P. Taylor and Graham Hough, now contribute happily." A year later they informed the Executive Committee that circulation had almost reached sixteen thousand, that is, a larger circulation than any comparable monthly review in the English language. Kristol had achieved his ambition of establishing "*the* English-language cultural periodical."

But Josselson and Kristol continued to be editorially at cross-purposes, and Kristol, himself a "lone wolf" and ahead of his time, was moving toward his neoconservative position, which was then beyond the Congress consensus. He finally resigned in 1958 to become editor of Max Ascoli's *The Reporter* in New York, and Melvin J. Lasky succeeded him in *Encounter.*

Kristol's editorship, which began with the Leslie Fiedler *succès de scandale,* ended with a Dwight Macdonald *scandale.* After Macdonald had finished his year on the *Encounter* staff (which he had "enormously enjoyed"), he submitted in 1958 the article "America! America!" which in a New Left spirit described the "sense of violence," the "lack of style," the "ugliness" of American life and its "lack of solidarity," as exemplified in the report that one out of every three American prisoners in Korea "was guilty of some sort of collaboration with the enemy." Spender liked the article; Kristol did not. It was, he wrote to Macdonald "almost John Osborne-ish" in its "unhealthy self-lacerating." But in view of Macdonald's close association with *Encounter,* they decided to publish it, with some cuts, to which Macdonald agreed. Nabokov then read it, shared Kristol's distaste, and said its publication would make fundraising in America harder. The article was accepted, then rejected, then accepted again—and finally rejected.

The article was published in *Dissent* in New York, in *Twentieth Century* in London, and in the Congress's magazine *Tempo Presente* in Rome.[51] In a prefatory note in *Dissent,* Macdonald wrote that "readers have a right to know when a magazine makes an editorial decision for extraneous reasons"—that is, on directions from "its great front-office Metternichs." Norman Birnbaum published "An Open Letter to the Congress for Cultural Freedom" in *Universities and Left Review,* in which he said of the Macdonald piece, "you have dishonoured the cause you profess, and the dishonour is not much diminished by the contemptible pettiness of its occasion."[52] Spender complained to Macdonald that his angry refusal to accept the editors' final decision that the article was not good enough to publish had led people like A. J. Ayer to stop writing for *Encounter.*

The damage was limited, however, when three letters replying to Birnbaum were published in the *Universities and Left Review.* Spender and Kristol wrote: "Had the editors wished to publish Macdonald's article in *Encounter,* it would have appeared. In the event, they decided otherwise"—there had been no "directives" from Paris. Nabokov's letter pointed out that the Congress's *Tempo Presente* had published the article. In his letter Macdonald agreed that, in his year on *Encounter,* he was never aware of any pressure

from Paris. He attributed the decision to reject the article to timid-
ity. *"Encounter* has been," he wrote, "an extremely good magazine—
lively, intelligent, free-spirited" and the matter of his rejected article was "an episode, an unhappy, mixed-up one, but—an episode."
Thereupon Birnbaum wrote that he wished "to apologise for
jumping to conclusions."[53]

There, for the moment, the matter remained. But the New Left
would strike again, and the rejected article would be put in evidence when the CIA's funding of the Congress was exposed in
1966–67. Meanwhile, Melvin J. Lasky moved to London from Berlin, and a new stage of *Encounter* began.

# 5
# *Magazines Against the Tide*

*Re: Damon Runyon Feature*

Mr. Melvin J. Lasky
DER MONAT

... Now it is known to one and all that *Freddy the Torte*
will not accept a business proposition if it comes from *Pall
Mall Mel,* or, for that matter, if it comes from anybody else.
He is one of those fat sloppy characters who do not care for
work in any form, shape, or manner.... As a matter of fact,
Freddy the Torte does not care for anything but food. He
does not even care for horses and dolls....

It is only a couple of weeks that Pall Mall Mel takes
Freddy the Torte to Wang Lum's Kosher Eatery in the city of
Berlin, Fla., and treats him to an order of gefilte Chinese
fish, a dish Freddy is very fond of indeed, and tells him how
much he appreciates what Freddy does for him in the
Racing Sheet he publishes. This sheet is pretty much of the
same kind like the one published by Pall Mall Mel, only in a
considerable smaller way, as *Baldy Bondy* and *Mandolin Mike*
who run the entire publishing racket around the tracks do
not wish Freddy to think he is in the market, and do not
ever permit him to hire a help, as opposed to Pall Mall Mel
who is associated with a citizen going under the monicker of
*Unser Hellmut.*

It is on problems like this he complains to Pall Mall Mel
while they are sitting at Kosher Lum's partaking of their

gefilte fish.... So Freddy the Torte is greatly amazed when
Pall Mall Mel now suggests that he should do a piece for
The Insider, and gives him a medium reproachful look, and
speaks to him as follows:

"Tut, tut, tut", Freddy the Torte says. "Tut, tut, tut, tut, tut.
Do I not tell you only the other day to cease and desist from
any such suggestions as far as I am concerned? You know
full well", Freddy says, "that I am tied up with my own blatt
to such an extent as to be unable to get a pause of
refreshment at least once in a while, and go on a nice little
trip, and maybe take along my everloving wife who in her
days is a very beautiful blond Judy if you like them blond,
and show her some places of historic interest, such as
restaurants. Also", Freddy continues, "I do not feel free to
engage in outside enterprises as I have nobody like Unser
Hellmut who would look after the blatt in the meantime.
And furthermore", Freddy concludes, "your idea will not
work out in the German lingo at all, and there are at least
ten other reasons why it stinks, and I am ready to name
them fast enough to outrun Jesse Owens, or at least give
him a photo finish. So you see", Freddy says, "it is an
impossible proposition, and I can not accept it. But", he
says, "I will ask you one question: how much do you pay?"

Friedrich Torberg
(Editor *Forum*, Vienna)[1]

*Encounter* was the flagship, but the Congress also sponsored (or
encouraged) a dozen other intellectual reviews around the world
in English, French, German, and Spanish (and later in Japanese,
Portuguese, and Arabic). For Lasky this was putting into practice
T. S. Eliot's ideal of an international "network of independent reviews" whose editors knew each other and exchanged ideas and
whose cooperation "should continually stimulate that circulation
of influence, of thought and sensibility, between nation and nation ... which fertilises and renovates from abroad the literature
of each one of them."[2] But this Lasky–Eliot formula overlooks, in
the Congress case, the extent to which its magazines were against
the current of the times, preaching, as it were, the "end of ideology" to the ideologically charged, or a liberal anti-Communism to
fellow-travelers. The initial publication of each of the magazines
was usually greeted with scorn or contempt. By the end of the

1950s—and especially after the Hungarian Revolution had proved them right—most of them had won respected niches in their countries, but it had been a long haul, and some, like the Spanish-language *Cuadernos,* never overcame its hostile reception in Latin America.

## Preuves

When the Executive Committee, meeting in Versailles in February 1951, discussed the need for a cultural-political magazine in the tradition of the great French reviews, Raymond Aron doubted that their circle could create an "essentially French" review. That would need (as Manès Sperber insisted) a French editor, and none was available; certainly neither Aron nor David Rousset was able to take it on. It would also require the support of French writers of high reputation, most of whom were tied to existing reviews. What might work, Aron suggested, was something that had failed before in France but was worth trying again—an international review in the French language modeled on *Der Monat* and drawing on the leading writers throughout Europe and the United States.[3]

That is precisely what *Preuves* became under the editorship of François Bondy, a Swiss writer whose mother tongue was German. (He was assisted by the French socialist journalist Jacques Carat and later by K. A. Jelenski and Jean Bloch-Michel.) Beginning with its ninth issue in November 1951, the polemical *cahier* and Congress news bulletin was turned into *une grande revue,* publishing, in that issue, articles by the Swiss writers Denis de Rougemont, Herbert Lüthy, and François Bondy; the Italians Ignazio Silone and Nicola Chiaramonte; the Spaniard Salvador de Madariaga; and the American Sidney Hook. In later issues (and years) it published the full range of Congress writers, from Daniel Bell, Franz Borkenau, and Jelenski to Jorge Luis Borges, Bertrand Russell, and Leslie Fiedler, as well as the French writers Aron, Thierry Maulnier, Carat, and Aimé Patri.

*Preuves* nevertheless faced what Sperber called *"une hostilité presque totale."* To establish his magazine in this climate, Bondy had to assert his independence of the Executive Committee and the Secretariat (as *Encounter* would have to do later). In June 1952 he wrote to Nicolas Nabokov that he would resign if the Executive Committee continued to discuss *Preuves* policy in the editor's absence and to claim the right to issue editorial instructions. The point was conceded, and what began as *Cahiers Mensuels* of the Congress were soon published *"sous les auspices"* of the Congress, and by 1953 became a *"Revue Mensuelle . . . publiée sous la direction de François Bondy."* To distance himself from the militant *Amis de la Liberté,* Bondy also formed *les mardis de Preuves,* a discussion group of a higher intellectual level than usually reached by *Les Amis.*

*Preuves* continued to inject its measured liberal anti-Communist perspective into the French debates, opposing the neutralism of *l'Observateur,* the pacifism of *Esprit* and the "coexistentialism" of *les Temps modernes.* During the Algerian conflict, *Preuves* consistently called for a liberal settlement. (Police in Algiers seized an issue of the magazine in 1958, and in 1962 the Organisation de l'Armée Serète [OAS] bombed the Congress office in Paris.) It enjoyed its greatest success after the Polish October and the Hungarian November of 1956. Albert Camus then said that *Preuves* was the only French magazine free of provincialism, and the editor of *Esprit,* J. M. Domenach, referred to *Preuves's* "reputation for objectivity." In his 1957 report to the Executive Committee, Bondy referred to his new contributors—Jean Bloch-Michel, Jean Daniel, Pierre Emmanuel, and Jean Duvignaud—who "come now to *Preuves* not because *Preuves* [has] changed, but because they have changed." In 1959 Bondy reported simply that: "the review has found its public"—a public in Eastern and Central Europe, Latin America, and francophone Africa as well as in France.

That was *Preuves's* high point. Its sales were three thousand, and it had become what Pierre Grémion (in 1987) called "one of the best intellectual and literary reviews of the postwar."[4]

## Cuadernos

The Congress launched three new reviews in 1953, *Cuadernos, Forum,* and *Encounter. Cuadernos,* in the Spanish language and published in Paris, was directed mainly at Latin American intellectuals and was edited by Julian Gorkin (born Gomez). Gorkin has referred to his life as a "savage battle,"[5] an accurate description. The son of a carpenter and an illiterate peasant girl, he became a novelist, playwright, polemicist, and revolutionary activist. In 1921 he founded the Communist Party of Valencia. At the age of twenty he fled the Spanish authorities and went underground in France, where the Comintern appointed him as its representative to the Spanish-speaking countries. He changed his identity several times ("I learned to forge passports with the greatest of ease") and traveled frequently to Moscow until his break with the Comintern in 1929. His published reasons for the break include the use by the Soviet secret police of a girl friend to spy on him and their attempts to persuade him to become an assassin. Nevertheless, after the break he experienced an emptiness that led him to consider suicide. A POUMist in the Spanish Civil War, he was arrested by the NKVD and subjected to a "Moscow Trial abroad" (organized by the Hungarian Stalinist Erno Gero). But the Barcelona judge would not condemn him, and he fled to Mexico, where he joined such other embittered former Bolsheviks as Victor Serge and Gustav Regler, and survived five attempts on his life, one of which left him with a hole in his skull. (It was at the time of this persecution that two hundred prominent Americans, including many who were later active in the Congress for Cultural Freedom, signed a letter of protest to the President of Mexico, and the letter resulted in a slackening of the persecution.)[6] After World War II, he was active in the socialist movement for a United States of Europe before joining the Congress for Cultural Freedom.

When *Cuadernos* began—as a quarterly reprinting articles from *Preuves*—Gorkin reported "a great distrust"[7] of the magazine in Latin America, a distrust inevitable in a continent of visceral and increasing anti-Americanism, especially among its *marxisant* intellectuals. The *only* way to produce a "trusted" intellectual magazine, he said, would be constantly to attack the United States and sing the praises of Sartre or Pablo Neruda! The situation grew worse as the decade progressed. The anti-American rage provoked by the U.S.-backed *coup* in Guatemala in 1953 was deepened by the Cuban Revolution of 1958. John Mander was to write, "The years 1958 to 1962 were . . . a period of euphoria for the Latin American Communists and their allies."[8]

Gorkin developed two ways of reducing this distrust. The first was to rely on figures of great prestige. He created an Honorary Board of former Ministers, former Ambassadors, and professors of wide culture and known progressivist views. They included Emilio Frugoni, the poet, a former Ambassador to the U.S.S.R. and a leader of the Uruguayan socialists; Romulo Gallegos, the first popularly elected President of Venezuela and in Gorkin's opinion "the greatest living novelist in the Spanish language"; and Jorge Manach, philosopher, biographer of the Cuban revolutionary national hero José Martí, and the man who drafted Fidel Castro's famous speech from the dock, *History will absolve me*. No other Spanish-language magazine, Gorkin boasted, had been able to bring together "so large a number of eminent figures." He also sought out contributors of great prestige, such as the Spaniards Luis Araquistain and Salvador de Madariaga and the Brazilian Gilberto Freyre.

This emphasis on literary luminaries brought *Cuadernos* a certain respect, however grudging, but as many of them were patriarchal figures, the young, whom the Congress wanted to reach, often turned away. The young intellectuals of Mexico reserved their greatest hatred, Keith Botsford later advised the Paris Secretariat, for "our dear don Salvador" (de Madariaga).

Gorkin's other technique was to open *Cuadernos*'s pages to such Latin American refugees as Victor Raul Haya de la Torre, the Peruvian founder of the APRA party (*Alianza Popular Revolucionaria Americana*). Many persons, Gorkin wrote in his report of January 1959, who

> ... now hold official positions or important teaching posts in the chief Latin American countries—such as Romulo Betancourt, who was recently elected President of the Republic of Venezuela—are ... contributors to *Cuadernos*. During my tour of Latin America, I was able to see that none of these presidents, cabinet ministers and professors had forgotten that during the last years of persecution and exile we had given them moral support and an opportunity to express themselves.[9]

*Cuadernos* supported, among others, Juan Bosch of the Dominican Republic, José Figueres of Costa Rica, and, at the beginning, Fidel Castro of Cuba—and, of course, the non-Communist opposition to Franco in Spain, especially its poets, artists, intellectuals, and academics.

With *Cuadernos*—and a large free list—Gorkin was able to put Congress writers and ideas into circulation and offer to the few willing to read it a more realistic view of the world than they would get from most of their *pensadores*. It was difficult to expect more, and Josselson remained loyal to *Cuadernos*, despite reports of its lack of influence, until the early 1960s.

*Forum*

In November 1953—a month after the Austrian general strike against the Occupation authorities—the Congress's Director of Publications, François Bondy, informed the Executive Committee at its meeting in Rome that the Congress's supporters in Austria, from the socialist Oscar Pollak to the Catholic Fritz Molden, had asked the Congress to help them start a modest magazine of liberal anti-Communist disposition to fill the void between, on the one hand, the lively Communist *Tagebuch* and, on the other, the serious Catholic *Wort and Wahrheit*. The Secretariat had agreed, and the new Viennese monthly, to be called *Forum,* would be edited by Friedrich Torberg (1908–79), the novelist, poet, critic, parodist, and translator, an Austrian refugee who had returned from New York to Vienna.

Born in Vienna as Kantor-Berg, Torberg worked in the Austro-Jewish literary tradition of Arthur Schnitzler, Franz Werfel, Alfred Polgar, and Karl Kraus. (He was sometimes called *ein Krausianer.*) His first novel, *Der Schüler Gerber hat absolviert* (*The Student Gerber Has Graduated*) (1930), was translated into ten languages. In 1938, fleeing the Nazis, he abandoned a literary and journalistic career in Vienna and Prague, served in the Czech Legion in France, and after the fall of France escaped through Spain and Portugal to the United States. In exile he wrote widely on Jewish themes, including a study of a concentration camp (*Mein ist die Rache [Revenge Is Mine]*, 1942). His anti-Nazi nausea was combined with an anti-Communist passion, which was the theme of his 1950 novel, *Die zweite Begegnung* (*The Second Meeting*). (The first meeting was with Nazis, the second with Communists.) As a writer he believed he could work at his best only in the Viennese ambiance, to which he returned in 1951—"the last Mohican of the Danube," in Koestler's words, "of an Old Vienna which perhaps existed only in our fantasy."[10] It was not an easy return: The Communists attacked him as "an American agent . . . slanderer . . . and informer," and he also experienced the Austrian distrust of its émigrés. But in time Torberg, the pig-headed, tolerant humorist-with-a-mission, became, in the words of Marcel Reich-Ranicki, "a Viennese institution, an Austrian miracle and a German scandal."[11]

*Forum* began in 1954. Its first editorial declared (in a still occupied Austria): "In the conflict of our time . . . between democracy and totalitarianism, we are against totalitarianism in all its forms, uncompromisingly." It developed the Congress themes of the 1950s—the "end of ideology" and the critique of neutralism—and published the regular Congress writers: Spender's satiric novella about East–West cultural exchanges, Silone's exchange with the Soviet editor I. Anissimov, and Jelenski on Poland. It also maintained a Danubian character, promoting such Austrian writers as Fritz von Hermanovsky-Orlando, exposing Austrian neo-Nazism (which led to the seizure by police of the March 1960 issue), and discussing the problems of an Austria that fell, in Hans Weigel's formula, between a "no longer" and a "not yet"—"no longer" an Empire but "not yet" a country. With its strong *Torbergsch* stamp, *Forum* combined (Manès Sperber said) the seriousness of metaphysical discussions and the lightness of the *Kaffeehaus*—a monthly edited as a weekly.

*Forum* was the natural base for the Congress's assistance to Hungarian refugees after November 1956. *Forumhilfe* provided emergency money, books, and advice to refugee writers and intellectuals, and arranged foreign language courses for Hungarian students, most of whom had only Russian as a second language. It was at this time that Josselson cabled Lasky in Vienna: "*Forum* has great role to play which ties in directly with ever increasing importance of Vienna and Austria in entire Danubian region. Our policy should be to strengthen *Forum* in every possible way."[12]

Josselson was not always satisfied with the irrepressible Torberg. *Forum's* reference to "Pandit Kadar" was "inexcusable," Josselson wrote to Torberg in February 1957, and "chances are it will be reported back to Nehru" and cause trouble for the Congress in India. Further, Torberg had reprinted from the pages of *National Review* an exchange between James Burnham and William Schlamm on the prospects of the withdrawal of Soviet troops from Eastern Europe. Josselson complained that "it is beneath the dignity of a Congress journal to reprint something from the completely discredited *National Review.*" "It will not happen again," a momentarily chastened Torberg replied.[13]

But while always in the shadow of *Der Monat* in the German-speaking world, *Forum* was one of Congress's successes in the 1950s. In 1958 the Austrian Government conferred the title "Professor" on the thoroughly unacademic Torberg.

## *Tempo Presente*

The Congress was not fully satisfied with its voice in Italy in the early 1950s—the Italian Association for Cultural Freedom and its bulletin *Libertà della Cultura*. They were anti-Communist (in a country where the Communists directed a mass party) and antifascist (while a neofascist nostalgia lingered), but their sometimes ferocious anticlericalism lacked the liberal civility which the Congress increasingly wanted to sponsor. In 1954 Alberto Moravia launched his magazine *Nuovi Argumenti* with a policy akin to that of Sartre's *les Temps modernes*, and it was time for the Congress to establish what Sperber called "the surest basis for our action": *une grande revue* to be edited by Ignazio Silone and Nicola Chiaromonte. It was to be called *Tempo Presente*.

Chiaromonte, the full-time editor, was born in Rapallo in 1905. Disgusted in his youth by Mussolini's dictatorship, he turned first to the antifascist underground organization *Giustizia e Libertà*, whose "idealistic banalities," in Gino Bianco's words, combined "Mazzini-type enthusiasm and ruthless realism."[14] But under the influence of Andrea Caffi, a Russian-Italian born in 1886 in St. Petersburg, who became Chiaromonte's "master," he joined the "novatori," the revisionists who sought to deepen antifascist thought and revive a libertarian, Proudhonian critique of both fascism and Communism. In a remarkable early essay of 1932, Chiaromonte wrote of the "morphological affinity" among the regimes of Mussolini, Stalin, and Hitler.[15] In Paris the Caffi group—living without plans, "since no future was possible"—became secessionists from the world of "established disorder."

Chiaromonte left this anarchist commune to fight in Spain during the Civil War, where he piloted one of what Enzo Bettiza called "the antiquated flying coffins of the Malraux squadron."[16] But he interpreted the Barcelona events of May 1937, when the Communists shot or imprisoned the anarchists and POUMists, differently from George Orwell, Arthur Koestler, and Julian Gorkin. They confirmed him in a new pacifism and in a conviction, as he wrote to Caffi, of "the absurdity and the inconsistency of all political action in the present situation. The inanity of every dogmatic standpoint must finally be recognized."[17]

Fleeing from the German invasion of France, he made his way

with 60,000 other refugees to Toulouse, then to North Africa and finally the United States, where he gravitated to the *Politics* circle and became an anarcho-pacifist guru for Dwight Macdonald. After the war he returned to Paris with his American wife, attracted by an appeal from Albert Camus (whom he had befriended in Algeria) to join the cultural battle to save Europe. He finally settled in Rome, resuming his old friendship with Silone.

Immersed in classical culture—in Malraux's *Man's Fate* he is the character Scali, who seems always to be reading Plato during the Spanish Civil War—this libertarian stoic, this "Renaissance man" (in Leo Labedz's words), this "sulky son of the south" (Enzo Bettiza's),[18] was out of tune with postwar Italy, and *Tempo Presente* gave him the opportunities to recreate, if not a monastic circle like the Polish *Kultura* group in Paris that he admired so much, at least a dissident circle like the old *Politics* group in New York.

The first issue of *Tempo Presente* appeared in April of 1956, a few weeks after N. S. Khrushchev's "secret speech." An editorial opposed ready-made ideas, mindless ideology, and grandiloquent rhetoric. The magazine would be not *engagé* but *degagé*, with a liberal tendency in ideas and socialist in politics. It would also be an international review: The first issue published Isaiah Berlin's "The Marvellous Decade" on Russia in the 1840s, Wayland Young's "London Letter," Lionel Abel's "New York Letter," and a story by Camus (*La donna adultera*), as well as articles by Moravia, Silone, and Chiaromonte. In subsequent issues and years it published all the leading writers associated with the Congress—Aron, Herbert Lüthy, Richard Löwenthal, Koestler, Milosz, Auden, Bondy, and others. It sought out American Leftists such as Macdonald, Mary McCarthy, and Irving Howe.

From the beginning one of its major themes was cultural freedom and human rights behind the Iron Curtain. Silone, representing *Tempo Presente,* was the dominant figure at the Congress-sponsored East–West conference of editors in Zürich in September 1956, and Silone's exchange with the Soviet editor I. Anissimov after the Hungarian Revolution, "The Impossible Dialogue," was widely reprinted ("a dialogue between us" Silone wrote, "is impossible and would have no meaning. The censorship constrains you to feign deafness").[19] *Tempo Presente* also opened its pages to the many defectors from the Italian Communist Party in the late 1950s—the writers Italo Calvino, Vasco Pratolini, and Libero de

Libero; the painters Antonio Sanfilippo and Carla Accardi; the composer Mario Zafred; and the younger writers Antonio Ghirelli and Cesare Vivaldi. It also frequently published dissident writers from the East, such as Boris Pasternak, Andrei Sinyavsky, Aleksandr Wat, and Marek Hlasko.

Its opposition to "ideological ruts" led it to collaborate with the young Catholic liberals associated with *Il Mulino* of Bologna and to introduce the writings of Andrea Caffi to Italian readers. It also campaigned against stage censorship and the harassment of religious minorities in Italy.

In this period of the Congress's greatest success, *Tempo Presente* quickly established itself. In 1957 the President of the Republic sent Silone his personal felicitations, and in January 1959, when reporting to the Executive Committee, the editors referred candidly to the magazine's success ("a source of great satisfaction to us"). They attributed it to its being "the first experiment of its kind in Italy," an international review, which was possible only because of the Congress and the fraternal support of *Encounter, Preuves,* and *Der Monat.* The Congress's dream of "a world family of magazines" was coming to life.

## Quest

The Congress's enduring problem in India was Prime Minister Nehru's distrust. The Congress supported him, despite his neutralism and his Leftist inclination, as a democratic alternative to Maoism in Asia and to Communism in general. But the Prime Minister treated the Congress and its Indian Committee as agents of the United States, and his distrust was deepened by the Indian Committee's publication, *Freedom First,* edited by Minoo Masani, an unrelenting critic, inside and outside the Indian Parliament, of Nehru's neutralism. To improve its standing in India, the Congress decided to launch a literary and cultural magazine whose politics would come through in a very low key.

The original idea was for the magazine to be edited by the famous Bengali poet and critic Sudhindranath Datta and published in Calcutta, whose intellectual life was strongly marked (in Nabokov's words in his report on his Indian tour in late 1954) "by neutralist, fellow-travelerish and direct Communist penetration."[20]

But Datta, disliking the idea of an editorial board probably dominated by the Indian Committee for Cultural Freedom, rejected the
invitation  (although he agreed to be an adviser). Nabokov could
find no other suitable editor in Calcutta, Delhi, or Madras, but in
Bombay he met a thirty-year-old poet and critic, Nissim Ezekiel, a
Ben-Israel Jew, who had a convincingly clear idea of what the proposed magazine should do. It would be a "a mouthpiece" (Nabokov's words) for Indian writers not published abroad. It would be
in English and "a bulwark against further deterioration of the English tongue" (already "appalling"). It would be an all-India, not a
Bombay journal. It would circulate Congress ideas but would not
be politically confrontationist in the style of Minoo Masani. Nissim Ezekiel suggested the name *Quest* to indicate the idea of
strengthening freedom, individuality, and creativity in traditionalist, caste-ridden, and individuality-deadening Hindu India.

The first issue of *Quest*—"a bi-monthly of arts and ideas"—appeared in August 1955 with Nissim Ezekiel's typical balance of literary and social criticism, poems, a short story, theater notes, and
book reviews. The articles included criticism of the Bhoodan
(land-gift) movement and of the attitudes and standards of Indian
students. It also published an interview with Silone. Later issues
under Nissim Ezekiel's editorship had articles by other Congress
writers, including Edward Shils, René Tavernier, Tomoo Otaka,
James T. Farrell, and Walter Laqueur, although most of the contributors were Indian.

Welcoming the first issue in Australia (more for its prose than
its poetry), the poet James McAuley wrote hopefully: "One notes
that the challenge of *Quest* was enough to send Krishna Menon
scurrying off to found a magazine to counteract its influence."[21]
In fact, its policy was too restricted for it to be able to have that
sort of impact. Politically, it was silent even on the Hungarian Revolution (although its coverage of the Suez War was, courageously
in the India of 1956, an article by Walter Laqueur that compared
Colonel Nasser to Mussolini and described the Egyptian regime as
"left-wing fascist").[22] Culturally it was limited by being in English, a
language for administration but rarely for creative literature; with
some exceptions, such as Dom Moraes and Buddhadeva Bose (both
of whom published poems in *Quest*) and R. K. Narayan, most creative writers worked in the vernacular languages, and the exceptions usually published abroad (or would if they could). Khush-
want Singh summed up the attitude: "I ignore English books

published in India."[23] *Quest* therefore relied more heavily than other Congress magazines on contributors who were administrators, academics, and lawyers. In his report to the Congress Executive Committee after two and a half years and fifteen issues, Nissim Ezekiel was defensive: Sudhin Datta had not cooperated; controversy had been hard to provoke; the standard of entries to a story competition was "not encouraging"; a special issue on Marathi literature had errors of selection and translation; and "on circulation, unfortunately, I am unable to report any great success ... 1,200 or so may be regarded as paid for."[24] (In Calcutta only forty were sold; *Encounter,* subsidized for India, was cheaper and sold much more.) The most promising sign that *Quest* was beginning to have an influence was that the Communists were attacking it for "insidious" American propaganda.

In 1958 the Congress tried a new tack. It retained Nissim Ezekiel as reviews editor in Bombay but moved the main editorial office to Calcutta and appointed two new coeditors—the fastidious philosopher Abu Sayeed Ayyub and the argumentative economist Amlan Datta. *Quest* now became "A Quarterly of Inquiry, Criticism and Ideas" and greatly reduced its literary content or (in Eugene Kamenka's phrase) its "arty-crafty" character. (Ayyub declared that Indian poetry and stories written in English were "freakish.")[25] It took up the issue of the struggle between tradition and modernity in India and the question of what is living and what is dead in Marxism. It sought a market among the teachers, journalists, lawyers, and officials, who were so susceptible to the Soviet myth.

After the first four issues produced in Calcutta, the Executive Committee in Paris sent the editors its congratulations. It never satisfied Minoo Masani (who does not mention *Quest* in his memoirs), but it never deserved John Kenneth Galbraith's sneer that it "broke new ground in ponderous, unfocused illiteracy."[26] Like *Cuadernos* in Latin America, it at least gave the Congress a niche in hostile, neutralist territory.

## Der Monat

The problem with Melvin Lasky's *Der Monat* in its early years was that despite its high standard—Sidney Hook in 1949 regarded it as "the best cultural magazine in the entire world"—and its editor's prickly independence, it remained formally a publication of the Information Services Division, Office of Public Affairs, High Commission, Germany (HICOG). Each issue carried a disclaimer to the effect that no contribution represented any official viewpoint, but the official auspices of *Der Monat* still weakened its reputation for independence. They also made it vulnerable to political critics— American or German—who opposed Lasky's generally social democratic politics, and to religious critics who opposed his humanism or criticized the space he gave to liberal critics of the Christian churches (such as Bertrand Russell or Benedette Croce) and to former "atheistic Communists." According to one church historian, for example, the Papal Nuncio—Bishop Alois Muensch (formerly bishop of Fargo, North Dakota)—did everything in his power to close *Der Monat* down or at least stop the American subsidy for it. "He appealed for support both to the American hierarchy and to government officials, and when the grant was finally cut off in 1954, Muensch claimed responsibility for it."[27]

In fact Lasky had long wanted to replace that subsidy and in 1953 arranged a three-year grant from the Ford Foundation for the years 1954 to 1956. *Der Monat* moved out of the U.S. Headquarters, and beginning with the October 1954 issue, its seventy-third, it adopted the subtitle "An International Magazine." It declared in an editorial: "From now on we are absolutely and completely free and independent." At the same time a new coeditor was appointed: Hellmut Jaesrich, the German writer whose literary career began only after the war because he had refused to be a licensed Nazi journalist under Hitler's regime. Under the new arrangement with the Ford Foundation, *Der Monat* moved farther into the European cultural circles established by the Congress.

There was no change in the basic policy, and *Der Monat* maintained its "transatlantic cultural mission" throughout the 1950s. It brought to German readers a range of Western writers often not otherwise readily available to them—from America (Edmund Wilson, William Faulkner, Philip Rahv, Norman Mailer), England (Cyril Connolly, J. B. Priestley, Denis Healey), France (Raymond Aron, Albert Camus, André Malraux), and Italy (Luigi Barzini, Alberto Moravia). It built up a circle of German-language writers from Switzerland (Herbert Lüthy, François Bondy, Fritz René Allemann), Austria (Hans Weigel, Alexander Lernet-Holenia), and increasingly Germany itself (Hans Schwab-Felisch, Klaus Harpprecht). It published extracts from Czeslaw Milosz's *The Captive*

*Mind* and Arthur Koestler's *The Age of Longing* early in the decade and from Milovan Djilas's *The New Class* later. It monitored developments in the East (documenting, for example, the June 17, 1953, uprising) and it baited the "showpiece" of East Berlin, Bertolt Brecht. (Lasky offered Brecht space to publish anything he pleased. Brecht replied, "Why not?" but when nothing arrived, Lasky published a blank page in the January 1955 issue with the headline "Bert Brecht: What I Think About Artistic Freedom.") *Der Monat* became the German forum for Congress debates on European unity or on George Kennan's "disengagement" of the superpowers from Europe. At the same time it always retained a certain unpredictability: Walter Lippmann, Evelyn Waugh, and the "incorrigible" revolutionary and former inmate of a Soviet labor camp, Wanda Bronska-Pampuch, would collaborate in *Der Monat's* pages. It was also the Congress host for visitors to Berlin, from Gary Cooper or Lotte Lenya to George Kennan and Thornton Wilder. When Lasky moved to London in 1958 to take over the editorship of *Encounter, Der Monat's* sales were over 25,000 (including underground sales in East Germany), making it the largest review of its kind in Europe.

If, to the Communist authorities in Berlin, Lasky was a *Schmutz-fink* and a *Dreigroschen-Junge* (a nauseating creature and a threepenny hireling) or, in one polemic "a pocket edition of Leon Trotsky," Bondy was able to say of Lasky's editorship: "A young American gave several generations of Europe not only a literary platform but something like a common intellectual homeland." Silone called him "den echtesten Weltbürger," the most genuine citizen of the world.

## Quadrant

The Australian quarterly *Quadrant,* the last of the Congress-related literary magazines established in the 1950s, was conceived in 1955 in the Russian Tea Room on Manhattan's West 57th Street, when Richard Krygier of the Australian Committee for Cultural Freedom complained to Irving Kristol, coeditor of *Encounter,* about the strong influence of the Communist Party and its fellow-travelers in Australian intellectual life. Kristol suggested to Krygier that he take up with Michael Josselson the possibility of starting a magazine akin to *Encounter* or *Preuves.* Josselson placed the matter on the agenda of the Executive Committee meeting in Paris in January 1956, and the Committee agreed.

Henry Richard Krygier was born in Warsaw in 1917. The shattering event of his youth had been the occupation of Poland by Hitler and Stalin in September 1939. Making his way with his wife to Lithuania, they were among the last few to obtain visas from a philo-Semitic Japanese consul who continued issuing them against instructions from Tokyo. They then traveled across a hungry, depressed, and depressing Soviet Union to Vladivostock and arrived in Sydney, via Tokyo and Shanghai, late in 1941, shortly before Pearl Harbor. This youthful survival of both the Holocaust and the gulag produced in Krygier a democratic, antitotalitarian illumination that the years would only strengthen. When the Yalta agreement closed down the Polish Consulate General in Sydney, where Krygier was a press officer, he set up business as a book importer and in 1951 became the Congress's Representative in Australia, distributing its publications and producing a bulletin made up largely of his translations from articles in *Preuves.* In 1954 he formed the Australian Committee for Cultural Freedom under the Presidency of Sir John Latham, a retired High Court judge, a former conservative political leader, and a still active member of the Rationalist Society of Victoria.

Krygier's choice of editor for the new magazine was the poet James McAuley. Also born in 1917, he had completed an intense ideological journey through an embittered bohemian anarchism to an immersion in Eastern mysticism and, finally, to a return to the Catholic faith of his fathers. In his poetics he had moved from a romantic modernism, which he had held up to ridicule in the "Ern Malley hoax" of 1946, to a new traditionalism. In politics he was deeply committed to the cause of liberal anti-Communism. When Krygier took him to meet Sir John Latham, this unlikely trio—the old Tory and agnostic judge, the Polish Jewish refugee businessman, and the aesthetic poet and Catholic convert—clicked, and together they decided to make a dent in the cultural history of Australia.

McAuley settled on the name *Quadrant.* He liked the metaphor from navigation, and it had a K sound to tack it into the memory. As for its policy, he acknowledged but could not entirely accept Malcolm Muggeridge's heroic advice to him that the only way to edit a magazine is to publish the truth and nothing but the truth, and then to make it as entertaining as possible. Certainly its literary policy would be frankly traditionalist, its political policy would be combative, and it would certainly not, in his hands (he wrote) "exemplify or promote that ideal of a completely colourless, odourless, tasteless, inert and neutral mind on all fundamental issues which some people mistake for liberalism."[28] It would also try to be a rallying point for gradually counteracting Communist influence. But all that had to be done tactfully, in such a way as not to repel those still lingering, as McAuley put it, "in no-man's land."

The first issue appeared late in 1956 with a characteristic balance of the literary and the political. McAuley's opening editoral "Comment" surveyed the state of the sciences (noting the synthesizing of a substance classed as living matter), of society (the crisis of authority), and of the arts (the bankruptcy of modernism). In a reference to the suppression of the Hungarian Revolution he wrote: "Suddenly this one huge glaring visage, this enormous mask made of blood and lies, starts up above the horizon and dominates the landscape, a figure of judgment speaking to each person in a different tone or tongue: And what do you think about *me?*" It concluded: "Truly an exhilarating time!—on condition that we have relevant principles worth living and dying for, and are not unnerved by the lightning and thunder, the whispers and temptations, the beatings and brainwashings . . . or by the rustle of dead leaves."[29]

The magazine inevitably attracted criticism. There is no room in Australia, one critic said, for a literary journal that opposes the Left. But John Wain's comment on the second issue in *The Observer* (London) was more typical: Read it, he wrote, and "then go out and brain the first oaf who tells you poetry is a dead art."[30] *Quadrant* became an Australian outlet for Congress writers and ideas and soon was a bimonthly and then a monthly. The English historian and poet Robert Conquest wrote of it: "*Quadrant* has survived and flourished in a jungle full of pygmies with poisoned arrows [and] has succeeded in McAuley's original aim. . . . Australia is lucky to have it. So are we, in the world at large."[31]

## Science and Freedom

The Congress publications in the 1950s were not all literary–cultural. It also sponsored *Science and Freedom, Soviet Survey,* and a news service, *Forum Service. Science and Freedom* was a biannual bulletin of the Committee on Science and Freedom, which was established under the chairmanship of Michael Polanyi to develop the basic theme of the Congress's conference on "Science and Freedom" in Hamburg in 1953—the idea of a self-governing scientific community. The Committee held international conferences—in Paris in 1956 and Tunis in 1959—and occasionally called public meetings, but its principal activity was its publication between 1954 and 1961 of its *Bulletin,* edited in Manchester by George and Priscilla Polanyi under the supervision of Michael Polanyi.

Of all the Congress's publications in the 1950s, it came closest to being a civil liberties journal. It drew attention to crises of academic freedom all over the world. It protested against the appointment of a "neo-Nazi" as Minister for Education in Lower Saxony in 1955, against government policies toward the University of Tasmania in 1955, against the academic color bar in Alabama in 1956, and against the mass arrest of Spanish academics in 1958. It campaigned persistently against *apartheid* in South African universities, publishing a special issue of the *Bulletin* on it, calling a public protest meeting in London to sponsor a mission of inquiry to South Africa, and launching a scholarship fund to help nonwhite students attend open universities. It also encouraged intellectual exchanges with the Soviet bloc, generally supporting Michael Polanyi's view that this bloc must gradually liberalize.

The *Bulletin,* with its short articles, polemical style, and flavor of a broadsheet, was lively and controversial. It had a mailing list of 5,500 people in more than fifty countries. But it lacked the intellectual solidity to advance the cause for which it had been established after the Hamburg conference, that is, the elaboration of the idea of a self-governing scientific community.

The Congress decided in May 1961 to close down the *Bulletin\** and sponsor a new and more scholarly quarterly to be edited by Edward Shils, who was "more deeply involved in the academic and

---

*The decision was made public in August 1961. The *New Statesman's* columnist "Critic," usually Kingsley Martin, alleged that the Congress had closed down the Committee on Science and Freedom and its bulletin in a fit of Cold War pique when it learned that the Committee had planned a public symposium on nuclear politics, which would provide a platform for the Communist scientist J. D. Bernal. Michael Polanyi replied that he did indeed believe that debating the Communist Party line with Bernal would be "unprofitable," but the Committee was continuing and expanding under Edward Shils.[32]

intellectual world" than George Polanyi. (The first issue of *Minerva* appeared in 1962. See chapter 11.)

## Soviet Survey

When Stalin died in 1953 and the cultural straitjacket he had imposed was slightly loosened, there was no magazine in the world closely monitoring developments in Russian writing, music, history, philosophy, or science and presenting the results to readers without the specialized jargon of the experts. In London Walter Laqueur, George Lichtheim, and Leopold Labedz suggested to Michael Josselson that the Congress sponsor a newsletter to fill this obvious need. Josselson agreed to a trial, and in 1955 a four-page mimeographed monthly called *Soviet Survey: An Analysis of Cultural Trends in the U.S.S.R.* was launched or, more accurately, posted to a few dozen people likely to be interested. It was edited and largely written by Walter Z. Laqueur. As the thaw developed and Russian cultural life became interesting again, the monthly newsletter took off and soon became a large quarterly.

Laqueur was born in Breslau in 1921 ("a bad year," he wrote later, "as far as chances of survival were concerned in those parts of Europe"). As a youth he witnessed the Nazi rallies for Hitler, Himmler, and Goebbels in the Hermann-Göring Stadium, and in 1938, as German Jews desperately besieged the foreign consulates, he was accepted as a student by the University of Jerusalem. It was in a kibbutz, in the valley of Esdraelon in the summer of 1942, that he decided his vocation.

> I was on guard duty, lying on the shade of a Palestinian tree to which a horse and a watchdog were tied. The grain was just about to be harvested, the birds chirping, and miles away there was the sound of a passing train. It was a most peaceful scene, and it occurred to me that I was very fortunate to be simply alive at a time when so many of my friends and European contemporaries had already perished. But I also reached the conclusion that, having been the plaything of historical forces over which there was seemingly no control, I might one day soon at least try to comprehend the events which had led up to that sudden and altogether inexplicable catastrophe.[33]

His first step was to establish himself a leading journalist in Jerusalem, with good contacts in the Mapai (Labor Party) and the Foreign Office. In the early 1950s he also became the Congress's cautious adviser on the Middle East: He warned that in the Arab world any Congress activity would face relentless attack from Nationalists and Communists, and that in Israel itself the Soviet myth was beginning to lose its appeal as a result of the Slansky trials in Prague and other anti-Semitic actions in the Soviet world.

It was when the Congress made him editor of *Soviet Survey* in 1953 that Laqueur began his career as a contemporary historian for whom the totalitarian world and movement, the creators of the Holocaust and the gulag, have been the central preoccupations. (But not his only ones; in 1986 his bibliography, which excluded his daily journalism, ran to sixty-six pages, listing studies of all aspects of twentieth-century European and Middle Eastern affairs.)

His associate editor was Leopold Labedz. Born of Polish parents in 1921 at Simbirsk (now Ulyanovsk, after the family name of another child of the town, Lenin), the infant Labedz and his parents were caught up in the maelstrom of the Russian Revolution and its aftermath. When his mother died in a typhoid epidemic, the father returned with his child to Warsaw (surviving the journey almost solely through the nourishment of the milk of a goat). Labedz was educated in Warsaw and later, at the time of the Spanish Civil War, in Paris, where he followed the writings of Boris Souvarine and Ante Ciliga and joined in "the Kronstadt debate" over Trotsky's savage suppression of the sailors' mutiny of 1921. (Trotsky's self-defense in *Their Morals and Ours* [1939] made Labedz "ill.") Although he predicted the Hitler–Stalin pact, he returned to his family in Warsaw and, in September 1939, fleeing Hitler's Panzers, was arrested by Soviet troops. His father, a doctor, was put to work in a sanatorium for the Soviet elite, where Labedz became a youthful "father confessor" to survivors of the Great Purge who spoke frankly to this precocious foreign prisoner about political matters they would not discuss with friends and family. He particularly befriended Stalin's film writer, Alexei Kepler (whom Stalin was later to deport to a labor camp because of his daughter Svetlana's affection for him).[34] Labedz completed his Soviet education on a collective farm, becoming by now an expert in what he called "comparative totalitarianism." He then left Russia to join the Polish Army in the Middle East. He later served in Italy in the battle of Monte Cassino and after the war settled in England in 1946.

The new magazine that Laqueur and Labedz produced, like the other Congress magazines of the time, filled a void and crackled with excitement. Its articles investigated the post-Stalin thaw, the struggles between "liberals" and "conservatives" in all departments of intellectual and artistic life in the Eastern bloc, the rehabilitation or condemnation of writers, the Polish October, the Hungarian Revolution, the rise of revisionism and polycentrism, and the emergence of the Sino-Soviet dispute. *Soviet Survey* (or *Survey*, as it later became, because the word *Soviet* aroused the suspicion of Egyptian censors) was soon the main source of information about the "Soviet orbit" in both the West and the East.

## Forum Service

With the launching in 1956 of *Tempo Presente* and *Quadrant*, it was clear that "notre grande famille," as Michael Josselson sometimes called the Congress, now had an international network of literary and cultural magazines in which to develop the characteristic themes of liberal, democratic, or humanist anti-Communism. (The network would be further expanded in later years.) But however influential, the magazines were—and were intended to be—of small circulation; the Congress was an elite built on the idea of influence "trickling down." In its early years it did little directly to popularize its ideas or to reach the general public, although many of its collaborators were experienced journalists—Aron, Laqueur, A. D. Gorwala, Bondy, and Arnold Beichman, among many others. But by the late 1950s and the era of decolonization, something more was needed. Many of the newspapers in the emerging states of the Third World could not afford to subscribe to the large commercial news services. Even where they could, those services often ignored developments that the Congress considered important. In practice the Third World newspapers increasingly relied on governmental news services, which were often fellow-traveling, anti-American, or neutralist. The result was that readers were left ignorant of what was going on in the world, especially in the Communist countries and within the Communist parties since Khrushchev's "secret speech."

In this situation the Congress departed from its usual programs of magazines, seminars, and festivals, and started its news service, *Forum Service,* for which Congress writers produced brief, expert reports and analyses of political, cultural, and intellectual developments, to be distributed free to newspapers and magazines around the world. Under the general direction of Melvin Lasky, the series began in October 1957 with K. A. Jelenski's report on the closing down of the dissident Warsaw journal *Po Prostu.* In its general policy *Forum Service* supported the independence of the new states, published sympathetic profiles of their emerging leaders, and attacked *apartheid,* racism, and the new dictatorships. In its coverage of British politics it usually supported the Labour Party, and in the United States the liberal wing of the Democratic Party. In the Soviet orbit it looked for a slow but real liberalization. It also republished such important articles as Imre Nagy's "Testament" and excerpts from such books as Howard Fast's *The Naked God,* which included Fast's exchange of letters with the Soviet writer Boris Polevoi over the murder of Jewish writers in the U.S.S.R. ("Why did you lie in so awful and deliberate a manner?" Fast asked.)

The *Forum Service* articles, usually written by journalists or academics—they included Aron, Edward Crankshaw, G. F. Hudson, Ronald Hingley, Karl Jaspers, Roderick MacFarquhar, and John Mander—appeared first in English, French, and Spanish, and later in nine Indian languages. The features finally reached six hundred newspapers and 5 million readers, a useful bridge between the Congress elite and the larger public, and one of the Congress's successes in the 1950s. Edward Shils expressed the general view when he wrote to Lasky about their reception in India: "I am sure that your Service must contribute a lot to the improvement of public opinion in India." Shils stressed the extent to which "sheer ignorance and a natural disposition toward fellow-traveling" had been sustained by the fact that the truth has not been easily available. "You are making it available."[35]

# 6
# Plato's Banquet

Remember Plato's Banquet. It contains the program of the Congress.

BERTRAND DE JOUVENEL[1]

Why is it ... that all of us here at this moment, whether sitting on the floor, or on the platform, are bored to death and wanting to go home? Why are we bored? Because this is a public meeting, that is to say, an occasion upon which nobody meets anybody! The reason for this Congress is that we are threatened by forces which would turn the whole of human existence into a continuous public meeting in which anyone who yawned would be deprived of his ration card, anyone who fell asleep, shot without trial.

Again if, when asked, I were to say that any of us should go away, as I shall go away, glad that this conference was held, it will be for us, not so much any resolutions that may have been drawn up, or even any practical effect they may have. It will not even perhaps be anything particular that was said by anyone. Speaking for myself, what I shall take away will be the memory of certain real faces, certain real encounters, over, I am sorry to say, non-alcoholic beverages, with real persons. Perhaps we shall never meet again, but a real encounter with anyone, if only for a second, and even if later

consciously forgotten, enters once and for all into the
structure and fabric of one's being.

W. H. AUDEN,
at the Indian Congress
for Cultural Freedom,
Bombay, 1951[2]

From its foundation the Congress for Cultural Freedom planned
to advance its cause by holding further international conferences.
At first they were usually large demonstrations, involving a hundred or more participants, often with a musical performance at
the opening ceremony and the adoption of resolutions at the closing ceremony. Gradually the conferences became smaller seminars, an "international round-table," a sort of seminar in permanent session to discuss Congress themes and issues of the Cold
War.

## HAMBURG, 1953

The Congress's first large-scale international conference after the
founding conference in 1950 was held in Hamburg in 1953. Called
"Science and Freedom," it had three themes. The first was to advance the idea of the freedom of science, teaching, and research,
of science without political control or "ideology." The second was
to arouse scientific opinion against the treatment of scientists and
scholars in the Soviet bloc. The third was to stress the freedom of
American science,* despite the damage to American prestige
caused by official obstacles to the travel of European scientists to
the United States and some harassment of scientists by Congressional investigating committees.

---

*This last was an urgent theme. In 1952 Edward Shils had edited a special
double issue of *The Bulletin of the Atomic Scientists* condemning the U.S.
visa policy, which stopped foreign scientists with past Communist associations from visiting the United States. Albert Einstein had contributed
to the issue, and several British and French scientists had written of their
humiliating experiences with U.S. consular officials. Shils wrote of the
"egregious wrong-headedness" of these policies, which "alienate our allies, comfort our enemies, enfeeble our free institutions, and traduce the
principles of liberty."[3] In the same issue Raymond Aron wrote that revision of American visa policy is "urgently needed": "Prestige is a factor
in the Cold War."

Michael Polanyi was the President of the Organizing Committee (along with Alexander Weissberg-Cybulski, Arthur Jores, and Nicolas Nabokov). He was an ideal choice. A renowned physical chemist, Polanyi also had a public record of anti-Nazi and anti-Soviet commitment and had been a leader in Britain of the liberal movement for the autonomy of science against the planners. He had also recently been humiliated by U.S. officials who had refused him a visa because of past political associations. In his own person he symbolized what the Hamburg conference stood for.

Born in Budapest in 1891, Polanyi was one of a family that Peter F. Drucker described as "the most gifted I have ever known or heard of."[4] Like his brothers and sister, he was educated by tutors in an isolated castle according to Rousseau's precepts in *Emile*. During World War I, in which he served as a medical officer in the Austro-Hungarian Army, he corresponded with Einstein on the application of quantum theory to the third law of thermodynamics and, while a patient in the hospital, completed the outline of his theory of the thermodynamics of adsorption, which was rejected at first, only to be accepted fifty years later. In 1933 he resigned from the Kaiser Wilhelm Institute in Berlin in protest against its dismissal of Jewish scientists. He took the Chair of Physical Chemistry at Manchester (and exchanged it in 1946 for a Chair in Social Studies).

His 1936 paper "Truth and Propaganda"[5] was one of the few to challenge the findings of Sidney and Beatrice Webb's *Soviet Communism: A New Civilisation?* (Polanyi's stance, in a period when Soviet prestige remained high, prompted Koestler to dedicate *The Yogi and the Commissar* [1945] to him.) Polanyi also campaigned strongly against the Marxist "social relations of science" movement, which flourished between 1932 and 1945 in Britain and, to a lesser extent, in France and the United States. A reaction to social and political decay during the world Depression, this movement, under the leadership of J. D. Bernal and the World Association of Scientific Workers, popularized the ideas that liberal democracy had failed and that science should be centrally directed and controlled as part of the process of economic planning.

The liberal counterattack began in 1939 with Polanyi's paper "The Rights and Duties of Science"[6] and John D. Baker's "Counterblast to Bernalism."[7] In 1940 Polanyi and others formed the Society for Freedom in Science, which by the middle 1940s had undermined the "social relations of science" movement and begun to

develop the alternative idea of a self-governing scientific community. That idea would play a central role in the Hamburg conference.

When Polanyi applied in 1951 for a visa to the United States to
take up a chair at the University of Chicago, he was, after eighteen
months of inquiries and discussions with U.S. consular officials,
finally informed by the American Consul General in Liverpool
that he was "ineligible to receive an immigration visa as a person
inadmissible into the United States." It turned out that he had
once allowed his name to be used as a patron of an anti-Nazi but
pro-Soviet front called the Free German League of Culture, which
he had addressed in December 1942 (a time of popular pro-Soviet
sentiment) on the persecution of scientists in the U.S.S.R. He had
also belonged, for a year in 1946–47, to the Society for Cultural
Relations between the Peoples of the British Commonwealth and
the U.S.S.R., along with such writers as Somerset Maugham, Walter
de la Mare, and Arthur Bryant. It may also be that his prewar visits
to the U.S.S.R. or the radical views of some members of his family
were held against him. In any case, his many writings in the liberal
anti-Communist cause did not convince State Department officials.[8] When he became chairman of the Hamburg Organizing
Committee, he had no illusions about what he called "harsh and
stupid conservatism."[9]

When 120 scientists and scholars gathered in the Free City of
Hamburg in July 1953, the mayor welcomed them, the Hanseatic
city put out its flags, and an orchestra played the pleasant first
movement of Gounod's *Little Symphony for Winds*. (No heroic *Egmont* this time. For the closing ceremony it played Mozart's urbane,
gracious *Serenade for Winds*.) No such assembly had ever gathered
before. The participants came from nineteen "Western" countries
(including Japan, but not Israel, which still discouraged association with West Germany). They were mainly natural scientists, including several Nobel laureates, but there were also several social
scientists and philosophers, among them Aron, Hook, and Shils.

Several had been victims of the Nazi regime. James Franck, the
Nobel laureate and physicist (and winner of an Iron Cross in
World War I) had resigned from the University of Göttingen in
protest at Nazi policies and had fled Germany. Hans Thirring had
been compelled to retire from his chair in Vienna because of his
anti-Nazi views. Lise Meitner, the Austrian physicist who had, with

Otto Frisch, coined the term "nuclear fission," had fled from Nazi Germany in 1938. Edgar Wind, the German art historian and philosopher, had moved with the Warburg Institute from Hamburg to London in 1933. Max Horkheimer had moved with his Institute for Social Research from Frankfurt to Geneva in 1933 and then to New York in 1934. Michael Polanyi had resigned from the Kaiser Wilhelm Institute in an anti-Nazi protest. While the physicist Max von Laue had remained in Germany, he became a symbol of independent science and its resistance to Hitler, resigning in protest from the Kaiser Wilhelm Institute in 1943.

Others had fled the Soviet Union, such as Theodosius Dobzhansky, the author of *Genetics and the Origin of Species,* and Fedor Stepun, the historian and sociologist. Still others had experienced both Nazi and Soviet regimes: the former Communist Alexander Weissberg-Cybulski (the founder of the Soviet *Journal of Physics*) and the physicist F. G. Houtermans, who had both been imprisoned by Stalin and then delivered to the Gestapo on the bridge at Brest-Litovsk at the time of the Hitler–Stalin pact.

The British scientists included the zoologist John D. Baker and the chemist E. F. Caldin, who had joined Polanyi to form the Society for Freedom in Science in 1940. Some of the American participants had been deeply involved in the postwar controversies concerning nuclear weapons and "nucleonics." Arthur Holly Compton, a Nobel laureate, had worked on the Manhattan Project as director of the Metallurgical Laboratory at the University of Chicago and in July 1945 had arranged a poll of 150 atomic scientists regarding the use of the atomic bomb against Japan. Samuel K. Allison had conducted the countdown for the Trinity atomic test explosion in New Mexico in July 1945, and James Franck had been chairman of the "Committee on Social and Political Implications," which advised the U.S. War Department in June 1945 against any unannounced use of the atomic bomb and called for international control of nuclear weapons. Eugene Rabinowitch, a Russian-born specialist in photosynthesis, had also worked on the Manhattan Project and later cofounded the *Bulletin of the Atomic Scientists* (with a nuclear doomsday clock on its cover, showing the world at 10 minutes to midnight). The *Bulletin* became the organ of the "scientists' movement" in the United States after World War II, which had some influence on the U.S. Government. (After months of public lecturing, barnstorming, and lobbying, it defeated the plan to turn all atomic energy installations over to the military forces and persuaded the U.S. Government, which then had a monopoly of atomic weapons, to adopt the Acheson–Lilienthal plan for the international control of nuclear energy, a plan approved by all governments except those of the Soviet bloc.) Shils, a social scientist, had also been active in the establishment and conduct of the *Bulletin of the Atomic Scientists*.

The Hamburg conference was not, and was not intended to be, a fighting conference like the Berlin Congress of 1950. Over four days the participants calmly debated the relations between pure and applied science, the plannability of science, and the freedom of science in fact and in principle in the West and in the Soviet bloc. At the end they sent fraternal greetings to their "unhappy" colleagues behind the Iron Curtain and looked forward to the day when they could work together as free men. (The Berlin message of 1950 had offered "material support" in any rebellion.) The conference also established a permanent Committee on Science and Freedom to develop the basic idea of an autonomous city of science in the free society.

Those results, in a tense period between the execution of the Rosenbergs as "atomic spies" and the charging of J. Robert Oppenheimer with being a security risk, justified Shils's description of the conference as "an enormous success."[10] A writer in the *Times Educational Supplement* described "the friendly mixing" of scholars, who disagreed on so many matters of philosophy and religion but were united in opposition to totalitarianism and in support of intellectual freedom, as "itself an object lesson in liberalism," although the writer wondered "whether such a coalition would hold together in a time of trial."[11] It was the mission of the Congress for Cultural Freedom, and its new Committee on Science and Freedom, to see that it did.

## MILAN, 1955

The next major conference was "The Future of Freedom" in September 1955 in Milan. Michael Polanyi was again a principal organizer, and again he wanted no crusade, rally, or demonstration in the spirit of Berlin 1950 ("I see no occasion for similar acts in the near future").[12] But he wanted it to deal with what was for him a "passionately controversial subject": the "new economic order" that would be neither socialist nor capitalist. As Shils put it, the idea had been "to forward the process of breaking the encrustations of liberal and socialist thought, to discover their common ground."[13] By the time the Conference met, the theme of a "new economic order" had been widened to include "the underdeveloped world" and the new economic developments in the U.S.S.R.

The 150 intellectuals who assembled for a week in Milan, this time mainly economists and social scientists, represented a wider range of countries—extending to Asia, Africa, and Latin America—than at the earlier conferences. If, when it was over, there were some who, like Hannah Arendt, had found the debates "deadly boring"[14] or, like Dwight Macdonald, thought that they had produced "no fire, no drama, no sparkle,"[15] there were more like Max Beloff, who recognized that the Conference had "in some important respects altered the shape of our mental world."[16] The Bandung Generation was about to take the world stage.

Five themes that emerged in the course of the week would be developed at later and smaller seminars. The first was implicit or below the surface (as it had been in earlier Congress activities). In an effort to find a unifying idea in the bewildering variety of papers, Edward Shils articulated a theme that made sense of the Milan conference—and also clarified the underlying mission of the Congress as a whole. In his article "The End of Ideology?" he wrote:

> The papers, despite their diversity of viewpoint and subject matter, circled over a single theme. Almost every paper was in one way or another a critique of doctrinairism, of fanaticism, of ideological possession. Almost every paper at least expressed the author's idea of mankind cultivating and improving its own garden, secure against obsessional visions and phantasies, and free from the harassment of ideologists and zealots. It was the intention of the conference's organisers to move thought further around the turning-point to which we have come in the last years. This turning point might be described as the end of ideological enthusiasm.

The Conference was a sort of celebration: "Communism had lost the battle of ideas."[17]

The second theme was subsidiary but explicit: Polanyi's theme that the dichotomy between "socialism" and "capitalism" is a false one, that state controls need not weaken freedom, and the debate

should be only over the degree and frequency of state intervention. The large British Labour Party "delegation" (Hugh Gaitskell, C. A. R. Crosland, R. H. S. Crossman, Denis Healey, Roy Jenkins, Stuart Hampshire, and W. Arthur Lewis) was not the only
group to welcome this theme. "Gaitskellism" (with which *Encounter*
became associated), was now an international movement. In 1959
it would triumph even in the Social Democratic Party of Germany,
which abandoned Marxism and adopted the *Godesberger Programm*.
Its triumph at Milan led Friedrich Hayek, adamant in his opposition to state intervention, to declare that the real agenda at the
conference was not to plan the future of freedom but to write its
obituary. But for the moment he had few allies.[18]

The third theme was the economic achievement of the U.S.S.R.,
or the Soviet Union as a superpower. In the July 1953 issue of
*Foreign Affairs,* Peter Wiles had published the article "The Soviet
Economy Outpaces the West." His statistics were challenged, although the idea gained dramatic support in 1957 when the Soviet
Sputnik defeated the United States in the race to place the first
object in orbit. The performance of the U.S.S.R. was debated at
Milan generally without rancor—and without reaching an agreed,
final view. But Polanyi issued a warning:

> Thus it would seem that some of the best equipped minds of
> Europe and America are unable to decide today whether
> Soviet Russia is surpassing us by far in economic growth or is,
> on the contrary, very much lagging behind. The lesson of this
> for the strategy of freedom seems to me clear and urgent. We
> must get to know and to know exactly what is the truth about
> the alleged economic dynamism of Soviet Russia. We are
> entering today on an intellectual and moral contest with the
> Soviet Government for the allegiance of men all over the
> world. Uncertainty concerning the most effective claims of
> our opponents must reduce our arguments to rhetoric or
> force us into evasive ambiguities.[19]

The fourth new theme was the "underdeveloped" world. The
Bandung Conference had taken place earlier in the year, but the
prospect of decolonization had not really sunk into the minds of
Western liberals. When the Milan conference debated economic
aid, few Westerners bothered to speak, and Beloff provoked a
storm when he objected to a note of blackmail in some of the statements: "Give us aid or we'll turn to the Soviets." Finally, when

Minoo Masani of India, backed by Chief Akintola of Nigeria, challenged the Westerners to speak out, the conference adopted a resolution expressing the solidarity of intellectuals in the free world with those of the underdeveloped countries and calling for programs of cultural aid. Polanyi referred to "the exhilarating perspective ... opened up to me of this immense area of new companionship."[20] Some, like George Kennan and Beloff, remained skeptical Columbuses. (Kennan thought there was little point for Americans in attending conferences with Asians, Africans, or Latin Americans: Misunderstanding of the United States would never be overcome.)[21] But the Westerners at Milan were in no doubt that the Bandung Generation had arrived and that the Congress for Cultural Freedom had to have a new agenda: The Soviet *mythos* may have been dead in the West, but it was alive and well in the Third World.

The final theme emerged almost accidentally. In his report on the conference for *The Economist,* the Oxford historian G. F. Hudson wrote:

> Although the conference showed such a great diversity of opinion, it was remarkable that debate could nevertheless be carried on with so much mutual toleration and effort at understanding. The founders of the organisation seem to have discovered a method of achieving a solidarity of the normally fragmented liberal intelligentsia without imposing articles of faith that would inevitably be unacceptable to large sections of those brought together in these conferences.[22]

This raised the possibility (despite Kennan's skepticism) of building a worldwide intellectual community of which the prototype was the scientific community adumbrated at Hamburg. This indeed soon became the Congress's supreme objective (when it concluded that it had won the battle against the fellow-travelers) and sustained all its programs—seminars, festivals, magazines, centers—for most of the remainder of its life.

## SEMINAR PLANNING COMMITTEE

The Milan conference gave the Congress new themes (above all, following Shils's article, the end of ideology as a framework for discussions). It also opened the way to trying to build a worldwide community of intellectuals, including those of the "underdeveloped world." Finally, it led the Congress to the view that large conferences were not always the best way to explore these issues and that small seminars might be more effective. It now created a Seminar Planning Committee, with Michael Polanyi as chairman, and the Ford Foundation agreed to fund a program of small seminars which would not (Polanyi explained) be dramatic demonstrations but sober discussions of "circumscribed" practical subjects.[23] At the same time the seminars would help create an international community, a permanent worldwide round-table, or what Shils called "a network or fellowship of liberal-spirited intellectuals all over the world, whose further thought on these hard problems would be encouraged and sustained by a feeling of affinity with their opposite members across boundaries of profession, generation, nationality, and continent."[24] The Seminar Program soon became a new arm of the Congress, complementing the magazines and the national committees.

Daniel Bell, the sociologist and journalist, became the first director of the Seminar Program in 1956–57, while on leave from his post as labor editor of *Fortune* magazine and before joining Columbia University as a professor of sociology. Born in 1919, Bell had grown up, he said, in the slums of New York, speaking only Yiddish until he was six years old. As a youthful socialist—he joined the Young People's Socialist League at the age of thirteen and was chairman of a Student Strike Against War at the age of eighteen— he was saved from becoming a Stalinist or Trotskyist by anarchist relatives who gave him Alexander Berkman's anti-Bolshevik pamphlets to read.[25] A graduate of the City College of New York, he became a staff member in 1940 and finally managing editor of the social democratic *New Leader*. One of the "twice-born" or disenchanted but radical antitotalitarian "generation of 1939," he, like most of that generation, came to support the war against Hitler (although uneasy about the alliance with Stalin and the British and French imperialists) and, after the war, remained a marginal radical (critical of the "three powers" peace, anti-Communist, anticapitalist, seeking a "third force"). But in the late 1940s he shared his generation's growing reconciliation with American life and its increasing rejection of Marxist ideological blinders. In his first major work, *The Background and Development of Marxian Socialism in the United States* (written in 1949 and 1950 and published in 1952), he concluded that American socialism had become "simply a notation in the archives of history."

Yet he remained "a lifelong Menshevik" or, in another formulation, a socialist in economics, a conservative in culture, and a liberal in politics. "The ethic of responsibility, the politics of civility, the fear of the zealot and the fanatic . . . are the maxims that ruled my intellectual life," he wrote. He is also a man of religion, steeped in Rabbinic lore. ("I was born in *galut*," he once declared, "and I accept—now gladly, though once in pain—the double burden and the double pleasure of my self-consciousness, the outward life of an American and the inward secret of a Jew. I walk with this sign as a frontlet between my eyes, and it is as visible to some secret others as their sign is to me."[26]) In 1960 he published a set of his 1950s studies under the title *The End of Ideology: On the Exhaustion of Political Ideas in the Fifties,* the first of his major books exploring the possibility of a public philosophy for what he came to call "the postindustrial society."

The Congress held five small but ambitious international seminars in the late 1950s on subjects ranging from the future of liberal institutions in the new states of Asia and Africa to the malaise of the West after "the end of ideology." The first, on "Problems of Economic Growth," was convened in Tokyo—for two reasons. The Congress had so far made little progress in Japan, where the intellectuals remained predominantly anti-American and fellow-traveling. But it had now established a new national committee, the Japan Cultural Forum, in place of the abandoned and ineffective Japanese Committee for Cultural Freedom (see chapter 8 below), and a major international seminar associated with the new Forum would give it a good start. Further, in the late 1950s there was both an almost universal commitment to the need for rapid economic growth and a rising concern at the failure to achieve it in many "underdeveloped" Asian and African countries, where the intellectuals (if not the economists) increasingly saw the option of "the Soviet model" as their only hope.[27] Japan's rapid economic growth, however, illustrated one of the seminar's themes: that such growth was possible without direct controls, let alone Sovietization.

The thirty economists from twelve Western, Asian, and African countries who assembled at International House in April 1957 included the writers of some of the classic texts on economic growth.

Colin Clark's *The Conditions of Economic Growth* (1940) had for the first time expressed in hard statistical terms the gulf between living standards in rich and poor countries, and Paul Rosenstein-Rodan's 1944 paper "The International Development of Economically Backward Areas" was the beginning of modern development economics.[28] The chairman, W. Arthur Lewis, was author of *The Theory of Economic Growth* (1955), and Peter Bauer wrote (with B. S. Yamey) *The Economics of Underdeveloped Countries* (1957). Several advisers to governments attended: D. R. Gadgil and M. L. Dantwala from India, Saburō Ōkita from Japan, Das Gupta from Ceylon, M. L. Qureshi from Pakistan, and Tun Thin from Burma. There were journalists, such as Rita Hinden of Britain, and politicians, such as Asoka Mehta of India.

Bell wrote to Josselson in Paris that, paradoxically, the conference was a tremendous success even before it began, as this was the first important, nongovernmental meeting held in Japan since before World War II, and the Japanese were flattered.[29] Japan had recovered its sovereignty only five years earlier under the Peace Treaty of San Francisco, and many Japanese, including Saburō Ōkita, had lively recent memories of being refused permission to speak at intergovernmental conferences because Japan was still an occupied country. Now some of the most famous economists in the world were coming to Tokyo, and the Japanese responded vigorously. A reception committee was formed of the president of the Bank of Japan, the presidents of the three leading universities, the head of the Japan Broadcasting Corporation, and the directors of the four leading newspapers. The opening session of the conference was broadcast, the press covered it daily, and there were several discussions on national radio.

But the debates themselves—on land reform, urbanization, trade unions, educational planning, and the role of intellectuals—lacked, in Bell's word, "fireworks." The "free enterprisers" (Colin Clark, Bertrand de Jouvenel, Peter Bauer) did not press their position against the planners, and while Jouvenel found the contrasting attitudes of the "Victorian" Japanese and the "post-Keynesian" Indians fascinating[30]—the one wanting to limit the public sector, the other to expand it; the one urging capital accumulation through profits, the other through taxation; the one wanting to eliminate small-scale industry, the other attached to it (as was Clark, who on this issue described himself as "a disciple of Mahatma Gandhi")—these differences never turned into lively confrontations. There was also an unexpected degree of agreement not only in opposition to Sovietization, especially the collectivization of agriculture, but also over the often unacknowledged "costs" of rapid economic growth, especially the costs in human relations and the quality of life. The high point of the latter was the storm provoked by M. L. Qureshi of the Pakistani Planning Board when he suggested that the public cost of education could be justified only to the extent that it contributed to economic growth. Ayo Ogunsheye of Nigeria and Edward Shils carried the conference with their argument that such a policy might produce servants of a government program but not the critical faculties to evaluate it. In this respect the conference was a precursor of the impending shift by development economists from an emphasis on growth of per capita income to one on the quality of life, social justice, and freedom as the true measure of development.[31] (On his return to Dr. Sukarno's "guided democracy," Dr. D. Sumitro, the Dean of the Djakarta School of Economics at the University of Indonesia, fled Djakarta and joined the doomed rebellion in Sumatra.)

Bell's second conference returned to one of the Congress's permanent themes when he brought together thirty of the world's leading authorities on the Soviet Union, mainly American and British, but also including Raymond Aron from France and A. D. Gorwala from India, to discuss "Recent Changes in the Soviet Union" and the possibilities of the liberalization of the regime. Merle Fainsod, Bertram D. Wolfe, Max Hayward, Aron, Richard Pipes, G. F. Hudson, A. D. Gorwala, G. H. Seton-Watson, and Bell himself prepared papers in advance and the seminar convened in St. Antony's College, Oxford, to discuss them in June 1957, at the very time Khrushchev was completing some further "changes" of his own in Moscow and expelling "the anti-Party group" (V. M. Molotov, G. M. Malenkov, L. M. Kaganovich) from the Presidium of the Communist Party Central Committee.

Two divisions dominated the debates.[32] The first was between those who, like Bertram D. Wolfe, the former Bukharinist Communist, saw the Soviet changes as "within-system" and not a fundamental breakup of totalitarianism (the West, Wolfe said, has always "found it hard to gaze straight and steadily at the head of Medusa") and those who, like Aron, raised the possibility that Soviet industrialization, with its need for literacy, competence, and rationality, would compel a normalization of society. (Aron amiably called Wolfe "the last great doctrinaire of Soviet society.") The phrase "within-system change" caught on like a slogan, and subsequent debates centered on it.

It also underlay the second major division at the seminar between those who saw the "ferment" among Soviet intellectuals as the beginning of a genuine liberalization and those who saw it as "within-system." Max Hayward, now beginning his career as the great English translator and interpreter of dissident Soviet writers, in Patricia Blake's words, "the custodian of Russian literature in the West, until it could be restored to Russia,"[33] delivered the basic paper, "Potentialities for Freedom: The Restlessness of Writers." Hayward had served in the British Embassy in Moscow during the Zhdanovist purges of writers and artists and retained all his life a loathing of the persecutors of culture and their apparatchiks. But he had also befriended many dissident writers and had wandered privately around the Soviet Union, trailed by secret police, absorbing the hostility of the Russian populace to the regime. The British Embassy had recently ordered him back to England after an alcoholic brawl in a Tiflis restaurant during which he had loudly and obscenely denounced Stalin from the top of a table. His paper at Oxford struck a note of cautious and sympathetic optimism.

Isaiah Berlin was more skeptical.[34] He had recently returned from a visit to Moscow, where he had met Boris Pasternak and spoken on the telephone with Anna Akhmatova (who believed it would not be safe for her to meet him). He spoke of the continued domination by contemptuously anti-intellectual "roughnecks and bureaucrats." (Kaganovich had asked him: "Is Hegel taught at Oxford?" "No, but Kant is." "Idealist! ... And who else?" "Hume." "Empirical monist!") Beneath them was a deadened, bullied, servile class of semi-intellectuals whose complaints were "within-system" and who had no political or "outside-the-system" direction. Berlin's note of "Moussorgsky mournfulness" angered George Katkov, the Russian philosopher of the *ancien régime,* who drew attention to the controversial "conspiracy of silence" among Russian intellectuals that *Pravda* was then denouncing—that is, the silent refusal to bow publicly to the dogmas of socialist realism. "And this you don't call political?" he asked. "I reel under Katkov's blows" was Berlin's unrepentant rejoinder.

The debates were unresolved, but Cyrus Sulzberger of the *New York Times* was not alone in finding them "fascinating." If, as Lasky saw, they marked the retreat of the anti-Soviet crusaders and the advent of the scholarly "Sovietologists" (Russia, he said, was no longer Churchill's riddle wrapped in an enigma and was becoming "a theory supported by a footnote and wrapped in a bibliography"), they also strengthened the Congress's determination to reach Soviet intellectuals and advance as far as it could the liberalization of Soviet society.

The Congress made a new departure in its third international seminar on "Workers' Participation in Management." Bell acknowledged that the topic might "at first blush ... seen to be far removed from 'cultural freedom,'" but he saw it as a way of exploring how, in an increasingly bureaucratized world, means may be found to give individuals a greater say over the control of their lives.[35] This was an early expression of his preoccupation with "humanizing a technocracy and taming the apocalypse" (which underlay a later international seminar at Princeton in December 1968). There was also a political point, in that the Soviet Union condemned the workers' councils that had emerged in Poland and Hungary in 1956, seeing them as centers of opposition to the Communist Party.

As had happened at the Hamburg conference with scientists, at Milan with social scientists, and at Tokyo with economists, this new departure brought a new range of participants within the Congress circle, as thirty union officials, plant managers, and industrial journalists, as well as scholars and such familiar figures as Ignazio Silone gathered from sixteen countries in September 1958 in Vienna to discuss the variants of workers' control: German and Austrian co-management, French producers' cooperatives, British joint consultation, Yugoslav workers' councils, the Olivetti experiment in Italy, the Tata enterprise in India, and the Histadrut industries in Israel.

There had never before been a conference like this. It was a further development of "the end of ideology," but more importantly it—with the follow-up conferences in Japan and Sweden and the book that grew out of the discussions, H. A. Clegg's *A New Approach to Industrial Democracy*—made a major contribution to the spread of the idea of "worker participation," including the adoption of it as "the democratic imperative" by the European Economic Community. It did not, however, remain a major Congress theme, although the underlying issue of humanizing industrial society did.

In the following month, October 1958, the Congress turned again to the question of the uncertain future of democracy in the new or emerging states. Edward Shils, the American sociologist, had investigated the intellectuals of India in the middle 1950s, where he observed the growing impatience of the modernizing intellectuals with traditional Indian society, its misery, apathy, and passionate parochialism, and their growing conviction that Soviet or Maoist methods may be necessary to transform India, that democracy was an obstacle to progress. It was a period when, as Richard Rovere put it, the lights were going out all over Asia, as Indonesia, Burma, Pakistan, and Thailand abandoned democracy, and the prospects in Africa were disheartening. What could be done, the Congress asked, to strengthen both liberal institutions and the will to meet social demands by democratic means?

Some forty intellectuals from twenty-three countries assembled in the Hôtel des Roses on the island of Rhodes to debate the issues. A mixture of scholars, politicians, officials, and journalists, they included Aron, Jouvenel, Gunnar Myrdal, Robert M. Hutchins, Judge Charles Wyzansky, Galbraith, Polanyi, Lasky, Bondy, Silone, Minoo Masani, Asoka Mehta, D. R. Gadgil, Ayo Ogunsheye, Thomas Diop, Maung Maung, Prince Kukrit Pramoj. (The crisis to be discussed prevented some from attending. The emergency in Ceylon, for example, kept Dudley Senanayake in Colombo, and the communal violence in Cyprus kept Hugh Gaitskell in London, although he sent a paper. One Lebanese who was to have been invited was by that time engaged in a civil war in the mountains.) The plan was to have a week of undogmatic discussion around a table—without speeches or the formal delivery of the papers—in the hope that, expecting the unexpected, the participants would advance understanding of both the problem and, if not the solution, at least the way ahead.

The discussion began with several questions: Is it reasonable to expect the institutions of political democracy, which is of Western origin, to take root in Asia and Africa and to cope with the problems of modernization? Does the collapse of democratic institutions have redeeming features? Is Hugh Gaitskell right when he says in his paper that the existence of two or more parties and of a legal and effective opposition to the government is *the* test of parliamentary democracy in any country?

Aron described the present experience as "without parallel in world history." We take institutions, he said, "which have grown up slowly in the West and we transplant them in countries where often neither *the state* nor *the nation* exists and where the tasks to be achieved are enormous—and were, in fact, never achieved in the West with constitutional procedures and party systems." The vital issue, he contended, was first to establish the state, the nation, the sense of citizenship. Yet while there was an almost universal belief that only popular elections gave legitimacy to a government, there was an almost equally universal distaste for actual politicians and parliaments (as was confirmed by Prince Pramoj of Thailand, Dr. Maung Maung of Burma, Professor Hussain of Pakistan, and Asoka Mehta of India). How can the new states in these circumstances encourage the sense of citizenship, of genuine participation? At the very least there should be less concern, for the moment, with questions of elections or bicameralism or procedures and more with the preservation of public liberties, the rule of law, and the building up of the national infrastructure—the professions, the universities, and the press. The collapse of first attempts at democracy need not be permanent.

No one was optimistic, but Aron detected no defeatism, only a cheerful pessimism. In words reminiscent of his description of the national mood in France following World War II, he found both a keen awareness of past failures and "a striking determination to make good," whatever the temporary setbacks and however massive the problems. Rhodes strengthened the Congress's commitment to building a liberal international community to help defend public liberties in the new states.[36]

While the Congress's international seminars so far had dealt with the Third World (Tokyo, Rhodes), the Soviet Union (Oxford), or a general issue (Vienna), the last seminar of the 1950s turned to the problems of the West. Entitled "Industrial Society and the Western Political Dialogue" and organized by Aron, it asked what was to be the West's public philosophy after "the end of ideology." What, Aron asked, does the West want beyond vast factories and a rising standard of living?

How could the West ever justify itself, either in its own eyes or the eyes of non-Westerners, if it were content with a science concerned only with the manipulation of natural forces and social beings and neglected the search for Reason which, beyond the realm of science or technique, is man's essential nature and his achievement throughout history?[37]

To discuss these questions Aron brought together twenty scholars (the smallest seminar yet), mostly Westerners, from ten countries. Some frequent *congressistes* were there: Polanyi, Shils, Jouvenel, and Mehta. There were some new faces: Eric Voegelin, M. M. Postan, and Jakob Talmon. There were also two Americans whom the Congress had supported during their "years of exile" or disputes with U.S. authorities—J. Robert Oppenheimer, who in 1954 had been declared a "security risk" by a Security Board of the Atomic Energy Commission, and George Kennan, who had been excluded from the Foreign Service in 1953. They all assembled in September 1959 in the old-fashioned, comfortable Saliner Hotel at Rheinfelden on the banks of the Rhine near Basel. The atmosphere remained, in Edward Shils's words, "elevated, grave and courteous."

The discussion began with an attempt to reach agreement over issues raised at earlier seminars about those states in relation to which the West in part defined itself—the U.S.S.R. as a rival and the Third World as a model. Now only Kennan remained optimistic about liberalization within the Soviet Union, and there was general agreement (the argument being carried mainly by Aron, Jouvenel, Postan, Voegelin, and Talmon) that there would be economic convergence ("the industrial society") but no political convergence between the West and the U.S.S.R. in the foreseeable future. The liberal West would remain in confrontation with an ideologized, one-party state. As for the Third World, the seminarists more strongly confirmed the concern that emerged in Tokyo over the cost of "unlimited" economic growth and the distinction made at Rhodes between the historic political institutions of the West (parliaments and parties), which might not take root in the new states, and the liberal ideas underlying them, which have a universal truth and which the West (and the Congress) must support.

The discussion then turned to the special theme of the seminar: Western industrial society and the good life. It produced the most wide-ranging critique of the postideological West yet made in a forum of the Congress, which for years had made "the end of ideology" its theme. Talmon stated a basic paradox: "Messianism" brings fanaticism, its absence smugness. Is there, the philosopher Jeanne Hersch asked, a middle course between the bovine life without an ideology and the "messianic" with one? Eugene Rostow spoke for the values of ordinary free life, of piecemeal progress in the service of ideals deliberately left vague. But the initiative fell to the critics of "ordinary life." Kennan complained of the increasing lack of privacy in the West, the growing loss of communion with nature and the pollution of the environment, which he attributed to the fetish of economic growth ("surely not all the values to be sought in Western life are to be found in quantitative increase") and its restriction of the consciousness of obligation to the needs of the present generation alone:

> I would plead for an end to this arrogant and hopeless attitude, and for the incorporation with the public philosophy of the West of the recognition of the obligation to pass this planet on to future generations in a state no poorer, no less fair, no less capable of supporting the wonder of life, than that in which we found it.

Robert Oppenheimer declared:

> I find myself profoundly in anguish over the fact that no ethical discourse of any nobility or weight has been addressed to the problem of the new weapons, of the atomic weapons ... what are we to make of a civilization which has always regarded ethics as an essential part of human life, and which has always had in it an articulate, deep, fervent conviction, never perhaps held by the majority, but never absent; a dedication to "ahimsa," the Sanskrit word that means "doing no harm or hurt," which you find in the teachings of Jesus and Socrates—what are we to think of such a civilization, which has not been able to talk about the prospect of killing almost everybody except in prudential and game-theoretical terms?

The seminarists did not all share the distaste for the postideological age shown by these two "icily lofty American saints" (as Shils called them). Voegelin also thought it premature to consider the postideological age at all: There was still an "iron curtain" within the West separating ideologists from the life of Reason, and even if everything went well, it would take at least a generation "before the Western stables are clean enough to make the power of the West, which rests on the life of reason, institutionally visible and persuasive again." But however cautiously, he foresaw "a renaissance of the life of reason," as did Aron, "in the long run." Mehta, on the other hand, supported Kennan and insisted that the new states of Asia and Africa rejected both the Western and the Soviet models and sought a new ideology, a "spiritual approach."

No agreement was sought in these debates. If for some it was an ominous surprise that a Congress seminar should produce so many angry or anguished criticisms of the free society, for others it marked a promising new stage, a move away from simple anti-Communism to an attempt to adumbrate a public philosophy in which both prudent conservatives and sensible radicals could find a home.

Intellectual response to the seminars was frequently critical. Bell reported to Josselson that the Tokyo discussions were "somewhat dull."[38] Richard Rovere reported that Rhodes "failed to provide anything very striking in the way of polemics," although there had been much "oratory and pedantry."[39] Peter Drucker described the book that transcribed the discussions at Rheinfelden as an example of "an increasingly common fraud: the bull session transcript that pretends to be a serious book by serious scholars."[40] University presses, he said, should not be party to this mischief.

But the Congress and Secretariat did not complain. As Arthur M. Schlesinger, Jr., remarked on another occasion: "I have never been to a conference which I would call a success."[41] The Seminar Program had two objectives. One, which was achieved, was to bring forward for discussion around the world (including in Congress magazines) a range of issues whose time had come. The other objective was to help build a liberal intellectual world community. For this purpose the spirit of the discussions was as important as their intellectual level, and the informal meetings as important as the formal ones. The seminars, moreover, reached people that the national committees, the magazines, and the festivals did not. To illustrate this Herbert Passin, who succeeded Bell as director of the Seminar Program, told the Executive Committee that in helping Shils plan the Rhodes seminar, he had been in touch with five hundred "outstanding people from all over the world" and that the Rhodes seminar had opened up contacts in Africa and the Middle East that simply had not existed before.[42] Polanyi regarded the seminars as "a breakthrough,"[43] and in the following years the Seminar Program would be greatly expanded.

# 7
# *The Impossible Dialogue*

✍

These people [the Hungarian insurgents] are our
closest allies ... we are wrong if we today maintain
we are anti-communists. We are not anti-communists. I
am not an anti-communist.

MICHAEL POLANYI, October 1956[1]

The Berlin Congress in June 1950 had adopted a resolution pledging "moral and material support" to writers and artists behind the Iron Curtain "who assert their right to freedom." But since, at that stage, it had no certain continuing resources, it adopted no precise plans. There was, however, no shortage of ideas in the Congress milieu. James Burnham, Josef Czapski, and Jerzy Giedroyc had their plan for a "university of exiles," which would train students in the professions that would be needed when the Iron Curtain was eventually "rolled back."[2] Sidney Hook wanted to get in touch with the underground intellectuals behind the Iron Curtain and provide them with light printing presses and radio transmitters.[3] Arthur Koestler had a plan for providing stipends to writers and artists who escaped to the West.[4] Ernst Reuter and the Social Democrats in Berlin were already developing a network of anti-Communist "contacts" in the Soviet zone of Germany, and Melvin Lasky's *Der Monat* (which had an influential "underground" circulation in East Germany)[5] was a rallying point for anti-Soviet intellectuals.

The Brussels conference of the Congress in November 1950 discussed these matters again. Nicolas Nabokov spoke of "la lutte se-

123

crète, intense and constante" behind the Iron Curtain, with the inevitable danger of death.[6] Ernst Tillich also spoke of this "action secrète." Tillich was a head of both the Association for Cultural Assistance (*Die Vereinigung fur Kulturelle Hilfe*), which gave support to anti-Communist intellectuals in the Soviet zone, and of the Fighting Group Against Inhumanity (*Die Kampfgruppe gegen Unmenschlichkeit*), which conducted missions of military sabotage. He urged the Congress to send books and magazines behind the Iron Curtain and to open a halfway house in West Berlin for refugee students, writers, and artists. But at the same conference Irving Brown urged caution: The Congress had limited resources, and the top priority must be the struggle against Stalinism and neutralism in still endangered France and Italy.

In fact, in its first two or three years the Congress did very little to meet its 1950 commitment of "moral and material" support to intellectuals behind the Iron Curtain. It opened a Congress House in West Berlin and provided a welcoming milieu for defectors like the Polish poet Czeslaw Milosz (in a Paris still cowed into refusing to translate *The Captive Mind* into French) or, later, the Polish composer Andrzej Panufnik. But most of the plans discussed in Berlin or Brussels were carried out by others, independently of the Congress. Koestler himself organized the Fund for Intellectual Freedom to support refugee writers; the university for refugee students was established without the involvement of the Congress; and Jerzy Giedroyc continued publishing his monthly *Kultura* in Paris without Congress help. The Congress in those early years remained too small, too tentative, and too busy—planning conferences, publishing *Preuves*, and organizing the huge Nabokovian Festival of the Twentieth Century—to give much time to Central and Eastern Europe. Some members were also influenced by the idea that the totalitarian world, as described in George Orwell's *1984*, Hannah Arendt's *The Origins of Totalitarianism*, and Czeslaw Milosz's *The Captive Mind*, was totally closed and therefore impenetrable.

The Congress never entirely abandoned the idea of a Central European program, and in 1952 it finally appointed K. A. Jelenski to develop it. But it still remained a low priority—until the situation changed dramatically with the death of Stalin and the first thaw. In the following years, at first slowly, cautiously and with many setbacks, and later more confidently, especially after the Polish October and the Hungarian Revolution, Jelenski and the Congress gradually built a program that, particularly in relation to Poland and Hungary, was one of the Congress's principal successes. It became the model for its programs in other dictatorships, such as Franco's Spain and Sukarno's Indonesia.

K. A. Jelenski (1922–87) was of the Polish nobility and had grown up in a Warsaw ambiance that was, he said, left-liberal, antichauvinist, anticlerical, and antifascist.[7] Educated in Austria, Switzerland, Scotland, and England, he left Poland in 1939 at the age of seventeen. During World War II he fought in Normandy in the Polish Armored Division. After the war he settled in Rome, where, trained as an economist, he worked for the Food and Agricultural Organization of the United Nations. When he was appointed to the Congress Secretariat, he was its youngest recruit at age thirty.

His appointment had been "not without difficulty,"[8] he wrote later. When Nabokov had offered him a position in 1951, Jelenski had rejected it, because he had (reasonably) considered the Congress's future to be uncertain. In 1952, however, he changed his mind, since he now wanted to live in Paris to be with the artist Leonor Fini, but the offer had been withdrawn, and it was only after strong pressure from Raymond Aron and others that he was appointed.

The appointment further consolidated the Congress's move away from the Koestlerizing anti-Communism of Berlin in 1950. The courtly Jelenski personified the "end-of-ideology"; his kind of anti-Sovietism did not preclude civil discussion or social life with Communist intellectuals, to whom, he believed, it was possible to appeal beyond their ideology. He retained a vivid memory of the Poland of his adolescence, where, in the higher levels of society, the Communist poet and editor Aleksandr Wat could dine at ease in Warsaw's literary café, the *Ziemianska*, with a Pilsudskist colonel and, when in prison, receive cases of vodka and caviar from Marshal Pilsudski's aide-de-camp. Jelenski himself recalled often dining with his grandmother, "a celebrated beauty of 1900 who dressed in Paris and divided her time between Karlsbad and Biarritz," and her brother, an influential Communist anthropologist. He believed that similar close, extra-ideological relations persisted in Communist Poland, and he distanced himself from the hardline anti-Communism of, for example, *Les Amis de la Liberté*, which he regarded as provincial or *petit bourgeois*. He also rejected the Koestler-Milosz thesis of "captive minds" that could not be reached.

But how to reach them? He proposed three lines of action. The first was to broadcast cultural radio programs, including excerpts from banned books or music. The second was to use the ordinary postal service to mail important books and articles, developing various devices to frustrate censorship and to prevent the persecution of addressees. (In the case of books, he proposed they be sent to libraries, bookshops, publishers, and newspapers. In the case of articles and poems, they would be sent in the form of private letters and posted from different places to a very large number of addressees regardless of professed political views.) The third proposed line of action was to dispatch parcels of goods, including medicines, to intellectuals in need. Jelenski also made two other proposals for action in the West: an organization to help refugee intellectuals and a journal both to publish their work and to monitor cultural life in the East.[9]

In time, all these proposals would be adopted and developed in one form or another, but progress was slow and fitful. A Committee for Central and Eastern Europe was formed, with Czapski, Mircea Eliade, and Milosz as members, but it was never active and soon faded away. The plan for broadcasts was more successful: In 1953 *Radiodiffusion Française* offered the Congress time on its Danube-Balkans network, and in July it began a weekly 15–20-minute broadcast, mixing literary, sociological, and Congress news and attempting to "demonstate Western values" rather than to attack Communist regimes in the style of Radio Free Europe in Munich. Diplomats, journalists, visitors, and refugees reported that the programs found an audience (especially in Armenia). But they were only a few minutes a week, and only in French.

The thaw that followed Stalin's death gave urgency to the expansion of the Congress's program. In 1953 Vladimir Pomerantsev published an essay calling for "sincerity" rather than the Party line in literature. Ilya Ehrenburg's novel *The Thaw* followed, and then Leonid Zorin's play *The Guests*, each criticizing the Soviet New Class. Aleksandr Tvardvosky circulated a poem satirizing Soviet censorship and actually referring to the Siberian labor camps. Selections from the formerly banned émigré writer Ivan Bunin began to appear. Love stories and novels exploring private life were published, in defiance of socialist realism. The Soviet leadership encouraged this "thaw," although the limits were indicated by the publicity given to the denunciation of "Hu Fengism" in China and the arrest of Hu Feng for advocating literature free of Party control.

The thaw moved more quickly and farther in some of the satellites, especially Poland and Hungary. In Warsaw in August 1955 Adam Wazyk published his famous *Poem for Adults* against the regime. ("They drink sea water and cry—Lemonade! They quietly return home to vomit, to vomit"), and in September the weekly *Po Prostu (Plain Talk)* began its series of exposures of the "New Class" and of Marxist orthodoxy. In Budapest, in November 1955, there was an extraordinary meeting of the Communist Party's Hungarian Writers' Association: Zoltan Zelk, poet and Kossuth Prize winner, received permission to read out a memorandum that respectfully condemned the persecution of Communist writers and the censorship of literature, and called for the acceptance of "a free and sincere and healthy and democratic atmosphere."[10] It was signed by fifty-nine writers and artists, the cultural elite of Hungary. The Stalinist dictator, Matyas Rakosi, called a meeting of Communist Party officials, who issued a "Resolution of the Hungarian Workers' Party's Central Committee Concerning the Rightist Phenomena Which Had Manifested Themselves in Hungarian Literary Life." It began: "Certain writers, among them Party members, have forgotten that literature must serve the people and that only by supporting the efforts of the Party can writers contribute to the people's advancement." When the first group of writers brought before the Central Control Committee refused to engage in self-criticism and admit their errors, they were expelled or reprimanded, and future royalties were withheld. To add to their humiliation, Rakosi ordered that the Resolution be published in the Writer's Association's weekly magazine, *Irodalmi Ujsag*. But his plan misfired, because publication meant that news of the writers' rebellion reached the newspapers of the world and received enormous publicity.

The Executive Committee of the Congress for Cultural Freedom met in Paris in January 1956 to discuss these dramatic developments. It accepted Daniel Bell's idea of establishing a Writers and Publishers Committee for European Cooperation to advance the thaw. It also decided to establish a new magazine, *Soviet Survey*, to monitor developments in the Soviet empire, and to hold an international seminar to debate the developments in detail.

The year 1956 was the *annus mirabilis*. In February, at the Twentieth Congress of the Communist Party of the Soviet Union, Nikita
S. Khrushchev delivered his devastating, if selective, denunciation
of Stalin's crimes, the murders and torture, the false confessions
and show trials, the mass arrests, the deportations of nationalities.
Millions of prisoners were soon released from the labor camps and
millions more posthumously rehabilitated. The thaw deepened. At
the same Party Congress, Mikhail Sholokhov had condemned the
Soviet Writers' Union as a racket run by Aleksandr Fadeyev, a barracks of dead souls who produced no books. (Fadeyev shot himself
in May.) Vladimir Dudintsev's novel *Not by Bread Alone* was a literary sensation, with its portrait of an honest man battling a corrupt
society and Communist Party. An anthology, *Literaturnaya Moskva*,
included A. Yashin's explosive anti-Stalinist short story, *The Levers*.

In Poland, Anton Slonimski, in an address before the Council
of Culture and Art, described socialist realism as a "precision tool
for destroying art by officials who for the past twenty years have
carried out the destructive procedures with zeal and application
sharpened by fear."[11] In Krakow, Jan Kott produced a *Hamlet* about
a Denmark/Poland where the Hamlet-intellectual was surrounded
by spies, informers, and murderers.[12]

In Czechoslovakia, at the Second Writers' Congress in April
1956, Jaroslav Seifert appealed on behalf of more than forty imprisoned writers: "Again and again we hear it said at this Congress
that it is necessary for writers to write the truth. That means that
in recent years they did not write the truth."[13] In Budapest in September, Julius Hay declared in *Irodalmi Ujsag*: "We have come to
the point where the most essential problem . . . is the question of
telling the truth. The best Communist writers, after much trouble,
grave errors, and bitter spiritual struggle, have decided that never,
under any conditions, will they ever write lies in the future."[14]

If these people are Communists, Michael Polanyi declared at a
meeting of the Executive Committee of the Congress for Cultural
Freedom in October 1956, then "I am not an anti-Communist."[15]
It had now become necessary to do more than monitor events, it
was essential to collaborate with this revolt against the Lie in Eastern Europe, to invite these "new voices" to meetings and publish
their work. Thus began the long debate in the Congress over "cultural exchanges." Some—Salvador de Madariaga, for example—
always remained skeptical of their value, maintaining that, as far
as the Russians were concerned, they would permit only obedient

functionaries to join in any exchanges. ("You can talk to a human being, but you cannot talk to a gramophone record.") Diana Trilling took a similar view: "[U]nder Communist totalitarianism, both the individual *and* his cultural ideals count for nothing except as political pawns." The Soviet Union, she wrote "has declared cultural war upon us and . . . therefore, in any cultural program which we undertake in the international field, we must proceed with enormous caution and acuteness, with the knowledge, indeed, that our lives are at stake."[16]

But the Congress as a whole did not take so cautious, skeptical, or hard a line. Silone considered that a minimum condition was that all participants in any East–West discussions be invited directly and individually and not through government offices; otherwise one would only meet servile, police-minded Soviet bureaucrats—men of stony looks, square shoulders, blue serge suits, and baggy pants, without culture and with nothing "to exchange." In this spirit the Italian Association for Cultural Freedom refused an invitation to meet the Italy–U.S.S.R. Association, and Spender declined an invitation to Poland.[17] Polanyi, and in most cases usually Spender, thought otherwise, considering any contact in almost any circumstances worth the trouble: After meeting scores of hacks, you might meet one on whom you could have some influence; there could be "a kind of flash," Spender said. Denis de Rougemont suggested, as a first step, a limited East–West seminar of writers on a precise and "safe" subject, such as "Social Responsibility or Art for Art's Sake?" Jelenski agreed: Such a seminar offered "a chance of dialogue" on which to build.[18]

The first "cultural exchange" involving Congress figures was not, in fact, a Congress initiative. It was organized by the Société Européenne de Culture, which Umberto Campagnola formed in 1949 to encourage East–West contacts. In March 1956 it held a meeting in Venice of seventeen intellectuals—to plan a larger meeting later. Spender and Silone—with Sartre and Maurice Merleau-Ponty—were among the seventeen. The Soviets had sent four representatives. One was the novelist Konstantin Fedin, a Stalin Prize winner who later initiated the harassment of Boris Pasternak and suggested putting Andrei Sinyavsky on trial. He was also largely responsible for the refusal to publish Aleksandr Solzhenitsyn's *Cancer Ward* in the U.S.S.R. (On his face, Solzhenitsyn wrote, "his every compromise, every betrayal, every base act, has superimposed its print in a dense cross-hatching.")[19] Another was Boris Polevoi, a novelist and former war correspondent who was later to demand "a fitting and extremely heavy punishment" for Boris Pasternak, this "literary Vlasov."[20] (Andrei Vlasov was a Soviet general who, captured by the Germans, had organized a Russian unit within the German Army and was later executed by the Soviets.) There was also a Soviet art historian, and a controller who came to be known as *le flic*. From Poland came the writer and editor Jaroslaw Iwaszkiewicz, and from Yugoslavia the essayist and former Ambassador to Paris, Marko Ristic.

At this improbable gathering (about which Spender was to write a comic novelette, *Engaged in Writing*) there was little East–West "communication" in a week of meetings. The extraordinary thing was that it happened at all, that writers from Russia and Poland were permitted to attend a meeting in the West with such anti-Communists as Silone. The Russians were patient, even when (to the dismay of Iwaszkiewicz) Silone delivered a long address asking what had happened to the great nonconformist tradition of Russian literature. Why had the horrors mentioned by Khrushchev in his "secret speech" not been reflected in Russian literature? He received no answer.

When it was over the Russians agreed that there should be more meetings, and Polevoi invited Spender to stay with him in Moscow. For his part, Silone said he would attend no more meetings with "delegations." When the Executive Committee, in April 1956, discussed the Venice meeting, Polanyi regretted Silone's decision:

> I think it is a pity. Any meeting is good enough, and if people like Silone are in a minority, so much the better, the more people do they address. I do not see anything wrong with this. It is the way an intellectual movement goes on—very slow and hazardous and patchy. But this is how it happens. I do not think one can do more than take every opportunity to go on with it.[21]

Jelenski, who had gone to Venice as an observer, gave an example of this "movement"—his conversation with Iwaszkiewicz's daughter, a young economist and a representative of Poland's contemptuous, anti-Stalinist Left. She called Poland "a dismal bordello for children," a corrupt and childishly conformist society. She also told him of a new unpublished but widely circulated poem, "Poem of the Unknown Poet" (by Kazimierz Wyka), which she thought was even more courageous than Wazyk's *Poem for Adults.* It dealt with Polish Communists assassinated by the Stalinists in the Spanish Civil War and those who were in the concentration camps of the U.S.S.R.

Nicolas Nabokov urged that the Congress now take the initiative itself and not leave it to such "dubious" organizations as the Société Européenne de Culture. He suggested an East–West meeting of editors, and Silone welcomed the idea, seeing it as one way of minimizing the Soviets' selection of the participants. It was agreed that the invitations would go directly to the editors in Russia and Poland, that the French invitees be Leftist and neutralist, and that, to avoid arousing distrust, the invitations would be in the name not of Silone but of Maurice Nadeau, the editor of the Leftist *Lettres Nouvelles.* Further, the conference would not be under the auspices of the Congress for Cultural Freedom but of *Lettres Nouvelles, Critique, Tempo Presente,* and *Encounter* (although the costs would be paid by the latter two magazines, and Jelenski would handle the arrangements). The object of it all would not be to make propaganda but to take "the thaw" one step further, to shake some Eastern intellectuals free from government controls. "The *'Gretchen-Frage'* which is really being put," Lasky wrote after a discussion with Silone,

> is: cannot private citizens ... meet privately? The first result is that the Russian editors will have to ask permission of the "VOKS" [The All-Union Society for Cultural Relations]. But obviously the Poles and Yugoslavs may have the freedom to say yes on their own, or at any rate to accept. Could then the Russians stay away? Once such an event takes place, the next step obviously would be to try and get Western magazines into a few Eastern bookshops.[22]

Twenty-two editors and collaborators finally assembled in Zürich in September. The French included Maurice Nadeau, Jean Duvignaud, Roland Barthes, and Clara Malraux from *Lettres Nouvelles,* and Georges Bataille from *Critique.* Spender, Jelenski, and Laurens Van der Post represented *Encounter,* and Silone and Chiaromonte, *Tempo Presente.* Iwaszkiewicz represented the Polish *Tworczosc,* and Eli Finci the Yugoslav *Knizevnost.* The Soviet *Znamya* (a Writers' Union monthly) sent V. Kozhevnikov, and *Inostrannaya Literatura* (devoted to non-Soviet writing) sent A. Chakovsky and I. Anissimov. Silone agreed to be chairman of the meetings, but only after he had insisted that the Soviet editors dispense with their translators, whom he regarded as spies. The "translators" withdrew.

Over the four days, the Poles and the French Leftists enjoyed lively exchanges, but discussion with the Russians was again formal and of a low level. Only Anissimov was of the literary-intellectual type familiar to Westerners; he seemed to Jelenski more like a librarian than a writer. Chakovsky struck Jelenski as a boring, philistine know-all (*Besserwisser*), and Kozhevnikov seemed to have modeled himself on a 1930s European idea of an American businessman. They did not understand the French *gauchistes* and certainly not Roland Barthes's "semiology." They had not heard of the famous critic Georges Bataille but knew about the popular romantic novelist Françoise Sagan. (When Chakovsky asked Bataille if he thought Sagan's second novel was better than her first, he replied, "I have not read it but I do not believe it could be worse.") But the editors agreed to consider exchanging articles, and Silone and Anissimov also agreed to continue, in correspondence, the discussion of the principal issue Silone had raised at the meetings, the censorship and control of Soviet literature.

In his report to the Secretariat and the Executive Committee, Jelenski declared the meeting a success. It had deepened contact with the Poles and had exposed some Russian editors to possible Western influence. As for the French *gauchistes,* contact with the Russians had been as unsettling if not disillusioning as it had been for Sartre and Merleau-Ponty at the Venice meeting in March; in both cases they finally realized that their attempts to interpret dull-ditted Russian statements as somehow profoundly Marxist did not work. Frederick C. Barghoorn took the same view of these "two extraordinarily, interesting intellectual encounters": "It seems certain that the Soviet participants underwent a severe ordeal. These dialogues probably played a part in the largely covert, but intense, re-evaluation of fundamental concepts stimulated on both sides of the ideological frontier by Khrushchev's exposure of Stalin's crimes."[23] Jelenski recommended more East–West meetings, with the involvement of Americans from the *Partisan Review* circle and more Western Leftists, even Communists.

But the Executive Committee meeting in October, which discussed the Zürich conference, was one of its angriest yet. For Aron, who had spent the past ten years exposing the dangerous illusions of the Marxist and fellow-traveling Left, it was outrageous that representatives of *Encounter* and *Tempo Presente* should attend a meeting from which *Preuves* had been excluded, and it was scandalous that the Congress should have sponsored an international conference at which France was represented by voguish Frenchmen "of the third order who have been fellow-travelers all these years." It was a serious political error, he said, to have given such prestige to these neutralists when the intellectual battle is still being fought in France. "This is the gravest thing that has happened to the Congress for a long time," he said. In words reminiscent of Koestler's when he heard in 1951 of the Secretariat's plan to invite Sartre, Simone de Beauvoir, and Thomas Mann to a Congress conference, Aron concluded: "I will not tolerate it twice."

The Executive Committee decided to classify the Zürich meeting as (in Manès Sperber's words) "une chose personnelle et silonienne," although it had had the support of Josselson, Nabokov, and Jelenski—an example of the division between the Executive Committee and the Secretariat that emerged from time to time within the Congress. A transcript of the debate was sent to Silone so that he would have the views of Raymond Aron and Manès Sperber in mind when he conducted his written "dialogue" with Anissimov. As it happened, the dialogue was soon suspended by the uprising in Budapest. Anissimov began his reply to Silone's questions on Soviet censorship with a lengthy reference to the "Fascist horror" that had emerged in Budapest, where Soviet soldiers had saved Hungary from Horthy's followers. He then, at some length, evaded all of Silone's questions. Silone replied that Anissimov's references to Hungary filled him with "indignation and disgust." He again summarized what had happened to Russian writers under Bolshevik rule, ridiculed "socialist realism," and said that, after the Hungarian events, "it is more important than ever that writers be recalled to a sense of the nobility and responsibility of their profession." Anissimov replied that "a dialogue between us is no longer possible." Silone's final letter concluded,

> . . . you are right: a dialogue between us is impossible and would have no meaning. The censorship constrains you to feign deafness. Therefore, we shall not renew the dialogue until you are in a position to reply fully to the questions I have asked and to those that I have in reserve, just as I have replied and am ready to continue to reply to yours. I hope that that time is not too far off.[24]

The Hungarian Revolution and its suppression by the Soviets (15,000 Hungarians killed and 5,000 arrested without trial) put a brutal end to these first tentative "dialogues." The need now was not for dialogue but for emergency action in response to the call for "help and support" broadcast by the Hungarian Writers' Association on November 4, 1956. The Hungarians appealed "to every writer in the world, to all scientists, to all writers' federations, to all scientific organizations, to the intellectual elite of the world."

The Congress's response had two aims. One was to mobilize world support for the Hungarian writers, artists, and scientists in the hope of having some influence on Soviet authorities; the other was to help the refugees, or in particular the hundreds of intellectuals among the 200,000 refugees.

Now for the first time, and in an almost exemplary way, the international network of national committees and magazines rallied to the call from Paris. In Santiago, Buenos Aires, New York, Hamburg, Bombay, Paris, Lyons, and elsewhere the affiliated committees held large public meetings of protest. In Australia, Japan, Indonesia, Cuba, Denmark, Lebanon, Italy, Pakistan, and Uruguay, the national committees issued public statements and distributed material provided by the Secretariat, such as the anti-Soviet statements of Camus and Sartre, and Denis de Rougemont's call for a cultural boycott of the Communist Party and of Communists. In Sweden the local committee arranged for eight Nobel Prize laureates to sign a cable of protest to Marshal Bulganin. In the United States, the American Committee, with the backing of the *New York Times*, telegraphed fifteen major universities proposing two minutes' silence in honor of Hungarian students. In India, Jayaprakash Narayan formed an Indian Committee for Solidarity with Hungary. In England, Polanyi's Committee on Science and Freedom appealed to everyone on the mailing list of its *Bulletin*, and more than a thousand professors from more than a hundred universities in twenty-five countries added their names to the committee's statement of protest. (The committee presented it to the Soviet Embassy; the Minister at the Hungarian legation refused to see them.) At the same time Koestler, Spender, and George Mikes telegraphed eighty British writers urging them to write immediately to the Hungarian Embassy asking for visas so that they might "investigate facts behind deeply disturbing reports." The telegram went on: "Unlikely visa request will be granted now but more visa applications the greater moral pressure on Russia for restraint."[25]

By January 1957, John Hunt, a young American novelist who had been appointed to the Secretariat in 1956, reported to the Executive Committee: "Never before have the actions of the various National Committees been so unified or strong."[26] Nevertheless, the unity was weakened by the conviction among Congress supporters in India, Indonesia, and Lebanon that condemnation of the Soviets must be coupled with an equal condemnation of France, Britain, and Israel over their invasion of Egypt in October–November 1956. Nicolas Nabokov sent a lengthy letter to all national committees arguing that the Congress was not a political organization, that its members disagreed on many political issues, and that they could speak with a common voice only on issues of cultural and intellectual freedom, which were raised by Hungary but *not* by Suez. That did not convince Minoo Masani: The Congress had from time to time taken up positions that were more political than cultural. It had condemned American racism in 1951 and Soviet action at Poznan in 1956 (later it would welcome Castro's victory in Cuba in 1958 and call for an international inquiry into the murder of Patrice Lumumba in the Belgian Congo in 1961). But those political interventions were few and usually had a cultural element, for example, in 1958 the wish to reestablish a Committee in Cuba or maintain its base among intellectuals in Léopoldville. In any case, division in the Congress over the Suez operation (and on President Eisenhower's actions against it) made a common stand impossible. Aron, for example, regarded the antitotalitarian Hungarian Revolution as belonging to "universal history" and Suez as a deplorable postimperial episode. One could condemn both, he said, but to "equate" the two was to reveal "the last degree of mental confusion." After a long debate, the Executive Committee voted to declare "its opposition to all forms of aggression," a feeble resolution but something for Masani to take back to India.

Congress agitation on behalf of Hungarian writers continued after the immediate crisis. In 1957 it published Lasky's *The Hungarian Revolution,* documenting in "White Book" detail the history of the uprising. It circulated throughout the world such books and brochures as *Nagy on Communism* and François Fejto's *La Tragédie Hongroise* on behalf of the imprisoned writers (Tibor Dery, Julius Hay, and others). When Imre Nagy was executed, it published a documented account, *The Truth about the Nagy Affair,* with a preface by Camus.

It is impossible to measure the influence on the Hungarian Kadar regime of all this pressure, supplemented as it was by worldwide pressure from other quarters, including those usually opposed to the Congress. But *Survey* published (in January 1962) a special issue examining Hungary five years after the revolution. Its editorial concluded: "In general the political and intellectual margin of relaxation in Kadar's Hungary is greater than in any other country in the Soviet bloc except Gomulka's Poland." In the same issue George Urban wrote that "russification has almost disappeared, the secret police has lost some of its teeth, and in the mood of the urban population there has been a return to that genial combination of irony and fatalism which makes Hungarians impervious to the heavy stuff of communist propaganda."[27] Some years later, in an interview in 1983 in a Hungarian *samizdat* periodical, Gyorgy Krasso (who had been sentenced to ten years' detention in 1957) said that "despite even the fact of its defeat, the Hungarian revolution brought more results for the Hungarians than any other movement in Eastern Europe."[28] This surely was the achievement of the Hungarians themselves, but the international pressure was a factor.

As for Congress's second response—its program for the refugees—it developed several "special projects." The first was emergency relief, in association with the Congress's Viennese magazine *Forum,* for writers and artists to whom they supplied living expenses, books, advice, and fares. It also helped reconstitute and finance the Hungarian Writers' Association and revived its magazine, *Irodalmi Ujsag,* in London. It paid short-term stipends to some ninety Hungarian intellectuals while they reestablished themselves. It financed lecture tours of various countries from India to Iceland by several Hungarian writers. Finally, it brought together seventy to eighty refugee musicians to form the orchestra known as Philharmonia Hungarica. The Congress financed this orchestra at Baden, outside Vienna, until the German city of Marl took it over in 1959.

Commenting on these projects in a report to the Executive Committee in January 1958, Marion Bieber of the Congress Secretariat wrote:

> It has not always been easy to separate the sheep from the goats in the face of language problems, the unavoidable intrigues of emigration and the fact that past activities of

refugees could not always be established beyond doubt. Nor could intellectual quality and integrity always be ensured in advance. Added to these were the peculiarities of Hungarian character and temperament, particularly among artists and intellectuals, and in many cases the experience of communist methods which in some had become second nature. There were also cases of careerists and those, though fortunately only a few, who saw in the Congress for Cultural Freedom a chance to jump on the dollar band wagon. Bearing in mind these difficulties, the Congress for Cultural Freedom can, on balance, claim to have succeeded in building up and uniting the intellectual nucleus of the new Hungarian emigration and with it to have played its part in keeping alive the real meaning of the Hungarian Revolution of October 1956.[29]

In 1968, at the time of the controversy over CIA funding of the Congress, Tamas Aczel, a Hungarian writer, once a winner of the Stalin Prize and by then a refugee in the West, wrote:

Perhaps the time has come to set the record straight ... it must be said, it seems to me, quite emphatically, that the Congress for Cultural Freedom performed an important and successful human, moral and organizational function in regard to a very large number of Hungarian intellectuals, students, artists, musicians and writers when it was most needed, namely, during the first and frightening yet unforgettable years of their exile.[30]

# 8

# *The Crusade for the World*

᭪

Many who went on the Crusades were actuated by base motives or were led into ignoble behaviour, but the Crusades still remained a noble enterprise. It is the same today.

MALCOLM MUGGERIDGE, 1953[1]

[T]here was little point in Americans attending conferences with Asians. . . . The work of explaining America to people was in many places absolutely useless.

GEORGE F. KENNAN, quoted by Stephen Spender, 1955[2]

In its first period, when the Congress considered itself a liberal anti-Communist "movement," it regarded its affiliated national committees as its "intellectual shock troops" (in Nicolas Nabokov's words). But they were in fact independent intellectuals, not subject to "democratic centralism" (as Michael Josselson sometimes wished they were), and their relations with the Paris Secretariat were often tense. As Stephen Spender pointed out at a meeting of the Executive Committee in January 1957, this was almost inevitable: If a national committee were inactive, as some were in Latin America, it was bad for the reputation of the Congress; but if it were too militantly active, that too would damage the Congress's reputation for liberal civility. In fact, some of the early national committees were closed down (England, Japan) and some were balanced by other Congress structures (India, France). Some persisted but failed to take root, as in Latin America. Others, in partic-

139

ular the American Committee in New York, were in frequent confrontation with the Secretariat in Paris.

## EUROPE

### FRANCE

The minutes of the first meeting of the steering committee, held at Koestler's home in Fontaine-le-Port on July 18, 1950, record: "First priority: France, Italy."[3] It was in those countries that the Stalinist hold on intellectuals was most powerful. It had survived the exposure of Soviet concentration camps, the excommunication of Tito, and the show trials and executions of Laszlo Rajk in Hungary and Traicho Kostov in Bulgaria in 1949. The dogmas that the U.S.S.R., despite its defects, was on balance on the side of historical progress and that the United States was the heartland of oppression, racism, and reaction still prevailed.

*Les Amis de la Liberté* was the first-born of the national committees. Koestler and his group planned it as a popular movement. "The idea is to set up in the big provincial towns committees in the form of luncheon clubs, etc., copied on the rotary club structure."[4] They would collect signatures for the Berlin Manifesto, organize counterdemonstrations against the Partisans for Peace, stick up anti-Communist posters, circulate anti-Communist pamphlets, and organize mass meetings on Korea, Persia, and Yugoslavia. It would be allied with General de Gaulle's Rassemblement du Peuple Français and would have a Gaullist organizer. By August 10, 1950, Koestler had written the first pamphlet for Les Amis: "Que veulent les Amis de la liberté?"

But as Koestler withdrew from the Congress, the Secretariat reconsidered the whole situation and changed direction. François Bondy, in February 1951, even referred to Les Amis as "an organization about whose future I have yet to be convinced."[5] In fact they survived, but not as Koestler had envisioned them. The Gaullist organizer was replaced by a socialist, Jacques Enock. Its agenda now was to establish reading rooms, study circles, and lecture circuits. Les Amis would still be a propaganda arm of the Congress, but in a lower key. Nicolas Nabokov was optimistic. Shortly after his arrival in Paris to take up his position as General Secretary he wrote to the American committee:

I am firmly convinced that these centers of *Les Amis de la Liberté* can perhaps become the most useful instrument of anti-communist activity in France. They could easily form the nuclea [*sic*] of reliable friendly elements upon whom we should be able to call on short notice.[6]

Les Amis formed centers—Maisons de la Liberté with libraries and meeting rooms—in Grenoble, Lyons, St. Etienne, Nice, and Bordeaux. They formed women's groups, film groups, and youth groups (which contested student elections). They conducted seminars. They organized demonstrations: In 1958, following the execution of Imre Nagy, they held a protest march on the Champs-Elysées in Paris and a rally of five thousand people in Lyons.

Always activist, always "a movement," in the twelve months between November 1956 and November 1957, for example, they organized 236 meetings, seven art and photographic exhibits, and fourteen concerts and music conferences. In the same period they also published three brochures on the Soviet bloc and one on the "underdeveloped world."

But while Les Amis provided a welcome platform for the Congress speakers, they remained a popular arm of the Congress and not an elite organization. It was to reach this opinion-forming elite that the Congress turned the bulletin *Preuves* into *une grande revue* and later created the mardis de *Preuves,* at which leading French intellectuals or foreign visitors would discuss issues of the day with their peers. Le Amis remained active, especially in its provincial centers, until about 1960.

## ITALY

A month after Koestler left Paris for the United States and a month before the Brussels conference of November 1950, François Bondy and Georges Altman journeyed to Rome for talks with Silone, whose standing with the Left was high and whose cooperation was essential to Congress work throughout Europe at a time when millions of people regarded the arrival of Russian tanks as (in Richard Löwenthal's words), "inevitable or, at any rate, highly probable."[7] As if to greet them on their arrival, *Corriere della Sera* published G. A. Borgese's harsh report on the "Manichean" Berlin Congress, which repeated Trevor-Roper's criticism.

Silone arranged three meetings with Roman intellectuals, none of which encouraged the visitors. The first was with the liberal *Il*

*Mondo* circle, who saw the Catholic Church as a greater threat than the Communist Party and who showed no trace of sympathy for intellectuals behind the Iron Curtain. "We attempted to tell these people that, in the present world context, Soviet imperialism and the Communist danger present specific problems, far more disturbing than the traditional, century-old struggle between clericalism and anti-clericalism in Italy. But our remarks were greeted with many reservations."[8]

Next they met the circle associated with Adriano Olivetti's magazine, *Comunità,* mostly members of Silone's Socialist Unity Party. After they had addressed the group, Bondy and Altman invited questions. Who's paying for all this? they were asked. By "freedom," do you mean American capitalism? Communist observers seemed to be present, and the meeting was unproductive (although, when it was over, several young writers *privately* expressed complete support).

The third meeting arranged by Silone was with the *La Via* circle, a group of the Christian Democratic Left. When Bondy and Altman had finished speaking, "everyone immediately changed the subject." A young priest called for a purely clerical state in Italy, which would by definition be the most tolerant and democratic in the world and would be in close touch with the Communist Party. This group seemed susceptible to what Jean-François Revel has called "the totalitarian temptation" and offered little to the Congress.

Talks with other Italian intellectuals were equally unproductive. Alberto Moravia was concerned more about neofascism than about Communism, and the European federalists mainly wanted to know how much financial help the Congress could give them.

In their report to Josselson, Bondy and Altman stressed the provincialism and anti-Americanism of Italian intellectuals. There were "great possibilities" for the Congress in Italy, they wrote, but it would have to be result of "slow, indirect, diversified and extremely discreet action."

The Paris Secretariat, however, was more interested in the "great possibilities" than in the slow and extremely discreet action. It wanted an Italian national committee, and Nabokov went to Rome after the Brussels conference to try to nudge along the Congress's cause. But he too found the intellectuals apathetic, and he heard "curious rumours" about the Congress. He also reported "tension with Silone" who still urged a "discreet" approach in Italy. Silone, at this stage, wanted Congress funds for his work in universities to help students defeat the Communists and fascists in student elections. He also wanted funds to help deepen the Communist Party crisis of 1951, which had led to the defection of the Parliamentary deputies Valdo Magnani and Aldo Cucchi, and their formation of the Movement of Italian Workers under the banner "Neither Russia nor America: Italy." In Silone's view it was absolutely essential to appoint an organizer, *un inspecteur,* to tour Italy in the interests of this movement. This, he said, was more important than an Italian Committee for Cultural Freedom.

Nevertheless, by the end of 1951 a compromise between the direct and the discreet approaches was reached. An Italian Association for Cultural Freedom was formed—an association rather than a committee, in that it formed a federation of independent cultural groups (in the end, about a hundred), to which the association provided speakers, books, pamphlets, and films and an internationalist ethos. The Italian Association produced a manifesto, written by Carlo Antoni, which did not mention totalitarianism or neutralism but proclaimed freedom of conscience, thought, and expression and called for international solidarity among intellectuals. (It was signed by the film director Roberto Rossellini; the former fellow-traveler and editor of *Politecnico* Elio Vittorini; the antifascist scholars Gaetano Salvemini and Lionello Venturi; and Guido Piovene, Eugenio Montale, and Mario Soldati, as well as Silone and Chiaromonte.)

In the following years the Italian Association, through its federal network, linked by offices in Rome, Milan, Florence, and Naples, emphasized antifascism and anticlericalism as well as anti-Communism. It campaigned for the abrogation of the old Fascist legal code. It conducted ceremonies in honor of such antifascist martyrs as Giacomo Matteotti. It produced the bulletin *Libertà della Cultura* and provided an intellectual home for former Communists and fellow-travelers as they defected in greater numbers in the 1950s. It attacked censorship and Catholic "inanities" in textbooks.

It was this anti-Catholicism that caused the Secretariat most concern. Nabokov wrote to Josselson in June 1954 that he thought little could be done about it. The members of the Italian Association, he said, were "profoundly steeped in Croceism" and are "drug-addicts of anti-Fascism." As for the Catholics, they resented the very presence of Benedetto Croce among the Congress's first honorary chairmen and refused to collaborate with Gaetano Salvemini, "who eats the Pope the way Levitas [and the *New Leader*] used to eat Uncle Joe" [Stalin]. In any case, liberal Catholics of the French type, who "will work with the non-and-anti-Communist Left," were rare in Italy. The best that could be hoped for, Nabokov said, was that the Italian Association might moderate its "quix-otic," "bellicose," and "arrogant" attitude to the Church and its organs. He would also ask Jacques Maritain, one of the Congress's honorary chairmen, to write "a long letter to the Vatican authori-ties" explaining that the Congress and the Italian Association had "different policies." In the end it might mean "a show-down with Silone."

But there was no showdown. Silone continued to follow his own course, and when the Congress launched its great Italian review in 1956, *Tempo Presente,* edited by Silone and Chiaromonte, Silone insisted that the title page carry no acknowledgment of Congress sponsorship.

GREAT BRITAIN

One of the first of the national committees for cultural freedom to be formed—and soon to close down—was in Britain. It began in January 1951 at a meeting at the Authors' Club in Whitehall Court called by Spender (to which he invited Julian Amery, T. R. Fyvel, Michael Goodwin, John Lowe, Richard Löwenthal, Bernard Wall, John Weightman, and David Williams). The meeting elected Spender chairman and Goodwin honorary secretary of what was called the "International Movement for Cultural Freedom (British Section)." It decided to call some public meetings and publish some pamphlets, and it agreed to include the Berlin Manifesto in a draft constitution. The headquarters of the "British Section" would be, for the time being, the office of the magazine *Nineteenth Century and After,* which the Congress was then subsidizing.

The "British Section" soon became factionalized in disputes over the editorial policy of *Nineteenth Century and After,* disputes which would not be settled until the Congress withdrew its sup-port from the magazine and concentrated on *Encounter.* Several members resigned in the first year, including, temporarily, the chairman, Spender. When Goodwin decided late in 1951 to call a postal ballot for executive officers of what had now been renamed the British Society for Cultural Freedom, the lawyers were called in and Spender urged the Paris Secretariat to suspend all funds to the Society.[9] But the ballot was eventually held, early in 1952,

In the years following World War II, the Soviet Union staged a series of glittering international "Peace Conferences," featuring famous artists and writers. The conferences duly denounced U.S. imperialism and praised Soviet progressivism. One of the most splendid of all was held in the Waldorf-Astoria Hotel in Manhattan in March 1949. Pictured above (*left to right*) are some of the participants: Alexandr Fadeyev, a novelist and official of the Soviet Writers' Union; Norman Mailer; Dmitri Shostakovich; Arthur Miller; and Olaf Stapledon, the English writer. (AP/Wide World Photos)

The Waldorf conference reinspired efforts to form an international organization of intellectuals to defend democracy and the free world against Soviet propaganda. Pictured (*left to right*) are Ernst Reuter, the social democratic anti-Communist mayor of Berlin, discussing the formation of the Congress for Cultural Freedom with Melvin Lasky, then an American editor resident in Berlin, and Sidney Hook, the philosopher.

One of the "back-room" founders of the Congress for Cultural Freedom was Michael Josselson of the CIA. After World War II he served in Berlin, first with the military government and then with the State Department. His assignment was de-Nazification and cultural politics. Josselson is pictured here (*left*) with Jürgen Fehling, the German theater director, whom he helped rehabilitate.

Mayor Ernst Reuter welcomed over one hundred participants to the founding Congress for Cultural Freedom in the Titania Palace, West Berlin, in June 1950—just as the North Korean army invaded South Korea.

Arthur Koestler (at podium) called on his "friends, fellow-sufferers, fellow-fighters" in Berlin to abandon their "contemplative detachment" and to acknowledge the world-wide emergency caused by Soviet totalitarianism. His scorn for the "clever imbeciles" who preached neutrality to the bubonic plague angered many participants, including the English philosopher A.J. Ayer. Pictured listening to Koestler at the dais are (*left to right*) Haakon Lie of Norway, Ernst Reuter of Germany, Jules Romains of France, Alfred Weber of Germany, and Sidney Hook of the United States. (The Department of Special Collections, The University of Chicago Library)

Two old ex-Communists, Franz Borkenau and Ignazio Silone in discussion. Silone, a gentle moralist, was an alternative leader to the pugnacious Koestler in Berlin. Borkenau's overwrought public speech welcoming President Harry S Truman's stand against North Korean aggression had won the applause of the frightened Berliners but alarmed the English historian Hugh Trevor-Roper, who thought he detected signs of a lingering Nazism in what was in fact a largely social democratic crowd. (The Department of Special Collections, The University of Chicago Library)

Thousands of West Berliners, fearful of Soviet expansion with the outbreak of the Korean War, sat through the first Congress's concluding outdoor rally in sweltering heat, at which a triumphant Arthur Koestler declared: "Friends, Freedom has seized the offensive!"

A follow-up conference was held in Bombay in March 1951—to the displeasure of Prime Minister Nehru, who always distrusted the Congress as an "American front." The Bombay meeting led to the formation of the Indian Committee for Cultural Freedom. Pictured at the conference are (*left to right*) Denis de Rougemont, W.H. Auden, Jayaprakash Narayan, and Bharati Sarabhai. Narayan's presence at the conference was a *coup* for the Congress. (Udit Gopal)

Some of the members of an early Executive Committee of the Congress. (*Left to right*), Irving Brown of the American Federation of Labor; Nicolas Nabokov, the composer and secretary-general of the Congress; Minoo Masani, the Indian writer and politician; Stephen Spender, the English poet; and Denis de Rougemont, the Swiss philospher and critic. (Associated Press photo)

The Congress for Cultural Freedom put itself on the map in Paris in May 1952 with a massive cultural festival it called "The Festival of the Twentieth Century"—organized by the Congress's Secretary-General, composer Nicolas Nabokov. Designed to illustrate the creativity of the free world, the Festival included performances of one hundred operas, ballets, symphonies, and concertos by seventy composers. Nabokov is pictured here (*left*) welcoming George Balanchine. (The Department of Special Collections, The University of Chicago Library)

Below: Michael Josselson (*right*) who, by the time of the Festival was beginning to establish his organizational leadership of the Congress, is pictured at a reception during the Festival talking with an unidentified woman and Mac Goodman (*center*).

Above: The Festival included literary debates, but in the anti-American Paris of 1952 the only French writer of international fame to join in them was André Malraux, who declared provocatively that "America is now part of Europe." Malraux is pictured here with (*left to right*) Salvador de Madariaga, Denis de Rougemont, and William Faulkner. (Sabine Weiss)

Right: One of the Festival's meetings of writers. In the front row, (*left to right*) André Malraux, Salvador de Madariaga, Denis de Rougemont, William Faulkner, and W.H. Auden. Behind them (*left to right*), Allen Tate, an unidentified woman, James T. Farrell, Robert Lowell, Glenway Westcott, and Katherine Anne Porter. (P.A. Constantin)

Irving Kristol (*right*), who with Stephen Spender founded the Congress's most famous magazine, *Encounter*, is pictured here with Edward Shils (*center*) and Robie Macauley, editor of the *Kenyon Review*. (The Department of Special Collections, The University of Chicago Library)

François Bondy (*left*), editor of the Paris-based *Preuves*, and Melvin Lasky (*right*), editor of the Berlin-based *Der Monat* and later *Encounter*, in discussion with two American "exiles," J. Robert Oppenheimer, "the father of the A-bomb" (*standing, center*), who had been declared a "security risk" in 1953, and George F. Kennan (*seated, center*), the author of the doctrine of containment, who had been "excluded" from the U.S. Foreign Service, also in 1953. (Maria Netter, Basel)

Below: Several of the Congress's magazines from various countries.

riedrich Torberg, editor, *orum*, Vienna. (The Department of Special Collections, The University of Chicago Library)

Leopold Labedz, editor, *Survey* (formerly *Soviet Survey*), London. (The Department of Special Collections, The University of Chicago Library)

Julian Gorkin, editor, *Cuadernos*, edited in Paris for Spain and Latin America. (The Department of Special Collections, The University of Chicago Library)

James McAuley, editor, *Quadrant*, Sydney. (© Bernard Leser Publications)

Michael Josselson points to the banner of the Congress's Hamburg Conference in July 1953 on "Wissenschaft und Freiheit"—Science and Freedom. The city put out its flags for the conference, which brought together 120 scientists and scholars to support the independence of science and "the end of ideology" in science. They also sent fraternal greetings to their "unhappy" colleagues behind the Iron Curtain.

Herbert Passin, organizer of the Rangoon Conference of February 1955 on Cultural Freedom in Asia, with Mrs. Prabakbar Padhye of India. With participants from all over Asia, it was an unsuccessful attempt to pre-empt Indonesian President Sukarno's anti-Western Bandung Conference a few weeks later. (The Department of Special Collections, The University of Chicago Library)

The Milan Conference in September 1955 on "The Future of Freedom" gave the Congress a new agenda—the problems of freedom in "the under-developed world." Hannah Arendt found the debates "deadly boring," but Max Beloff thought that they "altered the shape of our mental world." Pictured (*left to right*) at the conference are Mary McCarthy, George F. Kennan, and Arthur M. Schlesinger, Jr. (The Department of Special Collections, The University of Chicago Library)

Ezekiel Mphahlele, head of the Congress's African program. (The Department of Special Collections, The University of Chicago Library)

Michael Polanyi, chairman of the Seminar Planning Committee.

Daniel Bell, first director of the Congress's Seminar Program. (The Department of Special Collections, The University of Chicago Library)

Konstantin Jelenski, organizer of the Congress's East European Program. (The Department of Special Collections, The University of Chicago Library)

At the Congress's Tenth Anniversary Conference in Berlin, June 1960, on "Progress in Freedom," Congress leaders paid homage to an early inspiration of the Congress, Ernst Reuter, who died in September 1953. Shown at his graveside are (*left to right*) Michael Josselson, Nicolas Nabokov, Denis de Rougemont, and Minoo Masani. (The Department of Special Collections, The University of Chicago Library)

Raymond Aron (*left*), one of the leading participants in the Congress's conferences and a major influence on Congress decisions, with John Kenneth Galbraith (*center*) and Asoka Mehta (*right*) at the Rhodes Conference in October 1958 on the future of representative government in the new states of Africa and Asia—the first of the Congress's international conferences on this theme, following its emergence at the Milan Conference of 1955. (The Department of Special Collections, The University of Chicago Library)

In the 1960's, the French poet, Pierre Emmanuel, urged the Congress to explore essential "metaphysical" questions and minimize its pro-American politics. He arranged a series of meetings of poets and novelists, including those of Spain and Portugal. Pictured at the September 1964 International Meeting of Poets (and critics) in Berlin are Keith Botsford of the United States and Jorge Luis Borges of Argentina. (The Department of Special Collections, The University of Chicago Library)

John Hunt, a novelist originally from Oklahoma, pictured here (*left*) with Michael Josselson in a Geneva cafe. Hunt assumed increasing responsibility for the management of the Paris Secretariat when Josselson, suffering from a weak heart, moved to Switzerland in 1961.

(*Left to right*), Julius Fleischmann, Dwight Macdonald, and Michael Josselson. Fleischmann, a wealthy patron of the arts, was also President of the Farfield Foundation, one of the conduits for channeling CIA funds to the Congress for Cultural Freedom. Macdonald, a prominent journalist and editor, was for a time associate editor of the Congress's London-based magazine. *Encounter.* (The Department of Special Collections, The University of Chicago Library)

Thomas W. Braden's article in the May 20, 1967 issue of *The Saturday Evening Post*, through its authoritative revelation of CIA funding, written by a man who had arranged it, led to the final collapse of the Congress for Cultural Freedom. It appeared at a time when growing disaffection caused by the Vietnam War and CIA activities left few supporters of the Congress willing to defend the secret funding of their activities publicly. The successor organization, the International Association for Cultural Freedom, was free of any association with the CIA. But it never recaptured the vitality of the Congress. Its leaders were (*right to left*) Shepard Stone, president; Pierre Emmanuel, director; and Alan Bullock, chairman of the board of directors. (The Department of Special Collections, The University of Chicago Library)

and Harman Grisewood (the controller of the BBC's Third Programme) was elected chairman, Malcolm Muggeridge vice chairman, Fredric Warburg treasurer, and Michael Goodwin secretary. When Grisewood resigned (as did Goodwin), Muggeridge became chairman, and the Secretariat looked to him to reconstruct the British Society.

Malcolm Muggeridge fought the Cold War in the spirit in which he had fought World War II. It had been necessary to destroy Hitlerism, but Muggeridge had not believed in the Allies' battle cries, the "counterfeit words" *freedom* and *democracy*. They had died on him, he wrote, while writing editorials for the *Manchester Guardian* in 1932.[10] Now it was necessary to fight Stalinism, but he did not believe in—indeed, he came to despise—American liberal internationalism. He accepted American leadership for, as it were, the duration, as the only hope of containing the Soviet gulag. George Orwell called him a neo-Tory nationalist, but he is also an anarchist, a Christian, and (in his own words) Lear's Fool.

Born in 1903, the son of a Labour Party family, he was educated at Cambridge and after teaching in India and Egypt became an editorial writer and then Moscow correspondent for the *Manchester Guardian*. His book *Winter in Moscow* (1933) was one of the first exposures of the Soviet myth written from the Left, but it was professionally disastrous for him, since editors on the Left now blacklisted him and conservative editors still "rightly" considered him suspect. (He found work on the Calcutta *Statesman*.) During World War II he joined British Military Intelligence and received several French honors for his work as liaison officer with the French Securité Militaire. (He was later to write that he had never met anyone professionally engaged in intelligence work "whom I should care to trust in any capacity.") After the war he was Washington correspondent for the *Daily Telegraph* and became its deputy editor in 1950.

Throughout these years he wrote a series of plays and novels and several works of criticism, including a biography of the nineteenth-century novelist and essayist Samuel Butler, *The Earnest Atheist* (1936), of which Spender asked: Why does Mr. Muggeridge detest Samuel Butler so much?[11] The answer was that he saw in Butler a progenitor of the liberal progressivism he himself had imbibed as a youth and had come to see as the principal threat to civilization. All his work can be seen as a battle with Butler and his heirs, including the fellow-travelers of the 1950s.

Under Muggeridge's chairmanship, the British Society, like the other national committees, organized lectures and meetings on Cold War themes. Muggeridge, Warburg, Spender, Fyvel, and Louis MacNeice spoke in various English centers. Aron and Milosz made English tours. The Society distributed *Preuves* and other Congress publications, including David Mitrany's *Marx Against the Peasant*. It published such pamphlets as John Clews's *Students Unite* (with an introduction by Spender opposing "ideological think-ing"). But in a country with little ideological cleavage or passion at that time, the British Society never became an important force. Fredric Warburg in his memoirs ridiculed it: "Sterile discussions dragged on for months, and Muggeridge, an impatient man, pressed for our dissolution. 'There is altogether too much cultural freedom,' he is reported as saying, 'any man who hasn't got a plat-form to sound off from must be a fool.'" The Society, Warburg claimed, was "bored to death."[12]

In any case, when the Congress decided to start *Encounter*, that magazine became its center in Britain, and the British Society ceased to function. One of Muggeridge's last services, he said, was to arrange for the equivalent of the salary of any English coeditor of the proposed magazine to be paid by British intelligence, using his friend Lord Rothschild as a conduit, a sort of British Julius Fleischmann.[13] Neither Malcolm Muggeridge, in his published dia-ries *Like It Was* (1981), nor Stephen Spender in his *Journals 1939–1983* (1986), mentions the British Society.


## ASIA

### JAPAN

The Congress also made a false start in Japan when it established a short-lived Japanese Committee for Cultural Freedom in 1951. Japan was difficult terrain. Anti-Americanism was strong, fueled by the predominantly U.S. Occupation and intensified by the tri-umph of the Communists in China in 1949 and the early defeats and frustations of General MacArthur in the Korean War. Ayako Ishigati's *Yameru Amerika* (*Sick America*) was a best-seller in Japan (as was the Webbs' *Soviet Communism: A New Civilisation*). Although the Communist Party was banned, it was still able to control the streets, as it did during the May Day riots of 1952, when the veteran American Socialist leader Norman Thomas (who was visiting Japan for the Congress for Cultural Freedom) was driven from his speaker's stand by rioters waving North Korean flags and shouting, "Go Home, Yank."

When James Burnham visited Japan to celebrate the foundation of the Japanese Committee in March 1951, he found a group of determined anti-Communists who might have reminded him, in some respects, of New York. They key man was Jinji Kobori, the treasurer. He had helped found the Japanese Communist Party in 1922 but was now an anti-Communist, pro-American, and prorearmament Marxist. He also produced a newspaper, *The Workers' News,* which provided a corner in its office for the Japanese Committee. Kobori's wife, the famous "proletarian" and bohemian novelist Taiko Hirabayashi, was one of the Committee's principal local sources of funds. Both Kobori and Hirabayashi had been imprisoned for their revolutionary activities before the Pacific War, as had Takeo Naoi, now the Tokyo correspondent of the *New Leader.* Other members included the ex-Communist journalist Kanson Arahata; the surrealist painter Ichiro Fukuzawa, whose work included a series inspired by Dante's *Divine Comedy*; the liberal jurist Tomoo Otaka; and the scholar Kenzo Takayanagi, who was the Committee's chairman. Matsuhei Matsuo was the secretary and in that capacity received cables of congratulation from Karl Jaspers, Upton Sinclair, Salvador de Madariaga, Sol Levitas, Sidney Hook, Les Amis de la Liberté, and the Americans for Democratic Action (ADA).

The Japanese Committee published an anti-Communist bulletin, *Under the Flag of Freedom,* called public meetings, and kept in touch with the Paris Secretariat. (Hirabayashi represented the Japanese Committee at the 1952 Festival in Paris.) But when, two and a half years after its foundation, Aron called on the Committee in Tokyo, he found that it had "a phantom existence." They were honorable people, he reported to the Executive Committee, but they had the characteristic *déformations* of ex-Marxists, and they had no influence with the Japanese intellectuals, whose temper was still that of German Marxists of the 1928–33 period or of contemporary French Leftists (and who were shocked, Aron said, when he described Sartre as one of "yesterday's men"). As for the future, he recommended closing the Japanese Committee down and starting again under the guidance of the Tokyo-based American scholar Herbert Passin.[14] In any case, he said, it would not be easy: The Americans have let loose "a vague Westernization," but who knows what is going on in the Japanese subconscious? Accordingly, in December 1953 Josselson wrote to Matsuo:

> Based on the information from various members of our Committee who have visited Japan, which information has been corroborated by your own letters, the Executive Committee has reluctantly come to the conclusion that the present membership of the Japanese Committee does not allow for an expansion of our activities in Japan such as we would have liked to see. The Executive Committee therefore believe that it would be best to have this Committee die a natural death and to start from scratch after the present Committee will have passed away.

Herbert Passin, a thirty-eight-year-old social anthropologist from Chicago, had lived in Japan since 1945 and spoke Japanese. The son of migrants from the Ukraine who had suffered in the anti-Semitic pogroms that followed the Japanese victory over Russia in 1905, he had published a scholarly survey of the food habits of the Mississippi riverboat people and several studies of postwar Japanese and Korean society. He had also been a head of the Public Opinion and Sociological Research Division of the U.S. Occupation administration. He agreed to take responsibility for resuming Congress work in Japan on two conditions. The first was that preparations for any new organization should be slow and careful, with full allowance made for the Japanese sense of precedence and etiquette. (The preparations took more than two and a half years.) The second condition was that the new organization (unlike the Kobori splinter group) be a "broad front" of diverse groups that would identify with "the right socialist tendency"—the tendency which was, he believed, "our greatest asset" in Asia generally.

Passin gradually brought together intellectuals from four groups. The first comprised "elder statesmen" of scholarship and literature whose goodwill, rather than their active involvement, was essential: the philosopher Professor Yoshishige Abe (a former Minister for Education and now president of the Peer School, where the Crown Prince was a student); Professor Shinyo Koizumi (director of the Crown Prince's education); and the Supreme Court Justice Tanaka (who was a leading Japanese Catholic converted under the influence of Jacques Maritain and Vladimir Solovieff). The second group included the young professors who had attended the Milan Conference and showed some enthusiasm for the Congress: Tomoo Otaka, Kenzo Takayanagi (both of whom had also been in the first Japanese Committee), and Takeyasu Kimura. The third group were Right-wing socialists: Professor Yoshihiko Seki and Hobi Ishihara, who later became editor of the new review *Jiyu (Freedom)*. The fourth was made up of survivors of the old Committee: the novelist Hirabayashi and the painter Fukuzawa.

In March 1957 the new Japan Cultural Forum was finally established, and Daniel Bell, in Tokyo for the Congress's international conference on economic growth, informed the Secretariat that the new committee or Forum was "in many ways the model of what a Committee should be." In subsequent years it justified this confidence with a series of seminars, festivals, and exhibitions, an active publishing house, and the new magazine, *Jiyu*.

## INDIA

In no Asian country was the fellow-traveling mentality so strong as in India. Yet India was, in Nicolas Nabokov's words, "our last chance.... If India falls ... free institutions will disappear in Asia."[15] The Congress consequently made an enormous effort to establish itself in this often disheartening country, opening offices in Bombay, New Delhi, and Calcutta, starting magazines, organizing seminars, and conducting festivals. Throughout almost the whole period, it was handicapped by the often open hostility of Prime Minister Jawaharlal Nehru, who saw the Congress as merely "an American front."

Its first move was to call an Indian Congress for Cultural Freedom, broadly modeled on the Berlin Congress of a few months earlier, to be held in New Delhi early in 1951. But the Indian Government did not want it. A few days before the conference was due to begin, the government informed the original sponsors, the editors of the liberal magazine *Thought,* that the earlier official authorization had been withdrawn and that the conference could not now be held in New Delhi. The organizers thereupon transferred the venue to Bombay, where M. N. Masani's Democratic Research Service took over the management of the conference.

There were more than seventy Indian delegates, mainly writers, artists, and publicists, including a large group who had served prison sentences for anti-British agitation, such as the socialist leader Asoka Mehta. There were several foreign delegates, including the Congress president, Denis de Rougemont, and the poets Spender and Auden. Congratulatory messages poured in from around the world, including the usual one at this time from the Americans for Democratic Action.[16]

The two key figures among the Indians were the Parsee organizer, Minoo Masani, MP, and the charismatic *sadhu*, Jayaprakash Narayan. Born in Bombay in 1905, Masani completed his education in England, where he joined the British Labour Party and carried a red flag in the famous May Day March of 1926 at the time of the General Strike in Britain. Back in India he joined the anti-British Civil Disobedience movement and in 1932 had the first of what he called "three spells in prison." He later wrote nostalgically of his prison days and his long political debates with fellow prisoners. It was in prison that he helped Jayaprakash Narayan form the Congress Socialist Party, and it was in prison that he broke with that party over its decision to admit Communists. ("Minoo was right," Yusuf Meherally said later, "although we did not know it then.")[17] Always courageously and forcefully active in public affairs, he was in turn a "Quit India" agitator, a Mayor of Bombay, an Ambassador to Brazil, and a founder of the anti-Communist Democratic Research Service and its magazine, *Freedom First*. By 1950 he was a member of the Indian Parliament and a thorn in Nehru's side.[18]

If there was any truth in the jibe of the Communist leader, P. C. Joshi, that Masani was "an Angrez," that is, an Anglicized Indian, no such jibe could be made at Jayaprakash Narayan. Born in 1902, J. P., as he was known, was a Bihari and a Kayasth (one of the higher non-Brahmin castes) who was at various stages an orthodox Hindu, a Gandhian, a Communist, a terrorist, a democratic socialist, and a holy man. He served some ten years in prison for anti-British activities. As a youth he responded to Gandhi's call to boycott British-associated institutions and migrated to the United States, where he studied at the University of Wisconsin and came under the influence of Jay Lovestone. After his return to India in 1929 he founded the Congress Socialist Party (within the Indian National Congress), which formed a united front with the Communist Party. ("The experiment should never be repeated.")[19]

Arrested again in 1940, he escaped, went underground, and trained terrorists in sabotage (not killing) until he was recaptured and served three more years in prison. He was by then a legendary figure and regarded as a possible Prime Minister. But in the early post-Independence years he moved away from Party politics. In July 1951 he submitted to a three-week self-cleansing Gandhian fast, and in 1954 he solemnly offered his life—in a *jeevan-dan*—to the Sarvodaya (the uplift of all) and the Bhoodan (land gift) movements. A tall, moody, soft-mannered and handsome guru in a Gandhi cap, his support and presence was a coup for the Bombay Congress for Cultural Freedom, which Prime Minister Nehru had driven from New Delhi.[20]

The conference, however, was no triumph. It was held at a time of Indian famine when the U.S. Congress, angered by the Indian Government's pro-Peking policies, had held up a bill to give grain relief to India. At the same time the U.S.S.R. and China were offering India rice and wheat. (The American delegates cabled the Speaker of the House of Representatives: "Prompt dispatch of wheat imperative for American good name in Asia.")[21] In the debates, attacks on the West and America were frequent, but attacks on the Communists were greeted with indifference. The *New York Times* correspondent, Robert Trumbull, described some of the "involuted" Indian speakers as "antitotalitarian fellow-travelers."[22]

But the conference finally adopted a declaration, which condemned neutralism, and it agreed to establish a continuing Indian Committee. The real lesson for the Congress was the recognition of the difficulty it would have in establishing an effective base in India. Even Auden found it hard to connect: After watching Mrs. Shakuntala Masani's classical Hindu cobra-enticing, Siva-seducing dance, he pronounced, in a daze: "Not my cup of tea."[23]

The conference nevertheless was a start. It turned out to be a slow start, and it was only after the headquarters of the committee was transferred from the Delhi office of *Thought* to the Bombay office of the Democratic Research Service that Masani was able to put his energetic stamp on the Committee. Jayaprakash Narayan became its president, Prabhakar Padhye (a Marathi writer and editor, and an ex-Communist) its full-time secretary, and *Freedom First* its monthly magazine. It held meetings and seminars and distributed books and pamphlets, often in what it felt was an increasingly hostile atmosphere.

In a report on its activities at the end of 1954, the Indian Committee conceded that its work had touched "only the periphery of the vast problem" it faced. "The Committee has to contend against the basic fact that many of the values that it is seeking to propagate and establish appear rather foreign to the Indian mind. . . . The democratic tradition in the country is extremely weak . . . there is very little awareness in the country of the danger represented by communist totalitarianism."[24]

The Executive Committee discussed the Indian situation at its meeting in Rome at the end of 1953. Aron reported on his visit to India,[25] where he had formed a lively impression of the difficulties Masani's group faced: In Bombay, two Cabinet Ministers who had accepted invitations to meet Aron at a reception withdrew, on the insistence of Prime Minister Nehru. Aron made two suggestions to help the Congress increase its influence. The first was to widen its literary and arts program in India. The second was to adopt a more pro-Nehru allure; he himself had had an uninteresting half-hour with Nehru,[26] but the Prime Minister was after all the leading liberal alternative to Communist China in Asia. Both suggestions meant looking beyond Masani's group, which was almost exclusively political and deeply scornful of Nehru's neutralism.

The Congress for Cultural Freedom adopted Aron's advice. It launched the literary magazine *Quest* (which was so unpolitical that it did not even note the Hungarian Revolution) and opened a new office in New Delhi, which would have a "constructive" and pro-Nehru policy. It was called the "Asian Bureau" to denote its wider, pan-Asian ambitions. Prabhakar Padhye, who was appointed its secretary, was responsible to Paris, not to Bombay (the Asian Bureau had twelve honorary chairmen from various Asian countries and six honorary advisers).

The first task of the Asian Bureau was to organize in Rangoon in February 1955 a conference of forty intellectuals from ten Asian countries, on cultural freedom in Asia. It was the first time that any such gathering had ever taken place in Asia, and for some observers, such as Herbert Passin, it held great promise for the future. But the optimism proved ill-founded. When Nabokov visited Rangoon a year later, the conference seemed to have been forgotten. President Sukarno's Bandung conference, however, was well remembered. When the Paris Secretariat asked Prabhakar Padhye to issue a statement, signed by the Congress's Asian supporters, condemning the brutal suppression of the Poznan labor riots in Poland in June 1956, he could get no signatures from Japan, Thailand, or Indonesia and only a few from India (Masani's group). Padhye replied to Nabokov: "We therefore suggest that we drop the idea."[27] A depressed Nabokov considered closing down the Asian Bureau.

This was, however, the low point for the Congress, which pushed on, opening new centers—with libraries and meeting rooms—in Calcutta and elsewhere. International events also began to work gradually in the Congress's favor. Khrushchev's "secret speech," the Hungarian uprising (J. P. Narayan formed a Committee of Solidarity with the people of Hungary), and the first Chinese incursion into India in 1959 all had their impact on Indian opinion. At the same time the American social scientist Edward Shils became the principal adviser on the Indian program.[28] Acknowledging that fellow-traveling was "in a sense the 'natural' political outlook of the Asian intellectual,"[29] he sought not to confront but gradually to encourage a more independent and balanced position, less influenced by ideology or demagoguery. In India (and also in some of the African states) Shils saw the Congress's role as overcoming the intellectuals' sense of isolation, increasing their sense of belonging to an international community, and letting liberalism slowly take root.

Shils expected no easy victories. When Sidney Hook visited India in 1958, he was amazed at the "almost limitless credulity" of Indians about the U.S.S.R. and China. Neon signs everywhere lit the night sky with the message, "Read Soviet Books," and no one, he said, had added the words "especially *Dr. Zhivago*."[30]

This was to change a little in the 1960s, at least in relation to Mao's China.

## LATIN AMERICA

Irving Brown complained in 1952 that, although Latin America was on the agenda of every meeting of the Executive Committee and everyone agreed that something must be done, in fact "very little had been done."[31] That year, however, the Secretariat sent Julian Gorkin on a tour of Latin America to look into the possibility of establishing a network of national committees. He was accompanied by another Spaniard, El Campesino (Valentin Gonzalez), who had once been a Communist general in the Civil War and had just published, with Gorkin's help, his anti-Communist autobiography, *Listen Comrades*.

Gorkin's first report on his tour was optimistic. He envisioned committees in Santiago (to cover Chile, Peru, and Bolivia) and in Montevideo (to cover the Rio de la Plata region, including Para-

guay and Argentina as well as Uruguay). He also planned two committees in Brazil (in Rio de Janeiro and Saõ Paulo), one in Mexico,
one in Cuba, and one in Bogotà to cover Colombia, Ecuador, and
Venezuela. When they were all in operation, he proposed a pancontinental Congress for Cultural Freedom: "I will go so far as to
guarantee . . . that both the meetings of the *Committees* and the session of the *Congress* will create a tremendous stir throughout the
Latin American continent." Spender, who visited Brazil late in
1952, confirmed that "everyone I spoke to" wanted a Congress
presence in Latin America (although he warned that, if U.S. propaganda were suspected, knives might be drawn).

But when Gorkin returned to Latin America in 1954, he was less
optimistic. He now had *Cuadernos*, the Congress's Spanish-
language international review, to use as a calling card, but there
had also been the U.S.-backed overthrow of the Arbenz regime in
Guatemala in June 1954 and a consequent explosion of anti-
Yankee passions. "I was surprised," Gorkin reported to Paris, "at
the almost unanimously violent reaction of the democratic elements . . . in favour of Arbenz. . . . It cannot be denied that the
experience of their history and the position of most of the Latin
American countries, make them ideal subjects for communist
propaganda. . . . Whoever waves the anti-imperialist banner is sure
of a following." As for the national committees he had planned in
1952, Gorkin could report no real progress in Uruguay, Mexico,
or Brazil. In Cuba the committee had fallen under the control of
reactionaries and had to be reconstituted. There were, however,
promising signs in Chile.

The Secretariat now placed its hopes in an international conference to be held in Mexico in September 1956 on the theme "The
Future of Liberty." This was to be a Latin American "Rangoon,"
bringing the intellectuals of many countries together and laying a
basis for future work at a time when there was a revival of democracy in Latin America, with the overthrow of the Argentinian dictator Juan Domingo Peron in October 1955 and the free elections
in Peru in 1956. The Latin Americans at the conference included
the Colombian writer and journalist German Arciniegas (who had
been in Berlin in 1950); the Argentinian writer and editor Victoria
Ocampo; the Mexican poet and diplomat Alfonso Reyes; the Argentinian philosopher Francisco Romero; the Brazilian novelist
Erico Verissimo; the Peruvian writer and lawyer Luis Alberto Sanchez; and the Cuban lawyer Jorge Manach (who, as noted earlier,

drafted Fidel Castro's famous speech from the dock, "History will absolve me"). From the United States came Norman Thomas, John Dos Passos, Roger Baldwin, Ralph Ellison, and Arthur Whitaker. Salvador de Madariaga presided over the opening ceremonies.

Gorkin and Luis Alberto Sanchez reported to Paris that the conference "did not fully satisfy all the North American delegates," but in fact it angered them. Dos Passos complained to William Faulkner about the "violence and virulence"[32] of the attacks on the United States. Norman Thomas found the debates to be of a low intellectual level.[33] Irving Brown told Josselson he wanted nothing more to do with the Congress, and Jay Lovestone wrote to Gorkin: "I have washed my hands clean of the so-called Cultural Congress."[34] Back in New York, the American Committee organized a forum on "Anti-Americanism in Latin America."

Nevertheless the Secretariat pushed ahead, establishing national committees all over Latin American—in Argentina, Chile, Cuba, Mexico, Peru, Uruguay, Colombia, and Brazil. These committees held meetings, hosted visits, and distributed Congress publications, but they had little impact, especially among the young. For example, in 1960 François Bondy reported to Paris: "There is in Lima no 'Association' functioning, only one person who has established a *feudo*.... This situation is demoralizing, opens no prospects and should not be permitted to continue."

With the threat of the spread of *fidelismo,* the Secretariat decided to play down the national committees and appoint "permanent roving Congress representatives" with continental Latin American responsibilities. The men selected for this mission were the American novelist and critic Keith Botsford and the Spanish anarchist Luis Mercier Vega.

## AUSTRALIA

The Australian Committee for Cultural Freedom was one of the last national committees to be formed. When it was being organized in 1954, the Secretariat worked closely with Richard Krygier of Syndey in the hope of avoiding in Australia the sort of problems that had bedeviled its dealings with other national committees. In particular it urged him to form a small committee of eminent people who would not follow the practice of the American

Committee and become what Josselson called "a super Civil Liberties Union" for whom "nothing is allowed to pass without a protest, a resolution, a press release or what have you." ("The more one yells, the less likely one is to be listened to.")[35]

For Krygier, the need for an Australian Committee was urgent.[36] In the postwar years the Soviet *mythos* was more vibrant among Australian intellectuals than in any other English-speaking community, and when Krygier read about the Berlin Congress of 1950 in the *New Leader* and in *Kultura*, he wrote to Melvin Lasky in Berlin saying that he wanted to set up in Australia "something along similar lines."[37] It took more than three years to do this, but meanwhile Krygier became the Congress representative in Australia, distributing Congress publications and publishing a bulletin that reprinted articles by Congress writers and also served as calling card.

Finally, in June 1954—in an ideologically charged period shortly after the dramatic defections of Vladimir and Yevdokia Petrov of the Kremlin's MVD and the fall of Dien Bien Phu, and shortly before the epochal split in the Australian Labor Party on the Communist question—the Australian Committee was formed, under the presidency of Sir John Latham, a former Chief Justice of the High Court and former leader of the conservative Opposition in the Federal Parliament. Other members active at that time included John Kerr, a leading anti-Communist labor lawyer who some years later became Governor-General of Australia; R. N. Spann, who had come from Manchester to be Professor of Government at Sydney University; and the poet James McAuley. The Australian Committee (later Association) of this period was directed by idealistic mandarins who espoused "the end of ideology" and wanted to avoid "unnecessary" controversy. It issued judicious, practical statements on matters of public concern (for example, on censorship or immigration) but would not be drawn out on the Petrov Royal Commission in 1954 or the Communist-controlled "Peace Conference" in 1959. It also provided the more activist Krygier with a Sydney office, from which he distributed Congress publications; organized the Australian tours of Spender, Muggeridge, James T. Farrell, and Tibor Meray; edited a bulletin (*The Free Spirit*); and planned the literary magazine *Quadrant*. From this office he also organized a counter-conference in Melbourne in 1959 to frustrate the Communist-controlled peace conference, but in this case he acted as an individual and not as secretary of the Australian

Committee, whose Executive had resolved to keep its distance from "an unseemly shouting match." But the Paris Secretariat supported Krygier, meeting some of his expenses, using its influence to persuade Eleanor Roosevelt to withdraw her sponsorship of the "Peace Conference," and sending Tibor Meray to speak to it on behalf of imprisoned Hungarian writers. Krygier's work contributed significantly to the failure of this Communist enterprise.

Spender complained to the Paris Secretariat in October 1954 that the Australian Committee consisted of "all the stuffed shirts in Australia in one prodigious front of bores."[38] He found it to be as obsessed with anti-Communist politics as the Indian or the American Committee, and he advised Krygier to involve more poets and artists in the committee's activities. But Spender's view was not shared by the other visitors—Muggeridge, Farrell, Meray, and C. A. R. Crosland—and the committee retained the trust and confidence of Josselson (which made it a curiosity among the national committees of the 1950s). "You did well to remind me," Josselson later wrote to Krygier, "of the excellence of the people on the Australian Committee."[39]

## OTHER NATIONAL COMMITTEES

There were other national committees of "the international movement for cultural freedom" formed in the early and middle 1950s—for example, in Sweden, Denmark, Iceland, West Germany, and Pakistan. But the biggest, most influential, and most combative of all, and the most critical of the Congress and the Secretariat, was the American Committee, which requires a separate chapter.

# 9

# The "Obnoxious" Americans

✍

The American Committee has carried freedom's story to key intellectuals abroad while defending freedom here.

*New York Times,* 1955[1]

[I]f the American Committee chooses to disaffiliate [from the Congress for Cultural Freedom] well, it may be all to the good in the long run.

MICHAEL JOSSELSON, 1956[2]

I was regarded by the Parisian directorate as a representative of the obnoxious American Committee for Cultural Freedom.

SIDNEY HOOK, 1987[3]

The American Committee for Cultural Freedom was inevitably one of the most important constituents of the "international movement." At the same time, the American Committee, created in the spirit of the Berlin Congress of 1950 as a united front of liberals and conservatives determined to "take the fight to the enemy" (at a time when the Paris Secretariat had adopted a less militant strategy), was destined to be, in its half-dozen busy years, in a continual dispute with the Secretariat over the importance of the Congress festivals, American racism, McCarthyism, Bertrand Russell's anti-Americanism, and a host of lesser matters.

Its large membership—several hundred—included many internationally famous figures: novelists (Saul Bellow, John Steinbeck, Upton Sinclair), poets (Allen Tate, Auden, Delmore Schwartz), artists (Jackson Pollock, Robert Motherwell), critics (Lionel Trilling, Jacques Barzun), philosophers (Sidney Hook, Ernest Nagel, Arthur O. Lovejoy), political and social scientists and historians (Seymour Martin Lipset, Daniel Bell, Carl J. Friedrich, Merle Fainsod, Karl Wittfogel, Arthur M. Schlesinger, Jr., Boris Nicolaevsky, James Burnham), scientists (J. Robert Oppenheimer, Eugene Rabinowitch), labor officials (David Dubinsky, Irving Brown), and journalists and editors (Sol Levitas, Elliot Cohen, William Phillips, Murray Kempton, Jason Epstein, Dwight Macdonald, Whittaker Chambers). It included the theologian Reinhold Niebuhr, the filmmaker Elia Kazan, and the actor Robert Montgomery. Franz Borkenau and Arthur Koestler were also members.

The principal influence on the American Committee was Sidney Hook, who formed it as a legal entity in January 1951 and became its first chairman. Hook was born in December 1902 in Williamsburg, Brooklyn. In his memoirs he wrote of Williamsburg: "I have never seen or read of any other slum in New York that was worse in those years." The women worked like pack horses, he said, and his exhausted father would fall asleep at the dinner table, soupspoon in hand, but there was "always a feeling of hope," of "hope in America . . . nurtured by the public school" (although he also described his years at Boys' High School as "a succession of nightmares"). A youthful socialist and pacifist, he discovered philosophy as a student of Morris R. Cohen at the City College of New York, and at Columbia he came under the lasting influence of John Dewey and the pragmatist succession.

Hook learned about Communism from the inside. He was already a fellow-traveler in the 1920's and moved easily among the Communist factions—Stalinists, Trotskyists, Bukharinists. He helped prepare the first English translation of Lenin's *Materialism and Empiriocriticism* for the Communist Party. He worked in the Marx-Engels Institute in Moscow. He published a series of articles on Marxism, including one that bore the title "Why I Am a Communist" (and soon after it the Hearst press was calling for his dismissal from New York University). Those articles later culminated in the influential book *Towards an Understanding of Karl Marx,* which attempted to persuade Communists that Marxism was a sort of forerunner of Deweyan instrumentalism. In 1932, when the Left took it for granted that the capitalist order was about to collapse totally, Hook signed a public declaration in support of the Communist Party ticket in the Presidental elections (as did, among others, Edmund Wilson, Sherwood Anderson, and John Dos Passos). In 1933 the new leader of the Communist Party, Earl Browder, asked a shocked Hook to set up a Communist spy network in the universities.

But by then Hook was already disenchanted with the Kremlin-controlled Communist Party. Instead he helped form the anti-Communist American Workers' Party, which was to be based on American revolutionary traditions. He was now a public enemy of the Communist Party, "a counterrevolutionary reptile," according to one headline in the Communist press, and his supporters were "Hookworms."

But that was only a first step. However scornful Hook then was of Stalin and the Kremlin for disastrous errors of theory, judgment, and policy—for example, the doctrine of "social fascism"—he "never suspected that [Stalin] and the Soviet regime were prepared to violate every fundamental norm of human decency that had been woven into the texture of human civilization." The 1936–37 Moscow treason trials of Leon Trotsky (and his son, Leon Sedov) showed that they were. The trials and the Left's acceptance of them were "a decisive turning point" in Hook's life. He "discovered the face of radical evil—as ugly and petrifying as anything the Fascists had revealed up to that time—in the visages of those who were convinced that they were men and women of good will."[4] Hook writes that he could not rest or devote himself to anything else until the truth was established and published. Although strongly opposed to Trotsky and his doctrines (as Trotsky was to Hook and his), he organized the Commission of Inquiry under John Dewey, which in a quasi-judicial procedure carefully examined the evidence put forward by the accusers at the Moscow trials and the evidence for the defense put forward by Trotsky in Mexico. The Dewey Commission's painstakingly documented verdict was "not guilty." The trials were a frame-up.

Then a strange thing happened. The truth did not seem to matter. So powerful was the cultural influence of the Communist Party and the Popular Front that liberal opinion continued overwhelmingly to support the Kremlin in the controversy. This experience only deepened Hook's conviction of the importance of carrying the attack to the enemy, of exposing the calculated lie, of recording publicly the facts of the Communist terror and at the same time presenting the enduring values of the democratic way of life and free thought. It was in this mood in 1939 that Hook, with Dewey's help, formed the Committee for Cultural Freedom to defend free culture against both Nazi and Communist totalitarianism and to develop his idea that the great political contest of the age was not between capitalism and socialism but between democracy and totalitarianism. It was the forerunner—not only in its name and activities but also in the rage it produced among Stalinoid fellow-travelers—of the American Committee for Cultural Freedom of the 1950s.

When Hitler was finally defeated and the Kremlin resumed its policy of penetrating and sapping Western democracies, Hook watched with disgust and anxiety as it staged its great, star-studded international peace rallies at Wroclaw in 1948 and in New York and Paris in 1949—almost without opposition. Hook organized the *ad hoc* counter-rally in New York, but what he wanted was a permanent international organization for the defense of free culture. It was to advance this cause that he went to the Berlin Congress for Cultural Freedom in June 1950 and, in January 1951, incorporated its spirited and courageous American affiliate, the American Committee for Cultural Freedom.

Like the other national committees, the American Committee held public meetings, published pamphlets, and issued protests in the standard Congress manner. But from the beginning its policy of "taking the fight to the enemy" put it on a collision course with the Paris Secretariat. Many of its members, for example, scorned Nicolas Nabokov's huge and glittering Festival of the Twentieth Century in 1952. With "this kind of hoopla," Elliot Cohen wrote to Hook, "we are losing sight of our function and goals, and if we lose sight, who else is there around?"[5] Norbert Muhlen thought that the Festival, "appealing to snobs and esthetes," would destroy the Congress's reputation as "a serious intellectual power."[6] The American Committee also issued international protests, which, by implication, criticized the Congress's silence or inactivity: It attacked a death sentence imposed in East Germany on a politically dissident youth; organized a letter signed by Nobel Laureate scientists calling on Frédéric Joliot-Curie to produce evidence for his support of the worldwide, sensational Communist campaign alleging that the United Nations forces in Korea were waging germ warfare; and broadcast liberationist messages to Soviet writers. For its part the Secretariat in Paris complained that the American Committee was becoming "a super Civil Liberties Union."[7]

The basic issue that brought the Paris–New York conflict to a head and led to the *de facto* suspension of the American Committee early in 1957 was the idea of America itself, the assessment of American democracy. Faced with the Kremlin's massive campaign to depict America as a quasi-fascist, racist state that routinely persecuted liberals and lynched blacks, the Congress and the American Committee adopted different strategies, the former believing more than the latter that, to maintain credibility, it had to make concessions to critics of American justice.

The American Committee was barely formed in 1951 when the case of the "Martinsville Seven" in Virginia and of Willie McGee in Mississippi, both involving the execution of blacks for rape, became international news, often on the front pages in the Communist press. When McGee was executed in May 1951, the Assembly of the French Union observed one minute's silence in his honor. Such critics of the United States took it for granted that the accused men were innocent. The American Committee, on the other hand, considered the evidence that the men were guilty as charged to be overwhelming. It issued statements condemning the executions as "judicial crimes"—since white rapists had never been executed in Virginia or Mississippi—but refused to associate itself with the Communist campaigns, which it said had "hoodwinked the world." That was not enough to meet the Secretariat's need in Americophobic Paris.

These controversies were soon overshadowed by the Rosenberg case. In 1950, at the beginning of the Korean War, Julius and Ethel Rosenberg were arrested and charged with conspiracy to commit espionage by passing to the U.S.S.R. secret information concerning atomic weapons. When they were convicted in 1952 and sentenced to death, a spectacular worldwide Communist campaign claimed that the conviction was based on faked evidence. Again the Paris Secretariat wanted the American Committee to issue a strong call for clemency, but the Committee insisted that the "preeminent fact of the Rosenbergs' guilt must be openly acknowledged before any appeal for clemency can be regarded as having been made in good faith."[8] On June 10, 1953, an exasperated Josselson cabled a last appeal to Hook:

Consternation non-communist Western Europe over refusal
clemency reaching new pitch. Friends of Congress here
disturbed over absence our public statement urging clemency.
Is American Committee prepared to make such a statement?
If not we may have to issue statement here basing appeal on
purely humanitarian grounds. Appeal by American
Committee preferable. Please consult your immediate
associates and cable.

Finally Denis de Rougemont, in the name of the Executive Committee of the Congress, cabled President Eisenhower calling for
clemency, which, he said, "would serve the cause of freedom
throughout the world."[9]

When the Rosenbergs were executed in June 1953, Josselson
said the execution would live to haunt the Congress. About that
time Bondy wrote to Daniel Bell: "We feel quite often a difference
which comes near to a divorce of feeling between the American
Committee and ourselves. . . . It may be all a question of 'nuances'
of style and emphasis" but it embarrassed him, he said, that President Eisenhower, in one of his speeches, appeared to be more
alarmed about the deterioration of cultural freedom in the United
States than did the American Committee.

The misunderstanding between the Secretariat in Paris and the
American Committee in New York deepened over the committee's
policy toward Senator McCarthy and "McCarthyism." The committee (except for a few members, including Max Eastman and James
Burnham, who resigned) was overwhelmingly opposed to Senator
McCarthy; they differed only over how seriously to take him and
what tactics to use against him. After a public meeting in March
1952 (when Max Eastman declared that McCarthy's only faults
were his delicate sense of fair play and his excessive honesty), the
committee held a private meeting to discuss the issue. Two resolutions were adopted. The first concluded: "Communism and dema-
gogic anti-Communism nourish each other. In different ways the
Committee opposes both. For a long time to come the struggle for
cultural freedom will have to be conducted on two fronts." The
second called on Senator McCarthy to apologize publicly to Edmund Wilson (one of America's most distinguished literary critics)
for describing him as a writer of "obscene literature which follows
the Communist party line."

The committee also issued several public challenges to Senator

McCarthy. In March 1953 it denounced his procedures in investigating the Voice of America. In May, Hook published a letter in the *New York Times* calling for the Senator's retirement from public life.[10] In March 1954 Hook also published a ten-point code of ethics for political controversy, which was directed at McCarthy.[11] In 1954 the American Committee sponsored *McCarthy and the Communists,* a book by James Rorty and Moshe Decter, which showed how crudely the Senator combated Communism and how much harm he was doing to American life.

One might have expected that such a record would have satisfied the Paris Secretariat, but it did not. Some years later (in January 1968), when Mary McCarthy unfairly dismissed the American Committee as having been "actually divided within its ranks on the question of whether Senator McCarthy was a friend or enemy of domestic liberty,"[12] Josselson quoted the passage with approval.

The final and decisive conflict between New York and Paris arose over Bertrand Russell, whose association with the Congress had always been uneasy and whose attitude toward the American Committee (and America) had always been disdainful. He had already resigned three times from his honorary chairmanship of the Congress, once in 1950 because of Trevor-Roper's report on the Berlin meeting, once in 1953 because he thought the American Committee was "McCarthyist," and once in 1954 because he understood that *Les Amis de la Liberté* at St. Etienne were under the control of Catholic clergy. In each case he withdrew his resignation after hearing the facts. The fourth (and final) resignation resulted from the American Committee's response to a letter Russell published in the *Manchester Guardian* of March 26, 1956. The letter sought support for Morton Sobell, who had been sentenced to prison for thirty years for his part in the Rosenbergs' espionage activities, but who was, according to Russell, "an innocent man." Russell referred to "atrocities committed by the FBI" and compared America with "other police States such as Nazi Germany and Stalin's Russia."

The executive of the American Committee decided to write a letter of protest to Bertrand Russell and to publish its letter. It referred to his "extraordinary lapse from standards of objectivity and justice" and described his attacks on American justice as "a major disservice to the cause of freedom and democracy ... and a major service to the enemies we had supposed you had engaged in combat."

When Russell informed Stephen Spender that he intended to resign as honorary chairman, it was Josselson's turn to be angry—with the American Committee. Russell was, in Josselson's view "an old fool," but the Communists would regard his resignation as a coup. He wrote to Hook that the only way of saving the situation was for the Paris Executive Committee to rebuke the American Committee, to which Hook rejoined that any such rebuke would mean the American Committee's immediate withdrawal from the Congress. Josselson now felt free to give expression to his long festering indignation with "the obnoxious American Committee" (as Hook characterized the Paris attitude):

> You don't seem to realize what Russell's name on our masthead has meant to our international reputation, nor how very severely the loss of his name will affect the Congress and our friends who work for the Congress in non-committed areas where his name has helped offset some of the initial reluctance of people to associate with us—you should ask Passin about Japan, Padhye about India and Burma, Alisjahbana about Indonesia, Ghorayeb about the Middle East, Gorkin about Latin America, not to mention any of the European countries ... and you should project yourself into the near and far future when people say, "The Congress for Cultural Freedom?—that discredited organization that Bertrand Russell resigned from?"
>
> I'm sorry, Sidney, but I don't see how a rebuke to the American Committee can be avoided.... As always in my work, I will try to prevent any unnecessary damage, but if the American Committee chooses to disaffiliate, well, it may be all to the good in the long run.... The American Committee seems to recognize only one weapon in the fight against Communism: denunciation. Our methods are different. But because of this difference the American Committee no longer trusts us and, under such conditions, perhaps we each have to go our own way.

When the Executive Committee assembled in Paris on April 24, 1956, to consider the situation, only Raymond Aron thought that the Americans' action contained "an understandable element" in view of the years of lying Communist propaganda about the Rosenbergs they had endured. But in any case the Executive Committee only adopted a mild "opinion" which concluded plaintively:

"While it has never been the policy of the Congress to impose particular points of view on affiliated groups, it seems to us only right and proper that a national affiliate should consult with us when taking actions, within the body of the Congress, which can have serious international consequences."

Nabokov wrote to the American Committee that "we do not intend to make the above *Opinion* available to the press unless further developments require us to do so." For its part the American Committee would not accept the "opinion" or modify its own hostility to Russell's letter in the *Manchester Guardian*. Diana Trilling replied to Nabokov, summing up years of discontent with the Congress: "Russell published a fierce and totally ungrounded attack upon American institutions and freedom. And this attack constituted, we believe, an act of intellectual violence of a kind which puts it well outside the common realm of persuasive discourse." As to Russell's usefulness,

> ... how untruthful about America may a man be and still be useful to an organization which is pledged to truth and which numbers among its affiliates an American branch? ... Surely those who are won to the support of the Congress by Russell's present-day opinions and activities may turn out to be very uncertain friends of what Congress stands for tomorrow.

In May Nabokov visited Russell to urge him to reconsider his resignation. Russell's reply was that he would return to the Congress only if the American Committee made him a public apology or the Congress disaffiliated from the American Committee. The two-hour conversation ended, in Nabokov's account of it, with the two men agreeing about the Soviet menace and the importance of the Western nuclear deterrent.

There the matter rested for the time being, with Bertrand Russell's name still remaining on the Congress letterhead. But Russell revived the issue in November 1956, this time because of a statement from within the Congress, not from a member of the American Committee. In the final hours of the Hungarian Revolution, in response to the last appeal for help by Hungarian writers, Denis de Rougemont, Chairman of the Executive Committee, issued a passionate personal statement. Henceforth, he said, to "shake the hand" of any person—Communist, fellow-traveler, or whatever— who "justifies" the Soviet crime in Budapest would be to salute an accomplice. Bertrand Russell wrote to complain that Rougemont had not denounced the Anglo-French attack on Egypt and to announce that he, Russell, was not prepared to "shake the hand" of anyone who approved that. His resignation, he said, was now final.

The Congress formally accepted Bertrand Russell's resignation on February 12, 1957, some eleven months after he had told Spender of his intention to resign. In a last letter to Russell, Nabokov wrote:

> To compare the United States with Nazi Germany and Stalin's Russia is unjustified and to imply that the United States is a police state is in my opinion stretching semantics too far. To me, police state methods are symbolized by concentration camps, mass murders, rigged trials, the extraction of false confessions by means of torture and the deprivation of the right to appeal and the liberty to express opinion for their subjects. America may have many faults, but surely none of them puts her in that category.... As for not protesting against breaches of cultural freedom outside the Communist bloc, the charge is unjustified although we, as an organization, have to put first things first. It so happens that the greatest crimes were and still are being committed by the Soviet Union. The Communists still control a vast empire. Their hold over millions of minds and lives is still complete. Their subjects are still denied the right of appeal to justice.
>
> The tragic state of affairs in the USSR was brought particularly close to my own family recently. Not quite a month ago, my brother-in-law, the nephew of the Russian writer Dimitri Mirsky, who himself died in a concentration camp in Russia, returned from 11 years' hard labour behind the Polar circle, in Vorkuta. He lost his leg through gangrene caused by frost-bite and lack of medical care. In 1945, he had been kidnapped in Vienna, given no trial, and sentenced to 20 years' hard labour. I *know* that he was innocent. In his letters to me he speaks of millions of people, living under infamous conditions, herded together like beasts, dying under torture, from disease and cold. This is what I term conditions of a "police state" and I am sure that the description hardly fits the United States of America.

The long Russell episode marked the beginning of the end of the American Committee, which, unrepentant, suspended its activities a few months later. Before reaching that point its affairs were further confused by the circumstances of the resignation of its chairman since December 1954, James T. Farrell. On a Congress-sponsored world lecture tour of Australia, India, and the Middle East, Farrell had become angered by widespread anti-Americanism and in June 1956 had sent a letter from Istanbul to the isolationist *Chicago Tribune.* "We honest Americans," he wrote, "have taken enough, given enough, and have had enough of the blood of our boys spilled on foreign soil. From here on in, we should have a truly honest partnership in freedom, or else go it alone" and "retire to our own shores, and if necessary, fight it out to the death with communism."[13] It was not only the contents of the letter but the publishing of it in, of all papers, the *Chicago Tribune,* without consultation with the American Committee, that led to moves to replace him as chairman. To forestall this, he rang the *New York Times* late on August 27 to say that he had resigned. In a letter to the committee, he offered a rationale for resigning that ran directly opposite to the view he had given to the *Chicago Tribune*:

> Concerning our relationship with the Congress in Paris and its related committees, I led the struggle against the Paris office. But my direct experiences during my recent travels have convinced me that I was wrong, and that others on the Committee were wrong. I cannot say with definiteness that the Paris office is always sound, but, especially in Asia, they are dealing with problems which are extremely difficult. The views which many of us have held on anti-Communism are simply irrelevant to the Asians, and we must find a new way of approaching them. This is especially so in the case of India.

Farrell then cabled Josselson: "Have broken up American Committee. Your advantage. Have kept my word."

In November 1956, when Tito's police arrested Milovan Djilas for publishing a defense of the Hungarian Revolution in the *New Leader,* the American Committee issued its last international protest—in the absence of any response from the Congress in Paris. It sent (and published) a cable to Marshal Tito demanding Djilas's release and asserting that the arrest "violates every principle of freedom and decency cherished by the American people."[14] It was signed by Norman Thomas, Sidney Hook, John Dos Passos, George N. Shuster, Arthur Schlesinger, Lionel Trilling and Reinhold Niebuhr. The *New Leader* also sent a cable to Belgrade demanding an impartial inquiry. The Executive Committee in Paris considered the matter in January 1957 and decided to inform Marshal Tito that it supported the *New Leader*'s request.

The American Committee finally, in that same month, January 1957, decided "to suspend its active organizational life." Irving Kristol wrote to Josselson from New York that "the mourning seems to have been perfunctory; [there is] even a slight air of relief to be discerned." Almost ten years later, Josselson wrote: "Anybody, everywhere, who ever wants to attack the Congress can always find supporting material in the history of the American Committee." To which Diana Trilling might have replied by quoting her statement during the Russell controversy: "Surely those who are won to the support of the Congress by Russell's present-day [anti-American] opinions and activities may turn out to be very uncertain friends of what the Congress stands for tomorrow."[15]

# 10
# Changing Direction: "The New Enlightenment"

✍

In any case, the ideologists as we knew them in the
1930's, 1940's and 1950's are routed. But what do we
ourselves believe politically . . . ? There is an urgent need
to discover and enunciate our own principles of politics
broadly enough to serve Asia, Africa, and Europe and
America. I imagine we will come up with something akin
to the humane liberalism of the Enlightenment; but it
cannot be the same liberalism which stood so long and
then seemed to lose its power of attraction.

EDWARD SHILS[1]

The year 1958 was a turning point for the Congress for Cultural
Freedom. By then it had a sense both of past achievement and of
a need for new directions. But if there was debate or uncertainty
about the new directions, there was no doubt about the confidence
in what had been achieved in Europe. When the Executive Committee, with the Secretariat "in attendance," met in Paris on the
morning of Saturday, January 18, 1958, seven years and seven
months after the first stormy Congress for Cultural Freedom in
Berlin, there was an air of a victory party. The Communists and
their fellow-travelers were in disarray, and if Khrushchev's revela-
tory "secret speech" and his savage suppression of the Hungarians
in 1956 were largely responsible, the Congress had done much to
lay the foundation for the realistic public assessment of those

171

events. The days when *Pravda,* and the Left in general, would de-
fame Congress writers as "police informers," "turncoats," or
"scum" seemed to be over. (They would return.) People who once
attacked the Congress were now flocking to it. If ever there were
such a thing as anti-Communist *chic,* it was now.

The Congress had struck its form. It had established its methods,
and they worked. The British historian G. F. Hudson wrote after
the Milan conference in 1955: "The founders of the organization
seem to have discovered a method of achieving a solidarity of the
normally fragmented liberal intelligentsia without imposing articles of faith that would inevitably be unacceptable to large sections
of those brought together."[2] The seminar program, specifically
funded by the Ford Foundation and strengthened by jet travel and
simpler international telephone services, was expanding. The
Central and East European program was being developed, and African, Middle Eastern, and Indonesian programs were on the
agenda. The main Congress magazines, especially *Encounter* and
*Preuves,* were well established. It was about this time that George
Kennan wrote to Nabokov: "I can think of no group of people who
have done more to hold our world together in these last years than
you and your associates in the Congress. In this country [the
United States] in particular, few will ever understand the dimensions and significance of your accomplishment."[3]

As a token of Congress leadership, Melvin Lasky and François
Bondy had prepared a "Declaration," to be signed by intellectuals
inside and outside the Congress, which spoke for and supported
writers struggling for freedom of thought and expression throughout the world, whether in Peking, Johannesburg, or Djakarta, Moscow, Madrid, or Dublin. The struggle for school integration and
racial equality in Little Rock, Arkansas, was seen as part of this
same worldwide liberal struggle. The intellectuals of the world, the
Declaration said, are everywhere beginning to recover a sense of
mission, a new measure of confidence, a new solidarity, a common
devotion to the life of reason without ideological blinkers.[4]

Some were skeptical about this enthusiasm: If all this is so, Silone asked, why does the Congress not fold up, since it is no longer
needed?[5] The question was not entirely ironic. The Congress had
accomplished its primary mission against the fellow-travelers, and
it was not obvious in what direction it should now move. For his
part, Hook even believed that by this time the Congress "had outlived its usefulness." Matters had come to a head for him when, at

a meeting of the Executive Committee after the Soviet repression of the Hungarian Revolution, Spender objected to a reference to "the Soviet Empire," a term Spender considered "provocative." "What astounded me," Hook wrote, "was the failure of my politically sophisticated colleagues to react to Spender's reaction," a failure Hook regarded as "cowardly."[6] (Hook was not alone: Koestler, Burnham, Irving Brown, and Muggeridge shared, or came to share, his opinion, if for differing reasons.)

But Hook's diagnosis was premature, and the Congress still had several active years ahead of it in rapidly changing circumstances. In the coming years President Eisenhower would invite Khrushchev to the United States, President Kennedy would call for a constructive reexamination of the Cold War, and Pope John XXIII would convene Vatican Council II and, to ensure the attendance of bishops from the Communist states, would suspend a hundred-year Catholic tradition of anti-Communism. In the U.S.S.R. the thaw appeared to deepen, and in 1960 *Pravda* published the first literary denunciation of Stalin, A. T. Tvardovsky's canto, "How It Was," which was followed (in 1962) by Aleksandr Solzhenitsyn's *One Day in the Life of Ivan Denisovich* in Tvardovsky's *Novy Mir*. The possibility that "the end of ideology" would spread to the U.S.S.R. and that there would be a "convergence" of the Communist and liberal systems was widely debated. Within the Congress for Cultural Freedom itself there were also major changes of organization and personnel. By 1957 the most active national committee (the American) ceased to function. In 1958 Irving Kristol resigned as editor of *Encounter*. In 1961 Michael Josselson, suffering from a weak heart, moved his office to Geneva. In 1962 Nicolas Nabokov moved to Berlin to direct the Berlin Festival as a cultural arm of Willy Brandt's *Ostpolitik*, and was succeeded in Paris by Pierre Emmanuel. The management of the Paris office, including its dealings with the CIA, increasingly became the responsibility of John Hunt,* a novelist from Oklahoma, who had joined the Congress

---

*John Clinton Hunt contributed an autobiographical article to the *New Leader*'s series on "The Young Generation" (April 15, 1957), in which he described his "revulsion" from the abstractions of the 1930s, both anti-Stalinist and fellow-traveling. He described his generation, which came to social awareness in the 1940s, as "certainly far more concerned with tending one's own garden than with Utopia, an attitude more in the spirit of Melville than of Whitman. It is a generation groping for a kind of tragic affirmation of man based on what he is, with all his sins and

Secretariat in 1956 and remained with it until he resigned, with Michael Josselson, in 1967 at the height of the publicity over CIA funding.

An indication of the uncertainty of this period and of the tensions that would deepen in the 1960s was the Congress's large international conference on "Progress in Freedom" in Berlin in June 1960. Some 230 participants from fifty countries and all continents met in the *Kongresshalle,* where they had the choice of four study groups, one on the postideological age (Michael Polanyi's group), one on modernity and tradition (Edward Shils's), one on the future of democracy (Raymond Aron's) and one on the arts (Nicolas Nabokov's). As evidence of the seriousness and importance of the conference (despite some unfavorable publicity),[7] the Congress published three books of the papers and debates (as well as a Pollyanna-ish Forum Service report).[8]

Yet there was a general sense that the confident Congress consensus of the 1950s was faltering. This was partly reflected in the opening and closing addresses. In the one, J. Robert Oppenheimer declared, "We have to doubt the adequacy of our institutions to the world we live in,"[9] and in the other, George F. Kennan expressed his general sense of a "great helplessness."[10] More significant still were the debates during the week. Michael Polanyi presented to his group a "master paper" titled "Beyond Nihilism," in which he traced totalitarianism and its horrors to "moral excess," filling a void left by the rejection of all authority and transformed into ideological fanaticism. The "moral need of our time," Polanyi said, "is to curb our inordinate moral demands" and to restore a moderate civility based, perhaps, on a "reawakened national feeling," liberal religion and pragmatism. He saw this new civility as already emerging in both the West and the East—in "the end of ideology" in the one and in "revisionism" in the other. Polanyi regarded the Hungarian Revolution as "the paradigm" of a universal intellectual movement (outside China) that rejected the ideological lie, and *Poem for Adults* (by the Polish poet Adam Wazyk),

---

shortcomings." He concluded: "Surely we have suffered long enough from that hate-filled image of the fallen angel, yearning to be restored to heaven at any price." In 1956 he published a novel, *Generations of Men,* semi-autobiographical in style, about a young man's search for his roots among the Indians of Chetopa County, Oklahoma.

which depicts the "vomiting" forth of the lie, as a paradigmatic poem of the postideological age. Richard Löwenthal rebutted in a counterpaper, "Messianism, Nihilism and the Future," which claimed that, in tracing the origins of totalitarianism, Polanyi had overestimated the role of intellectuals and underestimated the impact of a stubborn conservatism, which had blocked necessary reforms. He also distinguished between kinds of totalitarianism, seeing Nazism as "satanic" but Marxism as retaining links with liberal humanism. For the future he saw the need for rapid social reforms and a "cultural revolution" to internalize morality. "Nor can I believe," he said, "that the necessary reforms can be achieved by general consent in all circumstances." With hindsight one can see in this debate between proponents of "civility" and proponents of a "cultural revolution" the rudiments of the conflict between a new conservatism and a New Left that would weaken the Congress and erode its "vital center" in the later 1960s.[11]

A similar tension marked the debates in the Shils group's discussion of the problems involved in modernizing traditional societies[12] and maintaining the quality of life in modern societies. The debates often turned into a contest between those who, like Shils, Daniel Bell, and Irving Kristol ("conservatives"), defended Western liberal civilization and those who, like Mary McCarthy, William Phillips, and John Kenneth Galbraith ("new Left"), who deplored the vulgarity, triviality, and conformism of Americanized "mass society," its consumerism, its automobiles, its popular media. When someone labeled Galbraith a "St. Francis" of our age, Melvin Lasky ironically discerned "a Franciscan Revolution" led by the new American saints, Galbraith, Oppenheimer, and Kennan. The exchanges were widely reported, usually unfavorably: Taya Zinkin declared that it all made "my housewife's blood boil,"[13] and Peregrine Worsthorne reported that the debates limited any meeting of minds between Westerners and Asians or Africans who hoped their countries might achieve some of the affluence being denounced in Berlin.[14] One Congress observer reported: "The question in my mind at the end of the conference is 'why are American intellectuals so unhappy?' In fact, a psychoanalysis of American intellectuals seems in order."[15] That question, and those divisions, would continue to bedevil the last years of the Congress.

Further, the conference atmosphere (and the international atmosphere) could hardly have been less like that of the Berlin Conference of 1950, whose tenth anniversary it celebrated. In 1950 a free world had welcomed President Truman's decision to support South Korea against the North Korean invasion; in 1960 the head-lines in the world press were about the anti-American riots in To-kyo, which led to the cancellation of President Eisenhower's visit to Japan. In 1950 there had been dramatic defections to the Con-gress from the East; now William Phillips of *Partisan Review* had stormed out of one session in protest at the Congress.[16] Then the sessions had sometimes become emotion-charged, antitotalitarian demonstrations; now François Bondy described them as "univer-sity tutorial classes."[17] Then the Cold War had been foremost; now it was barely mentioned (although there was a ceremony to com-memorate the rising in East Berlin of June 1953, and Nicolas Na-bokov's rendition of Boris Pasternak's poem "Hamlet" was, for one Australian lawyer, "unforgettable").[18]

The international conference in Berlin in 1950 had led to the formation of the Congress for Cultural Freedom; that in Hamburg in 1953 had produced the Committee on Science and Freedom; and the one in Milan in 1955 had given the Congress a new agenda ("the underdeveloped world"). But Berlin in 1960 was, if not a dead-end, a bad omen, a symbol of uncertainty. The Congress would hold no more large-scale international conferences.

The man who did the most to give the Congress a new sense of direction, and a hope of survival in the 1960s, was Edward Shils. Having vanquished all but the perennial and incorrigible fellow-travelers, the next task of the Congress should be, according to Shils, the creation and support of a worldwide liberal intellectual community that transcended the existing worldwide communities based on religion, race, ideology, or profession. He developed his ideas on this intellectual community in a characteristic series of essays, and if Polanyi and his *Logic of Liberty* (1951) or Aron and his *L'Opium des intellectuels* (1955) are representative figures and their books key texts in the first period of the Congress for Cul-tural Freedom, Edward Shils and his essays of the 1950s and early 1960s (collected later in *The Intellectuals and the Powers*)[19] fill those roles in the next period.

Edward Shils was born in 1910 in New England and was raised in Philadelphia. While he was a social worker in Chicago's Black Belt, he was invited to join the University of Chicago in 1933 as a research assistant to Louis Wirth. Now "pitched onto the peak of the sociological Parnassus," he attended Frank Knight's seminar on Max Weber ("reading Max Weber was literally breath-taking. Sometimes in the midst of reading him, I had to stand up and walk around for a minute or two until my exhilaration died down")[20] and attended the last courses given by Robert Park. He also collaborated with Talcott Parsons on *Toward a General Theory of Action* and translated (with Louis Wirth) Karl Mannheim's *Ideologie und Utopie,* which for many Americans was the first introduction to German sociology.

After World War II (in which he served in Washington and London in the Office of Strategic Services, studying German civilian and military morale), he returned to Chicago, where he helped launch *The Bulletin of the Atomic Scientists* and joined "the scientists' movement" for international and civilian control of nuclear energy—the beginning of his lifelong involvement in science policy, which culminated years later in his editing of the quarterly *Minerva.* In this period he also taught sociology at the London School of Economics (regarded as one of the leading university centers "of Africa and Asia"), which aroused his interest in the problems of intellectuals in the "underdeveloped world."

In 1955 he published *The Torment of Secrecy,* a polemic against "McCarthyism," especially as it affected scientists, and a plea for pluralistic, nonideological civility. It was his principal critique of the uncivil Right, and later essays include his critique of the uncivil Left—especially "collectivist liberalism" and its parasitic emancipationism. Central to his thinking is the concept of civility—the disinterested public spirit without which even a free, lawful, and democratic country is at risk, and he has looked especially to disinterested intellectuals ("the academic and amateur social scientists, highbrow journalists, literary critics, novelists, even poets")[21] to maintain this civility. He developed his ideas in a series of idiosyncratic essays that have attracted the adjective "Shilsian."[22]

In a paper he sent to Michael Josselson early in 1960, "Thoughts on the Congress in the Sixties," Shils set out his new perspective for the Congress.[23] Time, he wrote, had overtaken the themes with which the Congress began its career. In 1950 the world had been "full of frivolous fellow-travelers" and the work the Congress did in dispelling their illusions was exemplary. Since the Milan conference of 1955, the Congress had also sought to understand the situation in "underdeveloped countries" and to contribute to "the fortification of tendencies towards liberal modernity in Africa and Asia." "We must continue with these efforts to create a new, and for the first time, a world-wide intellectual community which cuts across academic specialities and national, ethnic and political boundaries" of all continents. But along with intellectual members, there must also be "an intellectual content," the discovering and delineating of which would not be easy. This world intellectual community was weak and barely existed. Its order was "still hidden." It had no corporate structure (unlike a professional association), no formal structure of authority (unlike universities), and no formal articles of faith (unlike churches). But it existed. There *was* a worldwide communion of universalistic values that linked an African novelist, a Japanese mathematician, and a British physicist. The Congress had been both an expression of this worldwide community and a means of strengthening it—the Congress as a New Enlightenment. But one thing was clear: Large-scale conferences like Berlin 1960 were not a way of strengthening it. Shils urged that more attention be given to small seminars and *conversaziones*. (The paper also touched on the problem of finding "the optimal compromise" between the Congress and the ruling oligarchs of the new states, if it was to be able to work in those states at all.)

Shils returned to the problem of the Congress's future a year later in a new paper (this time for the Executive Committee) called "Further Thoughts on the Congress in the '60's,"[24] which was discussed at length at a meeting of the Executive Committee in Zürich in March 1962. The Congress, he repeated, did not seek subscribers to an ideology, it sought to heighten the attachment of intellectuals to "universally valid standards of devotion to truth, to intellectual curiosity, and to the appreciation of creativity." But this internationalist liberal, humane, and generous orientation was only "in process of generation." It would be premature to define it too closely. The first task was "to discover" that outlook. "We must discover the implications of the general orientation which we feel links us with our fellow intellectuals. . . . We must practise and nurture that orientation until it becomes more elaborate within our consciousness and more capable of explicit and articulate formulation." Probably "we will come up with something akin to the humane liberalism of the Enlightenment."

As for the Cold War, Shils warned:

The new generation has no experience of the Communists of
the old days, and "fellow travelling" has become a more
complicated and obscure affair. The new generation does not
want to fight the old battles, partly because these battles
appear to them to be irrelevant and partly because the older
generation is engaged in these battles. What the older
generation is exercised about is almost automatically
discredited, either consciously or unconsciously; and by a
more subtle simplism than they followed in the 1920's and
1930's, the Communists have managed repeatedly to install
themselves in the minds of the callow and well-intended as
being on the right side. Furthermore, lacking the historical
knowledge and experience of the 1930's and 1940's, the
younger generation does not have the "apperception mass"
for interpreting Soviet policy that our generation has. The
younger generation, moreover, has—and rightly so—an
intolerance for the worn-out clichés of "free world" rhetoric,
and they are more sensitive and more irritated by these
clichés when used by our own politicians and intellectuals
than they are by the clichés of Communist politicians and the
utopians in the West who preach love and unilateral
disarmament. In this context, all I wish to do is to stress the
need for us to go beyond these clichés in our thought about
our relations with the Communist countries.

The new approach, in other words, should not be polemically
anti-Communist. It was a matter of building and consolidating the
newly emerging, still fragile worldwide international community,
especially in the Third World. The mode of operation would still
be primarily publishing magazines, pamphlets and books, but
Shils particularly defended the seminar program, despite widespread criticism of its lack of focus and the low level of discussion.
Shils summed up the criticism with the admission that "the discussions at seminars, judged by the Socratic standard, leave much to
be desired. They are certainly seldom satisfying to me." They did
not stick to the point; too many people made too-long speeches;
they seldom addressed themselves to each others' points; and
when they did, more often than not they addressed themselves to
points peripheral to the main theme. "Good chairmen do not exist; and, if an accident occurs and one is found, then the worst

windbags complain that they haven't had a chance to open their mouths—i.e., to deliver some cretinous twenty-minute oration. So if it was ever a dream of the Congress to conduct Socratic discussions at its seminars, that ideal should be renounced without further ado."

Should the seminar program be discontinued?

> To that I say: No. The fact is that most people like coming to and being at the seminars. They much enjoy meeting the other people, they like chatting and discussing with them outside the sessions, and they enjoy the chance to deliver themselves of some home truths which have lain stale on their chests for years. Their minds are often touched and alerted by things they hear in the discussion. It is not that they learn some new and fundamental proposition which they never understood or came near to understanding before. It is, rather, that they perceive some nuance hitherto overlooked or insufficiently appreciated, or they have underscored in their minds notions which they did not previously appreciate in sufficient measure. No less important is the impression made on them by the personalities they meet; they get new impressions of the quality of their fellow intellectuals in countries of which they knew little hitherto, and thanks to the good quality of our participants, the result is almost always heightened respect.

The seminar program was, in other words, consolidating at least the beginnings of a liberal international community.

There was general agreement with Shils's paper when the Executive Committee discussed it at Zürich. Aron cautioned against a too-rapid revision of ideas, as if everything had changed in the years since 1950. The Cold War would continue for two more generations, he said, and if what the Congress believed in 1950 was still true, it should not be ashamed to say so again. But he agreed that success in the future would mean finding the right idiom, forms, and techniques for the 1960s, keeping in touch with intellectuals everywhere, and not leaving "our people" isolated or in danger.[25]

The Congress had a second reason to defend the program of seminars: Because of their "circumscribed" and nonideological subjects, the dictatorships, "the ruling oligarchs," would sometimes allow their intellectuals to travel abroad to attend interna-

tional seminars. The Congress was able in this way to make contacts with the intellectuals of Indonesia, South Korea, Spain,
Portugal, and difficult parts of Africa, Latin America, and the Middle East. It was in those countries that the Congress now concentrated its energies. In its remaining five years it organized international and regional seminars all over the world from Poona and
Cairo to Madrid and Kampala, always "bringing together" in small
meetings Asian, African, American, and European intellectuals
(including Yugoslavs, Poles, and Hungarians) for discussion of
"circumscribed subjects." The most frequently chosen of the "circumscribed subjects" were economic growth, modernization, and
political developments in the "underdeveloped world." There
were also several gatherings of poets, novelists, and critics, and
several conferences on developments in the U.S.S.R. and Communist China. Bertrand de Jouvenel organized one on futurology,
Aron one on the conditions of world order, *Partisan Review* one on
"The Idea of the Future,"[26] and Oppenheimer and Nabokov one
that had no set subject or agenda beyond exploring the problem
of "communicability." George Urban organized, in several cities, a
set of seminars (combined with large public "teach-ins" involving
students) called the "European Seminar," aimed at revitalizing
"the European idea" and helping to get Britain into Europe. Most
of these seminars succeeded in contributing to the rudiments of a
world intellectual community.

Yet once again "a gypsy curse" hung over this Congress program. In 1967, at the height of worldwide liberal condemnation of
the Vietnam War, newspapers everywhere republished the disclosures of CIA funding of the Congress, and in Beirut, for example,
at a Congress seminar of Middle Eastern, Asian, and African
writers presided over by Kamal Jumblatt, speaker after speaker
vied with each other in denouncing the Congress for Cultural
Freedom, turning the seminar, as one witness reported, into "un
véritable fiasco." The disclosures overwhelmed and obscured the
contributions the seminars had made toward encouraging "a
world intellectual community" devoted to liberal democratic values. The same fate awaited the magazines as well.

# 11
# *Magazines of the Sixties*

*≤*

Each time we consider creating a review, with the
remarkable and competent personalities that we
draw on, I feel that the Congress can't lose, because the
reviews are the surest bases of our actions.

MANÈS SPERBER[1]

Writing in 1963, Philip Toynbee asked if readers of *Encounter* had
noticed the least change when Melvin Lasky replaced Irving Kristol as editor at the end of 1958. "And if not," he asked, "isn't this a
sign of a certain efficient impersonality?"[2] In fact, while *Encounter*
retained the liberal, cosmopolitan, polemical character that Kristol had given it and continued to draw on the familiar cross-
section of English, American, and European writers, Lasky inevitably made changes in *Encounter,* reflecting the times and the Congress's new priorities, especially in relation to the Cold War, the
Third World, and the British Labour Party.

One critic, A. Alvarez, had tendentiously noticed one of the
changes. Writing in 1961 he declared that "the paranoiac throb of
genuine propaganda is rarely heard in *Encounter* these days"[3]—an
acknowledgment that the Congress for Cultural Freedom had won
"the battle of ideas" and that it now gave a lower priority to documenting totalitarianism and a higher priority to cooperating,
where possible, with Central and East European dissidents and
revisionists, a process begun by Kristol himself in his unsuccessful
attempts to exchange articles with the aborted Polish *Europa.* Lasky
resumed those approaches with even more determination, plan-

183

ning, also without success, an East–West meeting of editors and a seminar of Western and Soviet writers. He published dissident Soviet writers—in 1960 "The Trial Begins" by "Abram Tertz" (Andrei Sinyavsky) and Vladimir Dudintsev's "A New Year's Fable," and in 1963 Aleksandr Solzhenitsyn's "Matryona's Home" and the anthology *New Voices* (prepared by Patricia Blake) including Akhmadulina, Voznesensky, Yevtushenko, and Vasily Aksynonov. In June 1963 he also published Herbert Lüthy's "Culture and the Cold War," calling for an end to "sterile polemics," to which S. Smirnov replied in *Pravda* denouncing Lüthy as an "imperialist propagandist" and *Encounter* as "the NATO mouthpiece in England." The thaw froze up again, and Lasky's overtures were met with the true "paranoiac throb" of Soviet propaganda.

As part of the Congress's "discovery of Africa" in the late 1950s, Lasky's *Encounter* paid greater attention both to Africa and the Third World as a whole. At Michael Josselson's suggestion, Lasky spent several months in 1961 in East and West Africa, meeting African writers, intellectuals, and politicians. The tour culminated in a series of *Encounter* articles (and a book) "Africa for Beginners." (They included a social democratic, humanist, internationalist "Manifesto" prepared one "argumentative, ideologized night in Ghana.")[4] *Encounter* published, as the first of its series of pamphlets, a booklet edited by Shils, *The Problems of Afro-Asian New States,* based on the debates at the Congress's conference in Berlin in 1960. Another in the series was Rita Hinden's *Africa and Democracy* (1962), a polemic against the claim that democracy would not work in Africa. Lasky in *Encounter* conducted a controversy over several months in 1961—mainly between Shils and Elspeth Huxley—on the prospects of liberal institutions in Africa. (Shils reserved some hopes, but Mrs. Huxley, not so optimistic, turned out to be right.) *Encounter* also regularly published reports on African developments by such "Africa hands" as Ulli Beier, Russell Warren Howe, Colin Legum, Colin MacInnes, Dan Jacobson, and W. Arthur Lewis. *Encounter,* in other words, contributed heavily to the Congress's mission in Africa—until it all collapsed in the late 1960s.

Finally, Lasky moved *Encounter* closer to the Hugh Gaitskell wing of the British Labour Party. After the socialists suffered their third consecutive electoral defeat in 1959, *Encounter* became one of the principal publications in which C. A. R. Crosland developed his "revisionist," social democratic, Keynesian program of which

"Radical Reform and the Left" (*Encounter,* October 1960) was typical. He called for higher taxation of the wealthy, increased welfare, an expanded public sector, the democratization of the public schools, protection of the consumer, conservation of the countryside, more technological education, liberalized laws on homosexuality, abolition of capital punishment, joining the European Economic Community, world government, racial equality, and support for NATO. In 1979, also in *Encounter,* Colin Welch could write of "the shabby, decaying slum, the haunted house,"[5] which Crosland's program, successfully carried out, had made of England, but in the early 1960s it seemed to many, including most of the *Encounter* circle, an enlivening, progressive vision. "Gaitskell has been very glad of our support," Lasky wrote (to John Hunt in October 1960) "and has written to me personally to express that gratitude." He also referred to "an enormous friendly feeling for *Encounter*"[6] in the center and the Right wing of the British Labour Party. This "friendly feeling" continued through the debates on nationalization, unilateralism, decolonization, science policy, censorship reform, and entry to the Common Market (which Gaitskell opposed and *Encounter* supported). In 1963 the special issue, with Arthur Koestler as Guest Editor, "Suicide of a Nation," could also be read as a call for a change of government to help put an end to "the British sickness." When Harold Wilson formed his Labour Government in October 1964, his Ministry included half a dozen regular *Encounter* writers (and Lord [C. P.] Snow was appointed Parliamentary Secretary in the Ministry of Technology).

Along with the new emphases that Lasky brought, *Encounter* continued publishing a range of widely discussed articles: Snow's lecture "The Two Cultures" and the resulting debate (but not F. R. Leavis's phillipic against Snow. Leavis was no *Encounter* man; he published in *The Spectator*); John Sparrow's "Regina v Penguin" on the buggery theme in *Lady Chatterley's Lover*; Henry Fairlie's critique of "The BBC"; and Wayland Young's "Sitting on a Fortune," about the lives of London prostitutes. By 1963 *Encounter*'s circulation had risen to 34,000, and it was a *success*. "Its list of bombshells is impressive," Alvarez conceded,[7] and "it gets around in the most remarkable way," Peter Duval Smith wrote in the *Financial Times,* "I recollect seeing the magazine on the coffee tables in Tokyo, Cairo, Cape Town, Addis Ababa." *Newsweek* attributed this success to its being "as open-minded, as animated, and as brilliantly bitchy, as a successful literary cocktail party."[8] (It was not entirely "open-minded": Lasky rejected an article by Malcolm Muggeridge that briskly dismissed all twentieth-century literature, music, and art; none of it, Muggeridge said, "will be of any conceivable *imaginative* interest to posterity."[9] But this meant dismissing the Western culture that Lasky's *Der Monat* and the Congress for Cultural Freedom had been created to affirm.)

A cloud appeared on the horizon at the time of the publication in 1963 of the book *Encounters,* an anthology of the first ten years of the magazine. Several of the English reviews were cool, detached, or critical. Conor Cruise O'Brien wrote that *"Encounter's* first loyalty is to America,"[10] and an editorial in the *Sunday Telegraph* referred to a secret and regular subvention to *Encounter* from "the Foreign Office."[11] After a denial by Lasky and Spender, the *Sunday Telegraph* published an apology the following week. But reports of British Government funding, supplementing reports of CIA or State Department subsidies threatened to damage *Encounter's* standing. Spender and Lasky looked for private "angels" and finally began negotiations with Cecil Harmsworth King, head of the *Daily Mirror* group. By July 1964 they were able to announce in *Encounter* that in future all financial and business affairs of the magazine would be handled by the International Publishing Corporation. A controlling Trust was established consisting of Sir William Hayter, Andrew Schonfield, Shils, and Schlesinger, and *Encounter* ceased to be sponsored by the Congress for Cultural Freedom. But it continued to be, in the words of Aron's *Mémoires* (1983), "the first, the best monthly review in English."

*Encounter* is the only one of the various European literary-cultural-political magazines sponsored by the Congress in the 1950s that has survived (along with the more specialized *Survey, Minerva,* and *China Quarterly*). In December 1963 the Austrian publishing house Hans Deutsch took over the Viennese *Forum.* When Hans Deutsch was charged in connection with alleged postwar restitution irregularities, the City of Vienna assumed financial responsibility for the magazine. In 1965 it became *Neues Forum,* under the editorship of Günter Nenning, who (to Friedrich Torberg's dismay) committed it to a Communist–Christian "dialogue." In 1965 *Cuadernos* published its last issue, as did Jørgen Schleimann's Danish *Perspektiv* in 1966, the Italian *Tempo Presente* in 1968, and the German *Monat* in 1971. *Preuves* survived longer, but with decreasing confidence: By the early 1960s Michael Josselson was criticizing it as having

become routinized and cliquish and for failing to represent a major current of French opinion; in the late 1960s Aron advised
writers not to publish in it because of the past CIA associations. It
survived with new editors, a new policy, and a fatuous subtitle (*"les
idées qui changent le monde"*) until the 1970s. By then it was unrecog-
nizable as the challenging *Preuves* of the Congress for Cultural
Freedom.

## *Jiyu*

After the dissolution of the first Japanese Committee for Cultural
Freedom, Herbert Passin recommended to the Congress that a
magazine by the center of all Congress activities in Japan—one in
the style of the *sogo zasshi,* a general magazine emphasizing politics
and the social sciences but also including literature and the arts.[12]
It should help, he said, to counter the anti-Western and anti-
American Leftism of the leading reviews, *Chūo Koron (The Central
Review)* and *Sekai (The World).* Progress was slow, however, and although a new committee, the Japan Cultural Forum, was formed
in 1957 and began its program of seminars, exhibitions, and lecture tours, publication of a magazine was deferred, and the intellectual climate remained discouraging: The enthusiasm of "the
China Boom" waxed in the 1950s and the successful Soviet *sputnik*
easily made up for the Hungarian disaster among Japanese intellectuals. "We may be in for a long, cold winter of this sort of
thing," E. G. Seidensticker wrote in *Japan Times.*[13] When Koestler
visited Japan early in 1959 as part of a Congress lecture tour, he
shocked his Japanese hosts (and the Paris Secretariat) by publicly
rejecting an invitation to address the Japanese chapter of PEN
after it had refused to condemn the Soviets for their treatment of
Boris Pasternak (and had actually condemned Pasternak's international supporters). "The SOB has given us a black eye," complained the ultra-sensitive tactician Josselson,[14] but the publicity
engendered by Koestler's gesture once again drew the Congress's
attention to the formidable influence of the Japanese Left and the
problems it created. A year later anti-American riots in Tokyo culminated in the cancellation of President Eisenhower's proposed
visit to Japan.

The Congress's monthly *Jiyu (Freedom)* was launched in this un-
promising atmosphere and quickly ran into difficulties. The first

issue placed it in the tradition of the *sogo zasshi:* It carried a liberal critique of Left and Right totalitarianism, an appreciation of Japanese traditions and methods of change, and short stories. Its cover was designed by Ichiro Fukuzawa, a surrealist painter. But when John Hunt went to Tokyo in April 1960, he found that the Japan Cultural Forum did not have complete control of *Jiyu* and that its publisher chose its articles with a view to sales and without regard to political or literary values. One issue carried a full-page advertisement for a Chinese Communist novel. "This is intolerable," Hunt wrote to Passin (then in the United States). After "a considerable amount of palaver," he went on, the Japan Cultural Forum agreed to take full charge.[15] Hunt returned to Paris unconvinced. In July he wrote again to Passin that "things are in a hell of a mess," as was illustrated by *Jiyu*'s response to the anti-American riots of June 1960: It "should have taken up [a] clear-cut stand on behalf of intellectual responsibility and democratic procedure," but in fact it swam with the tide and was scarcely distinguishable from the consistently anti-American reviews, *Sekai* and *Chūo Koron.*

Hunt decided to break entirely with the publisher and "go on our own with a team composed of one hundred per cent of our people. Japan is far too tricky ideologically to leave our magazine in the hands of a man who is not tried and true." He asked Passin to handle the new arrangements. Finally, Kenzo Takayanagi (scholar, man of letters, and political scientist) agreed to be the publisher, supported by an editorial committee: the historian Kentaro Hayashi, the novelist Taiko Hirabayashi, the economist Takeyasu Kimura, the historian Yoshihiko Seki, and the literary critic Michio Takeyama. Hoki Ishihara was appointed managing editor.

After those early troubles the magazine was at last established as an independent, liberal venture. By April 1961 Hunt wrote from Tokyo: "*Jiyu* is now generally regarded here as one of the big 4 of Japanese periodical publishing—a remarkable achievement. With more help, they can accomplish very important things." In the 1960s it became the principal outlet for pro-Western liberals and social democrats in Japan and helped to moderate anti-American opinion among Japanese intellectuals. Its circulation in 1967 was 5,600 and its subsidy from the Congress was $47,353—one of the largest magazine subsidies and an indication of the importance the Secretariat accorded it.

When the Japan Cultural Forum was dissolved and subsidies

from Paris ceased, Ishihara found other sources of funds. *Jiyu* continues to this day. "It will die with me," Ishihara has said.[16]

## *Hiwar*

Walter Z. Laqueur warned the Secretariat in the early 1950s that any Congress office in the Middle East would be denounced by nationalists and Communists as a tool of Western Imperialism and Zionism (unless the office itself joined in the anti-Western chorus!). Nevertheless, in the late 1950s the Congress opened a small bureau in Beirut to arrange seminars on nonpolitical themes, to distribute Congress publications, including *Adwa* (an Arabic *Forum Service*), and to organize lecture tours.

In 1961 it decided to take a further step and establish an Arabic literary magazine. To prepare the ground it held a seminar in Rome on "The Arab Writer and the Modern World," which "brought together" Arab and Western writers. Then it established a Novelists' Club in Beirut to sponsor literary prizes and translations into Arabic of Western novels. Jayaprakash Narayan called on President Nasser of Egypt to explain the Congress's aims, and Asoka Mehta discussed them with a range of Arab intellectuals. Finally, early in 1962, Tawfiq Sayigh (a Palestinian poet), Jamil Jabre (the Lebanese writer and Congress representative), Jamal Ahmad (the Sudanese Ambassador to Ethiopia), and Badr Al-Sayab (an Iraqi poet) met in Beirut to plan a bimonthly literary review called *Hiwar* (*Dialogue*), to be published in Beirut and edited by Tawfiq Sayigh.

The first issue, in October 1962, carried an article on "The Hero in Arabic Fiction," an interview with T. S. Eliot, and a plea by Silone for the independence of the writer and the autonomy of art. It maintained its literary emphasis throughout its four to five years of publication, hoping to appeal to young Muslims in Egypt, Syria, and Iraq and the Christians in Lebanon. Its politics were low-key but inevitably, as Tawfiq Sayigh put it, "Arab nationalist and left-wing liberal."

As Laqueur had predicted, the attack on *Hiwar* by Communists, Baathists, and Nasserites was relentless. The goals of *Hiwar*, said *Al Liwa* (a newspaper of the Muslim Brotherhood in Damascus, in a typical article), were

... to help Israel and the colonialists, to destroy the morals of the nation, to obliterate our history and our spiritual civilization, to kill the spirit of revolt, in our people.... The Congress tried to propagate its evil theories by spreading money here and there, by establishing attractive magazines and by giving big receptions and conferences.... In order to save our writers and our dignity, the Congress must be exposed and boycotted.[17]

To help counter such polemics, *Hiwar* announced in its October 1965 issue that it had awarded its literary prize of $2,800 to the most popular short story writer in the Arab literary world and "a lion of the Left," Yusuf Idris, who at first accepted the prize without reservation. But within twenty-four hours of his return to Cairo from a visit to Poland and Britain, and under pressure of attacks on him in the Egyptian press, he cabled Tawfiq Sayigh declining the prize. He would not be (according to one congratulatory Cairo editorial) "a Trojan horse."

It was, however, the *New York Times* report of April 1966 on CIA funding of the Congress that was the beginning of the end for *Hiwar.* In Beirut, the Lebanese police called Jamil Jabre in for questioning. In Cairo, *Hiwar* was seized and banned, and the headline in *Rose Al-Yousef* screamed "*Hiwar* Belongs to the CIA." Louis Awad (a Shakespeare scholar, literary editor of the Cairo daily *Al-Ahram,* and poet whose work had appeared in *Hiwar*) called for a universal boycott of the magazine, the resignation of Tawfiq Sayigh, and the "liquidation" of the Congress for Cultural Freedom. *Hiwar* survived until May 1967, when Thomas Braden's article on the Congress in the *Saturday Evening Post,* "I'm Glad the CIA is Immoral," led to its ceasing publication.

## Transition

Rajat Neogy, a thirty-year-old Uganda-born Bengali, launched *Transition* in November 1961 in Kampala shortly before Uganda became independent under Prime Minister Milton Obote. Subtitled *A Journal of the Arts, Culture and Society,* it followed the general style of *Encounter* and in its early issues published J. T. Ngugi, John Pepper Clark, Ezekiel Mphahlele, Julius Nyerere, Tom Mboya, Ivor Jennings, Gerald Moore, and Richard Le Fanu. After four issues, however, Rajat Neogy ran out of funds, and at the Congress's Kampala conference of African writers in 1962 he asked the director of the Congress's African program, Ezekiel Mphahlele, if it would help him. It did, and for the following six years Neogy produced the most talked-about and controversial literary-political magazine in Africa. It published African writers from East, West, and South Africa, and Western writers from the Congress circle (such as Lasky, Bondy, Jelenski, and James McAuley), as well as Conor Cruise O'Brien and even Milton Obote. Paul Theroux's satire on expatriates ("Tarzan Is an Expatriate") and Ali Mazrui's critique of African nationalists ("Nkrumah: the Leninist Czar" and "Tanzaphilia") aroused widespread debate.

*Transition*'s sales reached twelve thousand, including three thousand in the United States, where Lionel Trilling wrote to Neogy: "I must tell you that no magazine I can ever remember reading—except maybe the *Dial* of my youth—has ever told me so much about matters I did not know about."[18] Bondy described *Transition* as "the most exciting and colourful publication which we have ever had the luck of being associated with."[19] Paul Theroux encapsulated its reputation in this editorial comment:

> What is most interesting about reactions is that invariably the good ones come from afar. The *New York Times* says yes, the *Kenya Weekly News*, the Nigerian distributor and the local expatriate yahoos say no. *Transition* has been accused of taking things too seriously, not taking things seriously enough, being political, puritanical, unnecessarily licentious, demented, childish, pro-Indian, Afrophile, anti-African, CIA-inspired, left-wing, erotic, anti-white, anti-black, hippy, honkey, trendy, academic, mealymouthed, *au courant*, dirty-minded, immodest, and just plain boring. Arthur Schlesinger, Jr., takes special pains to renew his subscription and add his new address; Rudolf Augstein begins a new one; the weirdo bulldyke headmistress in Chad cancels hers when she sees the word orgasm staring out at her from the pages of issue 22 ... we'll go on printing the magazine because we really want people to see that we're pretty, honest, intelligent and tough. What more could a girl ask for?[20]

But *Transition*'s independence placed it in confrontation with the deepening dictatorship of Milton Obote, who in April 1966, in what he called "the Uganda Revolution," abolished the constitution, which had conceded a certain independence to the Kingdom of Buganda, ordered Idi Amin to storm the Kabaka's palace, forced the Kabaka into exile, and assumed the Presidency. Throughout this period *Transition* remained an outspoken critic of the regime. In 1967 the Ugandan poet Okot p'Bitek wrote in *Transition* that "the most striking and frightening thing about all African governments is this: that without an exception, all of them are dictatorships, and practise such ruthless discriminations as to make the South African *apartheid* look tame."[21] In another article in the same issue Abu Mayanja, a lawyer, described the proposed new constitution as "in many respects illiberal, authoritarian and dictatorial." When Akena Adoka, the head of the secret police, published in *Transition* a rejoinder to this article,[22] a student, Davis Sebukima, signing himself "Steve Lino" published a letter ridiculing Adoka.[23]

Okot p'Bitek was dismissed from the National Cultural Center (and emigrated to Kenya), and in October 1968 the police raided *Transition*'s offices and later arrested and imprisoned Rajat Neogy, Abu Mayanja, and "Steve Lino," charging them with sedition. Milton Obote ignored protests from abroad, usually scrawling the letters "CIA" on them. After six months in solitary confinement (more than half of them in a cell 8 by 5 feet for twenty-three hours a day) and an acquittal in court, Neogy was released and left the country, a wounded man. It was the end of *Transition* in Uganda. It was briefly revived in K. A. Busia's Ghana but never recaptured the zest or quality of the Kampala years.

## Censorship

In the 1960s the Congress joined the international campaign against literary controls and launched the British magazine *Censorship*, with the subtitle "a quarterly report on censorship of ideas and the arts." (The Paris office also produced a French *Censure contre les arts et la pensée*, edited by Jean Bloch-Michel, and a Spanish *Censura contra las artes y el pensamiento*, edited by Ignacio Iglesias, both of which were independent of *Censorship*.) Edited by Murray Mindlin, *Censorship* began in the autumn of 1964 and folded in the winter of 1967. Mindlin was an American-born writer who had been literary editor of the *Jerusalem Post* before settling in England.

One contributor to the journal described him as "a short, myopic, puckish, twinkling-eyed egg-shaped man" with a passionate dislike of censorship "in all its forms."[24]

His six lively issues dealt with the harassment of writers or the banning of books, films, and plays in all parts of the free world, the Communist world, and the Third World. "Mailed Fist in Portugal," "East German Freeze," "Indonesia: Writers Under Pressure," "Australia: Wowsers and Browsers," and "France: The New Puritans" were typical articles. Each issue (after the first) also carried a "Chronicle" briefly noting acts of censorship around the world. The "Chronicle" began with a summary of South African censorship and went on to deal with the dismissal of Robert Havemann from his academic post in East Germany (because of his critique of dialectical materialism), the suppression in Bratislava of Ladislav Mnacko's anti-Stalinist book *Delayed Reports,* the dissolution of the Portuguese Writers' Association, and the arrest of Wole Soyinka in Nigeria.

In one sense *Censorship* reflected the "Swinging Sixties" in its call for the total abolition of censorship, but it also had a sharp political point. When *Censorship* folded in 1967, the *New Statesman* lamented: "This is bad news for writers, publishers and artists everywhere. There is nothing else like it in the world . . . it is calm, objective, responsible and above all well-informed."[25] (*Index on Censorship,* launched by Stephen Spender in 1972, is a worthy successor to *Censorship.*)

## Mundo Nuevo

When Adlai Stevenson, the U.S. Ambassador to the United Nations, met with Michael Josselson and Nicolas Nabokov in Geneva in the middle of 1961, a few weeks after the Bay of Pigs imbroglio, to discuss the Latin American situation, Stevenson's view was that the magazine *Cuadernos* relied too much on "the great Hispanic humanists" (the Madariagas, the Romeros, and the Reyeses) and that younger writers had to be found to develop contemporary themes. It was at this meeting that Josselson suggested the non-Communist Left theme of *Fidelismo sin Fidel.*[26] *Fidelismo* had brought a new sense of urgency to the Congress for Cultural Freedom. In 1961 the Secretariat changed *Cuadernos* from a bimonthly to a monthly, and in

1962 it assigned Keith Botsford to Rio de Janeiro and Luis Mercier Vega to Montevideo in the hope of redirecting and revitalizing Congress activities in Latin America. In 1963 the Colombian writer German Arciniegas replaced Julian Gorkin as editor of *Cuadernos* and set out to attract younger writers and to open *Cuadernos*'s pages to debate and confrontation. But it proved impossible to overcome *Cuadernos*'s reputation as basically a magazine for aging Spanish émigrés. John Mander, after a tour of Latin America for *Encounter*, assured Josselson that "a majority of Latin American intellectuals" detested *Cuadernos*, confirming what Keith Botsford had also told him. Finally, after its hundredth issue, the Secretariat closed down *Cuadernos* and prepared to launch an entirely new magazine.

It was called *Mundo Nuevo*, and its founding editor was the Uruguayan literary critic Rodriguez Monegal, who had recently broken with the revolutionary "terceristas." Its first issue was in June 1966, a few weeks after the *New York Times* began the long controversy about the CIA's funding of the Congress. Monegal published "La C.I.A. y los intelectuales" in *Mundo Nuevo*, in which he pledged himself to the cause of "the independent writer" who will fight against "infiltration" by the CIA and who also accepts with equanimity the "slander and deceit" that is the price of independence.[27]

The new magazine quickly achieved a high standard, publishing fiction and criticism by established writers (Carlos Fuentes, Gabriel Garcia Marquez, Octavio Paz, and Mario Vargas Llosa) and poetry by young poets from all over the continent. (Each issue contained about ten new names.) It was also an "open" magazine, publishing such politically opposed writers as the Chilean Pablo Neruda and the Argentinian Jorge Luis Borges. While predominantly literary, it also published political articles, usually by such Congress writers as Leopold Labedz (on the Daniel–Sinyavsky case), François Fejto (on Cuba), and Richard Löwenthal (on Vietnam), but also by such Congress critics as Sartre. Two of its issues were banned in Argentina, and one was confiscated by the authorities in Brazil. By the time Monegal resigned in 1968 (he had insisted that *Mundo Nuevo* be edited in Paris, not in Latin America), it was becoming the sort of magazine that Michael Josselson had wanted, a magazine of *Fidelismo sin Fidel*. But by that time Josselson too had resigned, and the Congress had dissolved.

## China Quarterly, China Report, Informes de China

In August 1959 at the Lushan Conference of the Central Committee of the Chinese Communist Party, Minister of Defense Marshal Peng Teh-huai read out a memorandum bitterly attacking the "Great Leap Forward," in which some 20 million Chinese died. But despite important support for Peng, Mao survived the debate and Peng was arrested. A Lushan Resolution denounced "hostile elements within the country," and a campaign against "Right-wing opportunists" was launched. Peng, however, had had the support of the Kremlin, and the historic Sino-Soviet split, which had emerged with Khrushchev's "secret speech" against Stalinism, deepened.

There was no magazine in the world closely monitoring Chinese developments in the way in which *Soviet Survey* monitored the Soviet bloc. Leopold Labedz and Walter Laqueur, who had published a Chinese issue of *Soviet Survey* in 1958 and a pamphlet on the Chinese communes in 1959, discussed this void with Michael Josselson, who agreed that the Congress should fill it. Laqueur asked Roderick MacFarquhar, the London *Daily Telegraph*'s China specialist, who was editing a Congress-sponsored book on China, *The Hundred Flowers*, to edit it. He agreed, provided the magazine was a quarterly, not a monthly. *China Quarterly* then joined *Soviet Survey* in London's Summit House, Langham Place W1, and the first issue appeared in January 1960, editorially pledged to "rigorous and objective analysis" and featuring an appraisal of Communist China's first ten years by sinologists from around the world, ranging from C. P. Fitzgerald of Canberra to Karl A. Wittfogel of New York.

Its success from the start was due as much to the scholarly standard of its articles as to the fact that it then had no competitors. It occasionally published controversial exchanges, such as the 1960 dispute between Wittfogel and Benjamin Schwartz on Chinese history or the 1962 debate arising out of Joseph Alsop's "On China's Descending Spiral" (which also figured in debates in Peking). It sometimes ran newsworthy articles, such as "The Dismissal of Marshal Peng Teh-huai" by "David A. Charles" (the pseudonym of a China specialist with the British Government, who drew on covert East European sources). It also sponsored seminars (on Communist China's literature in 1962 and its historiography in 1964) and published several books, including *The Sino-Soviet Dispute* (1961) and *China Under Mao: Politics Takes Command* (1966), a selection of articles from *China Quarterly.*

*China Quarterly* remained apart from other Congress magazines, and there was little cross-fertilization (about which Josselson complained). It did not have the common Congress sense of commitment. It had, MacFarquhar said, no place in the political spectrum, and its pages and seminars were open to people ranging from a CIA sinologist to Owen Lattimore. If it often lacked "fight," its virtue in the 1960s was that it was "sober" and "balanced." Even Moscow's *Literary Gazette* called it "well informed."[28]

The Congress also filled sinological voids in India and Latin America. Marion Bieber reported to the Secretariat in 1961, after a visit to India, that "there are hardly any Indian experts on Soviet and Chinese affairs"[29] and no facilities for the study of them. Subsequently the Congress established the China Study Center in the Congress's Asian Bureau in New Delhi, and in December 1964 the first issue of *China Report,* edited by C. R. M. Rao, appeared. By its third issue it had become a bimonthly modeling itself in *China Quarterly,* although, with few Indian specialists to draw on, it was more journalistic in spirit. Finally, the Congress established *Informes de China* in Buenos Aires to serve Latin America.

### Minerva

Shils had seen the Hamburg Conference on Science and Freedom in 1953 as "an enormous success" not so much because of the high standard of the papers or the discussions—or because everyone enjoyed himself—but because it adumbrated the idea, still struggling toward clarity, of the autonomous scientific community in a pluralistic society. It was to advance this idea further that Shils in 1962 launched the quarterly *Minerva,* the last of the major journals to be founded under the auspices of the Congress.

Although not a natural scientist, Shils had long been involved in the affairs of the scientific community. He had participated in the scientists' movement for international control of the uses of atomic energy, had published the pamphlet *The Atomic Bomb in World Politics* for the National Peace Council in Britain in 1948, and had been a cofounder and member of the editorial board of the *Bulletin of the Atomic Scientists,* to which he was a frequent contributor on such issues as "the egregious wrongheadedness of our present visa policy" (he was the editor of a special double issue on the subject)[30] or the degradation of J. Robert Oppenheimer ("a heavy-handed stupid act of injustice").[31] In 1956 he published *The Torment of Secrecy,* which discussed the harm done to American science by overzealous security policies. He also served on the Congress's Committee for Science and Freedom.

For Shils the scientific community was one of the more important constituents of the wider international intellectual community that the Congress was attempting to build and to which no one was more committed than Shils himself. *Minerva* would be part of the institutionalization of this community. "The editor of *Minerva,*" he stated in an editorial in its first issue, "believes in the reality of the world-wide intellectual community and wishes *Minerva* to have a share in maintaining and strengthening that community"—a community that included creative scientists and scholars in Communist countries.

In particular *Minerva* chose as its subjects the issues that were only marginally dealt with in the existing journals of natural or social science: the problems arising from the increasing dependence of science and scholarship on government financial support; the expansion of universities everywhere, and the establishment of new ones in Asia and Africa; the selection of students for scientific careers; and threats to academic freedom. In later years new issues emerged: the politicization of universities; the reduced prestige of scientists; the utilitarianism of scientists; and the decay of the experience of contemplation. Each issue also published a "Chronicle" reporting university developments from Afghanistan to Zambia (for example, the dismissal of professors in Spain in 1965, the Knopfelmacher case in Australia in 1966, and the student riots in Japan in 1968).

Shils once described *Minerva* as "a work of artistry which no one looks at."[32] In fact it reached a circulation of two thousand in seventy-five countries, and more than any other Congress journal it both committed the Congress to high standards of scholarship and had "a share" in helping the universities (as Shils put it) to "hold on,"[33] to maintain civility in an uncivil period.

# 12

# *Liberal Hopes and Illusions in the "Underdeveloped" World*

I want to write on this theme when I get out [of prison]—on the need [for] and urgency of a continuing "liberal conspiracy."

RAJAT NEOGY, 1968[1]

How can there be international understanding without the binding link of international friendships?

BERTRAND DE JOUVENEL, 1964[2]

In our case a form of "democratic centralism" is a better method.

MICHAEL JOSSELSON, 1962[3]

## AFRICA

The Congress "discovered" Black Africa—the last major region in which it developed a program—in the late 1950s. There had been no Africans at its meetings before the 1955 Milan conference (which Chief Akintola of Nigeria and K. A. Busia of the then Gold Coast attended). But it was at the Milan Conference—held in the same year as the Bandung Conference attended by Kwame Nkrumah—that Michael Polanyi, speaking for the Congress, acknowl-

edged "the proud peoples of the ancient lands who are now coming into their own" in Africa (and Asia) and who opened up to
him "the exhilarating perspective . . . of this immense area of new
companionship." The pace soon quickened. In 1956 the World
Congress of African Writers and Artists met in Paris to proclaim
the values of *négritude*; in 1957 the Gold Coast attained independence as Ghana; and in 1958 the French African colonies voted
for independence, with the remaining British colonies soon to follow. (In 1958 too, the Soviet Union established an Africa desk in
its Foreign Ministry and began forming Communist Parties in the
various African states-to-be.) In 1960, "African Independence
Year," seventeen new African states were admitted to the United
Nations.

The Congress's African Program was inevitably tentative. The
problems for African liberals and democrats were obvious. Edward Shils, who was one of the most committed to the idea of
advancing "the possibility of a modern Africa which would be
alive, progressive, and decent," summed up the obstacles in an exchange with Elspeth Huxley that ran over several months in *Encounter* in 1961: African liberals are few in number; their countries
lack capital and technology; tribal loyalties weaken national coher-
ence and endanger the probity of the public services.

> Creative activity is slow in coming forth; traditionality, the
> preponderance of the aged and awe of ancestors, deadens the
> outward impulse. Their people have little civility; they are too
> submissive or too refractory in their relations with authority,
> and often excessively attracted by charismatic qualities in
> their leaders. Politicians find it too easy, in the face of the
> more intractable problems of economic growth, social welfare,
> educational development and administrative efficiency, to
> summon up the demons of tribalism, xenophobia,
> intolerance, revivalism, and demagogy.[4]

Nevertheless, the Congress had obligations both to beleaguered
African liberals who needed international support (including
thousands of young graduates now coming out of Western universities) and to the Congress's liberal values, which were held to be
"of universal validity": Their existence in Africa, Shils wrote,
"would make African societies better, even if practically no one
had been in their favor when they were initiated."[5] (Huxley's comment was that if practically no one was in favor of them, "they

would not last long.") To meet these obligations the Congress con-ducted its seminars and created a network of academic centers, li-braries, bookshops, galleries, magazines, and clubs, stretching across Africa from Ibadan and Brazzaville to Kampala and Nairobi.

It began in 1959, with an international seminar in Nigeria on representative government and public liberties in Africa. It was the first of its kind in Africa, a week-long conference in Ibadan with forty academics, politicians, lawyers, and journalists from both English-speaking and French-speaking Africa and from the United States, Israel, India, Britain, France, and West Germany. They included many who would be leaders of their countries after independence, including (briefly) Patrice Lumumba from the Bel-gian Congo. The main purpose of the conference was to challenge the ideal of a one-party state in Africa. But if the multiparty demo-crats won the argument in Ibadan, they did not prevail in Africa at large. In his introduction to the book that recorded the Ibadan Conference, *Africa: The Dynamics of Change,* published in 1963, K. A. B. Jones-Quartey of Ghana wrote that "since 1959 one-party governments have grown stronger than ever, and personal, press, and public liberties have been progressively and severely cur-tailed." These developments also made it harder and sometimes dangerous for the Congress to continue to be as openly political inside Africa as it had been in 1959. (Its next conference, dealing directly with African politics and entitled "Africa and the Soviet Bloc and China," with papers by Colin Legum, Ian Adie, Richard Löwenthal, and Walter Laqueur, was held in Uppsala, Sweden.)

The Congress nevertheless proceeded cautiously—emphasizing where possible nonpolitical themes—to develop its African Pro-gram, at first under Mercer Cook, a black American academic and diplomat, and later under Ezekiel Mphahlele, a South African writer. Late in 1959 it established an Institute of Congolese Stud-ies in Brazzaville to provide adult education classes in economics, history, constitutional law, and, later, music, theater, and film, for students from both sides of the Congo Pond and the Cameroons. In 1960 it held a seminar in Dakar, Senegal, on the needs of the press in Africa, and in 1961 a seminar in Freetown, Sierra Leone, on the needs of the universities. The first recommended establish-ing schools of journalism at the Universities of Dakar and Ibadan, and the second called for an association of West African universi-ties. (The Congress published a book on the Freetown seminar,

*The West African Intellectual Community*.) In 1961, the Congress sent
thirteen Africans to the Afro-Scandinavian Library Conference in
Copenhagen and announced a scholarship for training librarians.
(Amadou Mahtar M'Bow wrote a paper for the conference.) In
1963 it organized academics and writers in two seminars—one in
Freetown and one in Dakar—to promote (successfully) the inclu-
sion of courses in African literature at universities and schools.
(The Congress also published a book on these conferences, *African
Literature and the Universities*, in 1965.) In 1965 it organized an inter-
national seminar in Nairobi, Kenya, on "Economic Cooperation
in Africa."

The Congress also continued its forlorn campaign against the
one-party state, but mainly in meetings and publications outside
Africa. In 1961 it invited W. Arthur Lewis, the West Indian economist and at one time an adviser to Kwame Nkrumah, to tour West
Africa and prepare a monograph on the subject. He submitted his
report for discussion to a meeting in 1964 of a dozen specialists
at the Center of African Studies at Cambridge, and in 1965 he
published his report as *Politics in West Africa*. Writing in *Encounter*,
he argued:

> The single-party thus fails in all its claims. It cannot represent
> all the people; or maintain free discussion; or give stable
> government; or, above all, reconcile the differences between
> various regional groups. It is not natural to West African
> culture, except in the sense in which cancer is natural to man,
> since what would be natural in these countries would be two
> or three parties representing different regions. It is partly the
> product of the hysteria of the moment of independence,
> when some men found it possible to seize the state and
> suppress their opponents. It is a sickness from which West
> Africa deserves to recover.[6]

He called for the restoration of democracy and coalition governments, and he criticized those Western democrats who had given
up hope in Africa.

There were also frequent tours of Africa by other Congress figures, including Herbert Passin, Colin MacInnes, François Bondy,
Robie Macauley, and Melvin Lasky, who wrote *Africa for Beginners*,
a symbolic title since most of them were beginners. But it was discouraging work. The one-party state continued to spread and Congress associates to fall. Patrice Lumumba, in whom the Congress

had taken an interest because his Mouvement National Congolais looked beyond tribal ties, was murdered in 1961; Chief Akintola of Nigeria was assassinated in 1966; K. A. Busia remained exiled from Ghana until 1966 (and when he became Prime Minister some time after the fall of Nkrumah, his government was also over-thrown in a military coup, and he died in exile).

The Congress had for a time more success with its literary pro-gram, especially when it was able to collaborate with two existing and independent magazines and their circles. The first was Ulli Beier's *Black Orpheus* in Ibadan, Nigeria, and the second, Rajat Neogy's *Transition* in Kampala, Uganda. In April 1960 Michael Jos-selson wrote to Beier for advice. The Congress, he said, wanted to make a contribution to the celebrations of Nigerian independence in October 1960 and was considering a drama competition. Were there any good playwrights in Nigeria? Beier, thinking of Wole Soyinka's *A Dance of the Forest,* which he admired but which Nige-rian officials found too obscure, replied that indeed there were. Josselson invited Beier to Paris for further discussions, and the two men got on well together. (Beier attributed this to their common background in Weimar Berlin, "the cultural capital of the world.")[7] They agreed that *Encounter* should run the drama competition and that Stephen Spender, Ezekiel Mphahlele, and Beier should be the judges. Wole Soyinka's play duly won and was produced in Ibadan.

Ulli Beier now became a key figure. He was a characteristic Con-gress choice. A German Jew, born in 1922, he had migrated to Pal-estine, had been interned by the British, had settled in England, and after the war had become a teacher in Ibadan, Nigeria. His students were mainly adult Yorubas, whose language, art, music, and literature fascinated him. When he heard Aimé Césaire preach *négritude* at the World Conference of African Writers and Artists in Paris in 1956, he decided to devote himself to the promotion of African literature and art. A few months later he launched the magazine *Black Orpheus,* its title taken from Sartre's comparison of the black poet's search for identity with Orpheus's descent into Hades.

The magazine had two objectives. The first was "propaganda" (Beier's word) in support of African writers. (After early debates, *Black Orpheus* became a critic of *négritude.*) The second was to pub-lish African writers and artists from all parts of Africa and the Americas. Soyinka, Mphahlele, John Pepper Clark, Chinua

Achebe, Christopher Okigbo, Bloke Medisane, Dennis Brutus, Léopold Sedar Senghor, Aimé Césaire, and many others appeared in its pages. "What kept me going," he said later, "was simply the excitement of it."[8]

In response to a request from John Hunt for ideas for the Congress's African Program, Beier proposed that the Congress finance a club for Nigerian writers and artists. He found (in Ibadan) a rundown former Lebanese restaurant/nightclub with a concrete-paved courtyard (once used by the nightclub band), and the Congress agreed to pay the rent. This became the Mbari Club, a meeting place for the *Black Orpheus* and other African writers, a theater, a gallery, a library, and a publisher—the hub of the Nigerian "literary renaissance" and a Congress success, whose influence continued long after the club itself ceased to operate.

But the Congress also wanted a base in East Africa. A first step was taken in June 1962, when Ezekiel Mphahlele organized a Conference on African writers of English expression in Kampala. It was, once again, the first conference of its kind ever held in Africa, as forty-five writers, editors, critics, and publishers from East, West, and South Africa and from the Americas assembled at Makerere College for a week of discussion and readings. It achieved its purpose of breaking down the isolation of writers, creating a sense of community, and getting writers to know each other. Ngugi wa Thiong'o—then James Ngugi—attended the conference because he had long wanted to meet Chinua Achebe and Mphahlele and to get them to read his manuscript of a novel.

Ngugi said later that the absence of politics at the conference, the concentration on literary matters, was perhaps "a landmark in the cultural awakening of our continent."[9] However, a Nigerian critic, Obiajunwa Wali, detected "hidden politics" in the conference. He saw it as an expression of European cultural neocolonialism, an attempt to strengthen African literature in the English language. In an article (which Ngugi wa Thiong'o enthusiastically cited over more than twenty years later in Auckland, New Zealand) Wali claimed that the organizers of the conference had excluded the *négritude* school, all writers in tribal languages, and even writers in the nonliterary African-English vernacular, such as Amos Tutuola.[10] It promoted, he wrote, a literature without "blood and stamina," such as Wole Soyinka's prize-winning play for Nigerian independence, *Dance of the Forest,* which, he said, was understood by "less than one per cent of the Nigerian people." Those writers and "their Western midwives" would have to accept the fact that "any true African literature must be written in African languages"—Yoruba, Housa, Swahili, Kikuyu, Shona, and so on.

Since the Congress's objective had been to help create an international community, its main support would inevitably go to writers in the international, not the tribal, languages. As to the particular writers it promoted (Soyinka, Achebe), Ngugi wa Thiong'o himself said (in his Auckland lecture): "Who can deny their talent?" Wali was also wrong to call the socializing, getting-to-know-other-writers aspect of the conference its "only concrete achievement." It had also brought about the Congress's financing of Rajat Neogy's Kampala-based literary magazine *Transition,* a fruitful and fateful association.

The Congress now had a lively and sometimes brilliant presence in East Africa. It attempted to develop it further in 1963, when Mphahlele set up in Nairobi the Chemchemi (Swahili for "fountain") Creative Center to encourage new writers, on the model of Beier's Nigerian Mbari Club. This completed a Congress network across black Africa.

Then it all collapsed. The first to go was the Institute of Congolese Studies in Brazzaville. (Although situated in the French Congo, it served the former Belgian Congo, where civil war destroyed its hopes.) Then the Mbari Club, already divided, broke up in the Nigerian civil war. Ulli Beier left Ibadan in 1966. Christopher Okigbo was killed in the civil war. Chinua Achebe joined the Biafrans. Wole Soyinka was imprisoned. Ezekiel Mphahlele left Nairobi in 1966, and the Chemchemi Center folded through lack of interest.[11] *Transition* lasted the longest, but in 1968 Neogy and two of his contributors were arrested and imprisoned for several months by the Obote government and charged with sedition. (It survived for a short while in Prime Minister K. A. Busia's Ghana.) Josselson later referred to "our sad experience in Ibadan and Brazzaville," and he could have added Kampala and Nairobi.

## LATIN AMERICA

When the Congress Secretariat reassessed its program in Latin America in the late 1950s and early 1960s, it was clear that it had failed and that its cultural-intellectual network aiming at the climate of opinion was no match for the *fidelistas* aiming at revolutionary power. The national committees, from Mexico City to Buenos Aires, had not taken root. In Uruguay, Brazil, and Peru they had practically ceased to exist. Elsewhere anti-Communist activists had little appeal to the young. A new policy was obviously called for. The Secretariat decided to close down the remaining committees and try to replace them, again, with "centers of intellectual ferment" that would not so much defend cultural freedom as practice it. It would also make another attempt to reach the radical young and the non-Communist Left (in accordance with Michael Josselson's slogan, *Fidelismo sin Fidel*, revolution without dictatorship). In 1962 it sent Keith Botsford to Brazil and Luis Mercier Vega to Uruguay, the former to concentrate on writers, the latter on social scientists, and both to work together.

Keith Botsford (born in 1928), editor, critic, and novelist, who had just published *Benvenuto*, based on Mussolini's last days, had the harder task. A *yanqui* and a *gringo*, he was now working in an alien literary culture. No one in Latin America, he wrote to John Hunt, knew how to *read*.[12] People "do not grasp that Meaning applies to them, personally, directly." (A good editor, he said, would have to challenge his contributors' every word at every moment.) Further, almost no one in Brazil understood totalitarianism (and almost everyone disliked anyone who did—for example, Stefan Baciu, the Rumanian poet who was a Congress representative in Brazil). Botsford also told Hunt that Brazilian intellectuals regarded the Congress luminaries as *yanqui* fronts, and a bit old-hat besides. In these circumstances he suggested that the Congress become more discreet, modest, and "invisible," and support only those projects that had strong local support. But John Hunt entirely rejected this approach. "All over the world," he wrote to Botsford, "the problem is to push, push and push again."[13]

So Botsford pushed on in Brazil. He reorganized the Portuguese-language magazine *Cadernos Brasileiros,* circulated the news service *Informativo,* established a center for art exhibitions and study groups, and arranged lecture tours by Aron, Spender, Silone, Jelenski, David Rousset, Robert Lowell,[14] and Beier (who met the Yoruba artists in Brazil). After eighteen months Botsford left for Mexico, still dissatisfied with the Congress presence in Brazil.

In Mexico the prospects also appeared poor. The Paris Secretariat had withdrawn support from the Mexican Committee in 1962, and its former director, Rodrigo Garcia Trevino, now openly attacked the Congress for Cultural Freedom as a collection of fellow-travelers. The Secretariat had also tried to organize a group of *amigos de Cuadernos* as a replacement for the Mexican Committee, but (according to Botsford) "*Cuadernos* had very few friends" and "a large number of enemies."[15] The Congress's "natural allies" in Mexico, Botsford wrote to Hunt, were the writers associated with *Revista Mexicana de Literatura,* started by Octavio Paz and Carlos Fuentes, but they disliked *Cuadernos* so much that they refused to publish an advertisement for it. Botsford's recommendation was to form no Congress organization in Mexico, although he believed that since the government was the sole patron of the arts in Mexico, the Congress could discreetly offer an alternative sponsorship.

Finally, after eighteen months, Botsford gave up: He found "the sinister totem-Stalinism in that most subtly totalitarian of states so intolerable" that he drove, flat-out for twenty hours, north to Laredo, Texas, and "practically kissed the chiliburger-littered macadam of the Customs shed."[16]

Luis Mercier Vega, working largely with social scientists in Montevideo, had more success. Mercier was a Spaniard who had fought with the anarchists in Buenaventura Durutti's column on the Aragon front in the Spanish Civil War. He was one of those who considered the anarchists' decision to join the Communists in the Spanish Republic Government "a tragic error," and he continued to regard Communists (who had murdered Durutti) as part of "the counterrevolution."[17] After some years in Latin America he settled in France, working as a journalist and helping to develop the Force ouvrière and Les Amis de la Liberté.

Building on the ruins of the defunct Uruguayan Committee, Mercier found three helpful collaborators: Benito Milla, a Spanish bookseller and publisher who agreed to run a Congress office and publish *Temas,* a regional bimonthly magazine; Aldo Solari, a professor of sociology who agreed to run study groups; and Emir Rodriguez Monegal, a literary critic and a former *tercerista* of the neutralist "generation of 1945," who agreed to edit a new pancontinental Congress magazine. Mercier also arranged a series of study groups on social issues in other Latin American centers, and out of these came, first, a major international seminar in Montevideo in 1965 on the problems of developing modernizing elites in Latin America, organized by Solari of Uruguay and Seymour Martin Lipset of the United States,[18] and next, the establishment in January 1966 of the Latin American Institute of International

Relations (ILARI), an independent body, which took over the work of the Congress.

The ILARI had an International Advisory Council of social scientists and historians, its own statutes and legal status, and seven national centers—in Argentina, Bolivia, Brazil, Chile, Paraguay, Peru, and Uruguay (but not Mexico). Its basic work was social research and the publication of books and magazines, including *Aportes,* a social sciences quarterly edited by Luis Mercier. In a period torn between *fidelista* revolutionism and military dictatorships, this group did what it could to develop liberal elites and democratic cadres in Latin America.

## INDONESIA

By 1957 the Congress's early associates in Indonesia were in prison or exile, and Congress activity in the "guided democracy" took on something of the character of the *lutte secrète, intense et constante* that Nicolas Nabokov had described in the Congress meeting in Brussels in 1950 when referring to work behind the Iron Curtain. The novelists and editors Mochtar Lubis and S. Takdir Alisjahbana had both attended the Congress's Rangoon conference in 1955, but in 1956 Mochtar Lubis was arrested, and from 1957 on Takdir Alisjahbana found it prudent to remain abroad. The economist D. Sumitro had attended the Tokyo conference on economic growth in 1957 but, on his return to Indonesia, fled Djakarta to join the rebellion in Sumatra and, after its defeat, remained abroad. The Congress sent messages to the Sukarno government protesting against the harassment of Mochtar Lubis and Takdir Alisjahbana, but in a society increasingly in the grip (in Herbert Lüthy's words) "of a collective psychosis controlled by a charismatic leader,"[19] the protests were ineffective. There was "no chance" (as Takdir Alisjahbana told the Executive Committee in 1958) of creating a formal Congress organization in Indonesia.

In these circumstances, and under the direction of the Paris Secretariat's Ivan Kats, the Congress adapted its East European formula to Indonesia and its demoralized intellectuals. It sent books and magazines to more than a hundred intellectuals, including the poet W. S. Rendra, the lawyer and journalist P. K. Auwjong, the writer Gunawan Mohammad, the art critic Soe Hok Djin, and the poet Taufiq Ismail. It also sent thousands of otherwise

unobtainable books to twenty libraries. When it became clear that
the Indonesian authorities were sabotaging a Dutch scholarship
scheme, the Congress arranged its own scholarships for, among
others, the journalists Gunawan Mohammad and Arief Budiman.
It acted as a literary agent, sponsoring the translation into English
of Mochtar Lubis's novel *Twilight in Djakarta,* which he wrote in
prison. When it still could, it brought Indonesians to international
conferences, where they were able to renew their contacts with
the world: Soedjatmoko delivered the keynote paper at a Congress
conference in Manila in 1963 on "Religion and Progress in Modern Asia," which, often in Aesopian language, discussed the real
problems of the Third World.[20]

The Congress, in other words, did what it could to keep a sense
of liberal humanism alive in the Indonesian dictatorship and to
try to break down the isolation of its intellectuals. Its influence
was apparent in the "Cultural Manifesto" of August 1963, which,
signed by a thousand intellectuals, asserted the independence of
writers against the demands of both Nationalists and Communists.
(Publication of the Manifesto was banned, and its principal pro-
tagonist, H. B. Jassin, was forced to apologize abjectly to President
Sukarno.) When, after the failure of the Communist *coup* in 1965
(and for some time after the Army's slaughter of up to a million
Communists), Indonesia at last returned to a sort of normalcy
and stability, Mochtar Lubis and other prisoners were released,
Sumitro and other exiles returned, and the "Generation of '66"
had its chance to rebuild Indonesia.[21]

Similar programs were developed in other dictatorships in Asia,
particularly South Korea and Thailand, and in the Middle East.

# 13

# *Reaching Behind the Iron Curtain*

B ut coming to the specific case of having cultural
exchange with the Soviet Union and the East
European countries, my dilemma is that we betray
culture if we have such relations but we also betray it if
we refuse to have them. Those of us involved . . . are
faced with the morally uncomfortable situation of having
to entertain, meet, and be kind to a lot of hacks and
bureaucrats if we want to get through to the really
valuable and independent-minded people. . . . So one has
to meet the apparatchiks, including often sinister people,
and one has a tongue-in-cheek relationship with them.
They will be very genial, they will joke with you and even
give you subtly to understand that they too know
perfectly well the nature of the game you are playing.
There is double-talk on both sides.
   . . . But on the other hand, if—out of a sense of
integrity and solidarity with the persecuted writers and
intellectuals—you refuse to let yourself in for this game,
then you may not reach these persecuted or isolated
people at all.

FRANÇOIS BONDY, 1976[1]

Despite "the impossible dialogue" that had concluded the Congress's first attempts to reach Eastern bloc intellectuals in the hope

of advancing "liberalization," it resumed those attempts in the late 1950s. It had its best success in Poland and its greatest disappointment, despite persistent efforts, in Russia.

Even at the height of the controversy over the Hungarian Revolution, the Congress kept up its rapprochement with the Polish Writers Union. When the Union held its annual congress in late November 1956, *Encounter* sent a telegram of greetings, signed by more than twenty leading British writers of its circle, from Kingsley Amis to Leonard Woolf. *Preuves* also sent a letter signed by more than thirty of its circle, from Aron to Sperber. The *Encounter* message looked forward to "fruitful collaboration," that of *Preuves* to an "enriching confrontation." Similar messages were sent from *Tempo Presente, Cuadernos,* and *Perspektiv.* (In fact the *only* foreign messages received—other than those from the writers' unions of the Soviet Union and North Korea—were from the Congress groups.)

In April 1957 *Preuves* published a special Polish issue, in cooperation with the Polish Writers Union. It included contributions from younger writers (such as Marek Hlasko, whose work had been attacked by both the Communist Party and the Church) as well as from such established authors as Maria Dabrowska, Antoni Slonimski, Aleksandr Wat, and Jerzy Andrzejewski. (Czeslaw Milosz, who had lampooned Andrzejewski as "Alpha the Moralist" in *The Captive Mind,* contributed to the issue.) *Encounter* also agreed in 1957 to exchange articles with the proposed new Polish magazine *Europa,* but the plan collapsed late in 1957, when the Polish authorities withdrew *Europa*'s license to publish and banned its first issue, already in page proofs. *Po Prostu* was also banned, and Polish censorship and controls were gradually reimposed, although never as completely as before October 1956.

It was in this context of oscillating liberalization and restriction that K. A. Jelenski administered the Congress's Central European program, with its aim of strengthening Western values behind the Iron Curtain and of continuing what *Preuves* and *Encounter* had tried to do in the cause of "the thaw." It required judicious administration in order not to compromise the beneficiaries, but the Polish Jelenski understood the complexities of Poland, where, he remarked, atheists wrote for Catholic publications and were blessed by a Cardinal, where former fascists had become Communist propagandists and former Christians Maoists, and where Jewish Stalinists supported Colonel Nasser's crusade against Israel.

Some years later Jelenski illustrated this Polish situation by describing the funeral of the writer Maria Dabrowska. Dabrowska was a Left-wing atheist, condemned by the Polish Catholic Church, who refused to publish during the Stalinist period (although the Communist Party "annexed" her prewar books). In 1956 she was a leader of the liberal opposition, and in 1964 she was one of the thirty-four writers who signed a famous letter to the government condemning censorship. When she died in 1965, she asked in her will for a Catholic funeral in Warsaw Cathedral, as an act of homage to the thousand years of Christian tradition in Poland and as a tribute to the memory of Pope John XXIII. Despite opposition from the regime, the Cathedral held the funeral service, and several thousand attended. Her coffin was carried by Adam Wazyk, Pawel Hertz, Jan Kott, and Juliusz Zulawski—all avowed atheists, all prewar Communists who had left the Party in 1957, the first three Jewish. A regime propagandist who had been a fascist before the war was heard to comment to a neighbor: "They have stolen her from *us,* those Jews."[2]

One of the Congress's activities was to donate books and magazines to individuals and libraries. They were in four languages (English, French, German, and Italian) and all humanist disciplines. *Only* those publications requested—and every title requested, no matter how obnoxious to the Congress—were sent. (In some cases Communist books, in Western editions, were sent.) No spectacular results were expected, only to help maintain Western values, although Jelenski also belived that, by almost entirely creating the libraries in two sociological institutes, the Congress contributed significantly to the revival of Polish sociology. (One of those institutes—at Lodz—was abolished in 1959, and its head, Professor Chalasinski, dismissed.) The program was later extended to Hungary, Rumania, and Lithuania, and it became the Congress's regular method of entry in the dictatorships around the world.

Other elements in the Congress's Central European program included relieving intellectuals of financial problems (without informing the beneficiaries about the source of the relief); helping banned writers to find publishers in the West; helping *Kultura* publish books in Polish; running an East German Refugee Center in Berlin (on the pattern of the earlier one for Hungarian refugees in Vienna); subsidizing exhibitions of abstract artists at the Galérie Lambert in Paris; and publishing an anthology of Polish poetry edited by Jelenski.

The Congress also granted stipends to Polish writers, scholars, and artists and financed visits abroad (often remaining the anonymous donor and arranging for institutes or festivals to issue the invitations). Regarding such visits to the West, Leopold Labedz wrote: "One can hardly overestimate the effect of these intellectual peregrinations on the mental make-up of the Polish elite, in extending their knowledge, widening their horizons, and contributing to their *polish*—le mot juste—and sophistication."[3]

But despite successes in Poland (and to a lesser extent in Hungary) the Congress usually met a stone wall in the U.S.S.R. *Survey* and the other publications (including *Forum Service*), kept Congress circles well informed about Soviet developments, and the Congress magazines regularly published dissident Soviet writers, but its repeated attempts to establish continuing, direct contact with Russian intellectuals failed.

At an official press conference for Mikhail Sholokhov at the Soviet Embassy in London in April 1959, Melvin Lasky and Labedz raised the possibility of resuming the East–West meetings of editors and writers, on the pattern of the Zürich meeting of 1956. Sholokhov tentatively agreed in principle, and Khrushchev's speech on the importance of tolerance (at the Third Writers Conference in May 1959) encouraged further hopes. Spender and Lasky again raised the idea with K. A. Fedin and A. T. Tvardovsky in London in 1960, and this time they all agreed to have a small, informal private seminar of writers in Russia, England, or elsewhere in 1961. Fedin and Tvardovsky even mentioned the proposal ("this excellent initiative") in a friendly article in the Moscow *Literaturnaya Gazeta* (which *Encounter* reprinted): "Our young [Russian] writers could, without undue haste, prepare themselves for the seminar in the course of the next twelve months."[4] But there was in fact to be no such writers' seminar.

The propsal that *Encounter* and *Novy Mir* exchange articles, also enthusiastically agreed to by Tvardovsky, Fedin, Spender, and Lasky at their London meeting, came to the same dead end. "Dear Colleagues Fedin and Tvardovsky," Spender and Lasky had written, summarizing their agreement:

> Our proposal . . . for our first Editorial Exchange between *Novy Mir* and *Encounter* consists of the following . . . 1. An article by a leading Soviet critic (possibly an editor of *Novy Mir* or a frequent contributor to its pages) on the subject:

"Some Western Misunderstandings of the Nature and Evaluation of Russian and Soviet Literature" . . . 2. An article by a leading English critic on "Some Soviet Misunderstandings . . . "

The articles would appear simultaneously, possibly in December 1960. (Tvardovsky questioned Lasky in detail about *Encounter*'s printing schedules and deadlines.) "May our proposals," the letter concluded, "for cooperation and exchange go forward in the same spirit of confidence, friendship and intellectual eagerness!"[5] In fact no such articles appeared and no such exchange took place (although Tvardovsky permitted *Encounter* to publish Dudintsev's anti-Stalinist "A New Year's Fable" from *Novy Mir*).

The Congress succeeded in arranging one East–West meeting of scholars in 1960, but it was no breach of Soviet cultural defenses. In 1958 Nicolas Nabokov, on the suggestion of Leo Tolstoy's grandson, had proposed a conference to commemorate the fiftieth anniversary of the death of Tolstoy. Otherwise, he said, there would be no Western alternative to the forthcoming Tolstoy Festival in Moscow, which would present Tolstoy as a precursor of Bolshevism. The Congress adopted the proposal and decided to invite—directly, not through official Soviet channels—some sixteen Soviet scholars. It set up a sponsoring committee (including E. M. Forster, Salvador de Madariaga, Jacques Maritain, J. B. Priestley, Guido Piovene, Ignazio Silone, and Victoria Ocampo), commissioned papers (from Edmund Wilson, Karl Jaspers, Isaiah Berlin, George Kennan, and Jayaprakash Narayan), and selected the Venetian island of San Giorgio, one of Byron's favorites, as the venue. Finally, in June 1960, scores of prominent writers and scholars (including Alberto Moravia, Franco Venturi, Herbert Read, Iris Murdoch, John Dos Passos, and Raja Rao) assembled on the island. To his irritation and despite his interest, Arthur Koestler was not invited, lest foreknowledge of his presence deter Soviet cooperation.

But none of the invited sixteen Russians came! (One sent a message.) Instead, the Soviet authorities sent four of their own selection: Vladimir Yermilov, famed for his harassment of Vladimir Mayakovsky and for his role as a police informer; Georgy Markov, a neo-Stalinist secretary of the Executive Committee of the Union of Soviet Writers in the style of the notorious Fadeyev; Nikolai Gudzy, an old Tolstoy scholar; and an "interpreter." As expected, they presented Tolstoy as a precursor of the Bolshevik Revolution. Nabokov found Yermilov to be "an odious SOB ... a nasty little party hack,"[6] and Don Salvador de Madariaga complained to Josselson: "As a man who has made it a point of honour to have nothing to do with the thugs of Moscow, I felt unhappy discovering that we were to sit round the same table with a resigned historian of officially communist views, a Stalinist professor without prestige, and two men who either are NKVD agents or looked the part remarkably well."[7] The conference's attempt to make contact with independent Russian intellectuals failed: The dialogue was still "impossible," as it had been after Silone's Zürich conference.

The Congress never entirely abandoned the hope of reaching "liberal" or dissident Russian intellectuals, but there were no more East–West conferences with Russians during the life of the Congress. Beyond providing hospitality from time to time to Russian writers visiting the West (for example, K. G. Paustovsky, V. Nekrasov and A. Vozesensky), its main breakthrough came in 1962, when it was able to send the American critic and journalist Patricia Blake (who had been married to Nicolas Nabokov) to Moscow for two months to meet Russian writers and prepare an anthology of their work. This was in the period when the "liberals" had triumphed in the debate on the literary situation at the Twenty-second CPSU Congress in October 1961, when *Novy Mir* had published Solzhenitsyn's *One Day in the Life of Ivan Denisovich,* and when (shortly before Patricia Blake's visit) 14,000 people had gathered in a sports stadium to hear Akhmadulina, Voznesensky, and Boris Slutsky read their poetry. Blake attended another meeting where seven hundred cheering students filled an auditorium to hear Voznesensky, Bulat Okudzhava, and Yevtushenko read their works for six electrifying hours. (The crowd made Yevtushenko read *Babi Yar,* his attack on Russian anti-Semitism, five times.) After the reading, Yevtushenko took Patricia Blake to an actors' restaurant for supper:

> I had never seen anything like it in Moscow before. Pretty girls with beehive hairdos and green eyelids, wearing fuzzy sweaters over short pleated skirts, went from table to table greeting friends. At one table a group of young actors in over-tailored, over-tight suits were singing *Blue Suede Shoes* in something like English. It could have been a hip Greenwich Village nightclub.[8]

She met most of the writers she wanted to meet, got their ready agreement to her publishing their work in London, and with Max Hayward prepared her anthologies—a smaller one for *Encounter* and a larger one for the *Encounter* book *Halfway to the Moon.* The anthologies, with her lively introductions, introduced thousands of readers to the new Russian literature. But the *Encounter* issue was attacked at the Writers' Union in Moscow, and even before it appeared, Khrushchev in a 15,000-word speech (which *Encounter* published in full as a pamphlet) had declared that in the future any deviation from socialist realism would be considered an anti-Communist act. The thaw froze again. When Herbert Lüthy suggested in *Encounter,* in June 1963, that the West should abandon "the sterile polemics of the cold war"[9] and be more open-minded in meetings with the Soviets, S. Smirnov wrote in *Pravda* denouncing both Lüthy ("imperialist propagandist") and *Encounter* ("the NATO mouthpiece in England).[10] In the same year the KGB arrested and framed, Frederick C. Barghoorn, the head of the Department of Russian Studies at Yale (in circumstances similar to the arrest of the American reporter Nicholas Daniloff in 1986). In 1964 the promising but then unpublished young Russian poet Josef Brodsky was arrested and sentenced to five years' hard labor. (*Encounter* in September 1964 published a smuggled transcript of his trial.) When Khrushchev himself was overthrown later in 1964, the freeze deepened, and dissidents were imprisoned, confined to psychiatric hospitals, exiled, or deported.

There was little hope of "dialogue" in this situation. In any case, by the time Yuli Daniel and Andrei Sinyavsky were arrested in September 1965, the impending exposure in the *New York Times* of the CIA funding of the Congress handicapped it in offering that "moral and material" support it had so firmly pledged in June 1950 in Berlin. In the circumstances the Secretariat thought it prudent to keep the Congress's name out of the protests, although Nicolas Nabokov and John Hunt urged Congress associates around the world to write as individuals to the Kremlin. It was Leopold Labedz of *Survey* and his friends, with the help of International PEN (and its General Secretary, David Carver) and the publisher Collins (headed by Mark Bonham Carter)—but with little help from the beleaguered Paris Secretariat—who largely organized the great and portentous movement of protest at the trial and punishment of Daniel and Sinyavsky.

# 14

# *A Black Operation?*

✑

It was in the orthodox terminology, a black operation—
that is to say, an operation that is conducted through
cut-outs.

WILLIAM F. BUCKLEY, 1967[1]

There is also the question whether these operations were
allowed to drag on, with their flimsy cover arrangements,
past their need or usefulness. (Some years ago, the
initiator of these operations, now dead, surveying their
flourishing growth, remarked sadly, "And to think that we
set these up as emergency operations.")

"CHRISTOPHER FELIX (James McCarger)," 1967[2]

I would have served the CIA (had I known of its
existence) in the years following the war, with pleasure.

MICHAEL POLANYI, 1967[3]

In August 1964 the *New York Times* published a report that in the
course of a congressional inquiry into the taxation of private foundations, Representative Wright Patman had happened on the information that a number of foundations (the "Patman Eight") had
received funds from the CIA. Discussing the report editorially in
its issue dated September 14, 1964, the New York Leftist weekly
*The Nation* asked:

> [S]hould the CIA be permitted to channel funds to magazines
> in London—and New York—which pose as "magazines of

219

opinion" and are in competition with independent journals of opinion? Is it proper for CIA-supported magazines to offer large sums in payment of single poems by East European and Russian poets regarded as men of a character who might be encouraged to defect by what, in the context, could be regarded as a bribe? Is it a "legitimate" function of the CIA to finance, indirectly, variously congresses, conventions, assemblies and conferences devoted to "cultural freedom" and kindred topics?

A year later the *New York Times* ordered a team of reporters to spend several months investigating the CIA and its activities around the world.

Michael Josselson was now aware that exposure of the Congress's links with the CIA was inevitable and that what had seemed necessary and desirable in 1950 or 1951 would be presented as sinister in the 1960s. When the Congress had decided to continue its activities after the Berlin meeting in 1950, it had no reliable source of funds and no hope of getting adequate funds from the State Department, or (being basically Left of center) from the U.S. Congress or private foundations. The CIA had the obvious answer, and for Allen Dulles, Frank Wisner, Thomas Braden, and others in the CIA the Congress for Cultural Freedom was precisely the sort of organization they were looking for, a group of committed anti-Communist liberals and Leftists of clear integrity. It was also necessary to keep the arrangement secret, since otherwise European intellectuals would refuse to cooperate with the Congress. As Raymond Aron put it later: "The Congress could only accomplish its task—and it did accomplish it—by camouflage or, if one wishes, the lie of omission." Aron also noted, as did Sidney Hook, a culpable incuriosity about funding in Congress circles.[4]

Thus, "a major fault" (in Michael Josselson's own words) was built into the organization of the Congress. In fact the fault lay less in the initial CIA funding—the early postwar years were an "emergency"—than in allowing it to continue until 1966. After the early years it would surely have been possible to find other sources of funds: The Rockefeller Foundation had made possible the Hamburg Congress on Science and Freedom, and the Ford Foundation had funded the seminar program after 1956. If it had not been possible to find other sources of funds, it could be said in hindsight that it would have been better to have reduced the Congress's range of activities. In 1967 Arthur M. Schlesinger, Jr., wrote: "I admit my own error in not trying to do something more specific about the problem"[5] when he was in the John Kennedy White House. Referring to an analogous link between the CIA and the U.S. National Students' Association, Cord Meyer, Jr., also wrote in his 1980 book, *Facing Reality*: "I blame myself for that mistake in judgment," that is, for not having stopped the CIA funding before it was "exposed" in the media.

But the inevitable and pending exposure was a shadow over the last years of the Congress, even sometimes silencing it altogether (as in the case of Andrei Sinyavsky and Yuli Daniel). It also handicapped it in other ways: Jelenski wrote that Josselson had refused further help to *Kultura* through fear of the consequences for it when disclosure came.[6] In his hopes of limiting any damage, Josselson found himself in a race between reorganizing the Congress and the coming exposures. He considered changing the Congress's name. He renewed attempts to have the Congress entirely funded by the Ford Foundation and to cut the financial link with the CIA. He urged the magazines to separate from the Congress and find independent funding, as *Encounter* and *Forum* did in 1963. He also wanted to reorganize Congress activities in regional institutes, which would be independent, have their own boards and statutes, and be entirely funded by private foundations. (The Latin American Institute of International Relations, established in January 1966, was an example.)

But above all Josselson attempted to direct the Congress away from its Cold War perspective and to minimize the plausibility of any suggestion that the Congress was a tool of the U.S. Government in this Cold War—even if this caused some confusion and a sense of "a lack of focus." It was not a complete reversal, since the Congress continued for a time to organize protests against Soviet bloc infringements of cultural freedom (against Polish censorship in 1964, for example, and in support of Josef Brodsky in 1964). But Josselson told the Executive Committee at its meeting in London in October 1964: "I frankly wouldn't like to see the Congress's *raison d'être* to be the Cold War. I somewhat get the feeling that this is its *raison d'être*, and, frankly, I don't like it."[7] He stressed Congress activities that were not Cold War–like, such as the African Program, Pierre Emmanuel's series of seminars on writers, and the new magazines of the 1960s—*Minerva, Censorship, Mundo Nuevo,* and *Hiwar*. He closed down *Cuadernos* and sold *Forum Service* to a company in London called Forum World Service (closing down its French equivalent, *Preuves-Informations*). Needless to say, he objected to having a CIA specialist attend a seminar organized by the *China Quarterly.* During the Vietnam War, Josselson approved the antiwar positions of Galbraith, Schlesinger, and Richard Löwenthal, and disagreed with the Indian and Australian associates of the Congress who supported the U.S. commitment to save South Vietnam from Communism. Although he reluctantly agreed to subsidize the publication of a symposium on Vietnam produced by the Australian Association for Cultural Freedom, he wrote to its Secretary, Richard Krygier, in May 1967: "There is no point in our pursuing this correspondence because there is an unbridgeable gulf between you and me on this question. . . . I agree with Senator McGovern that our deepening military involvement in Vietnam is the most regrettable diplomatic, political, and moral failure in our national history."[8]

The *New York Times* series of articles on the CIA prepared by its team of reporters over seven months, appeared in April 1966. Harrison E. Salisbury, in the book *Without Fear or Favor* (1980), described how James Angleton of the CIA, Ambassador Charles Bohlen, and Secretary of State Dean Rusk tried without success to persuade the *New York Times* to abandon the story. In a compromise the *New York Times* agreed to submit its five articles, each between three thousand and four thousand words, to the Director of the CIA, John A. McCone, for his comments. McCone read the articles and made many suggestions, some of which were accepted. One not accepted was that references to the CIA's links with the Congress for Cultural Freedom and to the origins of *Encounter* be deleted. Consequently on April 27, 1966, the *New York Times* published its third article in the series with these paragraphs:

> Through similar channels, the C.I.A. has supported groups of exiles from Cuba and refugees from Communism in Europe or anti-Communist but liberal organizations of intellectuals such as the Congress for Cultural Freedom and some of their newspapers and magazines.
>     *Encounter* magazine, a well-known anti-Communist intellectual monthly with editions in Spanish and German [sic], as well as in English, was for a long time—though it is not now—one of the indirect beneficiaries of C.I.A. funds

through arrangements that have never been publicly explained. Several American book publishers have also received C.I.A. subsidies.

The article caused outrage in the Middle East; the Beirut police questioned the editor of the Congress magazine *Hiwar*, and a Cairo newspaper called for the "liquidation" of all Congress centers. In New Delhi the Parliament debated the matter, and in Manila the editor of the Congress-supported *Solidarity*, who was defamed as "a CIA agent" in one newspaper, wrote that "we will not be using the CCF name for a long time."[9] But in the West the reaction at this stage was calmer, and Josselson still hoped to survive the crisis. Nicolas Nabokov distributed a statement that the Congress "has never knowingly received support, directly or indirectly, from any secret source." Galbraith, Kennan, Oppenheimer, and Schlesinger wrote to the *New York Times* that "we can say categorically that we have no question regarding the independence of [the Congress's] policy, the integrity of its officials or the value of its contribution,"[10] and many others publicly expressed their agreement with the letter, including W. H. Auden, Daniel Bell, Leslie Fiedler, Hook, Lipset, Mary McCarthy, Yehudi Menuhin, and Lionel Trilling. When Kristol, Lasky, and Spender also wrote to the *New York Times* ("We know of no 'indirect' benefactions"; *Encounter*'s contributors "write as they please"), the *Times* added an editorial note to their letter: "*Encounter* is known as a distinguished journal of independent opinion,"[11] which led some European publications (the Copenhagen *Information* and the Hamburg *Stern*), which had rewritten the *New York Times*'s articles in a libelous way, to publish apologies. (The London *Times*'s original report had omitted the reference to *Encounter*.)

The Congress referred the *New York Times* article to its New York attorneys, Palmer, Serles, Delaney, Shaw & Pomeroy, who recommended that no action for libel should be brought, and there the matter rested for the moment, although Conor Cruise O'Brien attempted to reopen the issue with a lecture (published in *Book Week* and distributed to delegates at a PEN Congress in New York in July 1966) in which he described *Encounter* as published "in the interests—and as it now appears at the expense—of the power structure in Washington." O'Brien also sued the publishers of *Encounter* after Goronwy Rees ridiculed the lecture, and the matter then became *sub judice*.

The episode made even more urgent the negotiations between the Congress and the Ford Foundation over future funding of the Congress. In August 1966 James A. Perkins, the President of Cornell University and Chairman of President Johnson's General Advisory Committee on the U.S. Foreign Assistance Program, spent some days in Paris assessing the Congress, its staff, and its programs. He then prepared a memorandum for the Ford Foundation (now under the Presidency of McGeorge Bundy, who had until recently been Special Assistant to President Lyndon Johnson for National Security Affairs) on the prospects of the Congress in the light of the *New York Times* article. He found the program to be "unfocussed" ("one has the impression of able people struggling with a redefinition of their collective tasks"). He observed a "disintegration of leadership" ("Michael Josselson is still the mainspring but he is not well"), made worse by "the soul-wrenching problem of finance" ("it is difficult to imagine the bitter resentment that may arise if ever the financial facts of life are widely understood"). He continued:

> The summary fact is that the Congress still would seem to be an important organization, led by absolutely first-class people and directed at a matter of vital importance for the future of the free world. The question will have to be whether or not the Congress can be strengthened and survive, or whether it would be better to allow it to disappear and create a new structure. It is hard to believe that some structure like the Congress is not badly needed on the current world scene.

Phasing out the Congress would be the easiest decision, Perkins wrote, but the emphasis in his memorandum was on strengthening the Congress by finding new programs, new leadership, and new funding. To meet an annual Congress budget of $1.5 million, $1 million would have to come from the United States and $500,000 from elsewhere.

> Ford Foundation would have to be willing to put up three-quarters of a million a year for the next decade, if this venture were to have any prospects. . . . When all is said and done, a three-way ploy of leadership, program, and finance will have to be initiated by someone. At this writing, the current leadership of the Congress may not be up to it. The tough question will be whether the Ford Foundation will wish

to, itself, take the initiatives, even though indirectly urged, necessary to make the Congress a successful venture during the next decade. It would be a gamble, but an important one.[12]

The Ford Foundation decided to take the gamble: It agreed to finance the venture on the basis of new leadership, a new board, a new name, and a new program. But instead of Perkins's proposal of three-quarters of a million a year for ten years, it made a five-year grant of $4,650,000, which would meet the full budget in the first year and progressively less of it in the following years, compelling the new organization to find other sources of funds—or dissolve. The amounts were:

| 1968 | $1,300,000 |
| 1969 | $1,100,000 |
| 1970 | $900,000 |
| 1971 | $750,000 |
| 1972 | $600,000 |

Josselson lost no time advising Congress associates around the world of the good news. The decision, he wrote, was, in view of "the allegations published in the New York Times . . . a solid vote of confidence in both the past integrity and future program of the Congress." He also outlined a reorganization of the Congress as proposed in the Perkins memorandum. The old Executive Committee was to be replaced by a new Board of Directors chaired by Raymond Aron. It would also have new members: Galbraith and Oppenheimer from America, Alan Bullock from England, Countess Doenhoff from Germany, Cosio Villegas from Mexico, W. Arthur Lewis from Jamaica, J. P. Narayan from India, and Soedjatmoko from Indonesia. Silone and Shils from the old Executive Committee would remain. It would be an active Board and would take up new themes. The days of a "negative battle" against Communism and all other forms of totalitarianism were now over, Josselson wrote to Narayan. He went on: "I have heard . . . that you are particularly interested in doing something about the state of agriculture in developing countries. This is exactly the type of positive action which the Congress wishes to engage in from now on."[13]

Yet within a year Josselson had resigned. If the first blow in the destruction of the Congress came from the New York Times, the second, and more damaging, came from *Ramparts,* a muckraking San Francisco monthly ("they're out for the kill this time," Josselson wrote to Dwight Macdonald),[14] and the third from the *Saturday Evening Post.* In the March 1967 issue of *Ramparts* (published in February) Sol Stern wrote a long article describing how the CIA used various foundations to provide funds for the international program of the U.S. National Students' Association (NSA). The article was based on information provided by a radically inclined twenty-three-year-old NSA staff-member, Michael Wood, who had been told privately of the funding arrangements by a chatty and fully informed NSA officer ("my public trust as a citizen of the United States must transcend my private trust," Wood wrote).[15] *Ramparts* took out full-page advertisements for its scoop, and soon the leading newspapers and wire services were vying with each other to obtain the confidential tax records of tax-exempt foundations and to unravel, in lengthy reports, the CIA's use of foundations to fund secretly a wide range of organizations—labor unions, jurists, students, and intellectuals. But whereas the reporting of CIA activities a year before had been more or less "objective," it was now vengeful. What had changed was public (and the intellectuals') opinion on the Vietnam War. Early in 1966 there had still been little public opposition to the war, but by 1967 the opposition to it (and to the CIA's role in it) was mounting, including among writers once associated with the Congress, such as Dwight Macdonald and Mary McCarthy. "CIA: The Great Corrupter," the title of an article by Andrew Kopkind, and one sentence from it—"They were spies who came in for the gold"[16]—give an idea of the flavor of the attacks. Walter Lippmann wrote three articles in the *Washington Post* in February 1967 calling for the stamping out of "lying as a public policy" and for the abandoning of the CIA's "totalitarian method."[17] On February 15 President Johnson established a committee of three (composed of the Under Secretary of State Nicholas Katzenbach, Secretary of Health, Education, and Welfare John Gardner, and the CIA Director Richard Helms) to review—promptly—CIA relations with voluntary organizations. Six weeks later, on March 29, the committee recommended that "no Federal agency shall provide any covert financial assistance ... to any of the nation's educational or private voluntary organizations" and that the government should establish "a public–private mechanism to provide public funds openly for overseas activities or organizations which are adjudged deserving, in the national interest, of public support." President Johnson accepted this "state-ment of policy," but an eighteen-member committee under the chairmanship of Secretary of State Dean Rusk could not agree on the "public–private mechanism," and the U.S. Government's with-drawal became (in Cord Meyer's words) "an act of unilateral politi-cal disarmament."

The Congress for Cultural Freedom could no longer evade the issue by denials and reliance on its attested integrity. Michael Jos-selson prepared a memorandum for the Executive Committee meeting planned for May, in which he took responsibility for ac-cepting CIA funds in the past, when he could not obtain them elsewhere. He stressed that the funds had been given without strings, that CIA funding had ceased, and that the Ford Founda-tion was now the Congress's principal financial supporter.[18] He still thought the Congress would overcome the crisis, a view shared by many others. In a letter to Melvin Lasky, for example, about *Encounter*'s place in the affair, Cecil Harmsworth King expressed the widespread attitude that what had happened was regrettable, but one should look to the future:

> There are episodes in the archives of most successful publications—and of some institutions—which none of us regard with relish or pride.
>
> I quite appreciate that it is embarrassing to some of the distinguished supporters of "Encounter" not to have known, and not to have been told, that what they were dismissing as fiction is now realised to have been fact.
>
> The important point to me is that "Encounter" was not influenced in its editorial freedom in the past by this consideration and certainly is not influenced now. It would surely be folly for us to lose the baby with the bathwater.
>
> "Encounter" is the leading intellectual publication of its type appearing in the world today, and I am sure that what we all wish to ensure is its successful continuation and expansion.[19]

Sir Isaiah Berlin wrote to Lasky in similar terms: "The proper role of *Encounter* is simply to say that they acted as they did in ignorance. . . . Men of sense and good-will understand this; those who lack it will continue to snipe away."[20] Stephen Spender wrote to Josselson about "the importance of our letting controversy among ourselves cool off."[21]

This general "cooling off" still seemed possible, and as it prepared for the May meeting of the Executive Committee the Congress hoped the worst was at last over. Before the office closed for
Easter late in March, Josselson sent a memorandum to the Secretariat thanking its members for their "loyalty and solidarity" during "the unpleasant events of the past weeks." He went on:

> You will be glad to learn that letters of support have been
> coming in regularly from our friends and colleagues in other
> parts of the world expressing faith in the policies and
> programs of the Congress and a clear determination to
> surmount our present difficulties and carry on our work. For
> everything that each of you has contributed individually to
> the general atmosphere of calm and confidence, I wish once
> again to express my most profound appreciation.[22]

But the worst was not over. There was still the *Saturday Evening
Post* and the "Braden affair" to come. Early in May Thomas Wardell Braden, who had established the International Organization
Division of the CIA (which dealt with the Congress for Cultural
Freedom), published an explosive defense of the CIA in the May
20, 1967, issue of the *Saturday Evening Post.* When he had joined
the CIA in 1950, he wrote, the Kremlin was winning the Cold War
because of the success of its well-funded network of fronts—the
device, perfected in the 1930s by the Marxist propagandist Willi
Muenzenberg, of involving eminent people and the public at large
in apparently good causes that were totally controlled by the
Kremlin. Braden suggested (he wrote) to Allen Dulles that "the
CIA ought to take on the Russians by penetrating a battery of international fronts ... it should be a world-wide operation with a
single headquarters." When the International Organization Division was established, its rules included: "Limit the money to
amounts private organizations can credibly spend; use legitimate
existing organizations; disguise the extent of American interest;
protect the integrity of the organization by not requiring it to support every aspect of official American policy." The division particularly supported Leftists and socialists, because they were, in Braden's words, "the only people who gave a damn about fighting
Communism."

Drawing on his experience in the CIA in the early 1950s, Braden
gave details of CIA funding of student and labor organizations.
(Irving Brown of the American Federation of Labor had drawn

on CIA money, Braden wrote, to pay strongarm anti-Communist squads in Mediterranean ports in the late 1940s.) But the paragraphs that caused anguish and rage around the world were these:

> And then there was *Encounter,* the magazine published in England and dedicated to the proposition that cultural achievement and political freedom were interdependent. Money for ... the magazine's publication came from the CIA and few outside the CIA knew about it. We had placed one agent in a Europe-based organization of intellectuals called the Congress for Cultural Freedom. Another agent became an editor of *Encounter.* The agents could not only propose anti-Communist programs to the official leaders of the organizations but they could also suggest ways and means to solve the inevitable budgetary problems. Why not see if the needed money could be obtained from "American foundations"?
>
> As the agents knew, the CIA-financed foundations were quite generous when it came to the national interest.

The article was, with crude bravado, entitled "I'm Glad the CIA Is 'Immoral.'"

The effect was inflammatory. In Uganda, Rajat Neogy, the editor of *Transition,* now labeled "a CIA agent," was soon arrested and jailed. In Japan, Hoki Ishihara's house was fire-bombed, and he sought police protection.[23] In India, the government ordered an inquiry into all CIA and Congress for Cultural Freedom activities. In the West, reactions were more mixed. In Italy Silone and Chiaromonte decided not to issue a statement on the matter, because in Rome there was little public or press interest in it. In France and Germany, there was more interest in Braden's revelations about the CIA's involvement with labor unions than in what he said about the Congress. The debate in England, however, was long and bitter, although respect for *Encounter* and the wish to see it survive remained, generally, central. Spender and Frank Kermode resigned from *Encounter,* and Spender announced that he would start a new magazine to attract readers and contributors away from *Encounter.* (Nothing came of it, at least until 1972, when Spender helped relaunch an old Congress publication, *Censorship,* now entitled *Index on Censorship,* a good specialized magazine but no rival to *Encounter.*) Lasky, declaring that he was "nobody's agent," refused to resign, and Cecil King again supported him—a decisive consideration, since Shils was the only trustee of *Encounter* to insist that Lasky be retained as editor. Macdonald wrote to Schlesinger (another trustee): "There isn't any moral imperative I can see . . . that the Congress, or its off-shoots like *Encounter,* should continue to exist,"[24] but *Encounter*'s readers and most of its contributors disagreed with him. Leading authors like Max Beloff, D. W. Brogan, H. R. Trevor-Roper, and Colin MacInnes rallied to *Encounter*'s support. John Weightman wrote to Lasky that, since *Encounter* was always independent, he could not see that "any major moral issue is involved,"[25] and he joined *Encounter* as a contributing editor. After much anguish and heartbreak the magazine survived— and subsequently flourished.

But in America there was more than anguish and heartbreak. This was America at the height of the New Left attack on American institutions and U.S. foreign policy, especially the Vietnam War. For the New Left, the CIA was worse than a rogue elephant, it was an evil empire, and the Congress for Cultural Freedom was a contemptible supporter of a contemptible liberalism, "cold war liberalism." "Cockroaches in a slum sink"[26] was Norman Mailer's metaphor for the Congress intellectuals. The *Partisan Review* (published at that time by the American Committee for Cultural Freedom and partially supported by funds from Paris) issued a "Statement" condemning secret subsidies to magazines, which was signed by Hannah Arendt, Lillian Hellman, Macdonald, Norman Mailer, among others, including two from Britain, V. S. Pritchett and Angus Wilson.[27] The *Nation* gloated editorially and published Christopher Lasch's contemptuous appraisal of the Congress and its "corruption."[28] The *New York Review of Books* published Jason Epstein's account of the "underground gravy train."[29] Norman Podhoretz's *Commentary* published a long symposium, which debated the question whether covert CIA subsidies "prove that liberal anti-communism has been a dupe of, or a slave to, the darker impulses of American foreign policy."[30] In their contributions Daniel Bell, Sidney Hook, Arthur Schlesinger, Diana Trilling, and Lionel Trilling defended the Congress and its record, but the majority of the participants condemned American policies in general: "our totalitarian foreign policy" (Harold Rosenberg), the "diabolic" American establishment (Paul Goodman), the "President's genocidal crusade" in Vietnam (Dwight Macdonald), and Congress for Cultural Freedom personalities as "breezy, rootless, freewheeling, cynically anti-Communist orgmen" (William Phillips).

None of these critics attempted any assessment of the Congress's achievements or any answer to Schlesinger's argument:

> During the last days of Stalinism . . . the non-Communist trade-union movements and the non-Communist intellectuals were under the most severe, unscrupulous, and unrelenting pressure. For the United States government to have stood self-righteously aside at this point would have seemed to me far more shameful than to do what, in fact, it did—which was through intermediaries to provide some of these groups subsidies to help them do better what they were doing anyway.[31]

It was not only the Left that was on the attack. James Burnham, one of Congress's founders but long since disenchanted with its "soft liberalism," saw in the shambles proof of what he had long thought of as the Congress's wrong turning in the early 1950s:

> The fundamental flaw was political. CIA mounted most of these activities in the perspective of "the non-Communist Left." CIA estimated the NCL as a reliably anti-Communist force which in action would be, if not pro-Western and pro-American, at any rate not anti-Western and anti-American.
>
> This political estimate is mistaken. The NCL is not reliable. Under the pressure of critical events the NCL loosened. A large portion—in this country as in others—swung toward an anti-American position, and nearly all the NCL softened its attitude toward Communism and the Communist nations. . . .
>
> Thus the organizational collapse is derivative from the political error. This political error is the doctrine that the global struggle against Communism must be based on the NCL—a doctrine fastened on CIA by Allen Dulles. Cuba, the Dominican Republic, and above all Vietnam have put the NCL doctrine and practice to a decisive test. A large part of the organizations and individuals nurtured by CIA under the NCL prescription end up undermining the nation's will and hampering or sabotaging the nation's security.[32]

Above the battle, a *Time* magazine essay asked how these important movements, now "orphaned" by the CIA, would be cared for in the future. Returning to the Katzenbach committee's recommendation of "a public–private mechanism to provide public funds openly," it concluded that since the CIA's most important contribution had been not money but unconventional, imaginative ideas, any new mechanism should steer between a hard Cold War orientation and "an aimless benevolence."[33] (But it was many years before the recommendation of the Katzenbach Committee was reexamined.)

Meanwhile in Paris both Michael Josselson and John Hunt prepared their resignations from the Congress. When the General Assembly* met on May 13, 1967, to debate plans for the future, Josselson presented his last Report as Executive Director:

> Although the Congress for Cultural Freedom has worked in entire independence from the CIA, the condition of secrecy imposed upon me has been a grievous one to bear, since it placed me in the position of having to deceive the people I most respected, admired and liked, and who gave me their trust wholeheartedly. As a consequence, I now must submit my resignation to the members of the General Assembly. I shall be only too glad to help the Congress get over the present difficulties, but I can under no circumstances remain its Executive Director.[34]

James McAuley, the founding editor of *Quadrant,* attended the meeting as an observer and wrote a few days later about some of those present that "there was a contradiction between their wish to (1) support Mike [Josselson] in friendship—and in honesty because none of them had been *really* much deceived—and (2) take up a public position of outraged innocence."[35] In the event the meeting issued a press release that affirmed its pride in the Congress's achievements and condemned the CIA, whose covert actions had tended "to poison the wells of intellectual discourse." It "took note" of—but did not formally accept—the resignations tendered by Josselson and Hunt, expressed "renewed gratitude" to them for the way they had maintained "the complete independence and intellectual integrity" of the Congress, and asked them to "continue to perform their duties." Finally, it adopted the plans

---

*The members of the General Assembly were Minoo Masani (Chairman), Raymond Aron, Daniel Bell, Pierre Emmanuel, Louis Fischer, Anthony Hartley, K. A. B. Jones-Quartey, Ezekiel Mphahlele, Nicolas Nabokov, Hans Oprecht, Michael Polanyi, Denis de Rougemont, Yoshihiko Seki, Edward Shils, Ignazio Silone, and Manès Sperber.

for reorganization under the Board of Directors chaired by Raymond Aron and agreed to meet again in September.

By September, however, Aron had changed his mind. At the May meeting, "I was torn between contradictory feelings and in a highly emotional state."[36] He had later reconsidered the issues and concluded that the Congress should cease to exist. That a man of Aron's stature should withdraw was a serious blow, but the September meeting decided to proceed without him and appointed Shepard Stone of the Ford Foundation President and Chief Executive, and Pierre Emmanuel Director of the newly renamed International Association for Cultural Freedom. Josselson and Hunt now resigned.

Shepard Stone, born in 1908 in New Hampshire, had been director of the Ford Foundation's International Affairs Program for the preceding fourteen years. A former writer for (and a Sunday editor of) the *New York Times,* he had coedited *We Saw It Happen* (1938) with Hanson Baldwin and had written *Shadow over Germany: The Challenge of Nazi Germany* (1938). He had served in the U.S. Army during World War II and after the war had been Director of Public Affairs under John J. McCloy in the U.S. High Commission for Germany.

Pierre Emmanuel (a pseudonym of Noel Mathieu), born in 1916, was a poet and journalist who had been Literary Director of the Congress since 1959, organizing a series of writers' seminars, mainly in Spain, Portugal, and Scandinavia. In 1962 he became Deputy Secretary General of the Congress and replaced Nicolas Nabokov when the latter settled in West Berlin as director of the Berlin Festival. A Gaullist, an opponent of the Vietnam War, and an advocate of "de-Americanizing" the International Association, Pierre Emmanuel liked to stress the "metaphysical," rather than the political, dimension of cultural freedom.

Alan Bullock, who became Chairman of the Board of Directors (in place of Raymond Aron), was a university administrator and historian. He had written *Hitler: A Study in Tyranny* (1952) and *The Life and Times of Ernest Bevin* (2 vols., 1960, 1967).

George Kennan wrote to congratulate Shepard Stone on his appointment:

> I was delighted to see that you have taken the presidency of the Congrès. It is an institution of great value, which should have a permanent place, it seems to me, in the life of our

western world. The flap about C.I.A. money was quite
unwarranted, and caused far more anguish than it should
have been permitted to cause. I never felt the slightest pangs
of conscience about it, from the standpoint of the
organization. This country has no ministry of culture, and
C.I.A. was obliged to do what it could to try to fill the gap. It
should be praised for having done so, and not criticized. It is
unfair that it should be so bitterly condemned for its failures,
and should then go unpraised when it does something
constructive and sensible. And the Congrès would itself have
been remiss if it had failed to take money which came to it
from good intent and wholly without strings or conditions.[37]

The *National Review,* edited by William F. Buckley, Jr., also noted
the new development:

But will it perform any useful service? There has never been a
greater need for liberal anti-Communism. But the new
organization is liable to feel that in order to prove its
independence of its former patrons, it will have to go in for a
stylized anti-anti-Communism. In which case it will, like
cultural freedom in Russia, fade away into indistinction.[38]

# 15

# *The Aftermath:*
# *"No Consensus Emerged"*

⌇

Our approach must not be merely negative.

K. A. JELENSKI, 1968[1]

The minutes of recent Board meetings and discussions
would not suggest that any important ideas were being
generated.

ADAM WATSON, 1974[2]

The International Association for Cultural Freedom inherited
from the Congress for Cultural Freedom the remaining magazines
and national committees, the practice of international seminars,
the regional programs, and the ideal of a worldwide community
of intellectuals. There was also some continuity of personnel: If it
no longer had, or soon lost, the services of Michael Josselson, John
Hunt, Nicolas Nabokov, Denis de Rougemont, François Bondy,
Melvin Lasky, Raymond Aron, and Sidney Hook, the General Assembly still retained Daniel Bell and Minoo Masani (until 1970);
the Board (Executive), Edward Shils, Ignazio Silone (until 1970),
and Manès Sperber (until 1970); and the Administration (Executive), K. A. Jelenski. Now "CIA-free," funded almost entirely by the
Ford Foundation, and with the death agonies of the Congress behind it, the International Association set out to resume the work
of the Congress—in the year that brought the "student revolt" in

235

Paris, the Soviet occupation in Czechoslovakia, and the Tet Offensive in Vietnam (as well as the falsification of its results in the world media), and in a period that saw the resignation of President de Gaulle, the withdrawal of President Johnson, the Watergate scandal, and the U.S. defeat in Vietnam.

The International Association continued, at first, to subsidize the magazines, and it played an active role in securing the release from prison of *Transition*'s editor, Rajat Neogy, in Kampala. It extended its support to additional magazines in Asia: *Social Science Review* in Bangkok and *Horison* in Djakarta. It helped meet *Encounter*'s deficit in 1971. It sent several private letters of protest to governments that harassed intellectuals, for example, in 1971 to the Indonesian, Turkish, Greek, and Soviet governments. It made public protests against the U.S. prosecution of the Vietnam War in 1972. It created new national committees (in Madrid, Lisbon, and Morocco) and, curiously, opened an office in Cambridge, Massachusetts. It conducted a number of international seminars, especially in Europe. It maintained the *Fondation pour une Entr'aide Intellectuelle* for Central Europe, providing travel grants, sending books and magazines, publishing anthologies, and arranging exhibitions at the Galérie Lambert. In Asia it opened new centers in Thailand, the Philippines, and Indonesia. In Latin America it maintained ILARI (Latin American Institute for International Relations) and its magazines *Mundo Nuevo* and *Aportes*. In Africa it maintained a presence, especially in Ghana while its old associate, Dr. K. A. Busia, was Prime Minister: It held a seminar on the press in Accra, revived *Transition,* and supported the Center for Civil Education. (After the overthrow of the Busia government in a coup, the Association suffered restrictions.)

But the Association never regained the élan and the tense momentum of the Congress in the 1950s and early 1960s. The dominant policy also differed from that of the Congress in basic ways. Whereas the Congress attached great importance to mobilizing opinion around the world in protests against major Soviet infringements of cultural freedom, the Shepard Stone–Pierre Emmanuel International Association was *détentiste* and issued no public anti-Soviet protests, not even in support of the harassed Solzhenitsyn and Sakharov. (It did write some "private letters.") Whereas the Congress was predominantly critical of the irrationalism of fellow-travelers, the International Association was determined to "understand" the New Left and the Student Revolt: Its approach, said Jelenski, must not be "merely negative." Whereas the Congress's seminars almost always had a political and intellectual point, the point of some of the Association's seminars was obscure indeed. Regarding the seminar in Venice in 1971 on "The Present Position of History as a Concept and as a Value," Aron said that "it had not the least connection with political problems."[3] In time the International Association would divide, to the point of splitting, on these issues, especially on policy toward the New Left, with Labedz, the editor of *Survey*, and Shils, editor of *Minerva*, leading a minority opposition to the revival of the "smelly little orthodoxies" denounced by George Orwell and now encouraged (in Labedz's and Shils's view) by the International Association.

The high-point—and swan song—of Shepard Stone's International Association was its huge seminar, at Princeton, New Jersey, on "The United States: Its Problems, Impact, and Image in the World," held in December 1968, a time of mounting opposition to the Vietnam War (including a major protest march on the Pentagon) and shortly after Richard Nixon's victory in the U.S. Presidential election. For Jelenski, the seminar was an opportunity to debate the "great issues" of the resurgence of Leftist ideology and its confrontation of the idea that (in Daniel Bell's "postindustrial society" or Zbigniew Brzezinski's "technetronic age") future problems would be administrative, not ideological. More generally it would be a fulfillment of his old dream, a meeting of minds, a "dialogue" among the liberal-Left intellectuals from across the spectrum. He hoped that Herbert Marcuse, Jürgen Habermas, and Richard Hoggart would attend the conference.* They did not, but Lillian Hellman, Sam Brown, Stanley Hoffman, and Martin Peretz, from the New and Old Left, did.

About ninety intellectuals from twenty countries assembled at Princeton, and, judged by the publicity the seminar attracted in Europe and the United States, it was an impressive event and convinced at least Shepard Stone that the Association had overcome any CIA legacy. (The presence of so many "international" intellectuals and the attendance of Henry Kissinger, shortly to be Assis-

---

*He had also wanted Soviet representatives, but Brzezinski wrote to him that in the light of the Soviet occupation of Czechoslovakia, "they should be disinvited," preferably "one week prior to the conference, in order to make it even more painful for them."[4] In the event, no Soviet representatives came.

tant to the President for National Security Affairs, and of John McCoy and Brzezinski, ensured the publicity.) But the meeting of minds was not the fruitful engagement that Jelenski had envisaged. The liberals (including Galbraith and Schlesinger) outnumbered the New Left, but the latter held the initiative and won the headlines. Owen Harries summed it up in a report on the conference: When the flamboyant Sam Brown ridiculed Galbraith, who had expressed his "faith" in the capacity of American liberal institutions to meet the demands made on them, Galbraith replied that he had not meant what he had said, withdrew the word "faith," and explained that pessimism was sometimes misplaced. Harries reflected:

> This exchange . . . might serve as an epiphany of the
> relationship between two generations of "progressives"; one
> compromising and compromised, ambivalent, guilt-ridden and,
> however confident on the surface, badly rattled by recent
> events; the other arrogantly sure of its moral superiority,
> however confused intellectually, refusing all compromises and
> looking beyond the system in being.[5]

On one occasion Kennan spoke for his idea of conservative values against the slogans and activities of student and black "mobs," and on another Shils denounced the loss of self-confidence and self-respect of the authorities in the United States because of failure in Vietnam: "The WASPS have abdicated. What has taken their place? Ants! Fleas!"[6] But the dominant note of the conference, struck by the New Left, was one of contempt for American institutions. Inevitably it adopted resolutions calling for the end of the Vietnam War, a new attitude to China, and prompt arms control talks with the U.S.S.R. It also called on the United States to abandon its role as "policeman of the world."

William F. Buckley (who was not there) called the conference "one of the spectacular effronteries of the season."[7] Labedz called it "a pathetic disaster."[8] It was an early illustration of the intellectual gulf between on the one side, Labedz and Shils (supported by Lasky), who saw the meeting as a dismantling of the Congress for Cultural Freedom, as a sort of Wroclaw-across-the-Hudson, and, on the other, the dominant Stone–Emmanuel–Jelenski group, who did not want to hear anything critical of the new radicalism. This deepened in the ensuing months and came to a head at a large Board meeting in Paris in June 1970, when Labedz summed up his critique of the Association (and indeed of the last years of the Congress). The Association, he said, saw itself as a movement of "the vital center," but this center had fallen apart, and no coalition with "the barbarism of the New Left" was morally acceptable. The Congress and the Association had nurtured many illusions: There had been no "end of ideology," no real liberalization in the U.S.S.R., no "convergence" of the rivals in the Cold War, and no "worldwide community of intellectuals." But there had been, according to Labedz, "a long march through the institutions" by the New Left, which would destroy the universities, politicize cultural life, and appease the Soviets. He called for "clarity of purpose" against this threat and for the creation of "an extreme center."[9]

On the next day, Pierre Emmanuel replied on behalf of the International Association and its Administration. Looking like a poet-prophet (and speaking in French for the sake of precision), he said that he had been very moved "par l'accent passioné de notre ami Labedz," but he saw the current wave of protest and confrontation as much more positive than negative. The New Left was trying to fill the spiritual emptiness of modern technological life ("the man who goes to the moon is also a man of nothing"). His own son-in-law, after years in the Third World and now in Latin America, had become a Maoist, an apostle of the *tabula rasa,* of recommencement from zero. What are we to reply to him, if we are not to be journalistic cheats (*tricheurs*)? We must not turn our backs on these young people.

The matter was debated around the table, but, as the minutes record, "no consensus emerged."[10] No consensus ever emerged. The Administration and Board continued to direct international seminars (eighteen in ten years), which began with such themes as the student rebellion and political violence and turned increasingly to such cloudy themes as "knowledge," "history," and "belief." They were mainly in Europe or the United States and usually featured the tribunes of the Left (and their epigones): Ivan Illich, Roger Garaudy, and Conor Cruise O'Brien. On the other hand, the central issues raised by Labedz's critique were debated in the pages of his *Survey* or in magazines never or no longer connected with the floundering and ambivalent Association: Melvin Lasky's *Encounter* in London, Norman Podhoretz's *Commentary,* and Kristol's and Bell's *The Public Interest* in New York.

From the beginning the Association, with its annually declining grant from the Ford Foundation, was a contracting organization.

In 1968 *Tempo Presente* closed down, and the Association ceased subsidizing *Der Monat* (which survived until 1971) and *China Quarterly*. In 1971 it ceased subsidizing five magazines: *Mundo Nuevo, Cadernos Brasileiros* (both of which closed down), *Solidarity, Social Science Review,* and *China Report* (all of which found other sources of funds). In 1971 it stopped supporting the New Delhi and Calcutta offices, and in 1972 it closed down the Latin American Institute for International Relations (ILARI) and its magazine *Aportes,* and stopped supporting the Australian Association and *Quadrant*. Its affiliated European committees stopped receiving financial support, and the Fund for Intellectuals dried up. The English magazines *Survey* and *Minerva* found independent sources of funds.

By 1974, when Adam Watson replaced Stone as Director-General (and Pierre Emmanuel replaced Sir Alan Bullock as Chairman), it was clear that the International Association was doomed. Adam Watson, a former senior British diplomat, recently diplomatic adviser to the British Leyland Motor Corporation, and the author, under the pseudonym "Scipio," of *Emergent Africa* (1965) (he had been head of the African Department of the Foreign Office and had served in several African posts), could only preside over the dissolution of the Association. Shils ceased to be a member in 1975, the Paris office closed its doors in 1977, and the International Association for Cultural Freedom finally voted to dissolve itself in January 1979.

Michael Josselson in Geneva watched the decline of the International Association with a bitterness made worse by poor health. (After his resignation at the height of the controversy about the CIA, he suffered arterial obliterations and two strokes.) He condemned the Association's "lack of seriousness," writhed at the continual denigration of the work of the Congress, and deplored the developments in the United States in the 1970s. "What a gruesome society it has become since you and I opted for it," he wrote to Nicolas Nabokov in 1975.[11]

He devoted most of his time to writing, in collaboration with his wife, *The Commander,* a scholarly biography of Barclay de Tolly, the great Commander-in-Chief of the Russian Army against Napoleon in 1812, "with whose unjust humiliation, I began to identify."[12] Barclay's scorched-earth strategy of retreating before overwhelmingly superior French forces and of making an ally of the

Russian winter was justified by its ultimate success, but at the time it was unpopular with Russia's nationalists. After the fall of Smolensk, Barclay was defamed as a foreign traitor (he was a Livonian Balt of Scottish descent) and replaced as Commander-in-Chief. He later overcame his disgrace, was reappointed Commander-in-Chief, and entered Paris in triumph as a Field Marshal in 1814. But for the rest of his life the stigma of his disgrace remained. Josselson quoted Aleksandr Pushkin's famous lines about Barclay:

> In vain! Your rival reaped the triumph early planted
> In your high mind; and you, forgotten, disenchanted,
> The sponsor of the feast, drew your last breath,
> Despising us, it may be, in the hour of death.

It was Barclay's fate, Josselson wrote, "to serve his country and his countrymen and reap disgrace, then glory but never the heart's reward of simple recognition."[13]

The autobiographical note is plain, and Josselson received little "simple recognition" in his lifetime. Something of the anguish he endured is indicated in his account of Silone's visit to him late in 1969. His relations with Silone had always been formally correct, but on this occasion Silone kissed him on both cheeks and addressed him using "tu." Josselson wrote: "This was certainly one of the most moving moments of my life."[14] A few other old Congress colleagues remained loyal to him: Sperber, Lasky, Labedz, Bondy, and Shils. Aron became reconciled with him. But most of the others were rarely heard from.

Josselson died immediately after an operation in Geneva in January 1978, shortly after he had finished writing *The Commander*. (Oxford University Press published it in 1980 and it was well received by historians and critics. A French translation, *Le Général Hiver*, appeared in 1986.) The funeral service was small, simple, and private. There were no speeches. Only Richard Strauss's *Letze Lieder* were played. Lasky, who put a flower on the coffin, wrote to Hook: "Had he died on that occasion when they repaired his heart some 14 years ago, the funeral would have been a European, a Western occasion—a thousand would have been there to bid him farewell."[15]

Diana Josselson received messages of condolence and tribute from all over the world from novelists, poets, philosophers, critics, historians, and parliamentarians. *Survey* referred to Michael Josselson's "warmth, his loyalty, his steadfast courage in adversity,"[16] and *Encounter* wrote: "No one who knew him well will ever forget his remarkable virtues: intellectual integrity, cosmopolitan culture, heartwarming loyalty. . . . '*This was a man!*'"[17] But none of the world's newspapers took note of Michael Josselson's death. There were no obituaries.

# 16
# *The Congress in Retrospect*

"**P**lay It Again, Uncle Sam!"
title of an article by LEOPOLD LABEDZ[1]

Of the periods into which the seventeen years of the Congress for Cultural Freedom fall—its formative period in the 1950s, its moves to new directions between 1958 and 1963–64, and its final stage of retreat before the "exposé" of CIA funding—there can be little doubt about its success in its first period. Through its publications, conferences, and international protests, it kept the issues of Soviet totalitarianism and liberal anti-Communism to the fore in a frequently hostile environment. It cannot claim to have had the historic impact of Khrushchev's "secret speech" in 1956 (or of Solzhenitsyn later), but it took and held the initiative in public political education. By the end of the period, the propaganda of the Soviet Union and its fellow-travelers was no longer credible.

Sidney Hook, who had been a member of the Congress's Executive Committee, has claimed that after this first great period the Congress had become a "lost cause" and had "outlived its usefulness and promise." It no longer had its "heart in the anti-communist fight." Whatever truth there is in this assessment, it is also an overstatement. In the Congress's second period, it maintained its magazines (*Encounter, Survey, Preuves,* and *Tempo Presente,* among others), which Hook described as "most valuable contributions in the continuing struggle for cultural freedom."[2] It also started new publications, such as the news commentary *Forum Service,* which

243

gave a central place to Cold War issues, and the quarterly *Minerva,* which led the resistance to the politicization of the university. Further, it organized a number of important international protests: in support of Boris Pasternak in 1958 and Olga Ivinskaya in 1961, against Polish censorship in 1964 and the Portuguese arrest in Mozambique of an anti-apartheid editor in 1964, in support of Joseph Brodsky in 1964, against the Franco regime's suspension of professors in 1965. It conducted its invaluable Central European program of providing books, stipends, and travel expenses to intellectuals, especially in Poland.

It is true that in the Third World, where "Cold War" were dirty words, the Congress blunted its anti-Soviet edge in order to keep the possibility of having any influence at all. Certainly Hook himself at the time advocated this gradualistic approach. In 1959, after a tour of Asia that left him depressed at the strength of the pro-Communist and anti-American outlook among Asian intellectuals, he wrote:

> The intellectuals of the free world must find some way to reach them. . . . While there is still time we should find and multiply the occasions of bringing together the intellectuals of Asian (and African) countries with those of America and free Europe in common cultural projects.[3]

He suggested sympathetic discussions of Asian traditions and religions, and their relevance to modernization. That is precisely what the Congress tried to do.

Nevertheless, the softening of its anti-Sovietism was more than a tactic for the Third World. There was, as Hook perceived, some ideological fatigue. Edward Shils summed up the position some years later when he wrote that although the Cold War continued unceasingly, the "moral strain" of it proved too much for Western opinion, including, if not especially, that of the non-Communist Left, which increasingly grasped at the idea of "competitive coexistence" and emphasized the relaxing coexistence rather than the competitiveness. He found the source of the "moral strain" in "the burden of 1917," the liberal conviction that the Soviet Union, whatever its terrible imperfections, remains an "advanced" and "progressive" society, since it has abolished private property, capitalism, and the market. To eliminate that "burden," it is necessary to acknowledge that a free society is bound up with private property, capitalism, and the market, that there is "an inescapable affinity between socialists and communists."[4]

The leading Congress intellectuals—especially the Americans, such as Shils and Kristol—were increasingly taking this step away from the non-Communist Left, but they did so in journals and meetings outside, not within the Congress, which remained, officially (as it were) on the non-Communist Left, unwilling finally to slough off "the burden of 1917." The failure to do so weakened not only its anti-Soviet politics in the 1960s but its intellectual initiative, which passed to the "neo-conservatives." The Congress had conquered the fellow-travelers but seemed unwilling to follow the logic of its conquest.

The Congress in its second period, in short, continued its fundamental work in shifting world circumstances ("Peaceful Coexistence," Vatican II) but increasingly lost its drive, remaining in the dead end and contradictions of the non-Communist Left. The Congress's third period (1963–67) was, on the other hand, basically a time of winding down and retreat. The disclosures about the CIA hastened the process, but the Congress was by then almost exhausted, and it did not recover in its new incarnation as an International Association for Cultural Freedom.

Why did it sentimentally remain within the non-Communist Left and not follow its leading intellectuals toward "neo-conservatism"? James Burnham attributed this to the influence of the CIA.[5] Burnham did not regard the Congress as a "front" (as some senior CIA officers, including Thomas Braden and William Colby, did). He knew, as Hook put it, that it was "simply preposterous to believe that men like Ignazio Silone, Raymond Aron, Nicola Chiaromonte, Michael Polanyi, Haakon Lie, or Carlo Schmid . . . would dance to anyone else's tune."[6] But, according to Burnham, at a time when the leading Congress intellectuals were moving "to the right," the CIA used its influence to keep the Congress close to the non-Communist Left because of its misjudgment that this was where the leadership of the intellectual community remained. This, in Burnham's view, may have been true in the 1950s and in the time of Stalin and his fellow-travelers, but it was no longer true in the 1960s and the time of "competitive coexistence." Burnham's role as a founder of the Congress and a onetime CIA consultant must give weight to his views, but until CIA records become available, it is unlikely that its influence in the Congress will become much clearer.

The Katzenbach Committee had recommended in 1967 the "prompt creation" of a "public–private mechanism," possibly patterned on the British Council or the Smithsonian Institution, that would enable public funds, administered largely by private citizens, to be provided for the "overseas activities of organizations which are adjudged deserving, in the national interest, of public support."[7] But yet another committee, established to work out the details, could not reach agreement, and the proposal was dropped. Cord Meyer, as noted previously, described this withdrawal of the U.S. Government from the cultural struggle of the continuing Cold War as "an act of unilateral political disarmament."[8]

In fact, however, it is difficult to see how the latter group, the Rusk Committee, could have reached agreement, and difficult indeed to believe that the Katzenbach Committee expected it to do so. Kristol summed up the problem when the proposal was revived fifteen years later in the form of the National Endowment for Democracy, which would make open grants to foreign publications, trade unions, and educational institutions working in the democratic interest. Kristol described the proposal in 1982 as "one of the most inane foreign policy initiatives in living memory," which "will inevitably abort." One reason was that in many foreign countries it either was, or quickly would be, illegal for citizens to accept money from a foreign government. "Can anyone imagine the left-wing regime in Greece or the right-wing regime in South Korea allowing such goings-on?" A second reason was that any publication or union that accepted such funds would lose all credibility. "So, being neither stupid nor suicidal, they will not accept them."[9]

Kristol's prediction that the proposal would "inevitably abort" was mistaken. The National Endowment for Democracy (NED) was established in 1983, and its grants have helped a number of democratic causes—political parties, newspapers, trade unions, and schools around the world. The *New York Times* has referred to "the general success of the venture,"[10] and the *New Republic* declared: "Without NED, the U.S. has no way to embolden the hopeless except with empty rhetoric or with guns."[11] But Kristol was right in that its programs have been limited in their range—certainly when compared with those of the Congress for Cultural Freedom.

The Katzenbach Committee also reported that it expected U.S. private foundations (which had grown in number from 2,200 in 1955 to 18,000 in 1967) to take over the CIA's funding of international organizations. In fact the Ford Foundation became the principal source of funds for the International Association for Cultural Freedom; when the Association was dissolved, other foundations (in the United States and elsewhere) helped sustain surviving Congress magazines, for example, *Survey* and *Minerva,* and new magazines largely sympathetic to old Congress objectives, such as *The New Criterion.* The "Committee for the Free World," a sort of partial regrouping of Congress intellectuals (Aron, Hook, Kristol, and Labedz were among its founders), was established in 1983 and has also been privately funded by foundations. Under its Executive Director, Midge Decter, it holds international conferences and sponsors publications in defense of basic Western political institutions. But none of these activities is on the scale, certainly not the ambitious international scale, of the Congress for Cultural Freedom.

Few people have called for a resumption of covert CIA funding. One who has is the British philosopher Roger Scruton, who in 1985 deplored the fact that "the CIA is now utterly intimidated, refusing to engage even in its most honourable occupation—the support of those publications which tell the truth about the modern world."[12] It ought, he wrote, to support those who express uncomfortable truths. But after the events of 1966–67 and the fate of the Congress for Cultural Freedom, such a resumption of covert funding is highly unlikely. At the time of the 1967 disclosures, the well-informed James McCarger (writing under the name "Christopher Felix") argued that the point was not the immorality of covert funding, which—distinguishing integrity from purity—he regarded as necessary, but the failure to ensure secrecy or to devise proper "cover."[13] But the fact remains that in a democracy like the United States, such secrecy would not and could not be maintained, and the inevitable disclosures would damage reputations and careers and even endanger lives, as it did in the story of the Congress. In this respect the advantage in the continuing Cold War—even in a period of "thaw"—remains with the KGB.

The achievement of the Congress for Cultural Freedom was in its time to have placed some severe limits on the advantages of Stalinist Russia. Today almost everyone (including Mikhail Gorbachev) agrees with the Congress's once lonely assessment of Soviet totalitarianism, and in particular of the Soviet failure to accept human rights (in other words, cultural freedom). In contributing in so brilliant and timely a way to this public awareness throughout the world in a period of great danger, the Congress for Cultural Freedom was a historic success.

# A

# *Manifesto of Congress for Cultural Freedom (Berlin, 1950)*

(This was drafted by Arthur Koestler. The italicized words in paragraphs 10, 13, and 14 are the amendments added on the motion of Hugh Trevor-Roper and A. J. Ayer. This document was adopted.)

1. We hold it to be self-evident that intellectual freedom is one of the inalienable rights of man.

2. Such freedom is defined first and foremost by his right to hold and express his own opinions, and particularly opinions which differ from those of his rulers. Deprived of the right to say "no," man becomes a slave.

3. Freedom and peace are inseparable. In any country, under any regime, the overwhelming majority of ordinary people fear and oppose war. The danger of war becomes acute when governments, by suppressing democratic representative institutions, deny to the majority the means of imposing its will to peace.

   Peace can be maintained only if each government submits to the control and inspection of its acts by the people whom it governs, and agrees to submit all questions immediately involving the risk of war to a representative international authority, by whose decisions it will abide.

4.  We hold that the main reason for the present insecurity of the world is the policy of governments which, while paying lip-service to peace, refuse to accept this double control. Historical experience proves that wars can be prepared and waged under any slogan, including that of peace. Campaigns for peace which are not backed by acts that will guarantee its maintenance are like counterfeit currency circulated for dishonest purposes. Intellectual sanity and physical security can only return to the world if such practices are abandoned.

5.  Freedom is based on the toleration of divergent opinions. The principle of toleration does not logically permit the practice of intolerance.

6.  No political philosophy or economic theory can claim the sole right to represent freedom in the abstract. We hold that the value of such theories is to be judged by the range of concrete freedom which they accord the individual in practice.

    We likewise hold that no race, nation, class or religion can claim the sole right to represent the idea of freedom, nor the right to deny freedom to other groups or creeds in the name of any ultimate ideal or lofty aim whatsoever. We hold that the historical contribution of any society is to be judged by the extent and quality of the freedom which its members actually enjoy.

7.  In times of emergency, restrictions on the freedom of the individual are imposed in the real or assumed interest of the community. We hold it to be essential that such restrictions be confined to a minimum of clearly specified actions; that they be understood to be temporary and limited expedients in the nature of a sacrifice; and that the measures restricting freedom be themselves subject to free criticism and democratic control. Only thus can we have a reasonable assurance that emergency measures restricting individual freedom will not degenerate into a permanent tyranny.

8.  In totalitarian states restrictions on freedom are no longer intended and publicly understood as sacrifices imposed on the people, but are, on the contrary, represented as triumphs of progress and achievements of a superior civilisation. We

hold that both the theory and practice of these regimes run counter to the basic rights of the individual and the fundamental aspirations of mankind as a whole.

9. We hold the danger represented by these regimes to be all the greater since their means of enforcement far surpasses that of all previous tyrannies in the history of mankind. The citizen of the totalitarian state is expected and forced not only to abstain from crime but to conform in all his thoughts and actions to a prescribed pattern. Citizens are persecuted and condemned on such unspecified and all-embracing charges as "enemies of the people" or "socially unreliable elements."

10. We hold that there can be no stable world so long as mankind, with regard to freedom, remains divided into "haves" and "have-nots." The defence of existing freedoms, the reconquest of lost freedoms, *and the creation of new freedoms* are parts of the same struggle.

11. We hold that the theory and practice of the totalitarian state are the greatest challenge which man has been called on to meet in the course of civilised history.

12. We hold that indifference or neutrality in the face of such a challenge amounts to a betrayal of mankind and to the abdication of the free mind. Our answers to this challenge may decide the fate of man for generations.

13. *The defence of intellectual liberty today imposes a positive obligation: to offer new and constructive answers to the problems of our time.*

14. We address this manifesto to all men who are determined to regain those liberties which they have lost and to preserve *and extend* those which they enjoy.

# B

# Selective List of Conferences Sponsored by the Congress for Cultural Freedom

*Founding Conference*
    Berlin, June 26–30, 1950
    See *Der Monat,* no. 22/23, 1950.

*First Asian Conference on Cultural Freedom*
    Bombay, March 28–31, 1951
    See *Indian Congress for Cultural Freedom* (Bombay: Kanada Press, 1951).

*L'Oeuvre du XXème Siècle*
    Paris, May–June, 1952
    See *Preuves,* no. 15, May 1952, and the special supplement of this number.

*Science and Freedom*
    Hamburg, July 23–26, 1953, in cooperation with the University of Hamburg
    See *Science and Freedom* (London: Secker & Warburg, 1955) and *Wissenschaft und Freiheit* (Berlin: Grundwald Verlag, 1954).

*La Musica nel XX Secolo*
    Rome, April 4–15, 1954, in cooperation with the Italian Radio and Television

*Second Asian Conference on Cultural Freedom*
Rangoon, February 17–20, 1955, in cooperation with the
Society for the Extension of Democratic Ideals
See Herbert Passin, ed., *Cultural Freedom in Asia* (Tokyo:
Charles E. Tuttle, 1956).

*The Future of Freedom*
Milan, September 12–17, 1955
See *The Soviet Economy* (London: Secker & Warburg,
1956).

*Inter-American Conference of the Congress for Cultural Freedom*
Mexico City, September 18–24, 1956

*Problems of Economic Growth*
Tokyo, April 1–6, 1957
See M. K. Haldar and R. Ghosh, eds., *Problems of Economic
Growth* (New Delhi: Kaxton Press, 1960).

*Changes in Soviet Society*
Oxford, June 24–29, 1957, in cooperation with St. Antony's College

*Tradition and Change in Music*
Venice, September 16–23, 1958, in cooperation with the
Cini Foundation

*Workers' Participation in Management*
Vienna, September 19–25, 1958, in cooperation with the
Austrian Council for Economy and the Austrian Produc-
tivity Center
See H. A. Clegg, *A New Approach to Industrial Democracy*
(Oxford: Basil Blackwell, 1960).

*Representative Governments and Public Liberties in the New
States*
Rhodes, October 6–13, 1958
See *Afro-Asian Attitudes* (New Delhi, 1961).

*Representative Government and National Progress*
Ibadan, March 16–23, 1959, in cooperation with the Uni-
versity College of Ibadan
See H. Passin and K. A. B. Jones-Quartey, eds., *Africa: The
Dynamics of Change* (Ibadan: University Press, 1963).

*Junge Maler der Gegenwart*
Vietnam, July 24–August 15, 1959, in cooperation with
Institutes zur Förderung der Künste in Oesterreich

*Industrial Society and Western Political Dialogue*
Basel, September 20–26, 1959
See Raymond Aron, George Kennan, Robert Oppen-
heimer, and others, *Die Industrielle Gesellschaft und die drei
Welten* (Zürich: Evz-Verlag, 1961); *Colloque de Rheinfelden*
(Paris: Calmann-Lévy, 1960); *World Technology and Human
Destiny* (Ann Arbor: University of Michigan Press, 1963).

*Progress in Freedom*
Berlin, June 16–22, 1960
See K. A. Jelenski, ed., *History and Hope: Progress in Freedom*
(London, Routledge & Kegan Paul, 1962), also in French
(Paris: Calmann-Lévy, 1960), in German (Zürich: Evz-Ver-
lag, 1961), and in Italian (Bologna: II Mulino, 1962). See
also *La Democratie à l'épreuve du XX$^e$ siècle* (Paris: Clamann-
Lévy, 1960), and *The Problems of Afro-Asian New States* (Lon-
don), Encounter Pamphlet no. 1, 1961.

*Fiftieth Anniversary of Tolstoy's Death*
Venice, June 29–July 2, 1960, in cooperation with the
Cini Foundation

*Constitutionalism in Asia*
Canberra, August 22–26, 1960, in cooperation with the
International Commission of Jurists
See R. N. Spann, ed., *Constitutionalism in Asia* (London:
Asia Publishing House, 1963).

*The New Metropolis in the Arab World*
Cairo, December 17–22, 1960, in cooperation with the
Egyptian Society of Engineers
See Morroe Berger, ed., *The New Metropolis in the Arab
World* (New Delhi: Allied Publishers, 1963), also in Arabic
(Cairo, 1964).

*Tradition and Progress in Sudanese Society*
Khartoum, January 23–28, 1961, in cooperation with the
University of Khartoum
See *Tradition and Change in Sudanese Society* (Cairo, 1962)
(in Arabic).

*East–West Music Encounter*
Tokyo, April 17–May 6, 1961, in cooperation with the
Tokyo Metropolitan Society for International Cultural
Exchange
See *Music East and West* (Tokyo, 1961).

*Contemporary History in the Soviet Mirror*
    Geneva, July 16–23, 1961, in cooperation with *Survey* and l'Institut Universitaire des Hautes Etudes Internationales
    See John Keep, ed., *Contemporary History in the Soviet Mirror* (London: George Allen & Unwin, 1964).

*The Arab Writer and the Modern World*
    Rome, October 16–20, 1961, in cooperation with *Tempo Presente* and the Instituto per l'Oriente
    See *Contemporary Arab Literature* (Beirut, 1962) (in Arabic), and French edition (Beirut, 1962).

*Inter-University Co-operation in West Africa*
    Freetown, December 11–16, 1961, in cooperation with Fourah Bay College, Sierra Leone
    See J. T. Saunders and M. Dowuona, eds., *The West African Intellectual Community* (Ibadan: University Press, 1962).

*Futuribles: Conférence sur la Prévision*
    Geneva, June 25–28, 1962, in cooperation with l'Institut Universitaire des Hautes Etudes Internationales
    See Bertrand de Jouvenel, *L'Art de la Conjecture: Futuribles* (Monaco: Editions du Rocher, 1964), also in English (London: Weidenfeld & Nicolson, 1967).

*Soviet Literature*
    Oxford, July 2–8, 1962, in cooperation with *Survey* and St. Antony's College
    See Max Hayward and Leopold Labedz, eds., *Literature and Revolution in Soviet Russia* (London: Oxford University Press, 1963).

*Développement Economique et Social des Pays Méditerranéens*
    Naples, October 28–November 2, 1962, in cooperation with Centre de Sociologie Européenne (first of four conferences devoted to this subject)
    See *Problèmes du Développement Economique dans les pays Méditerranéens* (Paris: Mouton, 1963).

*African Literature and the University Curriculum*
    Dakar, March 26–30, 1963, in cooperation with the University of Dakar, and Freetown, April 3–8, 1963, in cooperation with Fourah Bay College
    See Gerald Moore, ed., *African Literature and the Universities* (Ibadan: University Press, 1965).

*Religion and Progress in Modern Asia*
> Manila, June 3–9, 1963, in cooperation with the University of Manila
> See Robert H. Bellah, ed., *Religion and Progress in Modern Asia* (New York: Free Press, 1965).

*Politics in West Africa*
> Cambridge, June 30–July 3, 1964, in cooperation with the Afro-Asian Center, Cambridge University
> See W. A. Lewis, *Politics in West Africa* (Toronto and New York: Oxford University Press, 1965).

*Contemporary Chinese Historiography*
> Oxford, September 6–12, 1964, in cooperation with *China Quarterly*
> See *China Quarterly*, nos. 22, 23, and 24, 1965.

*La Formacion de las Elites en America Latina*
> Montevideo, June 6–11, 1965, in cooperation with the Institute of International Studies, University of Montevideo
> See Seymour M. Lipset and Aldo Solari, eds., *Elites in Latin America* (London: Oxford University Press, 1967).

*Conditions of World Order*
> Serbelloni, June 12–19, 1965, in cooperation with *Daedalus* and the American Academy of Arts and Sciences
> See *Daedalus*, Spring 1966, and *Seminar Report* no. 8 by Stanley Hoffmann.

*Race and Color*
> Copenhagen, September 6–11, 1965, in cooperation with *Daedalus* and the American Academy of Arts and Sciences
> See *Daedalus*, Spring 1967, and *Seminar Report* no. 9.

*Economic Co-operation and Integration in Africa*
> Nairobi, December 13–18, 1965, in cooperation with the University College of Nairobi
> See R. H. Green and K. G. V. Krishna, eds., *Economic Cooperation in Africa* (London: Oxford University Press, 1967), and *Seminar Report* no. 11.

*Democracy and Development in South East Asia*
> Kuala Lumpur, February 21–24, 1966, in cooperation with *Quadrant* and the University of Malaya
> See *Quadrant*, May–June 1966, and *Seminar Report* no. 10 by James McAuley.

APPENDIX

# C

# Some of the Institutions That Co-Sponsored Congress Seminars

| | |
|---|---|
| AUSTRIA | Austrian Council for Economy<br>College for World Trade |
| BURMA | Society for the Extension of<br>Democratic Ideals |
| FRANCE | Centre de Sociologie Européenne<br>Faculté des Lettres et Sciences<br>Humaines, Université d'Aix-en-<br>Provence |
| GERMANY | Free University of Berlin<br>University of Hamburg |
| INDIA | Council for Cultural Relations<br>Gokhale Institute of Politics and<br>Economics<br>Indian Institute of Public<br>Administration<br>University of Bombay |
| ITALY | Cini Foundation<br>Istituto per l'Oriente<br>Faculty of Economics, Catholic<br>University, Milan |

| JAPAN | Society for International Cultural Exchange |
| | Tokyo Metropolitan Government |
| NIGERIA | University of Western Nigeria, Ibadan |
| PAKISTAN | Bureau of National Reconstruction |
| | Bengali Academy |
| | Dacca University |
| PHILIPPINES | University of the East |
| | University of the Philippines |
| | Philippine Pen Club |
| SENEGAL | Dakar University |
| SIERRA LEONE | Fourah Bay College (University College of Sierra Leone) |
| SPAIN | Facultad de Ciencias Politicas, Economicas y Comerciales, University of Madrid |
| SUDAN | University of Khartoum |
| SWEDEN | Scandinavian Institute of African Studies, University of Uppsala |
| SWITZERLAND | Graduate Institute of International Studies |
| | International Press Institute |
| TUNISIA | Free University of Tunis |
| U.A.R. | Egyptian Society of Engineers |
| UNITED STATES | Research Center in Economic Development and Cultural Change, University of Chicago |
| | *Daedalus*, Journal of the American Academy of Arts and Sciences |
| | University of California, Berkeley |
| UGANDA | Makerere University College |
| UNITED KINGDOM | St. Antony's College, Oxford |
| | Ditchley Manor, Oxford |
| URUGUAY | University of Montevideo |

# D

# Books Published by the Congress for Cultural Freedom or Its Affiliated Groups

✍

*Note:* Books preceded by a bullet are the result of seminars organized by the Congress for Cultural Freedom.

## AFRICA

### NIGERIA

- Moore, Gerald, ed. *African Literature and the Universities* (record of two seminars held at the University of Dakar and Fourah Bay College, in March and April 1963, on African Literature and the University Curriculum). Ibadan: Ibadan University Press, 1965.
- Passin, Herbert, and K. A. B. Jones-Quartey, eds. *Africa: The Dynamics of Change* (record of conference on Representative Government and National Progress, held at Ibadan, March 1959). Ibadan: Ibadan University Press, 1963.
- Saunders, J. T., and Modjaben Dowuona, eds. *The West African Intellectual Community* (papers and discussions of International Seminar on Inter-University Co-operation in West Africa, Freetown, December, 1961). Ibadan: Ibadan University Press, 1962.

Tregear, Peter, ed. *Handbook of West African Universities*. Ibadan: Ibadan University Press, 1962.

## ASIA

INDIA

- *Afro-Asian Attitudes* (selections from proceedings of Rhodes Seminar, October 1958). New Delhi: Congress for Cultural Freedom, 1961 (Basic Books).

  Aganbegyan. *Soviet Self-Criticism.* Calcutta: IPSS, 1965.

  Alisjahbana, S. Takdir. *Indonesia in the Modern World.* New Delhi: Congress for Cultural Freedom, 1961 (Basic Books).

  Ayyub, Abu Sayeed, and Amlan Datta, eds. *Ten Years of Quest* (Indian Committee for Cultural Freedom). Bombay: P. C. Manaktala & Sons, 1966.

- Berger, Morroe, ed. *The New Metropolis in the Arab World* (papers prepared for an international Seminar on City Planning and Urban Social Problems, Cairo, December 17–22, 1960). New Delhi, Bombay, Calcutta, etc.: Allied Publishers, 1963 (Basic Books).

  Boorman, Howard L. *Mao Tse-Tung: The Lacquered Image* (publication of the China Study Centre, New Delhi). Bombay: Manaktala, 1965.

  Bose, Nirmal K., and P. H. Patwardhan. *Gandhi in Indian Politics.* N.p., 1967.

  Chaudhuri, Ranjit. *Problem of Village Leadership.* Calcutta: IPSS, n.d.

  Cranston, Maurice. *Human Rights To-Day.* Bombay: Indian Committee for Cultural Freedom, Manaktala & Sons, 1966 (first published 1962).

- Datta, Amlan, ed. *Paths to Economic Growth* (proceedings of Poona Seminar on Paths to Economic Growth, January 22–28, 1961). New Delhi, Bombay, Calcutta, etc.: Allied Publishers, 1962; 2d ed., 1963 (Basic Books).

  Dave, Rohit. *The Chinese Bomb in Perspective.* Bombay: China Study Centre, 1965.

- *Democracy in the New States* (proceedings of Rhodes Seminar, October 1958). New Delhi: Congress for Cultural Freedom, 1959 (Basic Books).

- *East and South-East Asia Take a Second Look at Democracy* (report of the Delhi Conference, February 1961). New Delhi: Indian Institute for Public Administration and Indian Committee for Cultural Freedom, 1961. Also published in Tokyo.

- *T. S. Eliot* (papers and proceedings of a Seminar on T. S. Eliot held at St. Stephen's College, Delhi, February 27–28, 1965). Bombay: Manaktala, 1965.

- Haldar, M. K., and Robin Ghosh, eds. *Problems of Economic Growth* (report of Tokyo Seminar, April 1957). New Delhi: Congress for Cultural Freedom, 1960 (Basic Books).

  Hoang, Van Chi. *From Colonialism to Communism: A Case History of North Vietnam.* New Delhi, Bombay, Calcutta, etc.: Allied Publishers, 1964.

  Hutheesing, Raja, ed. *Tibet Fights for Freedom* (a White Book). Bombay: Orient Longmans, 1960.

- *Indian Committee for Cultural Freedom* (proceedings of Second Annual Conference, Madras, September 1953). Bombay: Indian Committee for Cultural Freedom, 1953.

- *Indian Congress for Cultural Freedom* (proceedings of First Asian Congress for Cultural Freedom, Bombay, March 1951). Bombay: Kanada Press, 1951.

  Kapur, Harish. *China and the Afro-Asian World.* New Delhi: China Study Centre, January 1966.

  Karnik, V. K. *China Invades India.* Bombay, New Delhi, Calcutta, etc.: Allied Publishers, 1963.

  Koestler, Arthur. *Criteria of Creativity in Science.* Calcutta: IPSS, 1965.

  Krishna, Daya. *Planning, Power and Welfare.* New Delhi: Congress for Cultural Freedom, 1959 (Basic Books).

  Krishna, Raj. *Food Price Policy.* New Delhi: Indian Committee for Cultural Freedom (Reprint Series no. 1), 1965.

  Kulharni, V. Y., comp. *Tolstoy, a Bibliography: Books of and on Tolstoy in Indian Languages.* Calcutta: Sree Saraswaty Press, 1960.

  Lüthy, Herbert; Pierre Emmanuel; and Burton Raffel. *Indonesia in Travail.* New Delhi: Congress for Cultural Freedom, 1966.

- Naik, J. P. *Long Term Educational Reconstruction in India* (background paper for Seminar on a National System of Education for India, convened by the University of Bombay and the ICCF, June 25–28, 1964). Bombay: ICCF, 1964.

Narayan, Jayaprakash. *Towards a New Society.* New Delhi: Congress for Cultural Freedom, 1958 (Basic Books).

Noorani, A. G. *Our Credulity and Negligence.* Bombay: Ramdas G. Bhaktal, 1963.

• *Problems of Maharashtra* (report of Bombay Seminar, May 1960). Bombay: ICCF, 1960.

Shah, A. B., ed. *Education, Scientific Policy and Developing Societies.* Foreword by E. Shils. Bombay: Manaktalas, 1967.

• ———. ed. *Goa: The Problems of Transition* (papers presented to the Seminar at Margao, Goa, November 1964). Bombay: Manaktalas, 1965.

———. *Higher Education in India.* Bombay: Lalvani Publishing House, 1967.

———. *India's Defence and Foreign Policies* (anthology). Bombay: Manaktalas, 1966.

———, ed. *Jawaharlal Nehru: A Critical Tribute.* Bombay: Manaktalas, 1965. 2d ed. 1967.

• ———, ed. *A National University* (papers and proceedings of Bombay Seminar, September 1962). Bombay: ICCF, 1964. 2d ed., 1967.

———. *Planning for Democracy in India and other Essays.* N.p., 1967.

———, and S. P. Aiyar, eds. *Gokhale and Modern India.* Bombay: Manaktalas, December 1966.

• Shah, A. B., and Nissim Ezekiel, eds. *A New Look at Communism* (Bombay Seminar, August 30–September 1, 1963). Bombay, 1963.

• Shah, A. B., and C. R. M. Rao. *Tradition and Modernity in India* (proceedings of the New Delhi Seminar, November 1961). Bombay: Manaktalas, 1965. 2d ed., 1967.

Sinha, K. K., ed. *Boris Pasternak.* Calcutta: CCF, 1959.

———. *Impressions of a Tour of Some South East Asian Countries.* Calcutta: IPSS, 1966.

JAPAN*

Aron, Raymond. *L'Opium des Intellectuels.* Tokyo: Ronso-sha, 1960.
*In Japanese unless otherwise indicated.

Bergson, Abram, and S. Kuznets. *Economic Trends in the Soviet Union.* Tokyo: Jiyu-sha, 1964

- *Changes in Soviet Society* (report of St. Antony's Conference, June 1957). Tokyo: Jiyu Press, 1958.

Draper, Theodore. *Castro's Revolution: Myths and Realities.* Tokyo: Ronso-sha, 1963 (orig. pub., New York: Praeger, 1962).

Hirabayaski, Taiko, ed. *Tragedy of Soviet Literature.* Tokyo: Shincho-sha, 1960.

Japan Cultural Forum, ed. *Modern Art of Asia: New Movements and Old Traditions.* Tokyo: Toto Shuppan, 1961 (in English).

- Japan Cultural Forum, ed. *Tradition and Change in Japanese Culture* (I). Tokyo: Shincho-sha, 1958.

- Japan Cultural Forum, ed. *Tradition and Change in Japanese Culture* (II): *Japanese Sentiment* (second seminar on Tradition and Change, Tokyo, 1958). Tokyo: Shincho-sha, 1964.

Kimura, Takeyasu, ed. *Cultural Freedom in Asia.* Tokyo: Charles E. Tuttle, 1956.

MacFarquhar, Roderick. *The Hundred Flowers Campaign and the Chinese Intellectuals.* Tokyo: Ronso-sha, 1963 (orig. pub., London: Stevens & Sons, 1960).

Mander, John. *Berlin: Hostage for the West.* Tokyo: Miyasaka Shuppan Sha, 1963.

- Murata, M., ed. *East and South-East Asia Take a Second Look at Democracy* (report of the Delhi Conference, February 1961). New Delhi and Tokyo: Indian Institute for Public Administration, and ICCF, 1961.

- *Music—East and West* (conference reports on 1961 Tokyo East–West Music Encounter). Tokyo, 1961 (in English).

- Passin, Herbert, ed., *Cultural Freedom in Asia* (proceedings of a Conference held at Rangoon, Burma, February 17–20, 1955, and convened by the Congress for Cultural Freedom and the Society for the Extension of Democratic Ideals). Tokyo: Charles E. Tuttle, 1956 (in English).

Rostow, W. W. *The Stages of Economic Growth.* Tokyo, 1967.

- Seki, Yoshihiko, ed. *Representative Government and Public Liberties in the New States* (proceedings of the Rhodes Conference, October 1958). Shiseido Publishing, 1959.

Sorensen, Theodore C. *Decision-Making in the White House.* Tokyo:

Jiyu-sha, 1964 (orig. pub., New York and London: Columbia University Press, 1963).

Tertz, Abram. *The Trial Begins.* Tokyo, 1967.

Wittfogel, Karl A. *Oriental Despotism.* Tokyo: Ronso Sosho, 1961.

KOREA

Kelsen, Hans. *The Political Theory of Bolshevism.* Seoul: Sasangge, 1962.

Kim, Jun-yop. *History of the Chinese Communist Party.* Rev. ed. Seoul: Sasangge, 1961.

• Kim, Yong-koo, ed. *Developments Under Freedom* (proceedings of Seoul Seminar, April 1961). N.p., 1962.

• ———, ed. *Tradition and Modernity* (a collection of papers presented at a series of seminars sponsored by the KCCF 1962–64). Seoul: Ch'unch'usa, 1965.

PAKISTAN

• Ahsan, Syed Ali, ed. *Islam in the Modern World* (proceedings of an International Seminar, Karachi, January–February 1959). Dacca: Pakistan Committee CCF, 1964.

• *Education and Freedom* (papers read at the Karachi Seminar sponsored by the Pakistan Committee, CCF, and Jamia Talim-e-Milli, January 1963), in *Jamia Educational Quarterly* (Karachi), vol. IV, no. 1 (January 1963).

• *Education and Religion* (papers read at the Karachi Seminar sponsored by the Pakistan Committee, CCF, and Jamia Talim-e-Milli, October 1961), in *Jamia Educational Quarterly* (Karachi), vol. III, no. 1 (January 1962).

• *Education and Society* (papers read at the Karachi Seminar sponsored by the Pakistan Committee, CCF, and Jamia Talim-e-Milli, April 1960), in *Jamia Educational Quarterly* (Karachi) vol. I, no. 4 (October 1960).

Guhathakurta. *State Aid to the Arts.* Karachi and Dacca: Central Printing Press, 1957.

• *Problems of Translation in Pakistani Languages* (papers read at the Karachi Seminar sponsored by the Pakistan Committee, CCF, and Jamia Talim-e-Milli, April 1964). Karachi: Jamia Institute of Education, 1964.

- *Tradition and Change in the Arts* (proceedings of a Karachi Seminar convened by the PCCF and University of Rajshahi, December 30–31, 1958, and January 1, 1959). Karachi: Pakistan Committee, CCF, 1959.

  *The Writer and his Social Responsibility.* Dacca: Pakistan PEN, 1961.

- *The Writer and the Idea of Freedom* (records of the Seminar held in Dacca in February 1957). Karachi: Pakistan Committee, CCF, 1961.

THE PHILIPPINES

Costa, Horacio de la. *The Background of Nationalism and Other Essays.* Manila: Solidaridad, 1965.

Golgay, Frank H., ed. *Philippines American Relations: The Elements That Have Created Both Alliance and Antagonism.* Manila–Bombay–New York: Solidaridad Publishing House, 1966.

- *Literature at the Crossroads* (Congress for Cultural Freedom symposia on the Filipino novel, Filipino poetry, and the Filipino theater, 1962). Manila: Alberto S. Florentino, 1965.

Romulo, Carlos P. *Identity and Change: Towards a National Definition.* Manila: Solidaridad, 1965.

Sionil José, F., ed. *Asian PEN Anthology.* Vol 1. Manila: Solidaridad, 1966.

———, ed. *Equinox 1: An Anthology of New Writing from the Philippines.* Manila: Solidaridad, 1965.

## MIDDLE EAST

EGYPT

*African Constitutions.* Cairo: Congress for Cultural Freedom, 1961 (in Arabic).

- Berger, Morroe, ed. *The New Metropolis in the Arab World* (proceedings of Cairo Seminar, December 17–22, 1960). Cairo: Congress for Cultural Freedom, 1964 (in Arabic).

- *Problems of Administration* (seminar on Comparative Studies, Cairo, 1959). Cairo: Congress for Cultural Freedom, 1959 (English and Arabic).

- *Tradition and Change in Sudanese Society* (report of the Khartoum Seminar, January 1961). Cairo: Congress for Cultural Freedom, 1962 (in Arabic).

## LEBANON

- *Contemporary Arab Literature* (proceedings of the Rome Seminar, October 16–22, 1961). Beirut: n.p., 1962 (in Arabic).
- *La Littérature arabe contemporaine* (travaux du colloque de Rome, du 16 au 22 Octobre 1961). Sommaire du texte arabe. Beyrouth, 1962.

## TUNISIA

- *The Role of the University in Society* (report of the Tunis Seminar on Freedom and Society: The Role of the Scholar in Society, April 1959). In special issue of *Al Fikr:* (Tunis), no. 1, October 1959 (in Arabic).

# EUROPE

## FRANCE

Arciniegas, German; Carlos Alberto Floria; and Salvador Cruz. *Tres Ensayos sobre nuestra America.* Paris: Cuadernos, n.d. (ILARI).

Aron, Raymond. *Trois Essais sur l'Age Industriel* (collection *Preuves).* Paris: Plon, 1965.

- ————; François Bondy; George Kennan; Herbert Lüthy; Jayaprakash Narayan; Arthur Schlesinger, Jr.; Carlo Schmid; et al. *La Démocratie à l'Epreuve du XXe Siècle* (colloques de Berlin, June 1960. Paris: Calmann-Lévy, 1960.
- Aron, Raymond; George Kennan; Robert Oppenheimer; et al. *Colloques de Rheinfelden* (September 1959). Paris: Calmann-Lévy, 1960.

Cheverny, Jules. *Les Deux Stratégies du Communisme* (collection *Preuves).* Paris: Juilliard, 1965.

Fagg, William. *Sculptures Africaines.* Paris: Fernand Hazan, 1965.

Forgues, Nadine, and Pierre Forgues, eds. *L'Affaire Siniavski-Daniel* (collection *Preuves).* Paris: Christian Bourgeois, 1967.

Gara, Ladislas. *Anthologie de la Poésie Hongroise du XIIe Siècle à Nos Jours.* Paris: Editions du Seuil, 1962.

————, ed. *Hommage à Gyula Illyes.* Paris: Occidental Press, 1963.

Jelenski, Constantin. *Anthologie de la Poésie Polonaise.* Paris: Editions du Seuil, 1965.

- Jouvenel, Bertrand de. *L'Art de la Conjecture* (collection Futuribles). Monaco: Editions du Rocher, 1964.

  Kende, Peter. *Logique de l'Economic Centralisée: Un exemple—La Hongrie.* Paris: Sedes, 1964.

  Lasky, Melvin J., and François Bondy. *La Révolution Hongroise* (Histoire du Soulèvement d'Octobre), precédée de *Une Révolution Antitotalitaire* par Raymond Aron. Paris: Plon, 1957.

  Lüthy, Herbert. *Le Passé Présent: Combats d'Idées de Calvin à Rousseau* (collection *Preuves*), Monaco: Editions du Rocher, 1965.

- *Problèmes du Développement Economique dans les Pays Méditerranéens* (actes du Colloque International de Naples, 28 October–2 November, 1962). Publiés par Jean Cuisenier. Préface de Raymond Aron. The Hague: Mouton, 1963.

  *La Vérité sur l'Affaire Nagy.* Préface de Albert Camus. Paris: Plon, 1958.

GERMANY

  Allemann, Fritz René. *25 Mal die Schweiz.* München: R. Piper & Co. Verlag, 1965.

  *Der Fall Imre Nagy: Eine Dokumentation.* Vorwort von Albert Camus. Köln and Berlin: Kiepenheuer & Witsch, 1959.

  Lasky, Melvin J., ed. *Die Ungarische Revolution* (ein Weissbuch). Vorwort von Karl Jaspers. Berlin: Colloquium Verlag, 1958.

- *Wissenschaft und Freiheit* (Internationale Tagung, Hamburg 23–26 Juli 1953). Berlin: Grunewald Verlag, 1954.

ITALY

- Aron, Raymond. *La Democrazia alla Prova del Ventesimo Secolo.* Bologna: Il Mulino, 1962.

SWITZERLAND

- Aron, Raymond; François Bondy; Michael Freund; Walter Hofer; George Kennan; Herbert Lüthy; Salvador de Madariaga; Robert Oppenheimer; Arthur Schlesinger, Jr.; and Carlo Schmid. *Die Bewahrung der Democratie im 20. Jahrhundert* (das Seminar von Berlin). Zürich: Evz Verlag, 1961.

- Aron, Raymond; George Kennan; Robert Oppenheimer; et al. *Die Industrielle Gesellschaft und die Drei Welten* (des Seminar von Rheinfelden). Zürich: Evz Verlag, 1961.

THE UNITED KINGDOM

Blake, Patricia, and Max Hayward, eds. *Half-Way to the Moon: New Writing from Russia.* London: Weidenfeld & Nicolson, 1964 (an *Encounter* Book).

• Clegg, H. A. *A New Approach to Industrial Democracy.* Oxford: Basil Blackwell, 1960 (outgrowth of the Vienna Conference on Workers' Participation in Management, Vienna, September 1958).

Goldenberg, Boris. *The Cuban Revolution and Latin America* (vol. V, Library of International Studies). London: George Allen & Unwin, 1965.

Griffith, William E. *The Sino-Soviet Rift* (vol. IV, Library of International Studies). London: George Allen & Unwin, 1964.

• Hayward, Max, and Leopold Labedz, eds. *Literature and Revolution in Soviet Russia* (papers given at a conference held at St. Antony's College, Oxford, July 1962). London: Oxford University Press, 1963.

Hoang, Van Chi. *From Colonialism to Communism: A Case History of North Vietnam.* London and Dunmow: Pall Mall Press, 1964.

• Jelenski, K. A., ed. *History and Hope: Progress in Freedom* (Berlin Conference of 1960). London: Routledge & Kegan Paul, 1962.

• Jouvenel, Bertrand de. *The Art of Conjecture.* Tr. from the French. London: Weidenfeld & Nicolson, 1967 (in part the outgrowth of the Congress-sponsored seminar, Geneva, June 1962).

• Keep, John, ed. *Contemporary History in the Soviet Mirror* (vol. II, Library of International Studies). London: George Allen & Unwin, 1964.

Labedz, Leopold, ed. *Revisionism: Essays on the History of Marxist Ideas* (vol. I, Library of International Studies). London: George Allen & Unwin, 1962.

Laqueur, Walter. *Russia and Germany: A Century of Conflict.* London: Weidenfeld & Nicolson, 1965 (an *Encounter* Book).

———, and George Lichtheim, eds. *The Soviet Cultural Scene, 1956–1957* (selections from *Soviet Survey*). New York: Praeger, and London: Stevens & Sons, 1958.

Lasky, Melvin J., ed. *The Hungarian Revolution* (a White Book). Intro. by Hugh Seton-Watson. London: Secker & Warburg, 1957.

Lewis, Bernard. *The Middle East and the West.* London: Weidenfeld & Nicolson, 1963, 1964 (an *Encounter* Book).

• Lewis, W. Arthur. *Politics in West Africa.* Toronto and New York: Oxford University Press, 1965 (basic paper delivered at the Seminar on Politics in West Africa, Cambridge, June–July 1964).

Li, Choh-Ming. ed. *Industrial Development in Communist China.* New York and London: Praeger, 1964 (first published in Great Britain in 1964 as a special issue of *China Quarterly*).

• Lipset, Seymour M., and Aldo Solari, eds. *Elites in Latin America* (outgrowth of Montevideo Seminar, June 1965). London: Oxford University Press, 1967 (ILARI).

MacFarquhar, Roderick, ed. *The Hundred Flowers* (Atlantic Books). London: Stevens & Sons, 1960.

Mancall, Mark, ed. *Formosa Today.* London, Praeger, 1964 (most of the material in this book was first published in Great Britain in 1963 in *China Quarterly*).

Nolte, Ernst. *Three Faces of Fascism.* London: Weidenfeld & Nicolson, 1965 (an *Encounter* Book).

Paloczi-Horvath, György, comp. *One Sentence on Tyranny: Hungarian Literary Gazette Anthology.* London: Waverly Press, 1957.

• *Science and Freedom* (proceedings of Hamburg Congress, July 23–26, 1953). London: Secker & Warburg, 1955.

• *The Soviet Economy* (a discussion by R. Aron, C. Clark, C. A. R. Crosland, B. de Jouvenel, G. Kennan, R. Löwenthal, M. Polanyi, E. Shils, P. Wiles, B. D. Wolfe, and W. S. Woytinsky). London: Secker & Warburg, 1956 (seminar, Milan, September 12–17, 1955).

• Spann, R. N. *Constitutionalism in Asia* (papers and discussions of Seminar on Constitutionalism in Asia, held in August 1960 at the Australian National University). London: Asia Publishing House, 1963.

Spender, Stephen; Irving Kristol; and Melvin Lasky, eds. *Encounters: An Anthology from the First Ten Years of "Encounter" Magazine.* London: Weidenfeld & Nicolson, 1963.

*The Truth about the Nagy Affair.* Preface by Albert Camus. London: Secker & Warburg, 1959.

Tütsch, Hans. *From Ankara to Marrakesh* (vol. III, Library of International Studies). London: George Allen & Unwin, 1964.

# THE AMERICAS

THE UNITED STATES

- Aron, Raymond; George Kennan; Robert Oppenheimer; et al. *World Technology and Human Destiny.* Ann Arbor: University of Michigan, 1963 (the Rheinfelden Seminar, September 1959).

- Bellah, Robert N., ed. *Religion and Progress in Modern Asia* (proceedings of Manila Conference on Cultural Motivations to Progress in South and Southeast Asia, June 1963). New York: Free Press, and London: Collier-Macmillan, 1965.

  Honey, P. J. *North Vietnam Today: Profile of a Communist Satellite.* New York: Frederick A. Praeger, 1962 (most of the material in this book was first published in *China Quarterly* in 1962).

  Hudson, G. F.; Richard Lowenthal; and Roderick MacFarquhar. *The Sino-Soviet Dispute.* New York: Praeger, 1961 (first published in Great Britain as a special supplement to *China Quarterly*).

  Laqueur, Walter, and Leopold Labedz. *The Future of Communist Society.* New York: Frederick A. Praeger, 1962 (first published in Great Britain in 1961 as a special issue of *Survey*).

  ———. *Hungary Today.* New York: Frederick A. Praeger, 1962 (first published in Great Britain in 1962 as a special issue of *Survey*).

  ———. *Polycentrism.* New York: Frederick A. Praeger, 1962.

  ———. *The State of Soviet Science.* Cambridge, Mass: MIT Press, 1965 (these essays originally appeared in *Survey*, no. 52, July 1964).

  ———. *The State of Soviet Studies.* Cambridge, Mass. MIT Press, 1965 (these essays originally appeared in *Survey*, nos. 50–51, January and April 1964).

  Löwenthal, Richard. *World Communism: The Disintegration of a Secular Faith.* New York: Oxford University Press, 1964 (an *Encounter* Book).

  MacFarquhar, Roderick, ed. *China Under Mao: Politics Takes Command* (a selection of articles from *China Quarterly*. Cambridge, Mass.: MIT Press, 1966.

  Passin, Herbert. *China's Cultural Diplomacy.* New York: Praeger, 1963 (*China Quarterly*).

  Rorty, James, and Moshe Decter. *McCarthy and the Communists.* Boston: Beacon Press, 1954.

Scalapino, Robert A. *North Korea Today.* New York and London: Frederick A. Praeger, 1963.

LATIN AMERICA

Agulla, Juan Carlos. *Federalismo y Centralismo.* Buenos Aires: Libera, 1967.

————, et al. *Del Sociologo y su compromiso.* Buenos Aires: Libera, 1966.

Arenas, Mario Castro. *La Novela peruana y la evolucion social.* Lima: Ediciones Cultura y Libertad, 1965. 2d ed., 1967.

Bustamente, Norberto R. *Los Intelectuales argentinos y su Sociedad.* Buenos Aires: Libera, 1967.

Campobassi, José S.; Carlos S. Fayt; Jose Luis de Imaz; Mario Justo Lopez; and Luis Pan. *Los Partidos politicos: Estructura y vigencia en la Argentina.* Buenos Aires: Cooperadora de Derecho y Ciencias Sociales, 1965.

Coda, Hector Hugo. *La Educacion y las comunicaciones de masa.* Buenos Aires: Libera, 1966.

Dimase, Leonardo; Alfredo Garofano; and Gerardo Andujar. *La Situacion gremial argentina.* Buenos Aires: Libera, 1964.

Dominguez, Ramiro. *El Valle y la Loma: Comunicaciones en comunidades rurales paraguayas.* Asuncion: Emasa, 1966.

Garmendia, Dionisio J. *Uruguay 1967: Una interpretacion.* Montevideo: Alfa, 1967.

Giberti, Horacio; Aldo Solari; Gino Germani; and Jorge a Ochoa de Equilear. *Sociedad, Economica y reforma agraria.* Buenos Aires: Libera, 1965.

Grossi, Hector, et al. *Censura en el cine.* Buenos Aires: Libera, 1966.

Heisecke, Guillermo. *Bibliografia sociologica en el Paraguay.* Asuncion: El Arte, 1965.

Inglese, Juan Osvaldo, and Carlos L. Yegros Doria. *Universidad y Estudiantes,* and Berdichevski, Leon. *Universidad y Peronismo.* Buenos Aires: Libera, 1965.

Kolapa, J. *Patrones variables como tiempo social y espacio cultural.* Asuncion: El Arte, 1965.

• Lipset, Seymour M., and Aldo Solari, eds. *Elites y Desarrollo en América latina.* Buenos Aires: Paidos, 1967.

Rivarola, Domingo M. *Migracion Paraguay.* Asuncion: C. P. de Estudios sociologicos, 1967.

Solari, Aldo. *El Tercerismo en el Uruguay.* Montevideo: Alfa, 1965.

Verga, Alberto; Nelson Dominguez; Leon Zafran; and Horacio Martorelli. *El Periodismo por dentro.* Buenos Aires: Libera, 1965.

# E

# Congress for Cultural Freedom, Summary of 1966 Expenditures

| | |
|---|---:|
| EXECUTIVE COMMITTEE | $ 7,500 |
| GENEVA OFFICE | 55,000 |
| *Encounter* AND *Encounter* BOOKS | 30,000 |
| INTERNATIONAL SECRETARIAT | 200,000 |
| LONDON OFFICE—COMPTROLLER | 55,000 |
| EUROPEAN COMMITTEE FOR CULTURAL AID | 100,000 |
| EASTERN EUROPEAN PROGRAM | 50,000 |
| INSTITUTE OF MEDITERRANEAN CULTURE | 80,000 |
| ARAB PROGRAM | 20,000 |
| ASIAN INSTITUTE OF INTERNATIONAL RELATIONS | 100,000 |
| LATIN AMERICAN INSTITUTE OF INTERNATIONAL RELATIONS | 264,500 |
| *Mundo Nuevo* | 80,000 |
| *Aportes* | 30,000 |
| *Cadernos Brasileiros* | 30,000 |
| *Temas* | 5,000 |
| INTERNATIONAL SEMINAR PROGRAM | 100,000 |
| LOCAL AND REGIONAL CONFERENCES | 50,000 |
| INDIVIDUAL FELLOWSHIPS, LECTURE TOURS, AND STUDY GROUPS | 40,000 |
| ARTS COMMITTEE | 10,000 |
| INDIAN COMMITTEE FOR CULTURAL FREEDOM | 60,000 |

| | |
|---|---:|
| *Quest*—CALCUTTA | 10,000 |
| CHINA STUDY CENTER | 10,000 |
| *China Report*—NEW DELHI | 10,000 |
| JAPAN CULTURAL FORUM | 20,000 |
| *Jiyu*—TOKYO | 50,000 |
| AUSTRALIAN ASSOCIATION FOR CULTURAL FREEDOM | 15,000 |
| *Quadrant*—SYDNEY | 8,000 |
| AFFILIATED PUBLICATIONS—DISTRIBUTION AND PROMOTION | 40,000 |
| *Preuves*—PARIS | 80,000 |
| *Der Monat*—BERLIN | 60,000 |
| *Tempo Presente*—ROME | 45,000 |
| *Perspektiv*—COPENHAGEN | 10,000 |
| *Hiwar*—BEIRUT | 30,000 |
| *Black Orpheus*—IBADAN | 2,500 |
| *Survey*—LONDON | 45,000 |
| *China Quarterly*—LONDON | 45,000 |
| *Minerva*—LONDON | 30,000 |
| *Censorship*—LONDON | 30,000 |
| *Transition*—KAMPALA | 25,000 |
| *New African*—LONDON | 15,000 |
| *Solidarity*—MANILA | 8,000 |
| BOOK PUBLISHING | 15,000 |
| CONTINGENCY FUND | 100,000 |
| *TOTAL | $2,070,500 |
| TOTAL NUMBER OF EMPLOYEES | 280 |
| TOTAL PERSONNEL COMPENSATION | $783,271 |
| TOTAL SOCIAL CHARGES | $101,773 |

*The figure given as the total of current expenditure includes the additional figures for personnel compensation and total social charges.

# Notes

### CHAPTER 1
### *Out of No Man's Land*

1. *Der Monat* (Berlin), July–August 1950, p. 472.

2. "The Prevention of Literature," *Polemic*, January 1946, reprinted in *The Collected Essays, Journalism and Letters of George Orwell* (Harmondsworth, Middlesex: Penguin Books, 1970), IV: 84, and "The 'Liberal' Fifth Column," *Partisan Review*, Summer 1946, reprinted in William Barrett, *The Truants* (New York, 1982).

3. "I have debated in my mind whether this book should be delayed. . . . I have sought the advice of those whom I consider politically wise. The decision was not lightly taken." Pp. vii–viii.

4. Quoted by Leo Valiani in his memoir "Koestler the Militant," *Encounter*, July–August 1984.

5. "Writers for the Defense of Culture," *Partisan Review*, 1984, no. 3.

6. *New Statesman and Nation*, July 6, 1935.

7. Gustav Regler, *The Owl of Minerva* (London, 1959), pp. 232–33.

8. Boris Shub, *The Choice* (New York, 1950); see also *New York Times*, October 8, 1947, and *Time*, October 20, 1947.

9. A. J. P. Taylor, "Intellectuals at Wroclaw," *Manchester Guardian*, September 2, 1948; Kingsley Martin, "Hyenas and Other Reptiles," *New Statesman*, September 4 (and discussion in Correspondence pages of *New Statesman*, September 4, 11, 18, and 25); Freda Kirchwey, "East Meets West at Wroclaw," *Nation* (New York), September 4, 1948; Margaret Marshall, "Notes by the Way," *Nation*, September 18, 1948; and Bryn Hovde, "The Conference of Intellectuals," *New Leader*, December 11, 1948. See also Feliks Topolski, *Confessions of a Congress Delegate* (London, 1949), reprinted in *idem, Fourteen Letters* (London, 1988); A.

J. P. Taylor, *A Personal History* (London, 1983); François Bondy, "Remembering Wroclaw," in his "European Diary," *Encounter,* June 1984; and *New York Times* reports, August 1948. For Stephen Spender's message to the Congress, see *Nation,* September 18, 1948, p. 326.

10. Sidney Hook, "The Communist Peace Offensive," in *Out of Step* (New York, 1987), pp. 382–96, and Nicolas Nabokov, *Bagázh* (New York, 1975), pp. 232–39.

11. Dwight Macdonald, "The Waldorf Conference," *Politics,* Winter 1949.

12. Dmitri Shostakovich, *Testimony,* as related to and edited by Solomon Volkov (New York, 1979).

13. Hook, *Out of Step,* p. 395.

14. Macdonald, "Waldorf Conference."

15. William Barrett, "Culture Conference at the Waldorf," *Commentary,* May 1949.

16. Nabokov, *Bagázh.* For the conference generally, see Irving Howe, "The Culture Conference," *Partisan Review,* May 1949; Freda Kirchwey, "Battle of the Waldorf," *Nation,* April 2, 1949 (and an exchange of letters with Sidney Hook, April 30, 1949); Margaret Marshall, "Notes by the Way," *Nation,* April 9, 1949; Tom O'Connor, "News Tailored to Fit," *Nation,* April 16, 1949; and Joseph P. Lash, "Weekend at the Waldorf," *New Republic,* April 18, 1949. See also Frank A. Ninkovich, *The Diplomacy of Ideas: U.S. Foreign Policy and Cultural Relations, 1938–1950* (Cambridge, 1981), pp. 162–64, and Leslie A. Fiedler, *Olaf Stapledon: A Man Divided* (New York, 1983), pp. 20–30.

17. Norman MacKenzie, "The Paris Dovecote," *New Statesman and Nation,* April 30, 1949, deals with the World Peace Congress. Sidney Hook, "Report on the International Day Against Dictatorship and War," *Partisan Review,* July 1949, discusses the rival conference. "Partisans v. Resisters," *New Republic,* May 9, 1949, discusses both.

18. Hook, "Report on International Day." See also Ninkovich, *Diplomacy of Ideas,* p. 164.

19. Daniel Aaron, *Writers on the Left: Episodes in American Literary Communism* (New York, 1961), p. 319.

20. T. R. Fyvel, *George Orwell: A Personal Memoir* (London, 1982), pp. 129–31.

21. Malcolm Muggeridge, *The Infernal Grove* (London: Fontana Books, 1975), p. 16.

22. Michael Heller, "Boris Souvarine 1895–1984," *Survey,* vol. 28, no. 4 (Winter 1984).

23. Arthur Koestler, *The Invisible Writing* (London, 1954), p. 491.

24. Elisabeth Young-Bruehl, *Hannah Arendt: For Love of the World* (New Haven: Yale University Press, 1982), p. 281.

25. J.-P. Sartre, *Situations* (Paris, 1964), vol. IV.

26. Quoted in Melvin J. Lasky, "Living with an Insult in a Mind-Free Zone," *Encounter,* September–October 1983.

27. *Washington Post,* March 12, 1967. Later, in June 1985, Galbraith told the author that he considered the Congress's seminars to have been "social entertainments" and not genuinely intellectual enterprises. But this retrospective view is less a serious assessment than an example of what Roger Scruton, in *Thinkers of the New Left* (London, 1985), called Galbraith's "sublime sarcasm."

28. June 19, 1959, CCF Archives.

29. Jeffrey Hart, *When the Going Was Good: American Life in the Fifties* (New York, 1982), p. 184.

30. February 28, 1957, CCF–AICF Archives.

31. Raymond Aron, "Does America Welcome American Leadership?" *Saturday Review,* January 13, 1951.

32. Malcolm Muggeridge, *Like It Was* (London, 1981), p. 193.

33. Quoted in Iain Hamilton, *Koestler: A Biography* (London, 1982), p. 142.

34. *Politics* (New York), Winter 1949.

35. Norman Podhoretz, *Making It* (New York, 1967).

36. Conversation with author, December 19, 1982. Edward Shils conceded there was some poetic license used here, in that Josselson was born in Estonia and Lasky in America. But the families of both may be called Russian Jews.

CHAPTER 2
*The 1950 Offensive*

1. *Politics* (New York), Winter 1949, p. 36.

2. *Der Monat,* July–August 1950.

3. Iain Hamilton, *Koestler: A Biography* (London, 1982); Herbert R. Lottman, *Albert Camus: A Biography* (New York, 1979), pp. 458–63; and Gilbert Walusinski, "Camus et les Groupes de liaison internationale," *la Quinzaine* (Paris), March 1–15, 1972, pp. 22–24.

4. Nathan Glick, "In the Bronx, and After," in *Melvin J. Lasky ... a 60th Birthday,* a tribute to Lasky published by *Encounter* in January 1980.

5. Daniel Bell, "Our New York Days," in *ibid.*

6. *Partisan Review,* Summer 1939, pp. 125–27.

7. George F. Kennan, *Memoirs 1950–1963* (New York, 1972), p. 192.

8. Peter Blake, "AMG in Germany," *Politics,* no. 3, 1948, p. 194.

9. *The Collected Essays, Journalism, and Letters of George Orwell* (Harmondsworth, Middlesex: Penguin Books, 1970), IV: 434.

10. *Time,* October 21, 1946.

11. Melvin J. Lasky, "Berlin Letter," *Partisan Review,* no. 1, 1948.

12. Sidney Hook Papers, Hoover Institution on War, Revolution, and Peace, California.

13. Richard Crossman, ed., *The God That Failed* (1949), p. 17.

14. *Ibid.,* p. 21.

15. *Time and Tide,* February 5, 1938.

16. Arthur Koestler Papers, London.

17. Hamilton, *Koestler,* p. 193, quoting an entry from Mamaine Koestler's diary.

18. Crossman, ed., *God That Failed,* pp. 99, 105, 106–12.

19. Ignazio Silone, *Emergency Exit* (London, 1969), pp. 96, 97, 98.

20. Quoted in Edmund Wilson, "Two Survivors: Malraux and Silone," *Horizon* (London), October 1945.

21. Darina Silone in letter to author, August 29, 1984.

22. The references to the Congress in this chapter are drawn from *Der Monat* (Berlin), July–August 1950, which reprinted (in German) the papers delivered. Those reprinted in English include Arthur Koestler, "The Right to Say 'No'" and "An Outgrown Dilemma," in *The Trail of the Dinosaur* (London, 1955); Franz Borkenau, "Return to the Old Values," *The Nineteenth Century and After* (London), November 1950; James Burnham, "Rhetoric and Peace," *Partisan Review,* vol. XVII, no. 8 (1950); and Elliot E. Cohen, "What Do the Germans Propose to Do?" *Commentary,* September 1950. Those reprinted in French include Raymond Aron, "Impostures de la Neutralité," *Liberté de l'Esprit,* September 1950; Josef Czapski, "Pour les Jeunes Evadés de l'Est," *ibid.,* November 1950; and Alfred Weber, "Nostra Maxima Culpa," *ibid.,* November 1950. For further discussions of the Berlin conference, see François Bondy, "Berlin Congress for Freedom," *Commentary,* September 1950; Sidney Hook, *Out of Step* (New York, 1987), pp. 432–44; and Pierre Grémion, "Berlin 1950," *Commentaire* (Paris), no. 34, Summer 1986.

23. Hugh Trevor-Roper, "Ex-Communist v. Communist," *Manchester Guardian,* July 10, 1950.

24. Unpublished letter to *Manchester Guardian;* copy in CCF–IACF Archives.

25. Peter de Mendelssohn, "Berlin Congress," *New Statesman and Nation,* July 15, 1950.

**CHAPTER 3**
*Good-bye to Berlin*

1. CCF–IACF Archives.

2. James Burnham Papers, Kent, Connecticut.

3. CCF–IACF Archives.

4. Donald Robinson, "Mr. Brown vs. Generalissimo Stalin," *Reader's Digest*, September 1952. For critical reports, see Sidney Lens, "Lovestone Diplomacy," *Nation*, July 5, 1965, and *Libération* (Paris), November 27, 1985. Brown died in Paris in February 1989.

5. CCF–IACF Archives.

6. *Ibid.*

7. Trevor-Roper, "Ex-Communist v. Communist," and G. A. Borgese, "Errore di Berlino," *Corriere della Sera*, October 8, 1950.

8. August 30, 1950, CCF–IACF Archives.

9. Iain Hamilton, *Koestler: A Biography* (London, 1982), p. 199.

10. André Reszler and Henri Schwamm, eds., *Denis de Rougemont* (Neuchâtel, 1976), for Rougemont's seventieth birthday, pp. 1, 108.

11. Eugène Ionesco, "Of Utopianism and Intellectuals," *Encounter*, February 1978.

12. Raymond Aron, *The Committed Observer* (Chicago, 1983), pp. 64–65.

13. *Ibid.*, pp. 95–96.

14. Robert Colquhoun, *Raymond Aron* (London, 1986), p. 2.

15. *Ibid.*, vol. 2, pp. 508–9.

16. Henry Kissinger, "Raymond Aron," in *Commentaire*, February 1985 (special issue on Aron), p. 129.

17. October 26, 1960, Diana Josselson Papers, Geneva.

18. Diana Josselson Papers, Geneva.

19. *Ibid.*

20. June 16, 1951, CCF–IACF Archives.

21. Melvin Lasky, in *Homme de lettres: Freundesgabe für François Bondy* (Zürich, 1985), pp. 23, 90.

22. Hamilton, *Koestler* (note 9 above), p. 218.

23. January 29, 1951, Arthur Koestler Papers, London.

24. January 29, 1951, James Burnham Papers, Kent, Connecticut.

25. January 22 and February 6, 1951, *ibid.*

26. July 19, 1951, CCF–IACF Archives.

27. Hamilton, *Koestler,* p. 201.

28. CCF–IACF Archives.

29. Sidney Hook, *Out of Step* (New York, 1987), p. 450.

30. CCF–IACF Archives.

31. Thomas W. Braden, "I'm Glad the CIA Is 'Immoral,'" *Saturday Evening Post,* May 20, 1967.

32. *Ibid.*

33. Cord Meyer, *Facing Reality* (New York, 1980), p. 67. The biographical details also come from this book.

34. CCF–IACF Archives.

35. Hook, *Out of Step*, p. 451.

36. CCF–IACF Archives.

37. Raymond Aron, "Does Europe Welcome American Leadership?" *Saturday Review*, January 13, 1951.

38. Malcolm Muggeridge, "An Anatomy of Neutralism," *Time*, November 2, 1953.

39. This and other references in the section, "The End of Ideology," are from the CCF–IACF Archives.

40. Silone's speech was published in *Der Monat*, February 1951, "Wer Ohren hat zu hören ..."

41. Edward Shils, "The End of Ideology?" *Encounter*, November 1955.

42. Raymond Aron, "The End of the Ideological Age?" (Paris, 1955).

43. Arthur Koestler, *Que Veulent les Amis de la Liberté?* (Paris, 1950).

44. *New York Times*, December 4, 1951.

45. Genêt (Janet Flanner), "Letter from Paris," *The New Yorker*, May 31, 1952. For detailed reports and discussions of the festival, see *Preuves*, May 1952 and June 1952, and Hellmut Jaesrich, "Brief aus Paris," *Der Monat*, July 1952.

46. July 3, 1952, CCF–IACF Archives.

47. Hamilton, *Koestler* (note 9 above), p. 243.

## CHAPTER 4
### Encounter: *"Our Greatest Asset"*

1. Irving Kristol, letter to M. J. Lasky, April 22, 1953, CCF–IACF Archives.

2. Raymond Aron, *Mémoires: 50 ans de réflexion politique* (Paris, 1983), p. 238.

3. Michael Josselson, letter to E. Shils, February 17, 1964, Diana Josselson Papers, Geneva.

4. Kristol, conversation with author, July 11, 1986.

5. CCF–IACF Archives for all references in this section (Lichtheim, Nabokov, Josselson).

6. Fredric Warburg, *All Authors Are Equal* (London, 1973), p. 156.

7. Irving Kristol, "Memoirs of a Trotskyist," in *Reflections of a Neoconservative* (New York, 1983), p. 12.

8. Geoffrey Norman, "The Godfather of Neoconservatism (And His Family)," *Esquire*, February 13, 1979.

9. Irving Kristol, "'Civil Liberties', 1952—A Study in Confusion," *Commentary,* March 1952.

10. *Ibid.,* May 1952.

11. *Ibid.,* July 1952. The WPA was a government agency created in 1935 to relieve unemployment as part of President Roosevelt's New Deal.

12. Reprinted in Kristol, *Reflections of a Neoconservative.*

13. Stephen Spender, *Journals 1939–1983* (New York, 1986), p. 356.

14. F. A. Voigt, in *Manchester Guardian,* February 2, 1937.

15. Stephen Spender, in *New York Times,* April 25, 1948.

16. Stephen Spender, "Message to Wroclaw," *Nation,* September 18, 1948.

17. Spender, *Journals 1939–1983,* p. 356.

18. *Ibid.,* p. 356.

19. Christopher Isherwood, "Autobiography of an Individualist," *The Twentieth Century* (London), May 1951.

20. Ian Hamilton, "Owning Up," *Times Literary Supplement,* November 22, 1985.

21. Quoted by Rupert Christiansen in "Spender the Man," *The Spectator,* November 30, 1985.

22. Isherwood, "Autobiography of an Individualist."

23. September 16, 1953, CCF–IACF Archives.

24. *The Observer* (London), October 4, 1953.

25. CCF–IACF Archives.

26. Transcript in CCF–IACF Archives.

27. "Review of Reviews," *The Spectator,* January 22, 1954.

28. Patrick Carpenter, "London Letter," *Meanjin* (Melbourne), vol. XIII (1954).

29. A. J. P. Taylor, "A New Voice for Culture," *The Listener,* October 8, 1953.

30. Quoted in letter from Spender to Josselson, October 22, 1953, CCF–IACF Archives.

31. *Times Literary Supplement,* October 9, 1953.

32. *Encounter,* January 1954.

33. See Ronald Radosh and Joyce Hilton, *The Rosenberg File* (New York, 1983).

34. Kristol to Josselson, July 31, 1953, CCF–IACF Archives.

35. Quoted in Josselson letter to Kristol, August 4, 1953, CCF–IACF Archives.

36. Taylor, "New Voice."

37. *The Observer,* October 4, 1953.

38. Transcript (note 26 above).

39. Forster and Milosz are quoted by Spender in his letter to Josselson, October 22, 1953, CCF–IACF Archives.

40. CCF–IACF Archives.

41. This and other references to Executive Committee meeting of January 1955 come from CCF–IACF Archives.

42. This and subsequent references to the American Committee—Norman Jacobs, Nicolas Nabokov, the exchange of letters between Kristol and Josselson, Arthur Schlesinger, Spender, and Muggeridge—are from CCF–IACF Archives.

43. Dwight Macdonald, "Politics Past (1)," *Encounter*, March 1957.

44. Dwight Macdonald, "Politics Past (2)," *Encounter*, April 1957.

45. Dwight Macdonald, "The Waldorf Conference," *Politics*, Winter 1949.

46. On Dwight Macdonald, see Stephen J. Whitfield, *A Critical American: The Politics of Dwight Macdonald* (1984), and Diana Trilling, "An Interview with Dwight Macdonald," *Partisan Review*, no. 4, 1984.

47. CCF–IACF Archives.

48. Quoted in James Burnham, "Politics for the Nursery Set," *Partisan Review*, Spring 1945.

49. Sidney Hook, "Three Intellectual Troubadours," *American Spectator*, January 1985.

50. This and subsequent references to correspondence (Josselson, Spender, Kristol, and Macdonald) are from CCF–IACF Archives.

51. Dwight Macdonald, "America! America!" *Dissent*, Autumn 1958; *Twentieth Century*, October 1958; *Tempo Presente*, April 1958.

52. Norman Birnbaum, "An Open Letter to the Congress for Cultural Freedom," *Universities and Left Review*, Autumn 1958.

53. *Universities and Left Review*, Spring 1959.

### CHAPTER 5
### *Magazines Against the Tide*

1. CCF–IACF Archives. The letter (February 17, 1957) from Torberg to Lasky was a reply to an invitation to write for *Der Monat*. The Runyonesque references are to Torberg, Lasky, François Bondy (of *Preuves*), Michael Josselson, and Hellmut Jaesrich (of *Der Monat*).

2. T. S. Eliot, *Notes Towards the Definition of Culture* (London, 1948), p. 116.

3. This and other references to *Preuves*, CCF–IACF Archives.

4. Pierre Grémion, "*Preuves* dans le Paris de Guerre Froide," *Vingtième siècle* (Paris), January–February 1987.

5. Julian Gorkin, *Canibales Politicos* (Mexico, 1941), and "My Experiences

of Stalinism," *The Review* (published by the Imre Nagy Institute for Political Research, London), October 1959.

6. "Letter to the President of Mexico," *Partisan Review,* March–April 1942.

7. CCF–IACF Archives.

8. John Mander, *The Static Society: The Paradox of Latin America* (London, 1969), p. 127.

9. CCF–IACF Archives.

10. Arthur Koestler, in Josef Strelka, ed., *Der Weg was schon das Ziel,* a *Festschrift* for Friedrich Torberg's seventieth birthday (Langen Müller Austria, 1978), p. 126.

11. Marcel Reich-Ranicki, in *ibid.,* p. 187.

12. November 3, 1956, CCF–IACF Archives.

13. February 1957, CCF–IACF Archives.

14. Gino Bianco, "Chiaromonte and Caffi," *Survey,* Spring 1982.

15. Nicola Chiaromonte, "Lettera di un Giovane dall'Italia," *Quaderni di Giustizia e Libertà,* December 1932, translated into English in *Survey,* Spring 1982.

16. Enzo Bettiza, "Chiaromonte: Citizen of the World," *Survey,* Spring 1982.

17. Quoted in Bianco, "Chiaromonte and Caffi."

18. Bettiza, "Chiaromonte."

19. See *Tempo Presente,* February and April 1957, and *Encounter,* July 1957.

20. CCF–IACF Archives.

21. James McAuley, in *The Free Spirit* (Sydney), November–December 1955.

22. Walter Laqueur, "Dilemma of the West in Egypt," *Quest,* October–November 1956.

23. Quoted in David McCutchion, "Indian Writing in English," *Quadrant* (Sydney), no. 4, 1962.

24. CCF–IACF Archives.

25. *Quest,* September 1960. For subsequent controversy, see Jyotirmy Datta, "Indian Creative Writers and English," *Quest,* January–March 1961, and P. Lal, "Indian Writing in English," *Quest,* April–June 1961. See also McCutchion, "Indian Writing in English."

26. CCF–IACF Archives.

27. Frederick Spotts, *The Churches and Politics in Germany* (Middletown, Conn., 1973), p. 86. For appreciations of *Der Monat,* see *Melvin J. Lasky, Encounter with a 60th Birthday* (London, 1980), especially the contributions by François Bondy, Luigi Barzini, Hellmut Jaesrich, Boris Shub, and Dieter Borkovsky.

28. *Quadrant* Papers, Sydney.

29. *Quadrant,* vol. 1, no. 1, Summer 1956–57.

30. Quoted in Peter Coleman, *The Heart of James McAuley* (Sydney, 1980), p. 74.

31. *Quadrant,* March 1983.

32. *New Statesman,* August 18, 1961, and September 1961.

33. Walter Laqueur, *Out of the Ruins of Europe* (London, 1972), p. x.

34. This and other details from an interview with author, April 10, 1984. See the collection of Leopold Labedz's papers, "The Use and Abuse of Sociology," *Survey,* March 1988, and the "Introduction" by Zbigniew Brzezinski.

35. CCF–IACF Archives.

CHAPTER 6

*Plato's Banquet*

1. CCF–IACF Archives.

2. *Indian Congress for Cultural Freedom* (Bombay, 1951), p. 76.

3. Edward Shils, "America's Paper Curtain," *Bulletin of the Atomic Scientists,* October 1952.

4. Peter F. Drucker, *Adventures of a Bystander* (New York, 1978), p. 126.

5. Michael Polanyi, "Truth and Propaganda," reprinted in *The Contempt of Freedom: The Russian Experiment and After* (London, 1940).

6. Michael Polanyi, "The Rights and Duties of Science," in *ibid.*

7. John D. Baker, "Counter-blast to Bernalism," *New Statesman and Nation,* July 29, 1939. See also William McGucken, "On Freedom and Planning in Science: The Society for Freedom in Science, 1940–46," *Minerva,* no. 1, 1978; John R. Baker, "Michael Polanyi's Contributions to the Cause of Freedom in Science," *Minerva,* no. 3, 1978; and Edward Shils, "A Great Citizen of the Republic of Science: Michael Polanyi, 1892–1976," *Minerva,* Spring 1976.

8. Michael Polanyi, "Some British Experiences," *Bulletin of the Atomic Scientists,* October 1952.

9. Michael Polanyi, "Protests and Problems," *Time and Tide,* July 25, 1953.

10. Edward Shils, "The Scientific Community: Thoughts After Hamburg," *Bulletin of the Atomic Scientists,* May 1954, reprinted in a slightly different form in Edward Shils, *The Intellectuals and the Powers and Other Essays* (Chicago, 1972).

11. *Times Educational Supplement,* February 18, 1955. The edited proceed-

ings of the conference, *Science and Freedom*, were published in 1955 (London).

12. CCF–IACF Archives.

13. Edward Shils, "The End of Ideology?" *Encounter*, November 1955.

14. *Hannah Arendt/Karl Jaspers: Briefwechsel* (Piper Verlag, 1985), pp. 304, 305.

15. Dwight Macdonald, "No Miracle in Milan," *Encounter*, December 1955.

16. Max Beloff, "L'Awenire della Libertà," *Spectator*, September 30, 1955.

17. Shils, "End of Ideology?"

18. Seymour Martin Lipset, *Political Man* (New York, 1981), pp. 441–42, and *Canadian Forum*, November 1955, p. 170.

19. CCF–IACF Archives, Chicago. See also a selection of the papers and discussions, *The Soviet Economy* (London, 1956). *Encounter* published three of the other papers delivered in Milan: Raymond Aron, "Nations and Ideologies" (January 1955); Michael Polanyi, "On Liberalism and Liberty" (March 1955); and Stuart Hampshire, "In Defence of Radicalism" (August 1955). *The Review of Politics* published Hannah Arendt, "Authority in the Twentieth Century" (October 1956). *Preuves* published Joseph Schmoler, "Opposition et résistance en Russie Soviétique" (November 1955); Bertrand de Jouvenel, "Identité d'essence des économies capitaliste et soviétique"; Hannah Arendt, "Autorité, tyrannie et totalitarisme"; and Aldo Garosci, "Nation, totalitarisme et démocratie" (all September 1956). *Ethics* (Chicago) published Edward Shils, "Tradition and Liberty: Antinomy and Interdependence" (April 1958). *Quest* published Tomoo Otaka, "Authoritarianism in Japan" (February–March 1956). *New Leader*, May 7, 1956, published a wide selection of excerpts from the papers. Daniel Bell, "America as a Mass Society" in *The End of Ideology*, and a part of his "The Break-up of Family Capitalism," in *Partisan Review*, Spring 1957.

20. CCF–IACF Archives.

21. Stephen Spender, "Notes from a Diary," *Encounter*, December 1955.

22. *The Economist*, September 24, 1955.

23. CCF–IACF Archives.

24. Edward Shils, "Old Societies, New States," *Encounter*, March 1959.

25. Daniel Bell, "First Love and Early Sorrows," *Partisan Review*, no. 4, 1981. See also Nathan Liebowitz, *Daniel Bell and the Agony of Modern Liberalism* (Westport, Conn., 1985), and Howard Brick, *Daniel Bell and the Decline of Intellectual Radicalism* (Madison, Wisc., 1986).

26. Daniel Bell, "Reflections on Jewish Identity," *Commentary*, June 1961.

27. See Daniel Bell's five "Asian Notebooks" published weekly in the *New Leader* from September 23 to October 2, 1957.

28. See H. W. Arndt, *Economic Development: The History of an Idea* (Chicago, 1987), p. 48.

29. CCF–IACF Archives for this and other references to Daniel Bell, unless other citations given.

30. Bertrand de Jouvenel, "Asia Is Not Russia," *Encounter,* October 1957 (a report on the Tokyo Conference).

31. The papers and some of the discussions were published in M. K. Haldar and Robin Ghosh, eds., *Problems of Economic Growth* (Delhi, 1960).

32. See Melvin J. Lasky "The 'Sovietologists,'" *Encounter,* September 1957; Richard Pipes, "Report on the Oxford Conference on Recent Changes in Soviet Society," *Russian Review,* October 1957; and C. L. Sulzberger's three reports in his "Foreign Affairs" column, *New York Times,* June 26 and 29 and July 1, 1957. Papers delivered at the conferences that were later published include Daniel Bell, "Ten Theories in Search of Reality," in *The End of Ideology* (1960), and Bertram D. Wolfe, "The Durability of Soviet Despotism," *Commentary,* August 1957.

33. Patricia Blake, ed., *Writers in Russia 1917–1978,* a collection of Max Hayward's essays (New York, 1983).

34. See "Meetings with Russian Writers in 1945 and 1956," in Isaiah Berlin, *Personal Impressions* (London, 1981).

35. Daniel Bell, "Report from Vienna," *Forum Service,* no. 88. His paper "Two Roads from Marx" was published in *The End of Ideology,* and Michel Crozier's paper "La participation des travailleurs à la gestion des entreprises" was published in *Preuves,* November 1958, with a discussion of the conference by K. A. Jelenski. The Austrian journal *Wirtschaftlichkeit* devoted a special number to the conference (Heft 3–4, 1958). H. A. Clegg, *A New Approach to Industrial Democracy* (Oxford, 1960), is a response to the papers and discussions at the conference. It also contains lists of the papers and the participants.

36. *Democracy in the New States* (New Delhi, 1959) and *Afro-Asian Attitudes* (New Delhi, 1961) published selections from the papers and discussions at Rhodes, as did *Preuves,* March 1959, and *Cuadernos,* January–February 1959. See also Edward Shils, "Old Societies, New States," *Enounter,* March 1959; Richard Rovere, "A Reporter at Large," *New Yorker,* November 8, 1958; François Bondy, "Asiatiques, Africains, Occidentaux," *Preuves,* March 1959; and *Forum Service,* nos. 84, 90, 92, and 94.

37. Raymond Aron, ed., *World Technology and Human Destiny* (Michigan, 1963), contains some of the papers and an edited transcript of some

of the discussion. See also Edward Shils, "Intellectuals on Ararat: The End of the Ideological Age," *New York Herald Tribune,* European edition, October 21, 1959.

38. April 2, 1957, CCF–IACF Archives.
39. Rovere, "Reporter at Large." Rovere asked whether the notion of trying to get at the truth by seating people around a table in a first-class hotel was "culture-bound and foolish." Compare the comment of the Japanese novelist Michio Takeyama on the 1955 Rangoon conference: "I was at a complete loss.... I am unable to speak well and debate skillfully in the conference room, even in Japanese." *Quadrant,* July–August 1966.
40. Peter F. Drucker, *Science,* March 29, 1963.
41. *Time,* December 13, 1968.
42. CCF–IACF Archives.
43. CCF–IACF Archives.

CHAPTER 7
*The Impossible Dialogue*

1. Executive Committee, October 27, 1956, CCF–IACF Archives.
2. James Burnham, *The Coming Defeat of Communism* (New York, 1949), pp. 217–19, and Josef Czapski, "Pour les Jeunes Evadés de l'Est," *Liberté de l'Esprit* (Paris), September 1950.
3. Sidney Hook, "To Counter the Big Lie: A Basic Strategy," *New York Times Magazine,* March 11, 1951.
4. Arthur Koestler, *Bricks to Babel* (London, 1981), pp. 263–67.
5. See Dieter Borkovsky, "A Tale from the Underground, 1948/1984," in *Encounter: Melvin J. Lasky ... a 60th Birthday* (London, 1980).
6. CCF–IACF Archives.
7. K. A. Jelenski, "*Kultura,* la Pologne en exil," *le Débat* (Paris), February 1981. See also François Bondy, "Kot," *Kultura,* July–August 1987, and René Tavernier, "Konstanty Jeleński czyli tajemnica przyjaźni" ("Konstantin Jelenski or the secret friendship"), *Kultura,* September 1987.
8. Jelenski, *"Kultura."*
9. CCF–IACF Archives.
10. Tamas Aczel and Tibor Meray, *The Revolt of the Mind: A Case History of Intellectual Resistance Behind the Iron Curtain* (New York, 1959), pp. 345–63, 367–77.
11. Quoted in Leopold Labedz, "Clamping Down in Poland," *Forum-Service,* no. 178, week of December 19, 1959.
12. See Jan Kott, *Shakespeare: Our Contemporary* (New York, 1966).

13. Quoted in Jan Vladislav, "Poets and Power: Jaroslav Seifert," *Index on Censorship*, April 1985.

14. *Irodalmi Ujsag*, September 22, 1956. Quoted in Melvin J. Lasky, ed., *The Hungarian Revolution* (New York and London, 1957), p. 35.

15. CCF–IACF Archives (note 1 above).

16. Diana Trilling, "Politics and Cultural Freedom," *New Leader*, November 2, 1959.

17. Stephen Spender, "Notes from a Diary," *Encounter*, February 1956.

18. CCF–IACF Archives.

19. Aleksandr Solzhenitsyn, *The Oak and the Calf* (London, 1980), p. 185.

20. Quoted in "Judgment on Pasternak," *Survey*, July 1966.

21. Executive Committee, April 24, 1956, CCF–IACF Archives. On the Venice conference, see Ignazio Silone, "Rencontre avec des écrivains soviétiques," *Preuves*, October 1956, and Stephen Spender's novella *Engaged in Writing* (London, 1958) and "Notes from a Diary," *Encounter*, June 1956. A transcript of the proceedings is published in the journal of the Société Européene de Culture, *Comprendre*, no. 16.

22. This and other references to the Zürich conference are from CCF–IACF Archives. See also Maurice Nadeau, "La Rencontre de Zurich," *Lettres Nouvelles* (Paris), November 1956, and Silone's comment on it, "Domande senza risposta" ("Questions without answer"), in *Tempo Presente*, November 1956.

23. Frederick C. Barghoorn, *The Soviet Cultural Offensive* (Princeton, N.J., 1960), p. 150.

24. *Encounter*, June and July, 1957.

25. *Encounter* Papers, London.

26. CCF–IACF Archives.

27. George Urban, "Hungary: the Balance Sheet," *Survey*, January 1962.

28. Gyorgy Krasso, "The Memory of the Dead," *A Hirmondo* (*Messenger*), no. 2, December 1983, translated in *Survey*, Summer 1984.

29. CCF–IACF Archives.

30. Tamas Aczel, *Nation*, January 15, 1968.

### CHAPTER 8
### *The Crusade for the World*

1. Malcolm Muggeridge, "An Anatomy of Neutralism," *Time*, November 2, 1953.

2. Stephen Spender, "Notes from a Diary," *Encounter*, December 1955.

3. CCF–IACF Archives.

4. CCF–IACF Archives.

5. Norbert Muhlen Papers, Boston University.

6. CCF–IACF Archives.

7. Richard Löwenthal, "The Politics of Atlantic Rearmament," *The Twentieth Century* (London), February 1951. "Millions of people in western Germany, France and Italy—businessmen as well as workers, intellectuals as well as farmers—cordially detest the prospect of Communist rule, but are not at present prepared to take a stand against it because they regard its arrival in the wake of Russian tanks as inevitable, or at any rate, highly probable."

8. This and other references in the following paragraphs to the Italian Association for Cultural Freedom are from CCF–IACF Archives.

9. CCF–IACF Archives.

10. Malcolm Muggeridge, *Chronicles of Wasted Time*, vol. II, *The Infernal Grove* (London: Fontana Books, 1975), pp. 13, 82, 172.

11. Stephen Spender, "A Distorted Portrait," *The Listener,* September 23, 1936.

12. Fredric Warburg, *All Authors Are Equal* (London, 1973), p. 155.

13. Malcolm Muggeridge, interview with author, June 2, 1983.

14. This and other references to the Japanese Committee for Cultural Freedom and the Japan Cultural Forum are from CCF–IACF Archives.

15. Nicolas Nabokov, "Report on My Trip to India" (November 20–December 1, 1954), CCF–IACF Archives.

16. *Indian Congress for Cultural Freedom* (Bombay, 1951).

17. Quoted in Bertram D. Wolfe, "Gandhi Versus Lenin: Memories of Yusuf Meherally," in *Strange Communists I Have Known* (London, 1966), p. 104.

18. See his memoirs, Minoo Masani, *Against the Tide* (New Delhi, 1981), and R. Srinivasan, ed., *Freedom and Dissent: Essays in Honour of Minoo Masani* (Bombay, 1985).

19. J. P. Narayan, *Socialist Unity and the Congress Socialist Party* (Bombay, 1941), quoted in Minoo Masani, "The Communist party in India," *Pacific Affairs,* March 1951.

20. See Minoo Masani, *Is J. P. the Answer?* (Delhi, 1975); Herbert Passin, "Journey Among the Saints," *Encounter,* February 1955; and Herbert Passin, "The Stages of Jayaprakash Narayan," *Forum Service,* no. 45.

21. CCF–IACF Archives.

22. *New York Times,* March 31, 1951.

23. Quoted in James Burnham, "Parakeets and Parchesi: An Indian Memorandum," *Partisan Review,* no. 5, 1951.

24. CCF–IACF Archives.

25. *Ibid.*

26. Raymond Aron, *Mémoires* (Paris, 1983), p. 243. "De ma demi-heure avec le Pandit Nehru, je ne tirai rien ou presque, bien que je fusse, comme tout un chacun, impressionné par une personnalité à laquelle l'Histoire réserva une destinée hors du commun."

27. CCF–IACF Archives.

28. See Edward Shils, *The Intellectual Between Tradition and Modernity: The Indian Situation* (The Hague, 1961).

29. "Asian Intellectuals," in Edward Shils, *The Intellectual and the Powers and Other Essays* (Chicago and London, 1972), p. 382.

30. Sidney Hook, "Grim Report: Asia in Transition," *New York Times Magazine,* April 5, 1959.

31. This and other references to Latin America are from CCF–IACF Archives, unless otherwise sourced.

32. Quoted in Townsend Ludington, *John Dos Passos* (New York, 1980), p. 469.

33. See W. A. Swanberg, *Norman Thomas: The Last Idealist* (New York, 1976), p. 389.

34. Diana Josselson Papers, Geneva.

35. CCF–IACF Archives.

36. Richard Krygier, "The Making of a Cold Warrior," *Quadrant,* June 1984, reprinted in *Quadrant,* November 1986. For a more detailed discussion of the Australian Committee, see Peter Coleman, "The Prodigal Sons," *Quadrant,* November 1986.

37. Australian Association for Cultural Freedom Archives, Canberra.

38. CCF–IACF Archives.

39. *Ibid.*

### CHAPTER 9
### *The "Obnoxious" Americans*

1. *New York Times,* March 25, 1955.

2. CCF–IACF Archives.

3. Sidney Hook, *Out of Step: An Unquiet Life in the 20th Century* (New York, 1987). This work is the principal source for the account of Hook in this chapter. See also "Sidney Hook at 80," a special issue of *Free Inquiry,* Fall 1982; Paul Kurtz, ed., *Sidney Hook: Philosopher of Democracy and Humanism* (New York, 1983), which includes a complete bibliography of Hook's writings between 1922 and 1980; Edward Shils's review-essay on *Out of Step,* "More at Home than Out of Step," *American Scholar,* Autumn 1987; and Peter Coleman "Sidney Hook and Cultural Freedom," *The National Interest,"* Fall 1987.

4. Hook, *Out of Step,* pp. 11, 218.

5. Copy in James Burnham Papers, Kent, Connecticut.

6. Copy in *ibid.*

7. CCF–IACF Archives.

8. *New York Times,* January 5, 1953.

9. This and other references to the American Committee for Cultural Freedom come from CCF–IACF Archives, unless otherwise sourced.

10. *New York Times,* May 8, 1953.

11. Sidney Hook, "The Ethics of Controversy," *New Leader,* February 1, 1954.

12. *New York Review of Books,* January 18, 1968.

13. *Chicago Tribune,* June 30, 1956.

14. *New Leader,* November 26, 1956.

15. For discussions of The American Committee for Cultural Freedom, see Hook, *Out of Step* (note 1 above); William L. O'Neill, *A Better World* (New York, 1982); Alexander Bloom, *Prodigal Sons* (New York, 1986); William Phillips, *A Partisan View* (New York, 1983); Mary Sperling McAuliffe, *Crisis on The Left* (Amherst, Mass., 1978); and Alan M. Wald, *The New York Intellectuals: The Rise and Decline of the Anti-Stalinist Left from the 1930s to the 1980s* (Chapel Hill, N.C., and London, 1987).

CHAPTER 10
*Changing Direction: "The New Enlightenment"*

1. Edward Shils, "Further Thoughts on the Congress in the 60's," 1961, CCF–IACF Archives.

2. *The Economist,* September 24, 1955.

3. June 19, 1959, CCF–IACF Archives.

4. CCF–IACF Archives.

5. *Ibid.*

6. Sidney Hook, *Out of Step* (New York, 1987), p. 449.

7. *La Démocratie à l'épreuve du XXᵉ siècle* (Paris: Calmann-Lévy, 1960), reporting Raymond Aron's study group; K. A. Jelenski, ed., *History and Hope* (London: Routledge & Kegan Paul, 1962), reporting Michael Polanyi's group; and *The Problems of Afro-Asian New States,* an *Encounter* pamphlet (London, 1961), reporting Edward Shils's group. Other published papers include Irving Kristol, "High, Low and Modern," *Encounter,* August 1960; Arthur Schlesinger, "On Heroic Leadership," *Encounter,* December 1960; and Denis de Rougemont, "Les incidences du progrès sur les libertés," *Preuves,* August 1960. See also *Der Monat,* August 1960, and *Preuves,* October 1960, for discussions of the conference.

8. "A Powerhouse of Thought," unsigned, *Forum Service*, no. 248.

9. J. Robert Oppenheimer, "A Time of Sorrow and Renewal," *Encounter*, February 1961.

10. George F. Kennan, "That Candles May Be Brought'..." *Encounter*, February 1961.

11. The papers are published in Jelenski, ed., *History and Hope*.

12. See *Problems of Afro-Asian New States*.

13. M. J. Lasky, *Guardian* (London), June 20, 1960, and Taya Zinkin, *Guardian*, June 22, 1960.

14. *Daily Telegraph and Morning Post* (London), June 21, 1960.

15. CCF–IACF Archives.

16. William Phillips, *A Partisan View* (New York, 1983), p. 155.

17. *Forum Service*, no. 253.

18. J. H. Wootten, *The Free Spirit* (Sydney), June–July 1960.

19. Edward Shils, *The Intellectual and the Powers and Other Essays* (Chicago, 1972). See also Edward Shils, "Totalitarians and Antinomians," an introductory essay to John H. Bunzel, ed., *Political Passages: Journeys of Change Through Two Decades, 1968–1988* (New York, 1988). A shortened version of this essay appears in *New Criterion*, May 1988.

20. Edward Shils, "Some Academics, Mainly in Chicago," *American Scholar*, vol. 50 (1981).

21. See Edward Shils, "The Prospect for Lebanese Civility," in Leonard Binder, ed., *Politics in Lebanon* (New York, 1960), and Edward Shils, "The Intellectuals and the Future," *Bulletin of the Atomic Scientists*, October 1967.

22. See "Symposium on Shils," *American Journal of Sociology*, November 1973.

23. CCF–IACF Archives.

24. *Ibid.*

25. *Ibid.*

26. Leslie Fiedler's paper "The New Mutants" was published in *Partisan Review*, Fall 1965.

## CHAPTER 11
### *Magazines of the Sixties*

1. CCF–IACF Archives.

2. *The Observer (Weekend Review)*, November 24, 1963.

3. *New Statesman*, December 29, 1961.

4. Melvin J. Lasky, *Africa for Beginners* (London, 1962), pp. 115–116.

5. Colin Welch, "Crosland Reconsidered," *Encounter*, January 1979.

6. *Encounter* Papers, London.

7. *New Statesman,* December 29, 1961.

8. *Newsweek,* November 25, 1963.

9. Malcolm Muggeridge, "I Like Dwight," reprinted in *Tread Softly for You Tread on My Jokes* (London, 1966).

10. *New Statesman* December 20, 1962. Kenneth Tynan popularized this criticism of *Encounter,* and other Congress magazines, in a satirical sketch, "Congress for Cultural Freedom," written for the BBC and printed in David Frost and Ned Skerrin, eds., *That Was the Week That Was,* published in the same year as *Encounters,* which incidentally carried "Bull Fever," Tynan's 1955 contribution to *Encounter.*

11. *Sunday Telegraph* (London) October 27, 1963.

12. CCF–IACF Archives.

13. Reprinted in *Forum Service,* no. 10.

14. Letter to M. J. Lasky, November 10, 1959, CCF–IACF Archives.

15. This and other references to *Jiyu* are from CCF–IACF Archives, unless otherwise sourced.

16. Conversation with author, September 30, 1983.

17. This and other references to *Hiwar* are from CCF–IACF Archives.

18. *Transition,* no. 18.

19. December 1967, CCF–IACF Archives.

20. *Transition,* no. 37.

21. *Transition,* no. 32.

22. *Transition,* no. 33.

23. *Transition,* no. 34.

24. *More* (United States), May 1978.

25. *New Statesman,* February 17, 1967.

26. CCF–IACF Archives.

27. *Mundo Nuevo,* August 1967.

28. CCF–IACF Archives.

29. *Ibid.*

30. *Bulletin of the Atomic Scientists,* October 1952.

31. *Ibid.,* May 1954.

32. Interview in *Times Higher Educational Supplement* (London), July 19, 1974.

33. *Ibid.*

## CHAPTER 12
### *Liberal Hopes and Illusions in the "Underdeveloped" World*

1. CCF–IACF Archives.

2. CCF–IACF Archives.

3. CCF–IACF Archives.

4. Edward Shils, "The False Prospero," *Encounter*, July 1961.

5. *Ibid.*

6. W. Arthur Lewis, "Beyond African Dictatorship," *Encounter*, August 1965.

7. Interview with author, December 27, 1984.

8. *Ibid.* On *Black Orpheus*, see also Peter Benson, "'Border Operators': *Black Orpheus* and the Genesis of Modern African Art and Literature," *Research in African Universities* (University of Texas Press), Winter 1983.

9. *Transition*, vol. 2, no. 5.

10. A shortened version of the lecture appeared in *New Left Review* (U.K.), March–April 1985.

11. Es'kia (formerly Ezekiel) Mphahlele gives an account of the Chem-chemi Center in his autobiography, *Afrika My Music* (Johannesburg, 1984).

12. March 12, 1963, CCF–IACF Archives.

13. March 29, 1963, CCF–IACF Archives.

14. Keith Botsford's account of Robert Lowell's "overwrought" tour of Argentina, culminating in a mental breakdown, appears in Ian Hamilton's biography *Robert Lowell* (New York, 1982).

15. Keith Botsford, "Report on Mexico," September 1964, CCF–IACF Archives.

16. "Yanqui Gringo," *Encounter*, September 1965.

17. Josep Alemany, *Entrevista con Luis Mercier Vega, Interrogations*, 13, *revue internationale de recherche anarchiste* (Milan), January 1978.

18. It was the basis of a book, S. M. Lipset and Aldo Solari, eds., *Elites in Latin America* (New York, 1967).

19. Herbert Lüthy, "Indonesia Confronted," *Encounter*, December 1965.

20. Robert W. Bellah, ed., *Religion and Progress in Modern Asia* (New York, 1965).

21. Ivan Kats, as guest editor, surveyed the beginnings of a post-Sukarno cultural revival in a special issue of *Quadrant*, September–October 1969.

## CHAPTER 13
### *Reaching Behind the Iron Curtain*

1. In G. R. Urban, ed., *Détente* (London, 1976), pp. 49–50.

2. CCF–IACF Archives.

3. Leopold Labedz, "The Polish Intellectual Climate," *Soviet Survey*, January 1961.

4. Konstantin A. Fedin and Aleksandr T. Tvardovsky, "In the Land of Shakespeare and Burns," *Encounter*, July 1960.

5. CCF–IACF Archives.

6. Nicolas Nabokov, *Bagázh: Memoirs of a Russian Cosmopolitan* (New York, 1975).

7. July 18, 1960, CCF–IACF Archives.

8. Patricia Blake, *Encounter*, April 1963.

9. Herbert Lüthy, "Culture and the Cold War," *Encounter*, June 1963.

10. *Pravda*, June 4, 1963, reprinted in translation in *Guardian*, June 12, 1963, and in *Encounter*, August 1963.

### CHAPTER 14
### *A Black Operation?*

1. William F. Buckley, Jr., on *Firing Line* (TV program), no. 92, England, February 27, 1968.

2. "Christopher Felix," "The Unknowable CIA," *Reporter*, April 6, 1967.

3. CCF–IACF Archives.

4. Raymond Aron, *Mémoires* (Paris, 1983), p. 238, and Sidney Hook, *Out of Step* (New York, 1987), p. 451.

5. Arthur M. Schlesinger, Jr., "Liberal Anti-Communism Revisited," *Commentary*, September 1967.

6. K. A. Jelenski, "*Kultura*, la Pologne en exil," *le Débat* (Paris), February 1981.

7. CCF–IACF Archives.

8. Australian Association for Cultural Freedom Papers, Canberra.

9. CCF–IACF Archives.

10. *New York Times*, May 9, 1966. Oppenheimer, in a letter to Nabokov, also described the Congress as one of the "great and benign influences" of the postwar years. October 28, 1966, Nicolas Nabokov Papers.

11. *New York Times*, May 10, 1966.

12. Ford Foundation Records, New York. See also Kathleen D. McCarthy, "From Cold War to Cultural Development: The International Cultural Activities of the Ford Foundation, 1950–1980," *Daedalus*, Winter 1987.

13. October 25, 1966, CCF–IACF Archives.

14. Diana Josselson Papers, Geneva.

15. *Ramparts*, March 1967.
16. *New Statesman*, February 24, 1967.
17. *Washington Post*, February 21, 23, and 28, 1967.
18. CCF–IACF Archives.
19. April 28, 1967, *Encounter* Papers, London.
20. April 18, 1967, *Encounter* Papers, London.
21. April 10, 1967, CCF–IACF Archives.
22. CCF–IACF Archives.
23. Interview with author, September 30, 1983.
24. April 20, 1967, Dwight Macdonald Papers, New Haven.
25. May 7, 1967, *Encounter* Papers, London.
26. Norman Mailer, *The Armies of the Night* (London, 1968), p. 85.
27. *Partisan Review*, Summer 1967.
28. *Nation*, September 11, 1967.
29. Jason Epstein, "The CIA and the Intellectuals," *New York Review of Books*, April 1967.
30. *Commentary*, September 1967.
31. *Ibid.*
32. *National Review*, March 21, 1967.
33. *Time*, May 19, 1967.
34. CCF–IACF Archives.
35. James McAuley, "C.I.A.," *Quadrant*, May–June 1967.
36. September 15, 1967, CCF–IACF Archives.
37. November 9, 1967, CCF–IACF Archives.
38. *National Review*, October 17, 1967.

CHAPTER 15
*The Aftermath: "No Consensus Emerged"*

1. CCF–IACF Archives.
2. *Ibid.*
3. Raymond Aron, *Mémoires* (Paris, 1983), p. 238. Some of the papers were published in *Survey*, Summer 1971.
4. October 7, 1968, CCF–IACF Archives.
5. *Quadrant* (Sydney), March–April 1969. See also the book of the conference, François Duchêne, ed., *The Endless Crisis: America in the Seventies* (New York, 1970); James H. Billington, "A Ferment of Intellectuals," *Life*, January 10, 1969; and Walter Goodman, "The Liberal Establishment Faces the Blacks, the Young, the New Left," *New York Times Magazine*, December 29, 1968.

6. Duchêne, ed., *Endless Crisis,* p. 170.

7. William F. Buckley, Jr., "The Anti-Nixon Clambake," *San Francisco Examiner,* December 5, 1968.

8. Interview with author, April 10, 1984.

9. CCF–IACF Archives.

10. CCF–IACF Archives.

11. Diana Josselson Papers, Geneva.

12. Diana Josselson Papers, Geneva.

13. Michael Josselson and Diana Josselson, *The Commander: A Life of Barclay de Tolly* (Oxford, 1980).

14. Diana Josselson Papers, Geneva.

15. Sidney Hook Papers, Stanford, California.

16. *Survey,* Spring 1977–78.

17. *Encounter,* April 1978.

CHAPTER **16**
### *The Congress in Retrospect*

1. *Encounter,* March 1980.

2. Sidney Hook, *Out of Step* (New York, 1987), p. 445.

3. *New York Times Magazine,* April 5, 1959.

4. Edward Shils, "The Burden of 1917," *Survey,* Summer–Autumn 1976, and *idem,* "The Social Ownership of the Means of Production," *Survey,* Autumn 1980.

5. *National Review,* March 21, 1967.

6. Hook, *Out of Step,* p. 451.

7. Report of the Katzenbach Committee, reprinted in full in the *New York Times,* March 30, 1967.

8. Cord Meyer, *Facing Reality* (New York, 1980), p. 106.

9. *Wall Street Journal,* June 16, 1982.

10. *New York Times,* March 13, 1987.

11. *New Republic,* January 20, 1986.

12. *The Times* (London) January 15, 1985. Compare the *New Republic* of January 20, 1986: "The democrats of Spain and Portugal ... know just how important U.S. government assistance was in keeping them alive during the Franco and Salazar years. That assistance was directed to them by the C.I.A.—yes, the C.I.A. And these were precisely the people who steered their countries away from the habits of fascism and the temptations of communism, into the constitution of mainstream of Western Europe."

13. "Christopher Felix," "The Unknowable CIA," *Reporter,* April 6, 1967.

# Bibliography

## INTERVIEWS

| | |
|---|---|
| Raymond Aron | June 1983 |
| Arnold Beichman | December 1982 |
| Ulli Beier | December 1984 |
| Sadao Bekku | September 1983 |
| Daniel Bell | January 1983, July 1986 |
| Ruth Berenson | January 1985 (telephone) |
| Gino Bianco | April 1984 |
| Marion Bieber | July 1983 |
| Patricia Blake | January 1985 (telephone), July 1986 |
| François Bondy | July 1983 |
| Thomas W. Braden | January 1985 |
| Irving Brown | January 1985 |
| Miriam Chiaromonte | April 1984 |
| Brian Crozier | July 1983 |
| J. K. Galbraith | July 1986 |
| Michael Goodwin | July 1983 |
| Anthony Hartley | July 1983 |
| Kentaro Hayashi | September 1983 |
| Paul B. Henze | August 1988 |
| Gertrude Himmelfarb | July 1986 |
| Sidney Hook | December 1982, July 1986 |
| John Hunt | January 1983 |

301

| | |
|---|---|
| Hoki Ishihara | September 1983 |
| Helmut Jaesrich | February 1984 |
| K. A. Jelenski | July 1983 |
| Diana Josselson | July 1983 |
| Tamio Kamakami | September 1983 |
| Ivan Kats | January 1983 |
| Yong-Koo Kim | October 1983 |
| Irving Kristol | January 1983, July 1986 |
| Richard Krygier | December 1982, December 1984 |
| Leopold Labedz | April 1984, July 1986 |
| Walter Z. Laqueur | May 1953 |
| Melvin J. Lasky | July 1983, April 1984, July 1986 |
| Roderick MacFarquhar | June 1983 |
| Minoo Masani | August 1982 |
| Tibor Meray | June 1986 |
| Cord Meyer | January 1985 |
| Murray Mindlin | July 1983 |
| Es'kia Mphahlele | November 1985 |
| Malcolm Muggeridge | June 1983 |
| Dominique Nabokov | January 1983 |
| Rajat Neogy | January 1985 |
| Michael Oakeshott | April 1984 (telephone) |
| Herbert Passin | January 1983 |
| Frank Platt | January 1983 |
| Norman Podhoretz | January 1983 |
| Lloyd Ross | August 1986 |
| Denis de Rougemont | July 1983 |
| Arthur M. Schlesinger, Jr. | January 1983 |
| Yoshihiko Seki | September 1983 |
| Edward Shils | December 1982, February 1985 |
| Darina Silone | April 1984 |
| Sulak Sivaraksa | March 1985 |
| Manès Sperber | June 1983 |
| Sol Stein | January 1983 |
| James L. Stewart | September 1983 |
| Shepard Stone | February 1984 |
| Robert K. Straus | July 1987 |
| Frank Sutton | January 1985 |

| | |
|---|---|
| Diana Trilling | January 1983 |
| George Urban | February 1988 |
| Jeanne Wacker | January 1985 (telephone) |

## MANUSCRIPT COLLECTIONS CONSULTED

*Manuscript Depositories*

By far the most important archive consulted is that of the Congress for Cultural Freedom and of the International Association for Cultural Freedom in the Special Collections of the Joseph Regenstein Library, the University of Chicago. Other public archives consulted include:

Nicolas Nabokov Papers, Harry Ransom Humanities Research Center, The University of Texas at Austin

Dwight Macdonald Papers, Yale University Library

Norbert Muhlen Papers, Boston University Library

National Archives, Washington Federal Records Center, Washington, D.C.

Australian Association for Cultural Freedom Papers, National Library, Canberra

Sir John Latham Papers, National Library of Australia, Canberra

*Private Collections*

Mrs. Diana Josselson's Papers, Geneva

James Burnham Papers, then (January 1985) at Kent, Connecticut; now at the Hoover Institute, Stanford, California

Sidney Hook–Melvin Lasky Correspondence, Stanford, California

Ford Foundation Archives, New York

Arthur Koestler Papers, London

*Encounter* Papers, London

*Quadrant* Papers, Sydney

*Freedom of Information Act Records*

Central Intelligence Agency, Langley, Virginia

U.S. Department of Justice, Washington, D.C.

Department of State, Washington, D.C.

Department of Foreign Affairs, Canberra, Australia

## BOOKS

Abel, Lionel. *The Intellectual Follies: A Memoir of the Literary Venture in New York and Paris.* New York, 1984.

Aczel, Tamas, and Tibor Meray. *The Revolt of the Mind: A Case History of Intellectual Resistance Behind the Iron Curtain.* New York, 1959.

Alsop, Stewart, and Thomas Braden. *Sub Rosa: The OSS and American Espionage.* New York, 1946.

Arendt, Hannah. *The Origins of Totalitarianism.* New York, 1951. British title: *The Burden of Our Time.* London, 1951.

———. *Eichmann in Jerusalem: A Report on the Banality of Evil.* New York, 1963.

Arndt, H. W. *The Rise and Fall of Economic Growth: A Study of Contemporary Thought.* Melbourne, 1978.

———. *Economic Development: The History of an Idea.* Chicago, 1987.

Aron, Raymond. *The Opium of the Intellectuals.* London, 1957.

———. *Eighteen Lectures on Industrial Society.* London, 1967.

———. *The Elusive Revolution: Anatomy of a Student Revolt.* London, 1969.

———. *Plaidoyer pour l'Europe décadente.* Paris, 1977. Instalments translated in *Encounter,* September and October 1977, as "My Defence of Our Decadent Europe."

Barrett, William. *The Truants: Adventures Among the Intellectuals.* New York, 1982.

Beauvoir, Simone de. *The Mandarins: A Novel.* London, 1957.

Beier, Ulli, ed. *Introduction to African Literature: An Anthology of Critical Writing from 'Black Orpheus.'* London, 1967.

Bell, Daniel. *The End of Ideology: On the Exhaustion of Political Ideas in the Fifties.* Glencoe, Ill., 1960.

———, ed. *The Radical Right: The New American Right.* New York, 1963.

———. *The Coming of Post-Industrial Society: A Venture in Social Forecasting.* New York, 1973.

Bellow, Saul. *Seize the Day.* New York, 1956.

———. *Humboldt's Gift.* London, 1975.

———. *The Dean's December.* London, 1982.

Beloff, Max. *The Intellectual in Politics, and Other Essays.* London, 1970.

Berlin, Isaiah. *Karl Marx.* London, 1939.

———. *The Hedgehog and the Fox.* London, 1953.

———. *Russian Thinkers.* New York, 1978.

———. *Against the Current.* New York, 1980.

Blake, Patricia. *Half-way to the Moon: New Writing from Russia.* Edited with Max Hayward. London, 1964.

Bloom, Alexander. *Prodigal Sons: The New York Intellectuals and Their World.* New York, 1986.

Borkenau, Franz. *Spanish Cockpit.* London, 1937.

———. *The Communist International.* London, 1938.

———. *The Totalitarian Enemy.* London, 1940.

———. *European Communism.* New York, 1953.

Brzezinski, Zbigniew (see also Friedrich, Carl). *Between Two Ages: America's Role in the Technetronic Era.* New York, 1970.

———. *Game Plan: A Geostrategic Framework for the Conduct of the U.S.–Soviet Contest.* New York, 1986.

Buckley, William F. *McCarthy and His Enemies.* With L. Brent Bozell. Chicago, 1954.

———. *Up from Liberalism.* New York, 1959.

———. *Odyssey of a Friend: Whittaker Chambers' Letters to William F. Buckley, Jr., 1954—1961.* New York, 1970.

Bunzel, John H., ed. *Political Passages: Journeys of Change Through Two Decades, 1968–1988.* New York, 1988.

Burnham, James. *The Case for De Gaulle: A Dialogue Between André Malraux and James Burnham.* New York, 1948.

———. *The Coming Defeat of Communism.* New York, 1949.

———. *Containment or Liberation?* New York, 1953.

———. *Suicide of the West.* New York, 1964.

Camus, Albert. *The Rebel.* London, 1953.

Caute, David. *Communism and the French Intellectuals 1914–1960.* London, 1964.

———. *The Fellow-Travellers: A Postscript to the Enlightenment.* New York, 1973.

Chamberlin, Brewster S. *Kultur auf Trümmern: Berliner Berichte der amerikanischen Information Control Section Juli–Dezember 1945.* Stuttgart, 1979.

Chiaromonte, Nicola. *The Worm of Consciousness and Other Essays.* Ed. Miriam Chiaromonte. New York, 1976.

Clay, Lucius D. *Decision in Germany.* New York, 1950.

Cohen, Theodore. *Remaking Japan: The American Occupation as New Deal.* Ed. Herb Passin. New York, 1987.

Colby, William. *Honorable Men.* New York, 1978.

Coleman, Peter. *The Heart of James McAuley: Life and Work of the Australian Poet.* Sydney, 1980.

Conquest, Robert, ed. *New Lines.* London, 1956.

———, ed. *Back to Life: Poems from Behind the Iron Curtain.* London, 1958.

———. *The Great Terror: Stalin's Purges of the Thirties.* London, 1968.

Crankshaw, Edward. *Russia and the Russians.* London, 1947.

———. *Krushchev: A Biography.* London, 1966.

Cranston, Maurice. *Freedom: A New Analysis.* London, 1953.

———. *Human Rights Today.* London, 1955.

———, ed. *The New Left: Six Critical Essays.* London, 1970.

Crosland, Anthony. *The Future of Socialism.* London, 1957.

———, *The Conservative Enemy: A Programme of Radical Reform for the 1960's.* London, 1962.

Crossman, R. H. S., ed. *The God That Failed.* London, 1949.

———. *The Diaries of a Cabinet Minister.* London, 1975–77.

———. *The Backbench Diaries of Richard Crossman.* London, 1981.

Dickstein, Morris. *Gates of Eden: American Culture in the Sixties.* New York, 1977.

Djilas, Milovan. *The New Class.* London, 1957.

———. *Conversations with Stalin.* London, 1962.

Dos Passos, John. *Adventures of a Young Man* (a novel). London, 1939.

Eastman, Max. *Artists in Uniform: A Study of Literature and Bureaucratism.* New York, 1934.

Ehrenburg, Ilya. *The Thaw.* Moscow, 1954. Trans. M. Harari. London, 1962.

———. *Memoirs: 1921–1941.* Trans. T. Shebunina. New York, 1964.

———. *Men, Years, Life.* Trans. M. Harari. London, 1962–66.

"Felix, Christopher" (James McCarger). *A Short Course in the Secret War.* New York, 1963. Reprinted with a new introduction, 1988.

Fiedler, Leslie. *An End to Innocence.* New York, 1955.

Friedrich, Carl, and Zbigniew Brzezinski. *Totalitarianism, Dictatorship and Autocracy.* New York, 1961.

Galbraith, J. K. *The Affluent Society.* Boston, 1958.

———. *Journey to Poland and Yugoslavia.* Cambridge, Mass., 1958.

———. *A China Passage.* New York, 1973.

———. *Annals of an Abiding Liberal.* Ed. Andrea D. Williams. London, 1980.

Gollancz, Victor, ed. *The Betrayal of the Left.* London, 1941.

Goodman, Celia, ed. *Living with Koestler: Mamaine Koestler's Letters 1945–51.* London, 1985.

Gorkin, Julian. *Cannibales politicos.* Mexico, 1941.

———. *Murder in Mexico.* With Salazar. London, 1950.

———. *Listen Comrades: Life and Death in the Soviet Union.* Trans. Ilsa Barea. London, 1952.

Gorwala, A. D. ("Vivek"). *India Without Illusions.* Bombay, 1953.

Grémion, Pierre. *Le Congrès pour la Liberté de la Culture (1950–1967).* Paris, 1988.

Gross, Babette. *Willi Münzenberg: A Political Biography.* Trans. Marian Jackson. Michigan, 1974.

Halle, Louis J. *The Cold War as History.* London, 1967.

Hamilton, Iain. *Koestler: A Biography.* London, 1982.

Hampshire, Stuart. *Freedom of Mind, and Other Essays.* London, 1972.

Hartley, Anthony. *A State of England.* London, 1963.

Hayward, Max. *Literature and Revolution in Soviet Russia, 1917–62.* Ed. M. Hayward and L. Labedz. London, 1963.

———. *On Trial.* Ed. M. Hayward. New York, 1967.

———. *Antiworlds and the Fifth Ace: Poems by A. Voznesensky.* Trans. W. H. Auden. Ed. P. Blake and M. Hayward. London, 1967.

———. *A Captive of Time: My Years with Pasternak—The Memoirs of Olga Ivinskaya.* Trans. M. Hayward. London, 1978.

———. *Writers in Russia: 1917–1978.* Ed. with an introduction by Patricia Blake. London, 1983.

Hellman, Lillian. *Scoundrel Time.* New York, 1976.

Hollander, Paul. *Political Pilgrims: Travels of Western Intellectuals to the Soviet Union, China, and Cuba 1928–1978.* New York, 1981.

Hook, Sidney. *Towards the Understanding of Karl Marx.* New York, 1933.

———. *John Dewey: An Intellectual Portrait.* New York, 1939.

———. *Heresy, Yes—Conspiracy, No.* New York, 1953.

———. *Out of Step: An Unquiet Life in the 20th Century.* New York, 1987.

Howe, Irving. *A Margin of Hope: An Intellectual Autobiography.* New York, 1982.

———, ed. *1984 Revisited: Totalitarianism in Our Century.* New York, 1983.

Jelenski, K. A., ed. *Anthologie de la poésie polonaise,* Paris, 1963.

Johnson, Paul. *Intellectuals.* London, 1988.

Kennan, George F. *Memoirs 1925–1950.* London, 1968.

———. *Memoirs 1950–1963.* New York, 1972.

Kirkpatrick, Lyman B., Jr. *The Real C.I.A.* New York, 1968.

Knopfelmacher, Frank. *Intellectuals and Politics.* Melbourne, 1968.

Koestler, Arthur. *Spanish Testament.* London, 1937.

———. *Darkness at Noon.* London, 1940.

———. *The Age of Longing.* London, 1951.

———. *The Trail of the Dinosaur.* London, 1955.

———. *Bricks to Babel.* London, 1981.

———. *Stranger on the Square.* With Cynthia Koestler. New York, 1984.

Kristol, Irving. *On the Democratic Idea in America.* New York, 1972.

———. *Reflections of a Neoconservative.* New York, 1983.

Kurzweil, Edith, and William Phillips, eds. *Writers and Politics: A Partisan Review Reader.* Boston, 1983.

Labedz, Leopold. *Solzhenitsyn: A documentary record.* London, 1972.

——, and Max Hayward, eds. *On Trial: The Case of Sinyavsky (Tertz) and Daniel (Arzhak)* (documents). London, 1967.

——, and Priscilla Johnson, eds., *Khrushchev and the Arts: The Politics of Soviet Culture, 1962–1964* (documents). Cambridge, Mass., 1965.

Laqueur, Walter Z. *Out of the Ruins of Europe.* London, 1972.

——. *The Struggle for the Middle East: The Soviet Union in the Mediterranean, 1958–68.* N.p.

——, and George Lichtheim, eds. *The Soviet Cultural Scene 1956–1957* (collection of articles from *Soviet Survey*). London, 1972.

Lasky, Melvin J., ed. *The Hungarian Revolution.* New York, 1957.

——. *Africa for Beginners: A Traveller's Notebook.* London, 1962.

——. *Utopia and Revolution.* Chicago and London, 1976.

Leys, Simon (Pierre Ryckmans). *Chinese Shadows.* New York, 1977.

——. *The Chairman's New Clothes: Mao and the Cultural Revolution.* New York, 1977.

——. *The Burning Forest: Essays on Chinese Culture and Politics.* London, 1983.

Lipset, Seymour Martin. *Political Man.* New York, 1960.

Lottman, Herbert R. *The Left Bank: Writers, Artists, and Politics from the Popular Front to the Cold War.* Boston, 1982.

Löwenthal, Richard (Paul Sering). *Jenseits des Kapitalismus: Ein Beitrag zur sozialistischen Neuorientierung.* Nürnberg, 1947.

——. *World Communism: The Disintegration of a Secular Faith.* New York, 1964.

Macdonald, Dwight. *The Ford Foundation: The Men and the Millions.* New York, 1956. Reprinted with a new introduction by Francis X. Sutton, 1988.

——. *Memoirs of a Revolutionist: Essays in Political Criticism.* Cleveland, 1958.

——. *Against the American Grain.* New York, 1962.

——. *Discriminations: Essays and Afterthoughts 1938–1974.* New York, 1974.

Mander, John. *Great Britain or Little England?* London, 1963.

——. *Static Society: The Paradox of Latin America.* London, 1969.

Masani, Minoo. *Communism in India.* London, 1954.

——. *The Communist Party of India: A Short History.* Bombay, 1954.

——. *Against the Tide.* New Delhi, 1981.

McAuley, James. *The End of Modernity: Essays on Literature, Art and Culture.* Sydney, 1959.

——. *The Grammar of the Real.* Melbourne, 1975.

McAuliffe, Mary Sperling. *Crisis on the Left: Cold War Politics and American Liberals 1947–1954.* Amherst, Mass., 1978.

Meray, Tibor. *The Enemy.* London, 1958.

———. *That Day in Budapest: October 23, 1956.* New York, 1969.

———, with Tamas Aczel. *The Revolt of the Mind.* New York, 1959.

Meyer, Cord. *Facing Reality: From World Federalism to the C.I.A.* New York, 1980.

Milosz, Czeslaw. *The Captive Mind.* New York, 1953.

Mphahlele, Es'kia. *Down Second Avenue.* London, 1959.

———. *The African Image.* London, 1962.

———. *The Wanderers.* London, 1971.

———. *Afrika My Music: An Autobiography 1957–1983.* Johannesburg, 1984.

Muggeridge, Malcolm. *Winter in Moscow.* London, 1934.

———. *Chronicles of Wasted Time,* I. *The Green Stick, and* II. *The Infernal Grove.* London, 1973.

———. *Like It Was: The Diaries of Malcolm Muggeridge.* London, 1981.

Nabokov, Nicolas. *Old Friends and New Music.* London, 1951.

———. *Bagázh: Memoirs of a Russian Cosmopolitan.* New York, 1975.

Narayan, Jayaprakash. *Socialism, Sarvodaya and Democracy: Selected Works.* London, 1964.

Ninkovich, Frank A. *Diplomacy of Ideas: U.S. Foreign Policy and Cultural Relations, 1938–1950.* Cambridge, 1981.

Oakeshott, Michael. *Rationalism in Politics and Other Essays.* London, 1962.

O'Brien, Conor Cruise. *Writers and Politics.* London, 1965.

O'Neill, William L. *A Better World. The Great Schism—Stalinism and the American Intellectuals.* New York, 1982.

Orwell, George. *Homage to Catalonia.* London, 1938.

———. *Animal Farm,* London 1945.

———. *1984.* London, 1949.

———. *The Collected Essays: Journalism and Letters.* 4 vols. London, 1968.

Paloczi-Horvath, George, ed. *One Sentence on Tyranny: Hungarian Literary Gazette Anthology.* London, 1957.

Pells, Richard H. *The Liberal Mind in a Conservative Age. American Intellectuals in the 1940s and 1950s.* New York, 1985.

Phillips, William. *The New Partisan Reader 1945–1953.* New York, 1953.

———. *A Partisan View: Five Decades of the Literary Life.* New York, 1983.

———, and Philip Rahv, eds. *The Partisan Reader: Ten Years of Partisan Review 1934–1944—An Anthology.* New York, 1946.

Podhoretz, Norman. *Making It.* New York, 1967.

———. *Breaking Ranks.* New York, 1979.

——. *Why We Were in Vietnam*. New York, 1982.

——. *The Bloody Crossroads: Where Literature and Politics Meet*. New York, 1986.

Polanyi, Michael. *The Contempt of Freedom: The Russian Experiment and After*. London, 1940.

——. *Science, Faith and Society*. London, 1946.

——. *The Logic of Liberty: Reflections and Rejoinders*. London, 1951.

Powers, Thomas. *The Man Who Kept The Secrets: Richard Helms and the C.I.A.* London, 1979.

Rahv, Philip. *Essays on Literature and Politics 1932–1972*. Boston, 1978.

Ranelagh, John. *The Agency: The Rise and Decline of the C.I.A.* New York, 1986.

Ray, Sibnarayan, ed. *Vietnam: Seen from East and West*. Melbourne, 1966.

Rees, Goronwy. *A Chapter of Accidents*. London, 1972.

——. *Brief Encounters*. London, 1974.

Reich, Richard, and Béatrice Bondy, eds. *Homme de Lettres: Freundesgabe für François Bondy*. Zürich, 1985.

Riesman, David. *The Lonely Crowd: A Study of the Changing American Character*. New York, 1950.

——. *Individualism Reconsidered, and Other Essays*. Glencoe, Ill., 1955.

Rorty, James, with Moshe Decter. *McCarthy and the Communists*. Boston, 1954.

Rositzke, Harry. *The C.I.A.'s Secret Operations*. New York, 1977.

Rostow, W. W. *The Stages of Economic Growth: A Non-Communist Manifesto*. London, 1960.

Russell, Bertrand. *Unarmed Victory*. London, 1963.

——. *Autobiography*. London, 1967–69.

Sartre, Jean-Paul. *Literary and Philosophical Essays*. London, 1955.

——. *Genocide: A Report* (to the International War Crimes Tribunal). Brisbane, 1969.

Schlesinger, Arthur M., Jr. *The Vital Center*. New York, 1949. In U.K., *The Politics of Freedom*. London, 1950.

Serge, Victor. *Mémoires d'un Révolutionnaire, 1901–1941*. Paris, 1951.

Shils, Edward. *The Torment of Secrecy*. London, 1956.

——. *The Intellectual Between Tradition and Modernity: The Indian Situation*. The Hague, 1961.

——. *The Intellectuals and the Powers and Other Essays*. Chicago, 1972.

——. *Center and Periphery: Essays in Macrosociology*. Chicago, 1975.

——. *Tradition*. Chicago, 1981.

Shub, Boris. *The Choice*. New York, 1950.

Silone, Ignazio. *Emergency Exit.* London, 1969.

Sivaraksa, Sulak. *Siam in Crisis: Collected Articles.* Bangkok, 1980.

Solzhenitsyn, Aleksandr. *The Oak and the Calf: Sketches of Literary Life in the Soviet Union.* London, 1980.

Souvarine, Boris. *Stalin.* London, 1939.

——. *A contre-courant: Écrits 1925–1939.* Paris, 1985.

Soyinka, Wole. *A Dance of the Forest.* London, 1963.

——. *The Man Died: Prison Memoirs.* London, 1972.

Spender, Stephen. *Forward from Liberalism.* London, 1937.

——. *Engaged in Writing* (novel). London, 1958.

——. *The Thirties and After: Poetry, Politics, People 1933–1975.* London, 1978.

——. *Collected Poems.* London, 1983.

——. *Journals 1939–1983.* 1986.

Sperber, Manès. *Like a Tear in the Ocean* (trilogy), I. *The Burned Bramble.* New York, 1951. II. *The Abyss.* New York, 1952. III. *Journey Without End.* New York, 1964.

——. *The Achilles Heel.* London, 1959.

——. *Ces Temps-là.* Paris, 1976, 1977, 1979.

Spotts, Frederic. *The Churches and Politics in Germany.* New York, 1973.

Swanberg, W. A. *Norman Thomas: The Last Idealist.* New York, 1976.

Taylor, A. J. P. *A Personal History.* London, 1983.

Theiner, George, ed. *They Shoot Writers, Don't They?* N.p.

Trilling, Diana. *We Must March My Darlings: A Critical Decade.* New York, 1978.

Trilling, Lionel. *The Middle of the Journey* (a novel). New York, 1947.

——. *The Liberal Imagination.* New York, 1950.

Urban, George R., ed. *Euro-Communism: Its Roots and Future in Italy and Elsewhere.* London, 1978.

——, ed. *Communist Reformation: Nationalism, Internationalism and Change in the World Communist Movement.* New York, 1979.

Wald, Alan M. *The New York Intellectuals: The Rise and Decline of the Anti-Stalinist Left from the 1930's to the 1980's.* Chapel Hill, N.C., and London, 1987.

Whitfield, Stephen J. *A Critical American: The Politics of Dwight Macdonald.* Hamden, Conn., 1984.

Wilson, Edmund. *To The Finland Station.* New York, 1940.

Wood, Neal. *Communism and British Intellectuals.* London, 1959.

# ACKNOWLEDGMENTS

I am grateful to all those listed in the bibliography who agreed to let me interview them, sometimes at great length. I also thank Edward Shils for giving me access to the archives of the Congress for Cultural Freedom and the International Association for Cultural Freedom held in the Special Collections, the Joseph Regenstein Library, the University of Chicago, whose curator, Robert Rosenthal, and staff were particularly helpful. The other libraries listed in the bibliography, as well as that of the Parliament of Australia, must also be thanked for their help, as must be the custodians of the private archives listed.

I also thank the Ford Foundation, which contributed significantly to meeting the costs of the research involved in preparing this book.

In every case where it has seemed appropriate I have attempted to reach the owner or owners of the copyright in text and photographs included in this book. In some cases I have been unable to locate the copyright owner. Any error or omission will be corrected in future printings.

# Index

315

Vittorini, Elio, 5, 143
Vivaldi, Cesare, 91
Vlasov, Andrei, 130
Voegelin, Eric, 11, 120
Voigt, F. A., 64
Voznesensky, A., 184, 216

Wain, John, 97
Wali, Obiajunwa, 204–5
Wall, Bernard, 144
Warburg, Fredric, 2, 61, 145, 146
Wat, Aleksandr, 91, 125, 212
Watson, Adam, 235, 240
Waugh, Evelyn, 95
Wazyk, Adam, 127, 174–75, 213
Webb, Beatrice, 146
Webb, Sidney, 146
Weber, Alfred, 28
Weber, Max, 177
Weidlé, Vladimir, 54, 60
Weigel, Hans, 94
Weightman, John, 144, 230
Weil, Simone, 76
Weissberg, Alexander, 60
Weissberg-Cybulski, Alexander, 105, 107
Welch, Colin, 185
West, postideological, 119–22
*West African Intellectual Community, The*, 202
"What Is Vulgarity?" (Dasnoy), 72
Whitaker, Arthur, 155
Wilde, Oscar, 60
Wiles, Peter, 110
Williams, David, 144
Wilson, Angus, 230
Wilson, Edmund, 77, 94, 161, 164, 215
Wilson, Harold, 185
Wind, Edgar, 107

*Winter in Moscow* (Muggeridge), 145
Wirth, Louis, 176
Wisner, Frank, 220
*Without Fear or Favor* (Salisbury), 222
Wittfogel, Karl A., 160, 195
Wolfe, Bertram D., 60, 115
Wood, Michael, 226
Woodcock, George, 76
Woolf, Virginia, 65
"Workers' Participation in Management" (seminar), 117
World Federation of Trade Unions, 34
World Peace Congress (1949), 6–7
Worldwide intellectual community, 111–12, 176–81
Worsthorne, Peregrine, 175
Wright, Richard, 7
Wroclaw Cultural Conference for Peace (1948), 4
Wyzansky, Charles, 118

*Yameru Amerika (Sick America)* (Ishigati), 146
Yamey, B. S., 114
Yashin, A., 128
Yeats, W. B., 66
Yergan, Max, 21, 51
Yermilov, Vladimir, 215–16
Yevtushenko, Yevgeny, 184, 216
Young, Wayland, 90, 185

Zafred, Mario, 91
Zdhanovite purges, 4
Zelk, Zoltan, 127
Zinkin, Taya, 175
Zorin, Leonid, 126
Zulawski, Juliusz, 213
*Zweite Begegnung, Die* (Torberg), 87